BEGINNER'S GUIDE TO
computer
CODing

LEARN TO CODE IN SCRATCH AND PYTHON

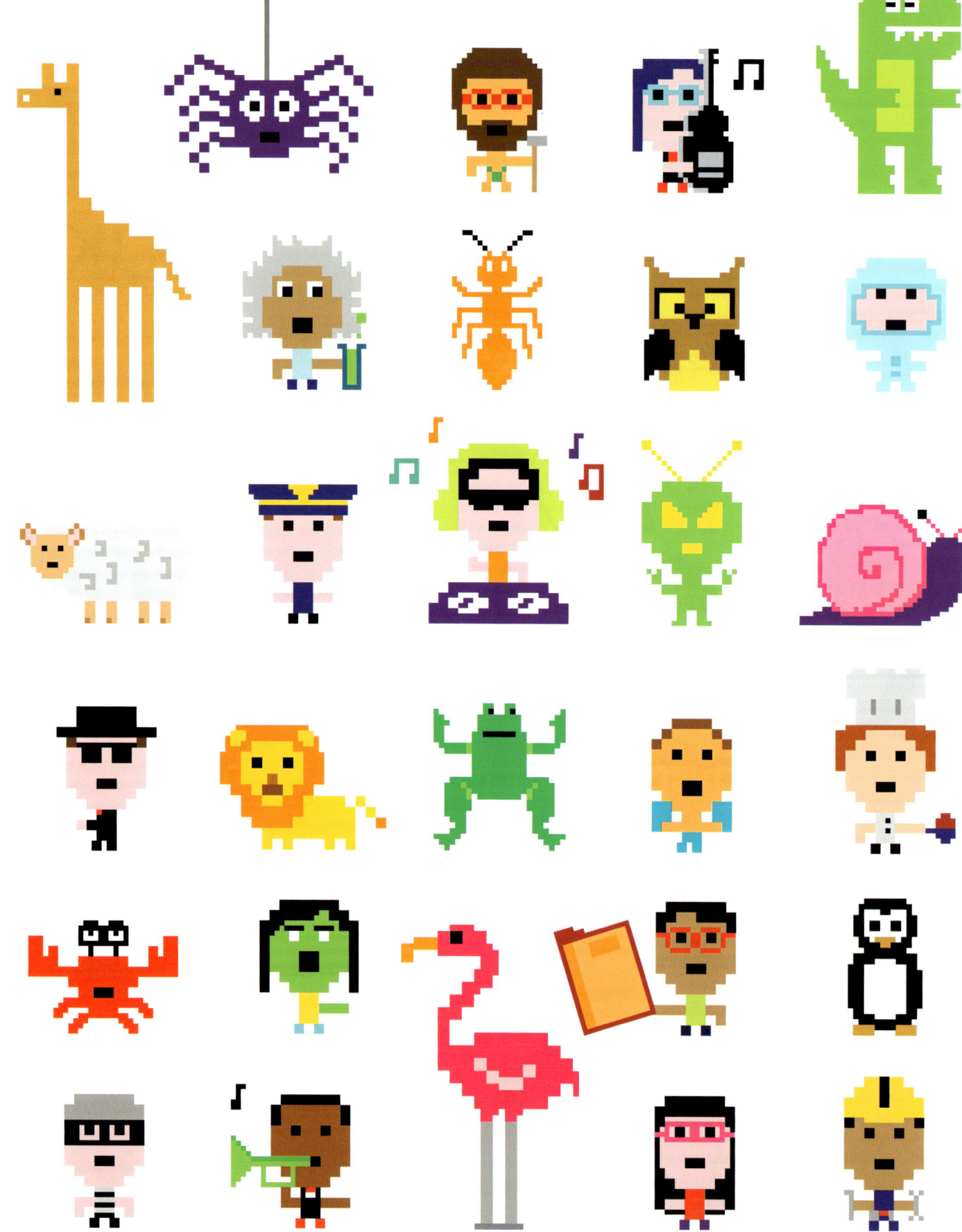

LONDON, NEW YORK, MELBOURNE,
MUNICH, AND DELHI

DK LONDON

Editors Sam Priddy, Sam Atkinson,
Lizzie Davey, Daniel Mills, Ben Morgan
Designers Fiona Macdonald, Simon Murrell
Managing editor Paula Regan
Managing art editor Owen Peyton Jones
Senior producer, pre-production Ben Marcus
Senior producer Mary Slater
Jacket editor Maud Whatley
Jacket designer Laura Brim
Jacket design development manager Sophia MTT
Publisher Sarah Larter
Art director Phil Ormerod
Associate publishing director Liz Wheeler
Publishing director Jonathan Metcalf

DK INDIA

Editors Suefa Lee, Neha Pande
Art editors Sanjay Chauhan, Devika Dwarkadas,
Vanya Mittal, Shreya Anand Virmani
DTP designer Sachin Gupta
Managing editor Rohan Sinha
Managing art editor Sudakshina Basu
Pre-production manager Balwant Singh
Jacket designer Suhita Dharamjit
Senior DTP designer Harish Aggarwal

Content first published in Great Britain in 2014 as
Computer Coding for Kids by Dorling Kindersley Limited
80 Strand, London WC2R 0RL
A Penguin Random House Company
Copyright © 2014 Dorling Kindersley Limited.

All rights reserved. No part of this publication may be reproduced, stored in a retrieval system, or transmitted in any form or by any means, electronic, mechanical, photocopying, recording, or otherwise, without prior written permission of the copyright owner.

ISBN: 978-0-2411-8678-7

Printed and bound in Italy by L.E.G.O. S.p.A.

See our complete catalogue at
www.dk.com

AUTHORS AND CONSULTANTS

DR JON WOODCOCK MA(OXON) has a degree in Physics from the University of Oxford and a PhD in Computational Astrophysics from the University of London. He started coding at the age of eight and has programmed all kinds of computers from single-chip microcontrollers to world-class supercomputers. Jon has a passion for science and technology education, giving talks on space and running computer programming clubs in schools. He has worked on numerous science and technology books as a contributor and consultant.

SEAN McMANUS learned to program when he was nine. His first programming language was Logo. Today he is an expert technology author and journalist. His other books include *Scratch Programming in Easy Steps*, *Web Design in Easy Steps*, and *Raspberry Pi For Dummies*. Visit his website at www.sean.co.uk for Scratch games and tutorials.

CRAIG STEELE is a specialist in Computing Science education. He is Project Manager for CoderDojo Scotland, which runs free coding clubs for young people. Craig has previously worked for the Scottish Qualification Authority, Glasgow Science Centre, and the University of Glasgow. Craig's first computer was a ZX Spectrum.

CLAIRE QUIGLEY studied Computing Science at Glasgow University where she obtained a BSc and a PhD. She has worked in the Computer Laboratory at Cambridge University and on a project that aimed to develop computational thinking skills in primary school pupils. She is a mentor at Coderdojo Scotland, a coding club for young people.

DANIEL McCAFFERTY holds a degree in Computer Science from the University of Strathclyde. Since graduating, he has been developing software for some of the world's largest investment banks. In his spare time, Daniel is a mentor at CoderDojo Scotland, a coding club for young people.

Contents

6   How it works

1 WHAT IS CODING?

10   What is a computer program?
12   Think like a computer
14   Becoming a coder

2 STARTING FROM SCRATCH

18   What is Scratch?
20   Installing Scratch
22   Scratch interface
24   Sprites
26   Coloured blocks and scripts
28   **Project 1: Escape the dragon!**
34   Making things moves
36   Costumes
38   Hide and seek
40   Events
42   Simple loops
44   Pens and turtles
46   Variables
48   Maths
50   Strings and lists
52   Co-ordinates
54   Make some noise
56   **Project 2: Roll the dice**
58   True or false?
60   Decisions and branches
62   Sensing and detecting
64   Complex loops
66   Sending messages
68   Creating blocks
70   **Project 3: Monkey mayhem**
78   Time to experiment

3 PLAYING WITH PYTHON

82   What is Python?
84   Installing Python
88   Introducing IDLE
90   Errors
92   **Project 4: Ghost game**

94	Ghost game decoded	134	Variables and functions
96	Program flow	136	**Project 6: Drawing machine**
98	Simple commands	144	Bugs and debugging
100	Harder commands	146	Algorithms
102	Which window?	148	Libraries
104	Variables in Python	150	Making windows
106	Types of data	152	Colour and co-ordinates
108	Maths in Python	154	Making shapes
110	Strings in Python	156	Changing things
112	Input and output	158	Reacting to events
114	Making decisions	160	**Project 7: Bubble blaster**
116	Branching	172	What next?
118	Loops in Python	174	Glossary
120	While loops	176	Acknowledgments
122	Escaping loops		
124	Lists		
126	Functions		
128	**Project 5: Silly sentences**		
130	Tuples and dictionaries	Find out more at:	
132	Lists in variables	www.dk.com/computercoding	

How it works

The following pages introduce all the essential concepts needed to understand computer coding. Fun projects throughout put these ideas into practice. Everything is broken down into small chunks so that it's easy to follow and understand.

Pixel people give hints and tips along the way

Each topic is described in detail, with examples and exercises

"See also" boxes list other subjects that are linked to the topic

166 PLAYING WI...

BUBBLE BLAS...
Working out the di...
In this game, and lots of oth... between two objects. Here... formula to have the compu...

11 This function calculates the d... two objects. Add this bit of co... the code you wrote in step 9.

```
from math import sqr...
def distance(id1, id...
    x1, y1 = get_coc...
    x2, y2 = get_coc...
    return sqrt((x2...
```

38 STARTING FROM SCRATCH

Hide and seek
Welcome to the special effects studio! Using the purple "Looks" blocks, find out how to make sprites vanish and reappear, grow and shrink, and fade in and out.

SEE ALSO
‹ 34–35 Making things move
Sending messages 66–67 ›

Sizes and effects
Scripts can be used to change the size of a sprite and add special effects to it.

change size by (10) — Type in positive numbers to make sprites bigger and negative numbers to make them smaller

set size to (100) % — Higher numbers make sprites bigger and lower numbers make them smaller. 100 is normal size

△ **Changing a sprite's size**
These two blocks can be used to make a sprite bigger or smaller, either by a set amount or by a percentage of its size.
Resets all the effects

Hiding sprites
To make a sprite disappear, use the "hide" block. The sprite is still on the stage, and it can still move around, but it can't be seen unless the "show" block is used to make it visible again.

Use the "hide" block to make sprites disappear in games

▷ **Hide and show**
To make a sprite vanish, use the "hide" block. When you're ready for it to be seen again, use the "show" block. These blocks are found in the "Looks" section of the blocks palette.

hide
show

Colourful illustrations highlight different programming concepts

▽ **Disappearing cat**
Try this script using the cat sprite. It disappears and reappears but it keeps moving, even when you can't see it.

Programming scripts and code are explained line by line

when ⚑ clicked
forever
  wait (1) secs
  hide ← This block hides the cat
  turn ↻ (90) degrees ← This block rotates the cat clockwise
  move (100) steps
  wait (1) secs ← The cat still moves even when hidden
  show ← This block shows the cat again

EXPERT TIPS
Showing sprites
Select a sprite in the sprite list. Click the "i" button on it to open the information panel. There you can also use the "show" tick box to show or hide a sprite.

Sprite1
x: 84 y: -69   direction: -90°
rotation style: ↻ ↔ ●
can drag in player: ☐
show: ☑ ← Show a hidden sprite

Using effects to teleport
Add a ghost sprite from the "Fantasy" category of the sprite library, and create the script shown below. It makes the ghost appear to teleport when clicked.

when this sprite clicked
clear graphic effects
repeat (20)
  change [ghost ▼] effect by (5) ← The "ghost" effect fade slightly; by block 20 times th... away completely
glide (0.1) secs to x: pick random (-150) to (150)
repeat (20)
  change [ghost ▼] effect by (-5)
← Using this block mak... sprite fade back in

Labels help explain each step

Instructions show what to click, drag, or select

HOW IT WORKS

7

Seven projects build up coding skills. Project pages are highlighted with a blue band

Simple step-by-step instructions guide you through each project

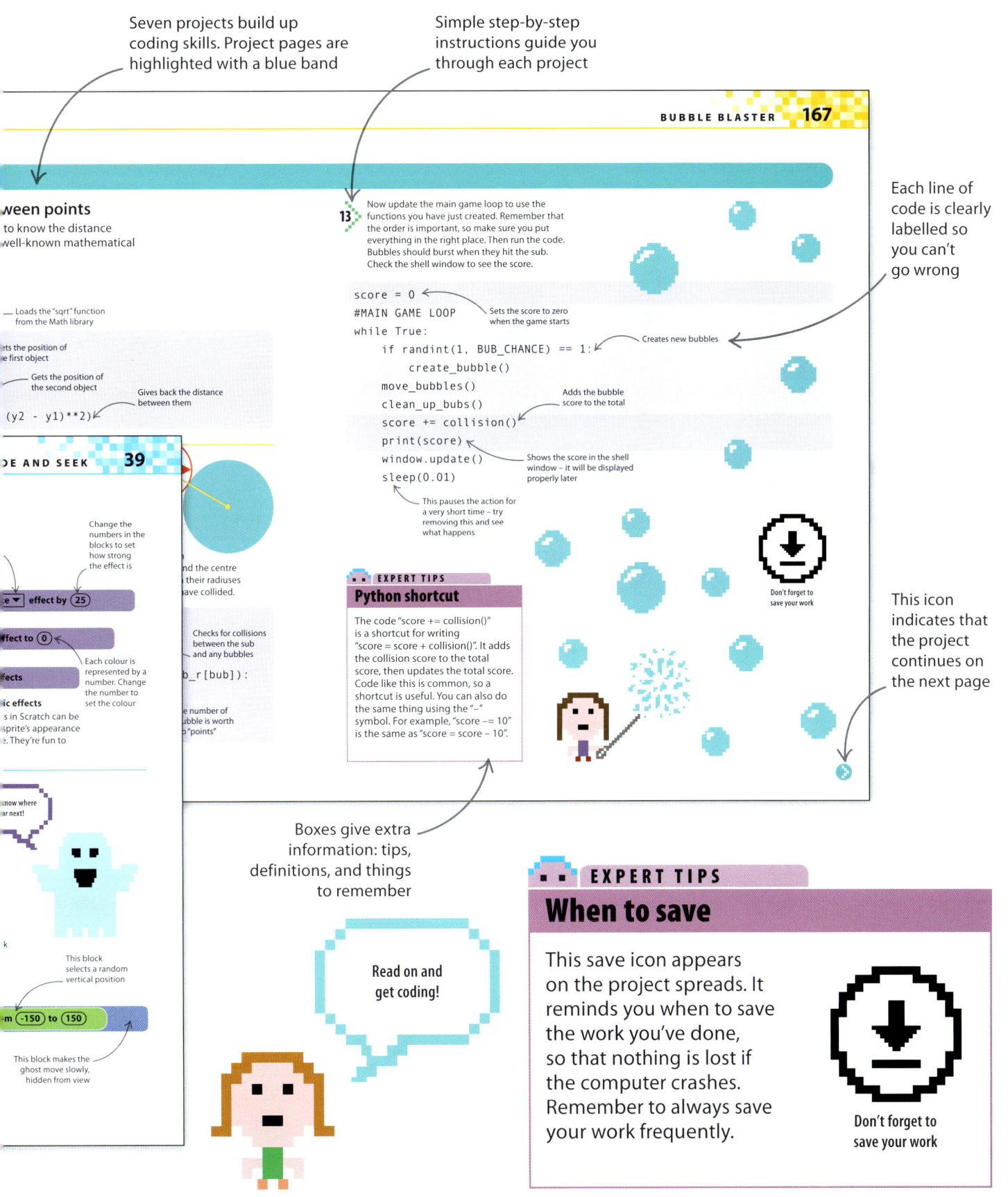

Each line of code is clearly labelled so you can't go wrong

BUBBLE BLASTER **167**

13 Now update the main game loop to use the functions you have just created. Remember that the order is important, so make sure you put everything in the right place. Then run the code. Bubbles should burst when they hit the sub. Check the shell window to see the score.

```
score = 0
#MAIN GAME LOOP
while True:
    if randint(1, BUB_CHANCE) == 1:
        create_bubble()
    move_bubbles()
    clean_up_bubs()
    score += collision()
    print(score)
    window.update()
    sleep(0.01)
```

Sets the score to zero when the game starts

Creates new bubbles

Adds the bubble score to the total

Shows the score in the shell window – it will be displayed properly later

This pauses the action for a very short time – try removing this and see what happens

EXPERT TIPS
Python shortcut

The code "score += collision()" is a shortcut for writing "score = score + collision()". It adds the collision score to the total score, then updates the total score. Code like this is common, so a shortcut is useful. You can also do the same thing using the "–" symbol. For example, "score –= 10" is the same as "score = score – 10".

Don't forget to save your work

This icon indicates that the project continues on the next page

Boxes give extra information: tips, definitions, and things to remember

Read on and get coding!

EXPERT TIPS
When to save

This save icon appears on the project spreads. It reminds you when to save the work you've done, so that nothing is lost if the computer crashes. Remember to always save your work frequently.

Don't forget to save your work

What is coding?

WHAT IS CODING?

What is a computer program?

A computer program is a set of instructions that a computer follows to complete a task. "Coding", or "programming", means writing the step-by-step instructions that tell the computer what to do.

> **SEE ALSO**
> Thinking like **12–13**〉
> a computer
> Becoming **14–15**〉
> a coder

Computer programs are everywhere

We are surrounded by computer programs. Many of the devices and gadgets we use each day are controlled by them. These machines all follow step-by-step instructions written by a computer programmer.

△ **Computer software**
Everything a computer does, from browsing the Internet to writing documents or playing music, works because of code written by a computer programmer.

◁ **Mobile phones**
Programs allow you to make a phone call or send text messages. When you search for a contact, a program finds the correct phone number.

◁ **Games**
Consoles are just another type of computer, and all the games that run on them are programs. All the graphics, sounds, and controls are written in computer code.

△ **Washing machines**
Washing machines are programmed to follow different cycles. Computer code controls how hot the water is and how long the wash takes.

▷ **Cars**
In some cars, computer programs monitor the speed, temperature, and amount of fuel in the tank. Computer programs can even help control the brakes to keep people safe.

WHAT IS A COMPUTER PROGRAM?

How computer programs work
Computers might seem very smart, but they are actually just boxes that follow instructions very quickly and accurately. As intelligent humans, we can get them to carry out different tasks by writing programs, or lists of instructions.

1 Computers can't think
A computer won't do anything by itself. It's up to the computer programmer to give it instructions.

Without instructions a computer is clueless

2 Write a program
You can tell a computer what to do by writing a set of very detailed instructions called a program. Each instruction has to be small enough that the computer can understand it. If the instructions are incorrect, the computer won't behave the way you want it to.

This is a computer program counting down to launch

```
for count in range(10, 0, -1):
    print("Counting down", count)
```

3 Programming languages
Computers can only follow instructions in a language they understand. It's up to the programmer to choose which language is best for the task.

```
for count in range(10, 0, -1):
    print("Counting down", count)
```

All programs are finally converted into "binary code", a basic computer language that uses only ones and zeroes

LINGO
Hardware and software
"Hardware" means the physical parts of the computer that you can see or touch (all the wires, the circuits, the keyboard, the display screen, and so on). "Software" means the programs that run on the computer and control how it works. Software and hardware work together to make computers do useful things.

WHAT IS CODING?

Think like a computer

A programmer must learn to think like a computer. All tasks must be broken down into small chunks so they are easy to follow, and impossible to get wrong.

> **SEE ALSO**
> ⟨ 10–11 What is a computer program?
> Becoming 14–15 ⟩ a coder

Thinking like a robot

Imagine a café where the waiter is a robot. The robot has a simple computer brain, and needs to be told how to get from the café kitchen to serve food to diners seated at tables. First the process has to be broken down into simple tasks the computer can understand.

> **LINGO**
> ### Algorithm
> An algorithm is a set of simple instructions for performing a task. A program is an algorithm that has been translated into a language that computers can understand.

1 Waiter robot program 1
Using this program the robot grabs the food from the plate, crashes straight through the kitchen wall into the dining area, and puts the food on the floor. This algorithm wasn't detailed enough.

1. Pick up food
2. Move from kitchen to diner's table
3. Put food down

◁ **Disaster!**
The instructions weren't clear: we forgot to tell the robot to use the door. It might seem obvious to humans but computers can't think for themselves.

2 Waiter robot program 2
This time we've told the robot waiter to use the kitchen door. It makes it through the door, but then hits the café cat, trips, and smashes the plate on the floor.

1. Pick up a plate with food on it
2. Move from kitchen to diner's table by:
      Move to door between kitchen and dining area
      Move from door to the table
3. Put plate down on the table in front of the diner

△ **Still not perfect**
The robot doesn't know how to deal with obstacles like the cat. The program needs to give the robot even more detailed instructions so it can move around safely.

THINK LIKE A COMPUTER **13**

3 **Waiter robot program 3**
In this version of the program, the robot successfully delivers the food to the diner avoiding any obstacles. But after putting the plate down, the robot remains standing at the table while food piles up in the kitchen.

1. Pick up a plate with food on it holding it level at all times
2. Move from kitchen to diner's table by:
    Move to door between kitchen and dining area
        checking for obstacles and steering around them
    Move from door to the table
        checking for obstacles and steering around them
3. Put plate down on the table in front of the diner

△ **Success at last?**
Finally the robot can deliver the food safely. But we forgot to give it instructions to go back to the kitchen and get the next plate.

Real-world example

The waiter robot might be imaginary, but algorithms like this are in action all around us. For example, a computer-controlled lift faces the same sort of problems. Should it go up or down? Which floor should it go to next?

1. Wait until doors are closed
2. Wait for button to be pressed
    If button pressed is higher than current floor:
        Move lift upwards
    If button pressed is lower than current floor:
        Move lift downwards
3. Wait until current floor equals button pressed
4. Open doors

◁ **Lift program**
For the lift to work correctly and safely, every step has to be precise, clear, and cover every possibility. The programmers have to make sure they create a suitable algorithm.

14   WHAT IS CODING?

Becoming a coder

Coders are the people who write the programs behind everything we see and do on a computer. You can create your own programs by learning a programming language.

SEE ALSO
What is Scratch? **18–19** ⟩
What is Python? **82–83** ⟩

Programming languages

There are a huge range of programming languages to choose from. Each one can be used for different tasks. Here are some of the most popular languages and what they are often used for:

C	A powerful language for building computer operating systems.	**MATLAB**	Ideal for programs that need to carry out lots of calculations.
Ada	Used to control spacecraft, satellites, and aeroplanes.	**Ruby**	Automatically turns lots of information into web pages.
Java	Works on computers, mobile phones, and tablets.	**Javascript**	A language used to build interactive websites.
Scratch	A visual language that's ideal for learning programming. This is the first language covered in this book.	**Python**	A text-based language that can be used to build all kinds of things. It's the second language covered in this book.

What is Scratch?

Scratch is a great way to start coding. Programs are created by connecting together blocks of code, instead of typing it out. Scratch is quick and easy to use, and also teaches you the key ideas you need to use other programming languages.

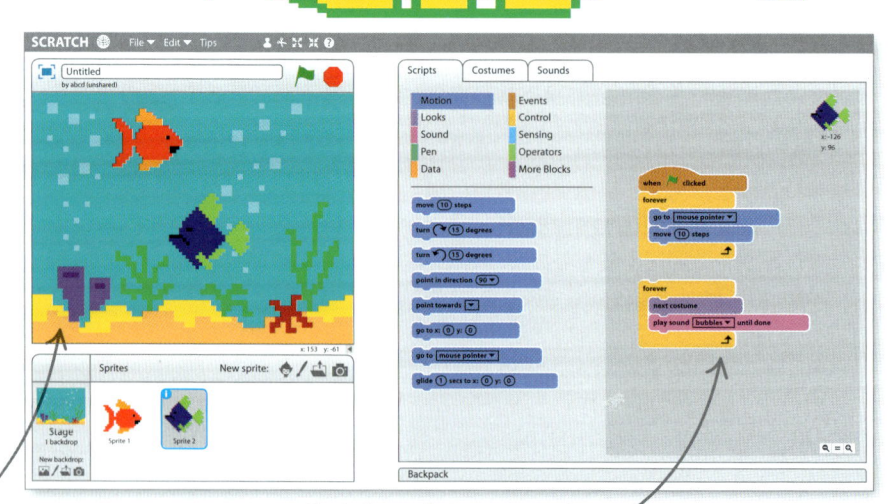

The program appears on this side of the screen

Code is made by connecting coloured blocks together

BECOMING A CODER   15

What is Python?

People around the world use Python to build games, tools, and websites. It's a great language to master as it can help you build all kinds of different programs. Python looks like a mixture of recognizable words and characters, so it can be easily read and understood by humans.

```
IDLE   File   Edit   Shell   Debug   Window   Help
ghostgame
# Ghost Game
from random import randint
print('Ghost Game')
feeling_brave = True
score = 0
while feeling_brave:
    ghost_door = randint(1, 3)
    print('Three doors ahead...')
```

A program written in Python

Getting started

It's time to start programming. All you need is a computer with an Internet connection. This book starts with Scratch – the perfect language to help you on your way to becoming a coding expert. Get ready to jump into the exciting world of computer coding.

EXPERT TIPS
Enjoy experimenting

As a programmer you should experiment with the code and programs you make. One of the best ways to learn programming is to play about and see what happens when you change different parts of the code. By tinkering and fiddling, you'll discover new ways of doing things. You'll learn much more about computer programming and have even more fun.

Starting from Scratch

18 STARTING FROM SCRATCH

What is Scratch?

Scratch is a visual programming language that makes coding simple. It can be used to make all sorts of fun and interesting programs.

> **SEE ALSO**
> Installing and **20–21**
> launching Scratch
> Scratch **22–23**
> interface
> Coloured blocks **26–27**
> and scripts

Understanding Scratch

Scratch is perfect for making games and animations. It has large collections (or "libraries") of cool graphics and sounds that you can play around with.

1 Start programming
Scratch is a programming language. There's not much typing, and it's easy to get started.

2 Put together programming blocks
Scratch uses coloured blocks of code. Blocks are selected and joined together to make a script, which is a set of instructions.

Blocks lock together like jigsaw pieces

Write your first program in Scratch!

3 Make sprites move and speak
Objects such as people, vehicles, and animals can be added to a program. These objects are called sprites. Scripts make them move and speak.

Sprites like me can be programmed to talk in speech bubbles.

> **LINGO**
> ## Why is it called Scratch?
> "Scratching" is a way of mixing different sounds to make new music. The Scratch programming language enables you to mix pictures, sounds, and scripts to make new computer programs.
>
>

Sprites can be programmed to walk, run, and dance

WHAT IS SCRATCH? **19**

A typical Scratch program

Here is an example of a Scratch program. All of the action takes place in an area on the screen called the "stage". Background images and sprites can be added to the stage, and you can write scripts to make things happen.

The red button stops a program

The green flag runs a program

▷ **Running a program**
Starting a program is called "running" it. To run a program in Scratch, click the green flag above the stage.

Background image

Adding a script makes the shark sprite move

Several sprites can be on the stage at once

▷ **Scripts make sprites move**
Scratch contains blocks that can be used to make scripts. This script makes the shark bounce around the screen. The "next costume" block makes it open and close its mouth with each movement.

The "forever" block keeps the sprite moving endlessly

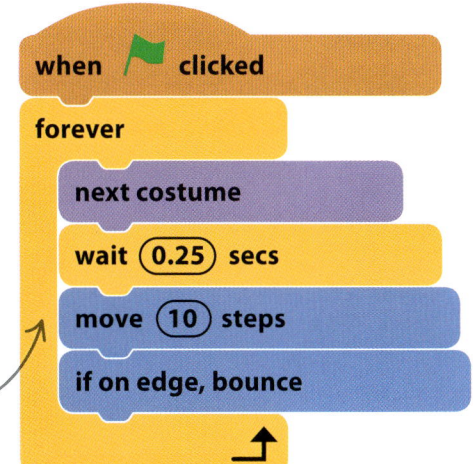

REMEMBER
Scratch programs

In Scratch, when you save your work it is called a "project". A project includes all the sprites, backgrounds, sounds, and scripts you're working with. When you load a project again later, everything will be where it was when you saved it. A Scratch project is a computer program.

STARTING FROM SCRATCH

Installing and launching Scratch

To start programming in Scratch, you need to have the Scratch software. It can be installed on a computer, or it can be used online.

> **REMEMBER**
> **Scratch website**
> Find the Scratch website at:
> **http://scratch.mit.edu/**

Create a Scratch account

A Scratch account can be used to share the programs you make on the Scratch website. It's also used to save work online. Visit the Scratch website at: **http://scratch.mit.edu/** and click "Join Scratch" to create your account.

▷ **Getting started**
The way Scratch is set up depends on whether it's used over the Internet (online) or from downloaded software (offline).

1 Set-up

2 Launching Scratch

Online

Visit **http://scratch.mit.edu** and click "Join Scratch". Fill in the form to create a username and password. Make sure you get permission from your parent or carer to join the website.

Once you've joined the Scratch website, click "Sign in", and enter your username and password. Click "Create" at the top of the screen to begin a new program.

Offline

Download the software version of Scratch at: **http://scratch.mit.edu/scratch2download/**. Run the installation program and a Scratch icon will appear on your desktop.

Double-click the icon on the desktop and Scratch will start, ready to begin programming.

INSTALLING AND LAUNCHING SCRATCH   21

> **EXPERT TIPS**
> ### Mouse control
>
> The "click" instruction means press the left mouse button if there is more than one. "Right-click" means use the right mouse button. If a mouse only has one button, hold the "CTRL" key on the keyboard and press the mouse button to perform a right-click.

Different versions of Scratch

This book uses Scratch 2.0, the latest version of Scratch. Use this version if possible. An older version will differ slightly.

△ **Scratch 1.4**
The older version of Scratch has the stage on the right of the screen.

△ **Scratch 2.0**
The latest version of Scratch has some new commands and the stage is on the left of the screen.

3 Saving work

When you're logged in, Scratch automatically saves work for you. To find your work, click your username at the top right of the screen and click "My Stuff".

Click the "File" menu at the top of the screen and choose "Save As". Ask the person who owns the computer where you should save your work.

4 Operating systems

The web version of Scratch works well on Windows, Ubuntu, and Mac computers. It needs Adobe Flash software, though, so it won't work on some tablets.

The offline version of Scratch works well on Windows and Mac computers. It doesn't work well on computers that use Ubuntu. If a computer uses Ubuntu, try the online version instead.

Ready? Let's go!

Scratch interface

This is Scratch's screen layout, or "interface". The stage is on the left and programs are created on the right.

▽ **Experiment**
Click the buttons and tabs to explore and experiment with the Scratch interface. The projects that follow explain how to use them.

EXPERT TIPS
Menu and tools

MENU OPTIONS
This is what the menu options at the top of the screen do.

- **File** — **Save work** or start a new project.
- **Edit** — **Undo any mistakes** or change the stage size.
- **Tips** — **If you get stuck,** find help here.

CURSOR TOOLS
Click on the tool you want to use, and then click on the sprite or script that you want to use it on.

- **Copy** a sprite or script.
- **Delete** a sprite or script.
- **Enlarge** a sprite.
- **Shrink** a sprite.
- **Get help** on a block.

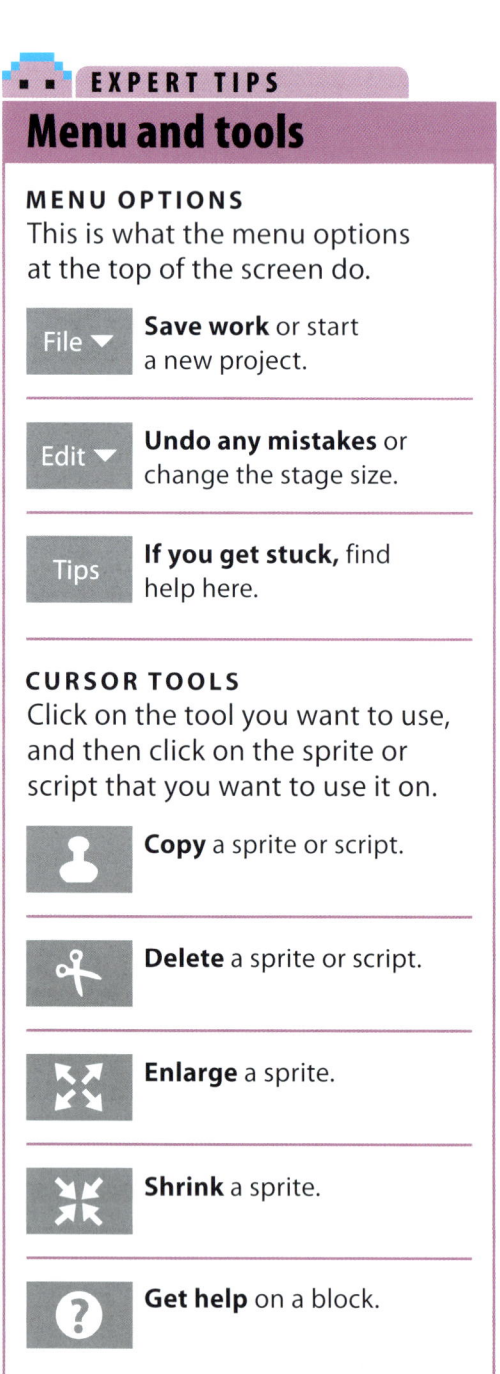

Click for full screen view

Change language

Menu options

Cursor tools

Program name box

Click a sprite on the stage or in the sprite list to select it

Buttons to change the background

Blue box around the selected sprite

Buttons to add new sprites

SCRATCH INTERFACE 23

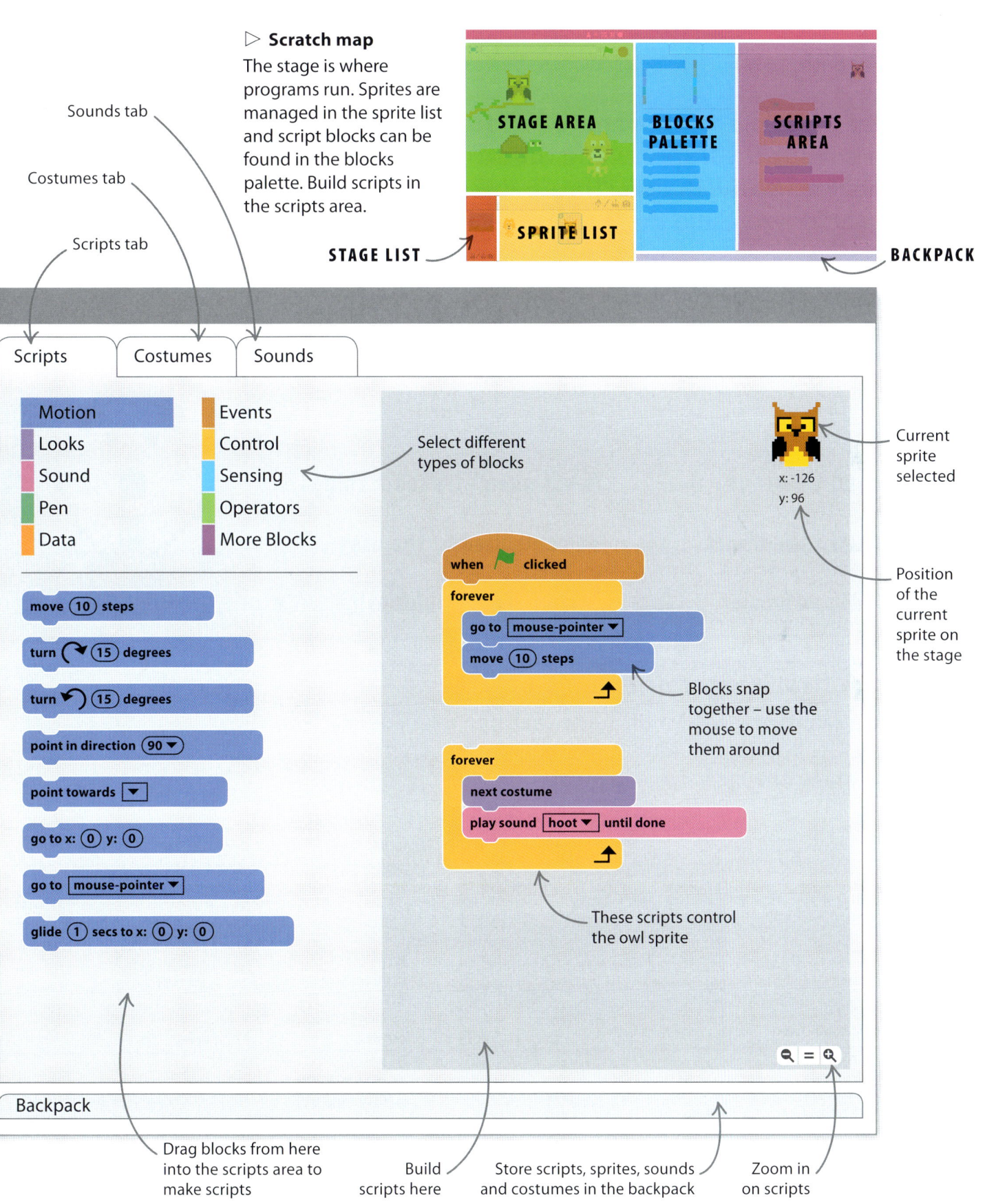

▷ **Scratch map**
The stage is where programs run. Sprites are managed in the sprite list and script blocks can be found in the blocks palette. Build scripts in the scripts area.

Sprites

Sprites are the basic components of Scratch. Every Scratch program is made up of sprites and the scripts that control them. The "Escape the dragon!" program on pages 28–33 uses the cat, dragon, and donut sprites.

> **SEE ALSO**
> ⟨ 22–23 Scratch interface
> Costumes 36–37 ⟩
> Hide and seek 38–39 ⟩

What can sprites do?

Sprites are the images on the stage. Scripts are programmed to make them do things. Sprites can be instructed to react to other sprites and the user of the program. Here are a few things sprites can do:

Move around the stage	React when they touch things
Change their appearance	Be controlled by the user
Play sounds and music	Talk in speech bubbles

We can make lots of different sounds.

Sprites in the Scratch interface

Each project can have several sprites, and each one can have its own scripts. It's important to add scripts to the correct sprite, and to know how to switch between them.

Select different sprites by clicking on them

The scripts being shown belong to the sprite shown here

▷ **Sprites and scripts**
A project can have lots of sprites, and each sprite can have lots of scripts.

SPRITES   25

Creating and editing sprites

Games are more exciting when there are more sprites to hit, dodge, or chase each other around the stage. It's simple to create, copy, and delete sprites.

▽ Create a sprite
Use the buttons above the sprite list to add or create a sprite for your program.

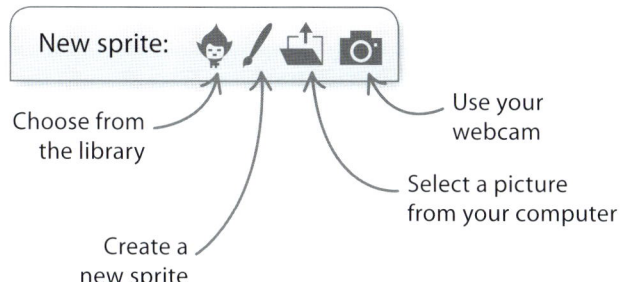

Choose from the library
Create a new sprite
Select a picture from your computer
Use your webcam

▽ Copy or delete a sprite
To copy a sprite and its scripts, right-click on it in the sprite list and choose "duplicate".

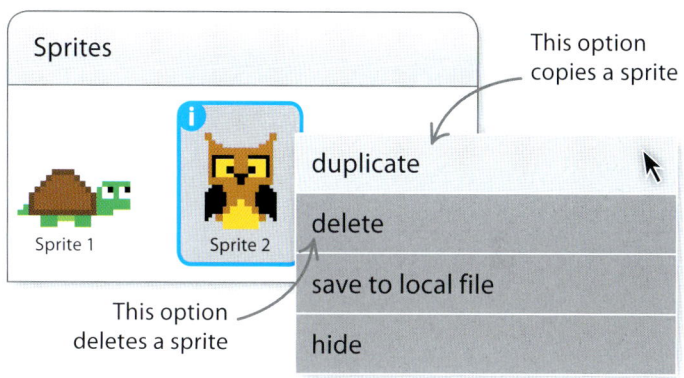

This option copies a sprite
This option deletes a sprite

Naming a sprite

When you start a new program in Scratch the cat sprite is called "Sprite1". It's easier to write programs if you give your sprites more meaningful names. It also makes it easier to understand and manage scripts.

1 Select the sprite
Select a sprite in the sprite list, and then click on the blue "i" button in the corner.

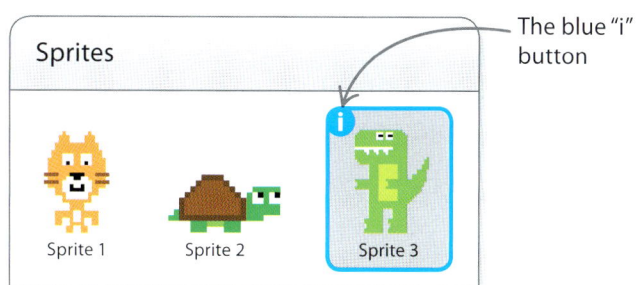

The blue "i" button

2 Change the name
When the information panel opens, click on the text box and use the keyboard to change the name of the sprite.

Type the sprite's new name here

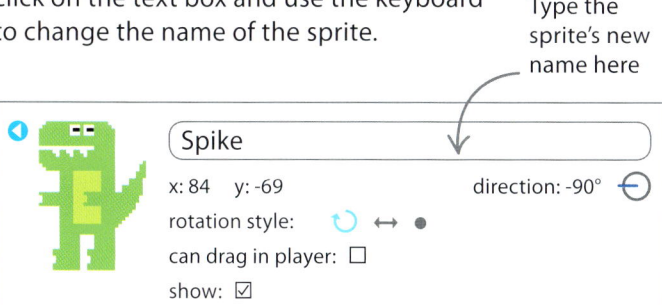

3 Renamed sprite
Click the blue arrow to the left of the sprite to close the information panel.

The sprite's new name appears in the sprite list

Coloured blocks and scripts

SEE ALSO

⟨ **22–23** Scratch interface

Escape the **28-33** ⟩ dragon!

Blocks are colour-coded depending on what they do. Putting them together builds scripts that run in the order in which they are placed.

Coloured blocks

There are ten different types of blocks in Scratch. Switch between them using the buttons in the blocks palette. Click on a colour to see all the blocks in that section.

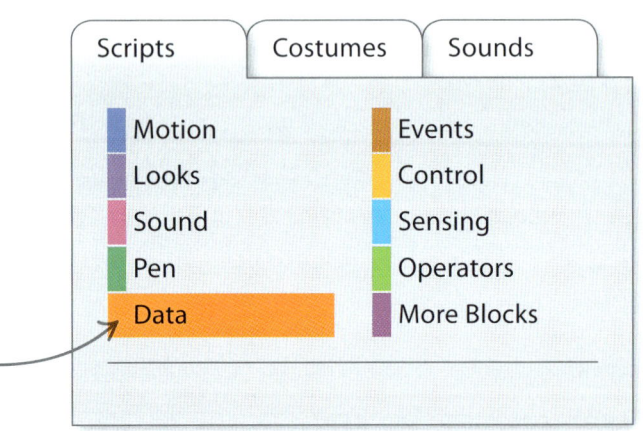

Button to show the orange "Data" blocks

Functions of blocks

Different types of blocks do different things in programs. Some of them make sprites move, some manage sounds, and some decide when things happen.

▽ **Motion, looks, sound, and pen**
These blocks control what a sprite does on screen – this is called the output of a program. Pick a sprite and try each block to see what it does.

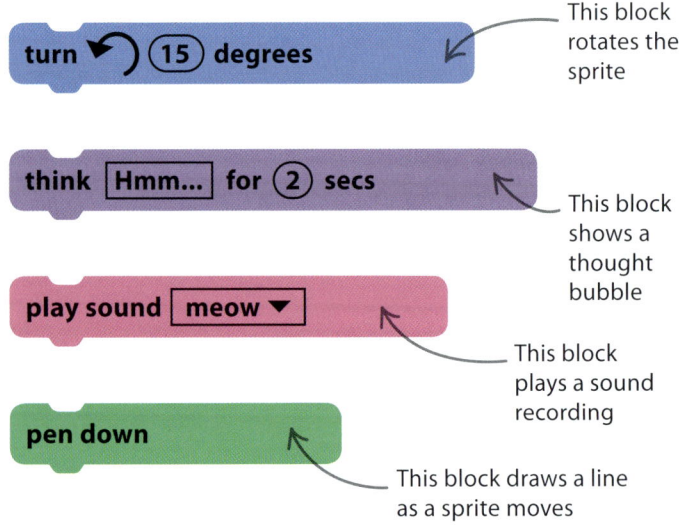

This block rotates the sprite

This block shows a thought bubble

This block plays a sound recording

This block draws a line as a sprite moves

▽ **Events and sensing**
Brown "Events" blocks make things happen. Light blue "Sensing" blocks detect information about the keyboard, mouse, and what a sprite is touching.

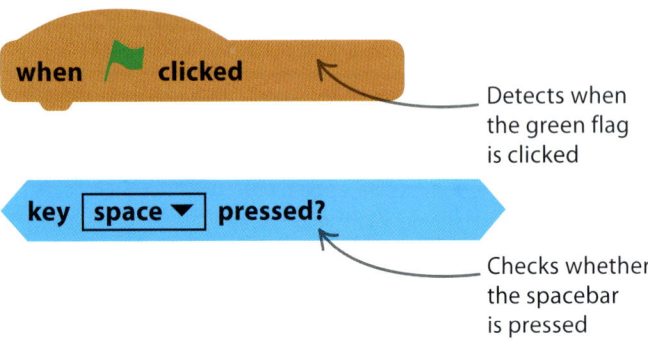

Detects when the green flag is clicked

Checks whether the spacebar is pressed

COLOURED BLOCKS AND SCRIPTS

▽ **Data and operators**
Orange "Data" blocks and green "Operators" blocks store numbers and words and do things with them.

▽ **Control**
The "Control" blocks make decisions about when blocks run. They can be programmed to repeat instructions.

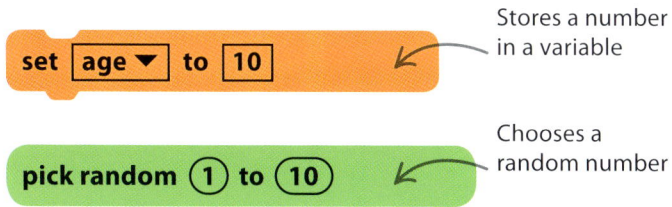

Stores a number in a variable

Chooses a random number

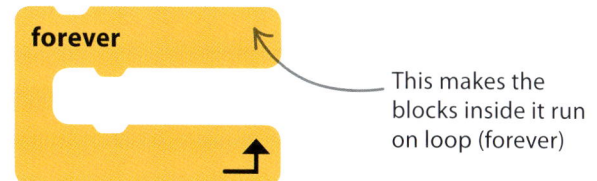

This makes the blocks inside it run on loop (forever)

Flow of scripts

When a program runs, Scratch carries out the instructions on the blocks. It starts at the top of the scripts and works its way down.

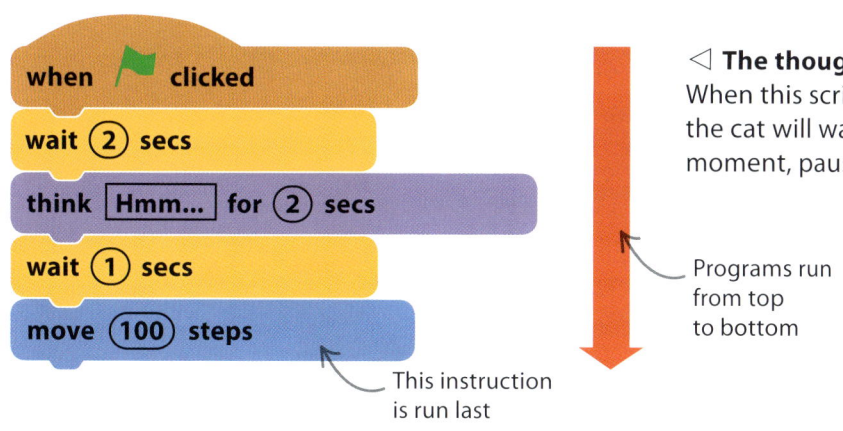

◁ **The thoughtful cat**
When this script is used with the cat sprite, the cat will wait 2 seconds, think for a moment, pause 1 second, and then move.

Programs run from top to bottom

This instruction is run last

Running scripts

When a script is running, it glows. Use the green flag button on the stage to run a script or click a script or a block to make it run.

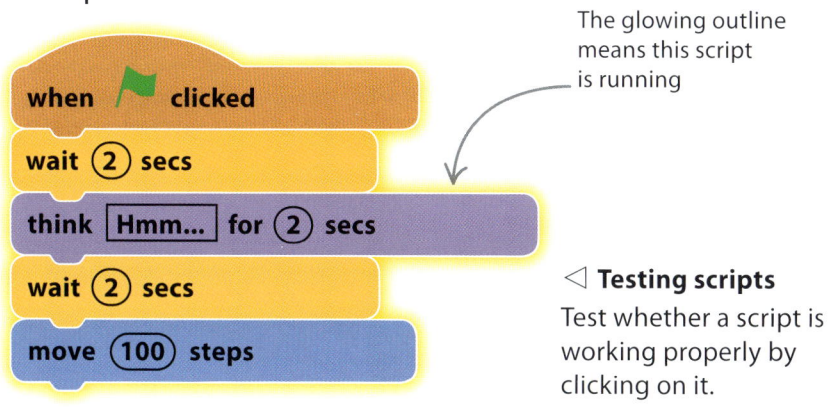

The glowing outline means this script is running

◁ **Testing scripts**
Test whether a script is working properly by clicking on it.

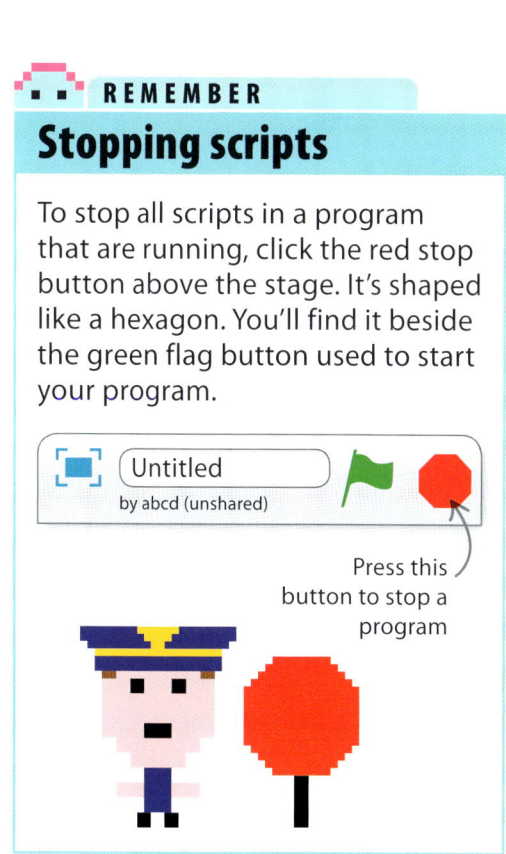

REMEMBER

Stopping scripts

To stop all scripts in a program that are running, click the red stop button above the stage. It's shaped like a hexagon. You'll find it beside the green flag button used to start your program.

Press this button to stop a program

28 STARTING FROM SCRATCH

▶ PROJECT 1

Escape the dragon!

This project introduces some basic Scratch coding. It shows how to make a game to help the cat sprite dodge a fire-breathing dragon.

> **SEE ALSO**
> ‹ **20-21** Installing and launching Scratch
> ‹ **22–23** Scratch interface

Make the cat move

This stage explains how to make the cat sprite move around and chase the mouse-pointer. Follow the instructions carefully, otherwise the game might not work.

1 ▷ Open Scratch. Click "File" on the menu and select "New" to start a new project. The cat sprite appears.

Every new project in Scratch includes me, the cat sprite.

2 ▷ Click the yellow "Control" button in the blocks palette. Then click the "forever" block, keep the mouse button pressed down, and drag the block into the scripts area on the right. Release the button to drop the block.

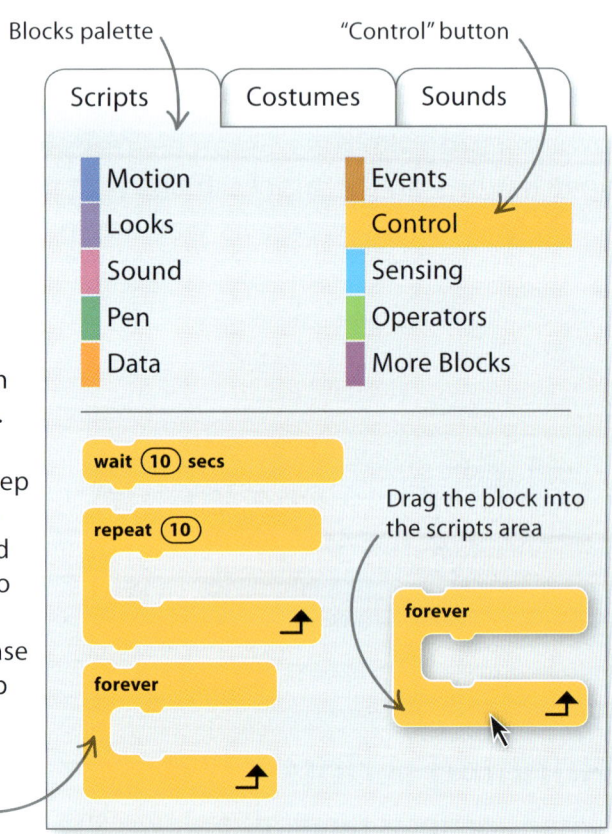

Blocks palette

"Control" button

Drag the block into the scripts area

Click this block

3 ▷ Click the blue "Motion" button in the blocks palette. The blue "Motion" commands will appear. Drag the "point towards" block into the scripts area and drop it inside the "forever" block. Click the black arrow in the block and choose "mouse-pointer".

Click the drop-down menu and select "mouse-pointer"

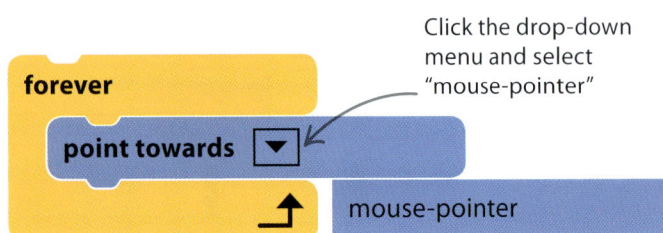

4 ▷ Click the "Events" button in the blocks palette. Drag the "when green flag clicked" block into the scripts area. Join it to the top of your script.

This block snaps to the top of the script

The menu shows "mouse-pointer" has been chosen

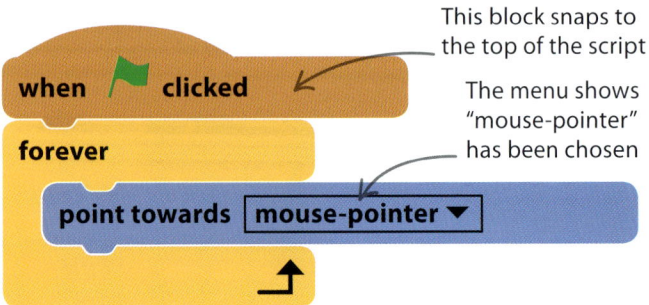

ESCAPE THE DRAGON! 29

5 Try running the program by clicking the green flag at the top of the stage. As you move the mouse around the stage, the cat turns to face the mouse-pointer.

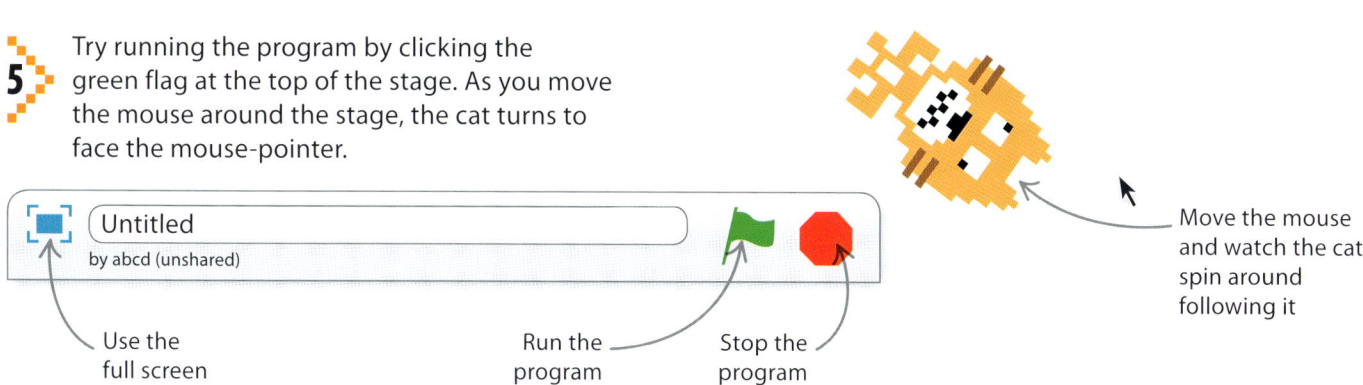

Use the full screen

Run the program

Stop the program

Move the mouse and watch the cat spin around following it

6 Click the "Motion" button again, and drag the "move 10 steps" block into the scripts area. Drop it inside the "forever" block. Click the green flag button so the cat chases the mouse-pointer!

7 The picture behind the sprites is called a backdrop. To the left of the sprite list is a button to add a backdrop from the library. Click it, then select the "Space" theme from the list. Click the "stars" image and then click the "OK" button at the bottom-right.

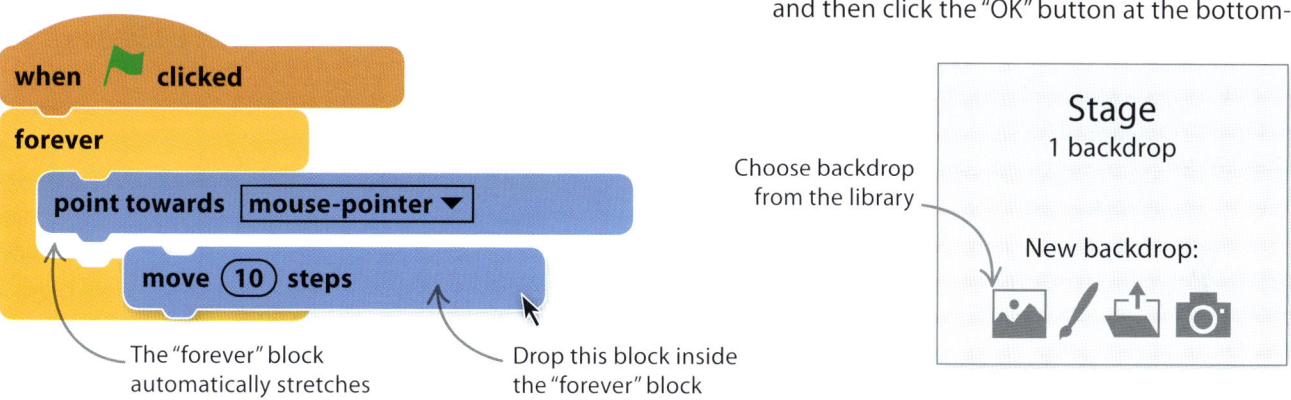

The "forever" block automatically stretches to make room

Drop this block inside the "forever" block

Choose backdrop from the library

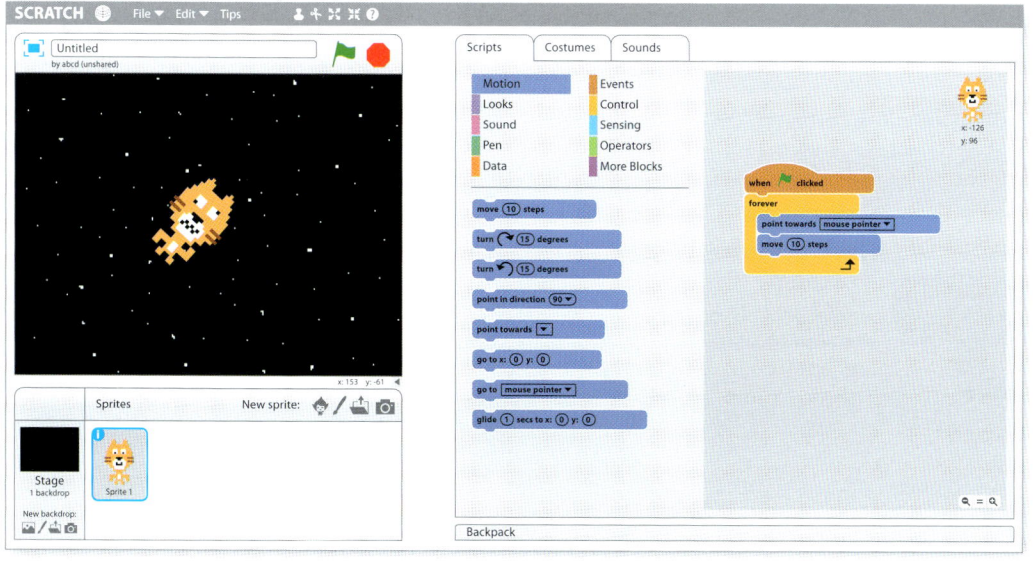

◁ **Cat in space**
The Scratch interface now looks like this. Run the program and the cat chases the mouse-pointer through space.

Scratch automatically saves work if you're online. To save work while offline – click "File" and select "Save As".

30 STARTING FROM SCRATCH

⏵ ESCAPE THE DRAGON!

Add a fire-breathing dragon

Now that the cat can chase the mouse, make a dragon to chase the cat. Don't let the dragon catch the cat, or it will get scorched.

8 ▸ Above the sprite list is a button to add a sprite from the library. Click it, choose the "Fantasy" category from the menu on the left, and select "Dragon". Click the "OK" button in the bottom-right of the screen.

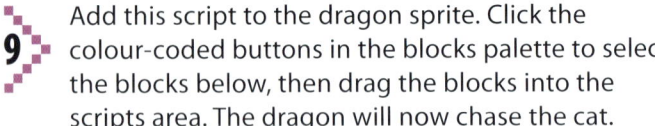
Add a sprite from the library

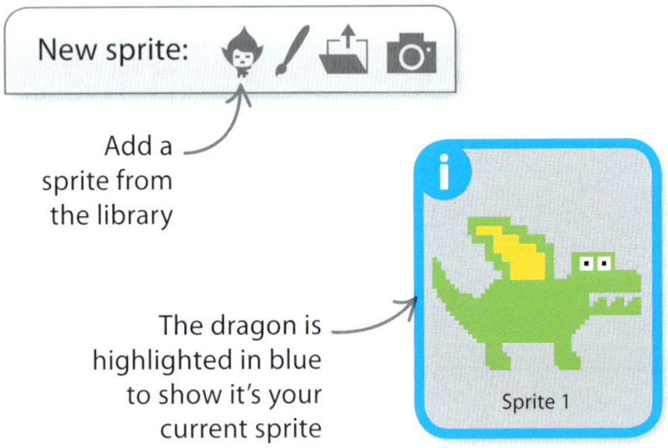

The dragon is highlighted in blue to show it's your current sprite

9 ▸ Add this script to the dragon sprite. Click the colour-coded buttons in the blocks palette to select the blocks below, then drag the blocks into the scripts area. The dragon will now chase the cat.

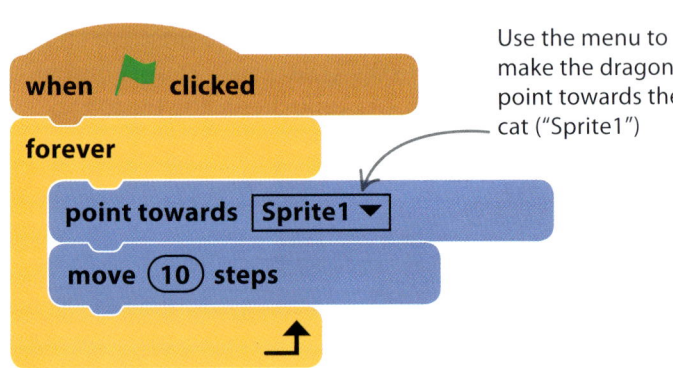
Use the menu to make the dragon point towards the cat ("Sprite1")

10 ▸ Click the blue "Motion" button and drag the "go to x:0 y:0" block into the script. Click the number boxes in the block and change them to -200 and -150. Click the purple "Looks" button and add the "switch costume to" block to your script.

11 ▸ With the dragon sprite highlighted, add this second script to the scripts area. The "wait until" block is found in the "Control" section, and the "touching" block is in the "Sensing" section. The dragon now breathes fire when it touches the cat.

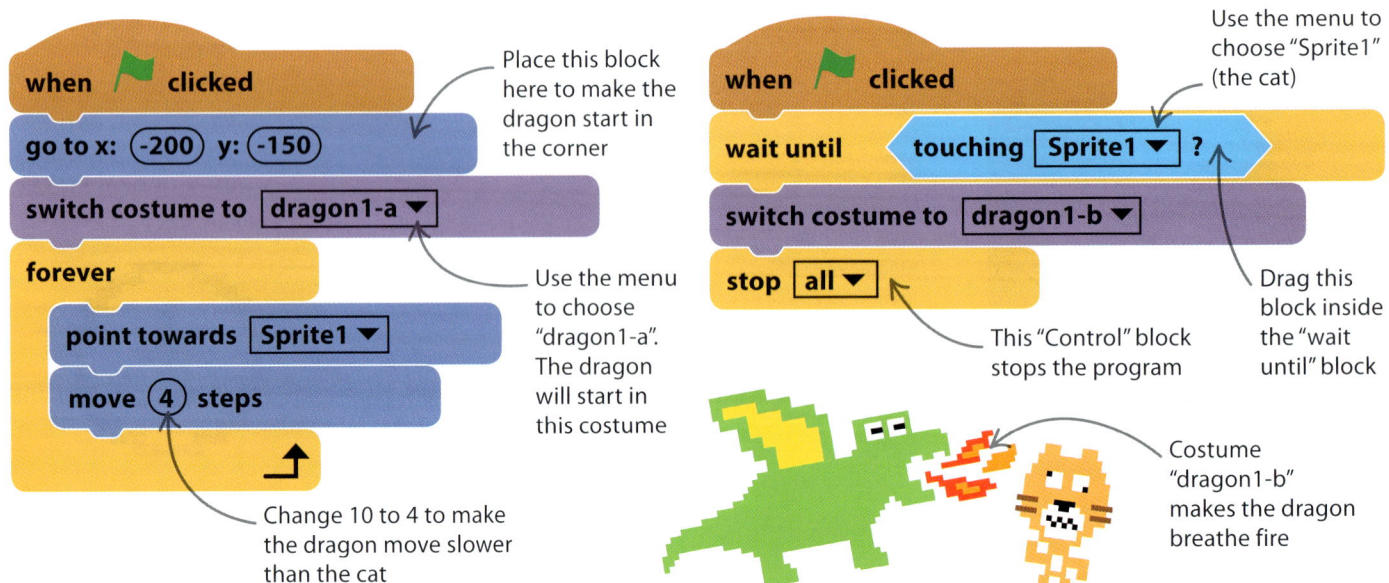

Place this block here to make the dragon start in the corner

Use the menu to choose "dragon1-a". The dragon will start in this costume

Change 10 to 4 to make the dragon move slower than the cat

Use the menu to choose "Sprite1" (the cat)

Drag this block inside the "wait until" block

This "Control" block stops the program

Costume "dragon1-b" makes the dragon breathe fire

ESCAPE THE DRAGON! **31**

12> In coding, a "variable" is used to store information. This step uses a variable to create a timer to measure how long a player survives before getting toasted. Click the "Data" button and then click "Make a Variable".

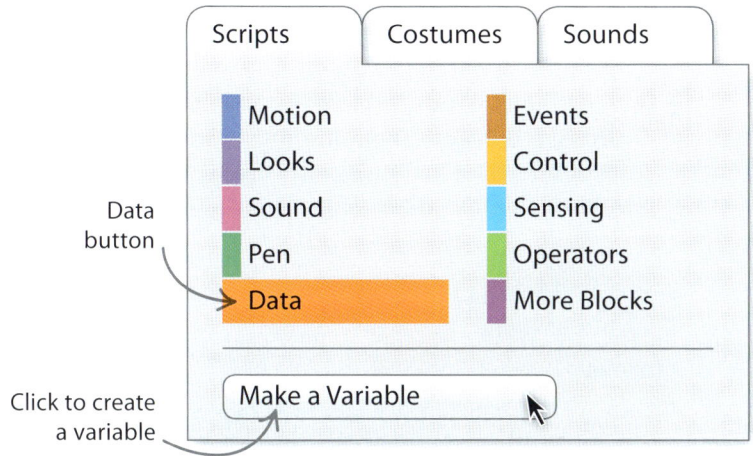

Data button

Click to create a variable

> **EXPERT TIPS**
> ## Make the game harder
> Try changing the speed or size of your sprites.
>
> **Make the dragon faster:**
>
>
>
> **Make the dragon larger or smaller:**
>
> Click this icon and then click a sprite to make it larger.
>
> Click this icon and then click a sprite to make it smaller.

13> Type in the variable name "Time" and make sure the "For all sprites" button is selected underneath, then click "OK". This means that the cat, dragon, and any other sprites can use the variable.

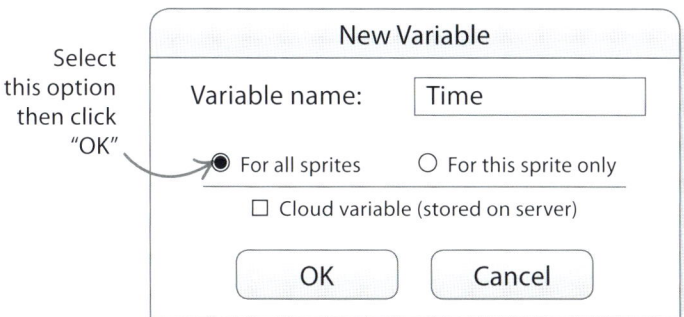

Select this option then click "OK"

14> The variable name and the number in it appear on the stage in a small box. Right-click it and choose "large readout". This shows just the number in the box.

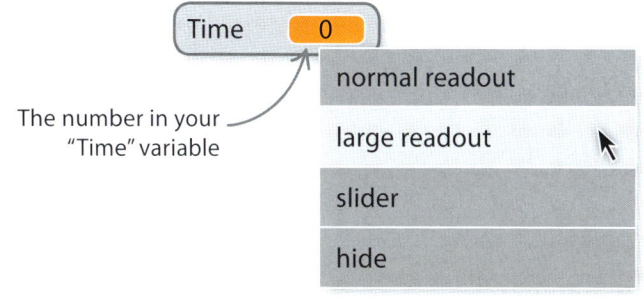

The number in your "Time" variable

15> Making a variable adds new blocks to the "Data" section of the blocks palette. Drag the "set Time to 0" and "change Time by 1" blocks from the "Data" section to the scripts area to make this new script. You can give this script to any sprite.

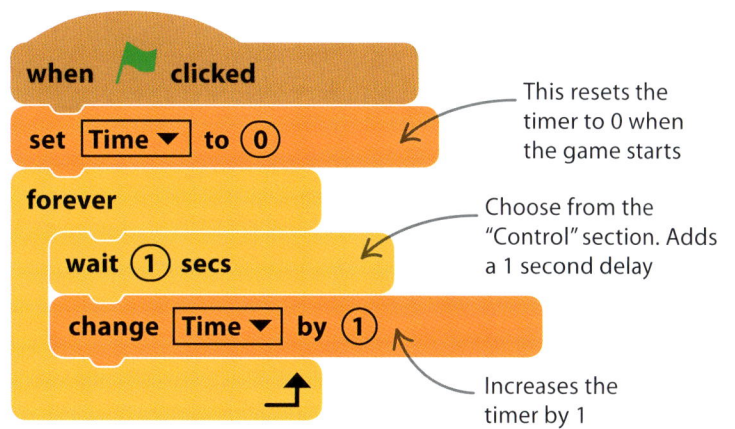

This resets the timer to 0 when the game starts

Choose from the "Control" section. Adds a 1 second delay

Increases the timer by 1

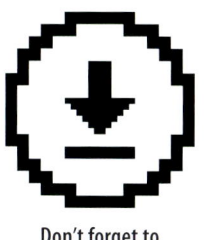

Don't forget to save your work

ESCAPE THE DRAGON!

Add a delicious donut

Scratch comes with lots of sprites in its library. Make the game trickier by adding a donut sprite to the program for the cat to chase.

16 ▸ Click the button above the sprite list to add a new sprite from the library. Select "Donut" from the "Things" category on the left and click "OK".

17 ▸ Add this script to the donut. The "mouse down?" block can be found in the "Sensing" section, and the "go to mouse-pointer" block in the "Motion" section. This script makes the donut follow the mouse-pointer when the mouse button is clicked.

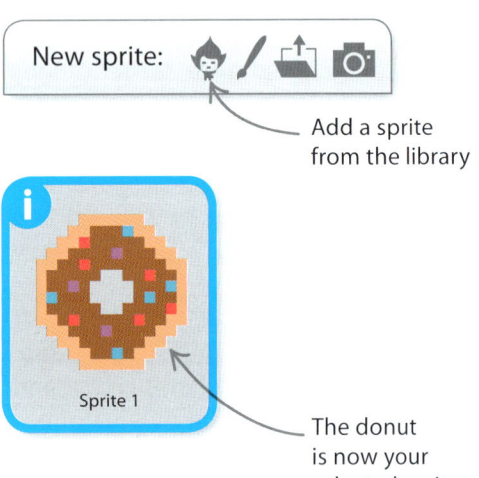

Add a sprite from the library

The donut is now your selected sprite

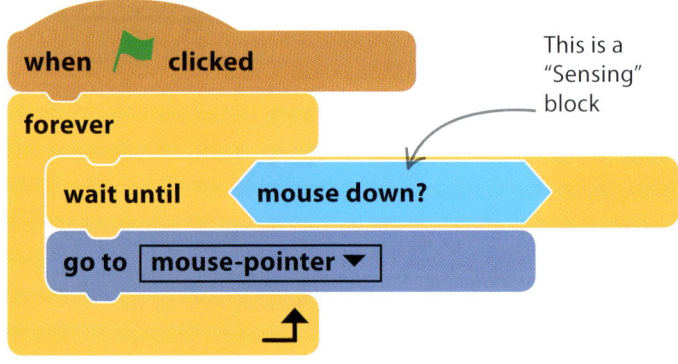

This is a "Sensing" block

18 ▸ Select the cat in the sprite list so its script appears. Click the menu in the "point towards mouse-pointer" block. Change it so that the cat follows the donut instead of the mouse-pointer.

19 ▸ Click the green flag button to run the program. Press the mouse button and the donut moves to the mouse-pointer. The cat follows the donut, and the dragon chases the cat.

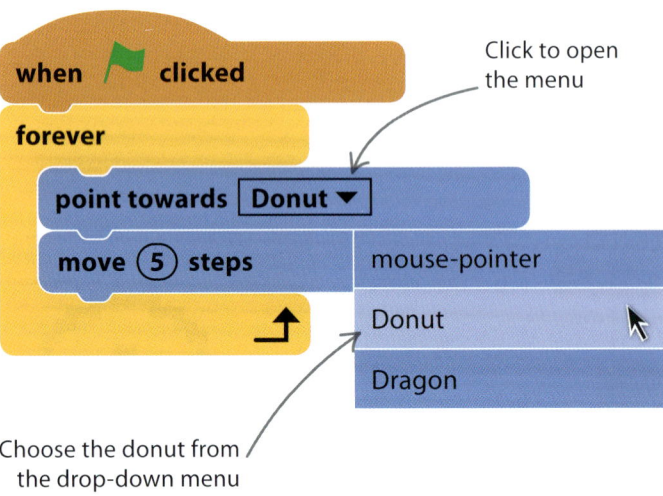

Click to open the menu

Choose the donut from the drop-down menu

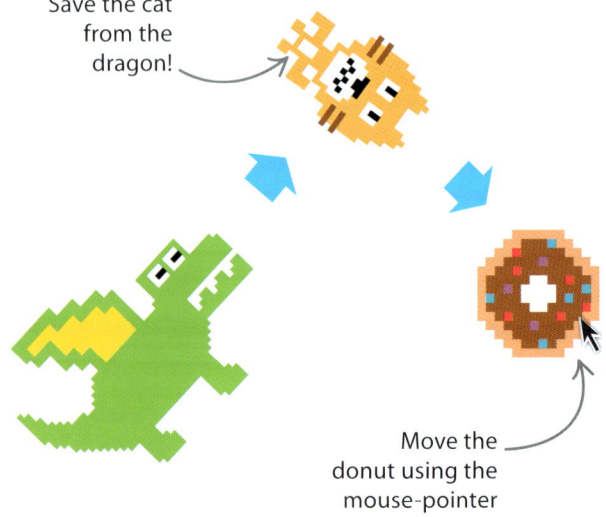

Save the cat from the dragon!

Move the donut using the mouse-pointer

ESCAPE THE DRAGON! 33

20 Now add some music. Click the "Sounds" tab above the blocks palette. Each sprite has its own sounds, and they are managed here. Click the button on the left to add a sound from the library.

21 Select the "drip drop" sound and click the "OK" button at the bottom-right. The sound is added to the cat sprite, and appears in the "Sounds" area.

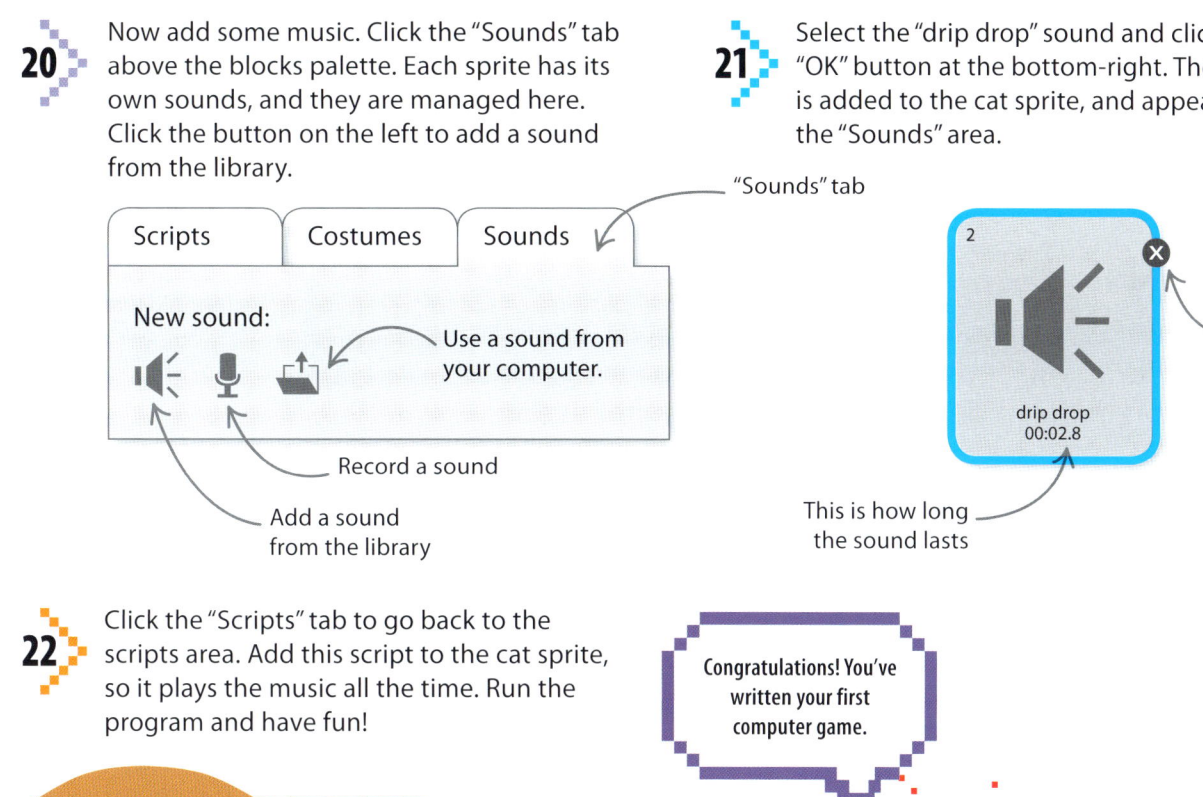

22 Click the "Scripts" tab to go back to the scripts area. Add this script to the cat sprite, so it plays the music all the time. Run the program and have fun!

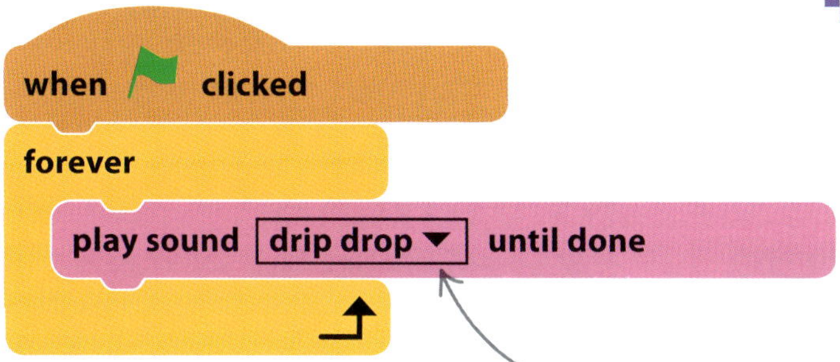

Congratulations! You've written your first computer game.

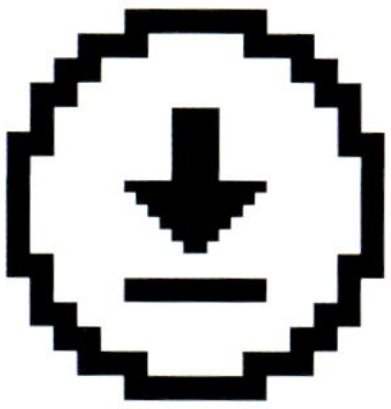

Don't forget to save your work

REMEMBER
Achievements

This project has shown some of the things Scratch can do. Here's what you've achieved.

Created a program: By combining blocks of code into scripts, you've put together a game.

Added pictures: You've used both backdrops and sprites.

Made sprites move: You've made sprites chase each other.

Used a variable: You've created a timer for your game.

Used costumes: You've changed the dragon's appearance using different costumes.

Added music: You've added a sound, and made it play when your program runs.

34 STARTING FROM SCRATCH

Making things move

Computer games are all about firing, dodging, catching, and escaping. Characters might run, fly spaceships, or drive fast cars. To create great games in Scratch, you first need to learn how to make sprites move.

> **SEE ALSO**
> ‹ 24–25 Sprites
> Co-ordinates 52–53 ›

Motion blocks

The dark blue "Motion" blocks make sprites move. Start a new project by clicking the "File" menu and choosing "New". The new project begins with the cat in the middle of the stage, ready for action.

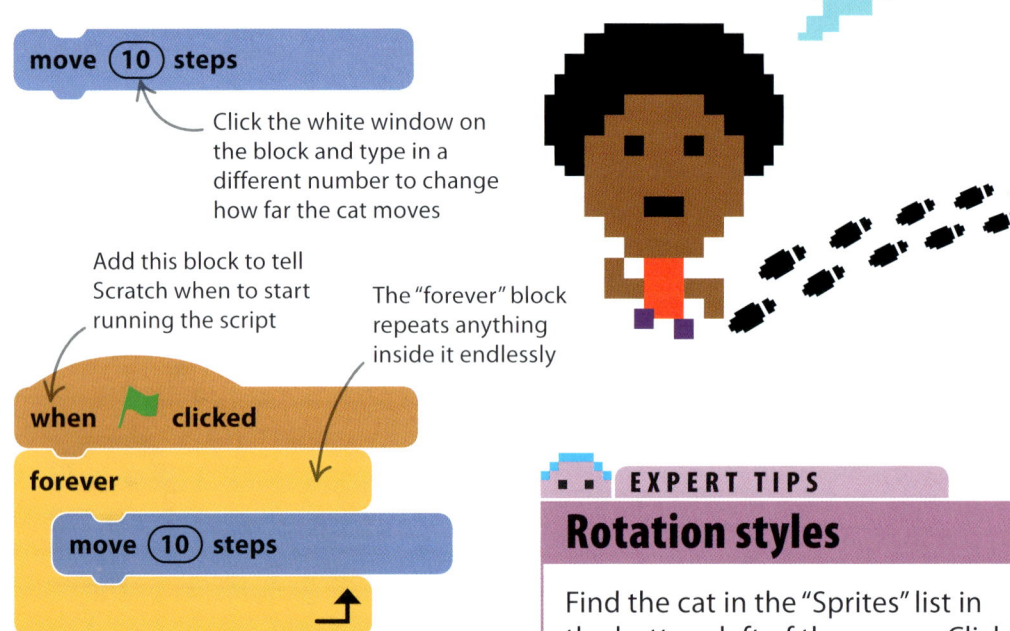

Scratch won't let sprites walk off the stage, so you'll never lose us.

1 First steps
Drag the "move 10 steps" block from the "Motion" section of the blocks palette and drop it into the scripts area to its right. Each time you click the block, the cat moves.

Click the white window on the block and type in a different number to change how far the cat moves

2 Keep on moving
Drag a yellow "forever" block from the blocks palette and drop it around the "move 10 steps" block. Click the green flag on the stage to run the program. The cat moves until it hits the edge of the stage.

Add this block to tell Scratch when to start running the script

The "forever" block repeats anything inside it endlessly

3 Bouncing
Drag an "if on edge, bounce" block inside your "forever" block. Now the cat bounces when it hits the edge of the stage. The cat is upside down when it walks to the left.

Try changing 10 to 30 to make the cat sprint!

This block makes the cat turn around when it hits the edge of the stage

▪▪▪ EXPERT TIPS
Rotation styles

Find the cat in the "Sprites" list in the bottom left of the screen. Click the "i" button in the top left of the frame. Here you'll find a button to change the cat's rotation style – so it doesn't walk around on its head!

↻ The cat faces the direction it's walking in, sometimes upside down.

↔ The cat faces left or right, and is always the right way up.

• The cat doesn't rotate at all.

MAKING THINGS MOVE

Which direction?

The cat is now marching left and right across the screen. It's possible to change the cat's direction, so it walks up and down, or even diagonally. The "Motion" blocks can be used to make a game of cat and mouse.

The direction -90° means "left"

△ **Compass**
Directions are measured in degrees, from 0° at the top. You can use any number between -179° and +180°.

4 Heading the right way
Drag the "point in direction" block into the scripts area and open its drop-down menu. There are four directions to choose from. Or, click on the number in the window and type in a new direction.

Click the block to make the cat change direction

Select or type in a new number to change the direction of the cat

point in direction (45 ▼)

(90) right
(-90) left
(0) up
(180) down

The drop-down menu gives you four options

The cat will follow the mouse-pointer

5 Cat and mouse
Remove the "move 10 steps" and "if on edge, bounce" blocks from the script. Now drag a "point towards" block into the "forever" block. Open the menu and choose "mouse-pointer".

when ▶ clicked
forever
  point towards mouse-pointer ▼

Click the green flag to start the program

As the mouse-pointer moves, the cat turns to face it

REMEMBER
Sprites

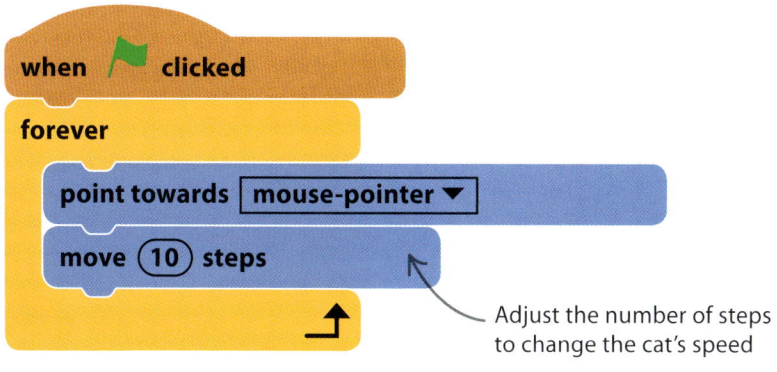

Sprites are objects in a Scratch program that you can move around (see pp.24-25). Every new project stars the cat sprite, but you can add cars, dinosaurs, dancers, and all sorts of other sprites from the library. You can even have a go at designing your own.

6 Chase the mouse
Can the cat catch the mouse? Drag a "move 10 steps" block into the "forever" loop. Now the cat walks towards the mouse-pointer.

when ▶ clicked
forever
  point towards mouse-pointer ▼
  move (10) steps

Adjust the number of steps to change the cat's speed

35

Costumes

To change what a sprite looks like, its expression, or its position, you need to change its "costume". Costumes are pictures of a sprite in different poses.

> **SEE ALSO**
>
> ‹ **34–35** Making things move
>
> Sending **66–67** › messages

Changing costumes

Different costumes can make your sprite look like it's moving its arms and legs. When you switch between the cat's two costumes, it looks like it's walking. Start a new project and try this example.

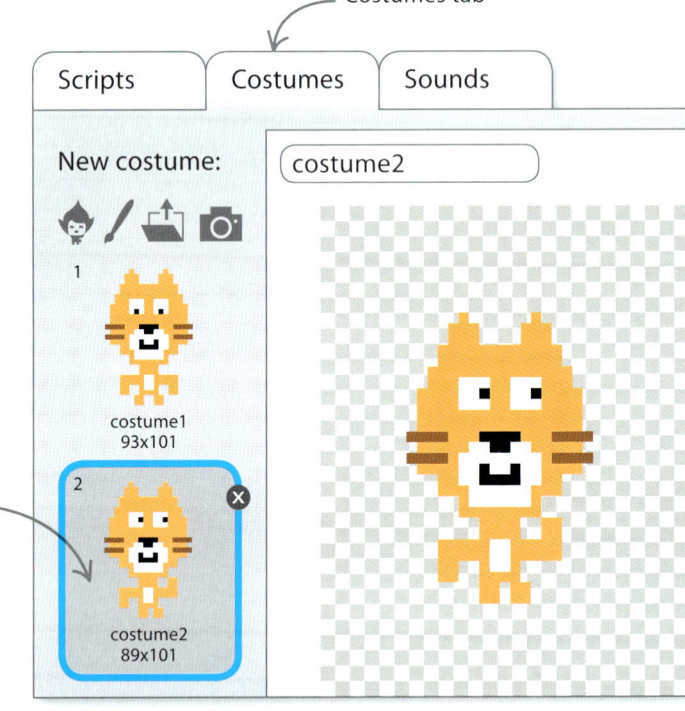

Costumes tab

One of the cat's costumes

1. **Different costumes**
   Click the "Costumes" tab to see the cat's costumes. They show the cat with its legs and arms in two different positions.

2. **Make the cat walk**
   Add this script to make the cat walk. When it moves, it slides across the screen without moving its legs, because its picture always stays the same.

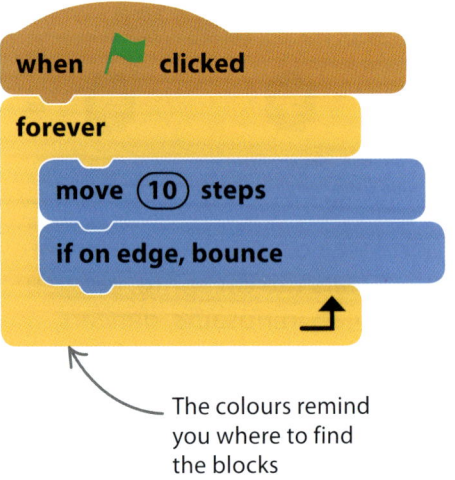

The colours remind you where to find the blocks

3. **Change the cat's costume**
   Add the "next costume" block from the "Looks" section of the blocks palette, so the cat changes its costume with each step. This makes its legs and arms move.

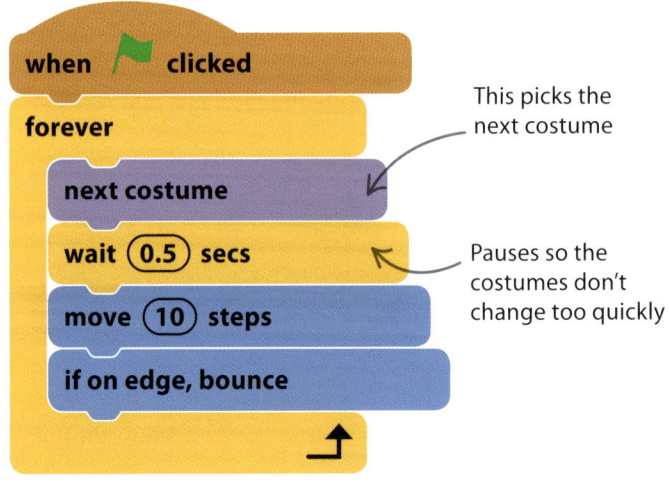

This picks the next costume

Pauses so the costumes don't change too quickly

Dancing ballerina

Now try making a ballerina dance. Add the ballerina sprite from the library. Select your cat in the sprite list and drag its script on to the ballerina in the sprite list. This copies the script to the ballerina.

Sprite 1

Drop the script on to the ballerina in the sprite list

The green flag starts the ballerina's dance

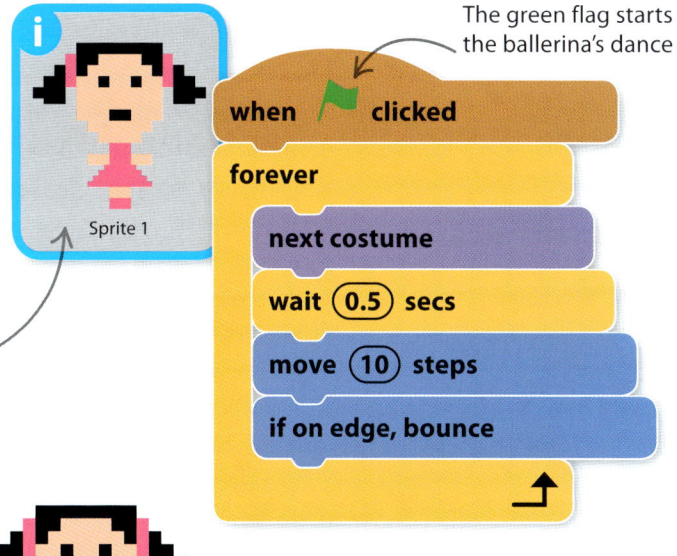

```
when [green flag] clicked
forever
    next costume
    wait (0.5) secs
    move (10) steps
    if on edge, bounce
```

△ **Ballerina's script**
The same script works for the ballerina and the cat. The ballerina has four costumes, and she uses them all as she dances on the stage.

EXPERT TIPS
Switching

You can choose to show a specific costume for your sprite using the "switch costume to" block. You can use this block to choose a particular position for your sprite.

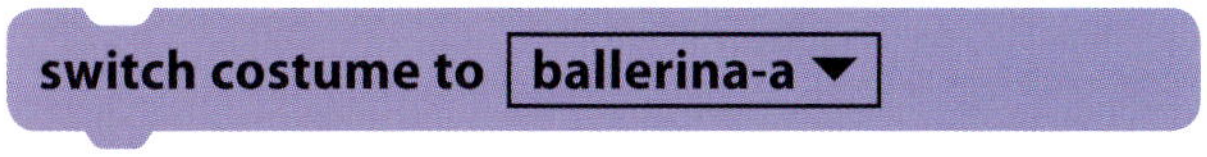

`switch costume to [ballerina-a ▼]`

Switch costumes: Use the menu in the block to choose a costume.

`switch backdrop to [backdrop1 ▼]`

Switch backdrops: Change the picture on the stage with this block.

Adding speech bubbles

You can add speech bubbles to make your sprites talk when they change costumes. Use the "say Hello! for 2 secs" block and change the text in it to make your sprite say something else.

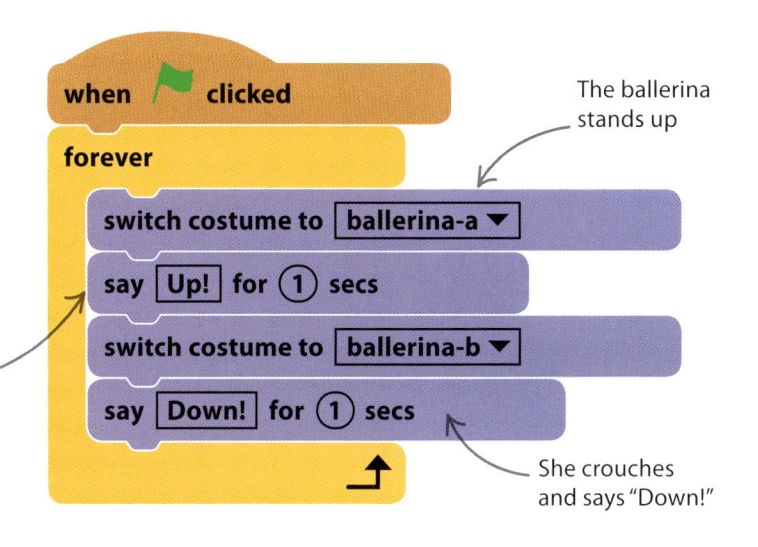

The ballerina says "Up!"

The ballerina stands up

```
when [green flag] clicked
forever
    switch costume to [ballerina-a ▼]
    say [Up!] for (1) secs
    switch costume to [ballerina-b ▼]
    say [Down!] for (1) secs
```

She crouches and says "Down!"

Hide and seek

Welcome to the special effects studio! Using the purple "Looks" blocks, find out how to make sprites vanish and reappear, grow and shrink, and fade in and out.

> **SEE ALSO**
> ‹ **34–35** Making things move
> Sending **66–67** › messages

Hiding sprites

To make a sprite disappear, use the "hide" block. The sprite is still on the stage, and it can still move around, but it can't be seen unless the "show" block is used to make it visible again.

Use the "hide" block to make sprites disappear in games

▷ **Hide and show**
To make a sprite vanish, use the "hide" block. When you're ready for it to be seen again, use the "show" block. These blocks are found in the "Looks" section of the blocks palette.

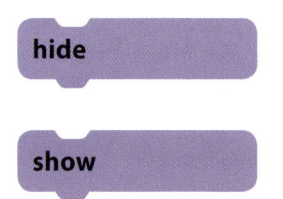

`hide`

`show`

▽ **Disappearing cat**
Try this script using the cat sprite. It disappears and reappears but it keeps moving, even when you can't see it.

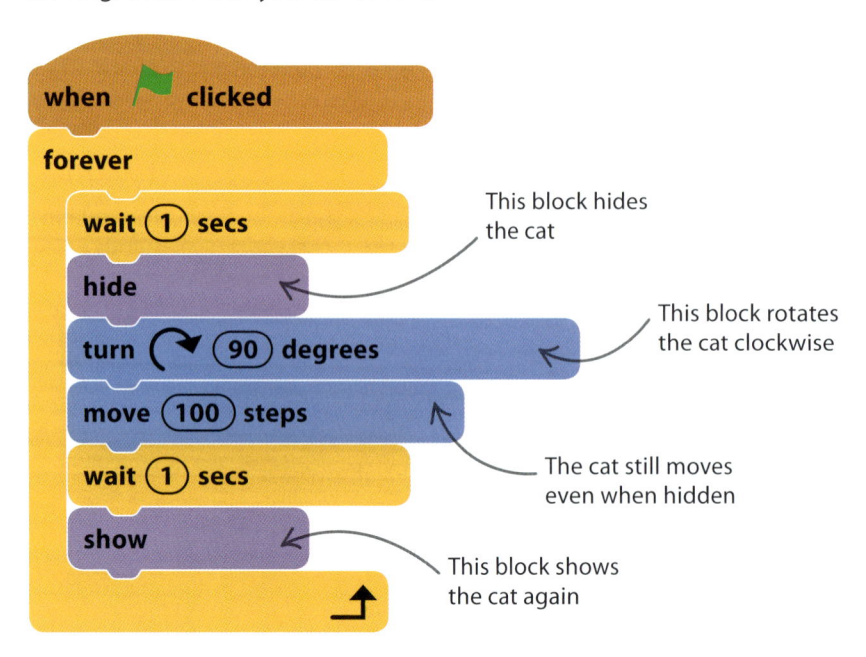

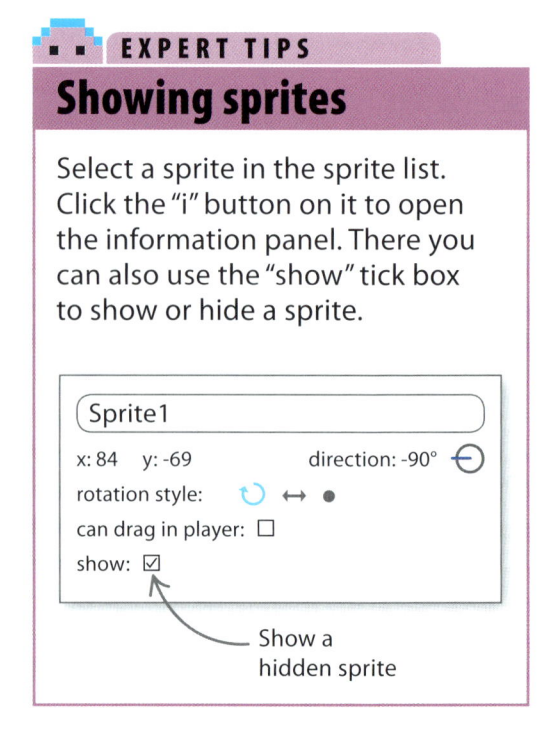

```
when ⚑ clicked
forever
    wait 1 secs
    hide
    turn ↻ 90 degrees
    move 100 steps
    wait 1 secs
    show
```

This block hides the cat

This block rotates the cat clockwise

The cat still moves even when hidden

This block shows the cat again

> **EXPERT TIPS**
> ## Showing sprites
>
> Select a sprite in the sprite list. Click the "i" button on it to open the information panel. There you can also use the "show" tick box to show or hide a sprite.
>
> ```
> Sprite1
> x: 84    y: -69          direction: -90°
> rotation style:  ↻  ↔  •
> can drag in player: ☐
> show: ☑
> ```
>
> Show a hidden sprite

HIDE AND SEEK   **39**

Sizes and effects

Scripts can be used to change the size of a sprite and add special effects to it.

`change size by (10)` — Type in positive numbers to make sprites bigger and negative numbers to make them smaller

Choose the type of effect from the drop-down menu. The "pixelate" effect makes the sprite become blurred

Change the numbers in the blocks to set how strong the effect is

`change [pixelate ▼] effect by (25)`

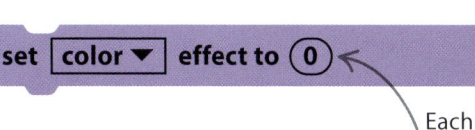

`set [color ▼] effect to (0)`

Each colour is represented by a number. Change the number to set the colour

`set size to (100) %` — Higher numbers make sprites bigger and lower numbers make them smaller. 100 is normal size

`clear graphic effects` — Resets all the effects

△ **Changing a sprite's size**
These two blocks can be used to make a sprite bigger or smaller, either by a set amount or by a percentage of its size.

△ **Adding graphic effects**
The graphic effects in Scratch can be used to change a sprite's appearance or distort its shape. They're fun to experiment with.

Using effects to teleport

Add a ghost sprite from the "Fantasy" category of the sprite library, and create the script shown below. It makes the ghost appear to teleport when clicked.

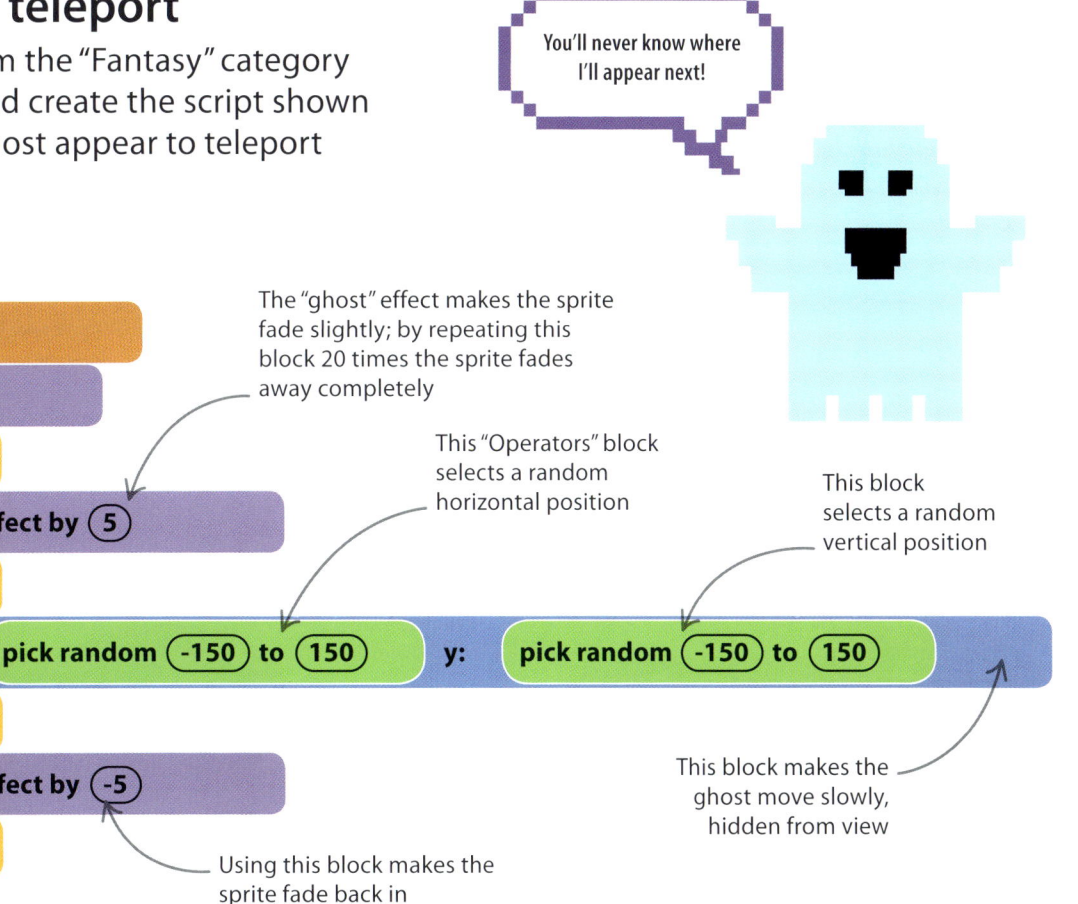

You'll never know where I'll appear next!

```
when this sprite clicked
clear graphic effects
repeat (20)
    change [ghost ▼] effect by (5)
glide (0.1) secs to x: (pick random (-150) to (150))  y: (pick random (-150) to (150))
repeat (20)
    change [ghost ▼] effect by (-5)
```

The "ghost" effect makes the sprite fade slightly; by repeating this block 20 times the sprite fades away completely

This "Operators" block selects a random horizontal position

This block selects a random vertical position

This block makes the ghost move slowly, hidden from view

Using this block makes the sprite fade back in

Events

The brown "Events" blocks in Scratch start scripts when certain things happen. For example, when the user presses a key, clicks a sprite, or uses a webcam or microphone.

> **SEE ALSO**
> Sensing **62–63** ⟩
> and detecting
> Sending **66–67** ⟩
> messages

Clicking

A script can be added to a sprite that makes it do something if the sprite is clicked while the program is running. Experiment with different blocks to see what a sprite can do when clicked.

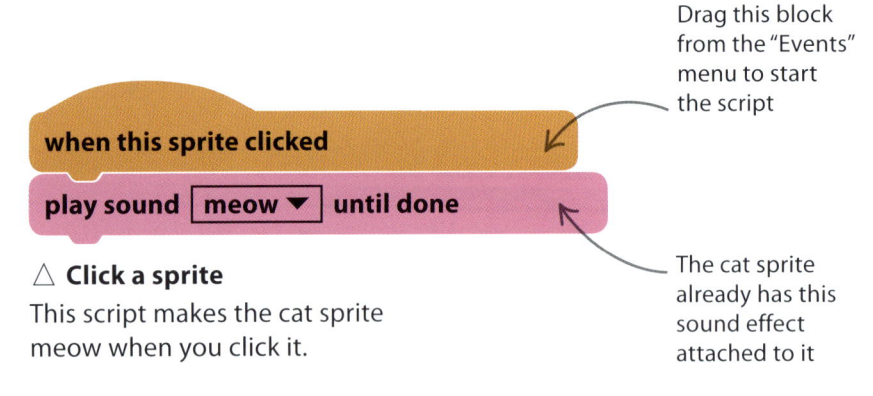

Drag this block from the "Events" menu to start the script

`when this sprite clicked`
`play sound [meow ▼] until done`

The cat sprite already has this sound effect attached to it

△ **Click a sprite**
This script makes the cat sprite meow when you click it.

> **LINGO**
> ### What is an event?
> An event is something that happens, such as a key being pressed or the green flag being clicked. The blocks that look for events go at the top of a script. The script waits until the event happens, and then it runs.

Key presses

Programs can be built to react when different keys on the keyboard are pressed. For another way of using the keyboard that's better for creating games, see pages 62–63.

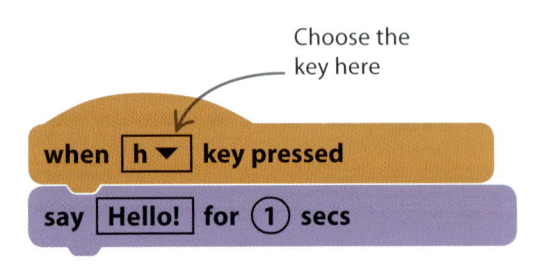

Choose the key here

`when [h ▼] key pressed`
`say [Hello!] for (1) secs`

△ **Say hello**
Add this script to a sprite and when the H key is pressed, the sprite says "Hello!"

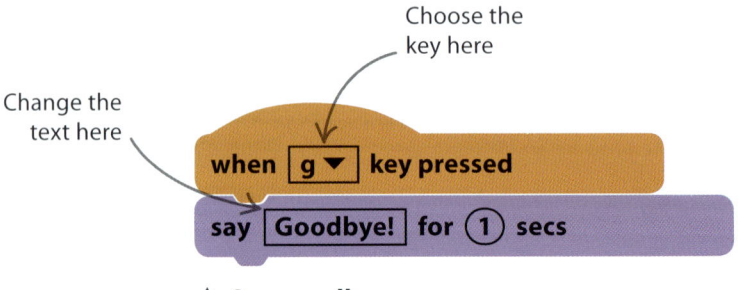

Change the text here

Choose the key here

`when [g ▼] key pressed`
`say [Goodbye!] for (1) secs`

△ **Say goodbye**
This script uses the G key to make a sprite say "Goodbye!"

EVENTS   41

Sound events

If your computer has a microphone, sprites can detect how loud the sounds in a room are on a scale of 0 (very quiet) to 100 (very loud). Use the "when loudness > 10" block to make a script start when the sounds are loud enough.

> **EXPERT TIPS**
> ### Asking permission
> Scratch asks for permission to use your webcam and microphone. When the box pops up, click "Allow".

1 Make the cat sensitive to noise
Start a new project, and add the "room3" backdrop image from the backdrop library. Drag the cat sprite on to the chair and add the script shown here.

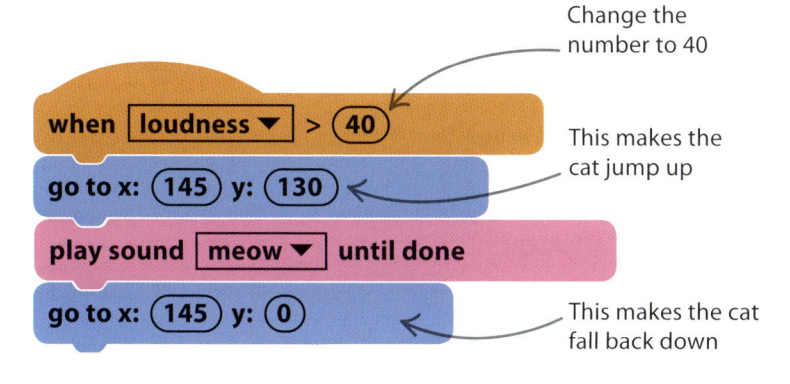

2 Shout at the cat
Shout into the microphone – the cat will jump out of its seat with fright and meow. It will also respond to music and other sounds if they are loud enough.

```
when loudness ▼ > 40
go to x: 145 y: 130
play sound meow ▼ until done
go to x: 145 y: 0
```

Change the number to 40
This makes the cat jump up
This makes the cat fall back down

Webcam motion detector

If you have a webcam, it can be used with Scratch too. Add this script to the cat, and when you wave at it through the webcam, it will meow back.

```
when video motion ▼ > 40
play sound meow ▼ until done
```

Change the number to 40

△ **Detect motion**
Use the "when loudness > 10" block. Click the menu to change "loudness" to "video motion". The script will start when you're moving around enough.

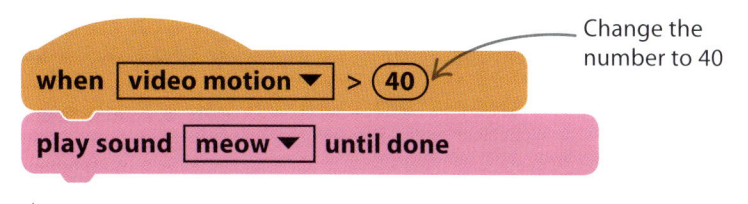

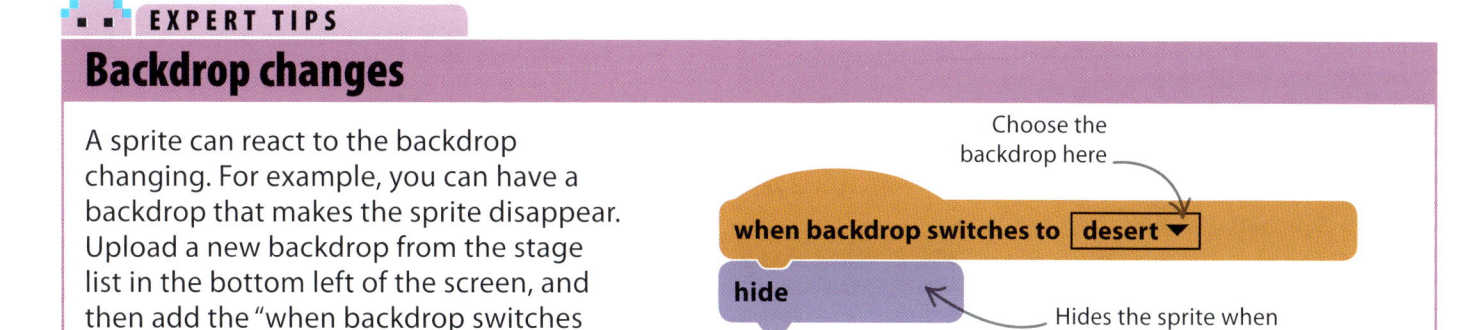

> **EXPERT TIPS**
> ### Backdrop changes
> A sprite can react to the backdrop changing. For example, you can have a backdrop that makes the sprite disappear. Upload a new backdrop from the stage list in the bottom left of the screen, and then add the "when backdrop switches to backdrop1" block to do this.
>
> ```
> when backdrop switches to desert ▼
> hide
> ```
>
> Choose the backdrop here
> Hides the sprite when the backdrop changes

Simple loops

A loop is a part of a program that repeats itself. The loop blocks (from the "Control" section) tell Scratch which blocks to repeat, and how many times. They save us from adding the same blocks over and over again.

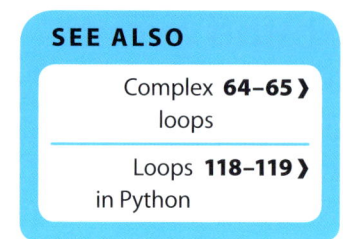

> **SEE ALSO**
> Complex **64–65** ⟩
> loops
> Loops **118–119** ⟩
> in Python

Forever loop

Whatever you put inside the "forever" block repeats itself forever. There's no option to join anything at the bottom, because a "forever" loop never ends.

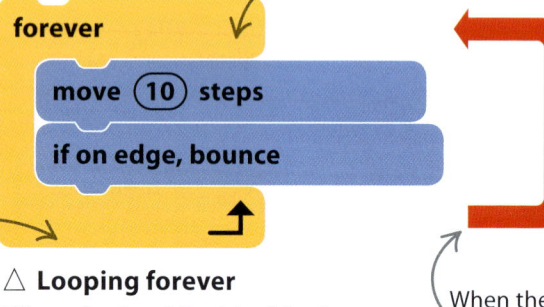

No option to add more Scratch blocks

Drop blocks inside this loop to repeat the actions forever

△ **Looping forever**
When the last block inside the loop ends, the loop goes back to the start again.

When the actions finish the program goes back to the start of the loop again

Repeat loop

To repeat an action a certain number of times, use a "repeat 10" block. Change the number in it to set how many times the loop will repeat itself. Add the "Dinosaur1" sprite to a new project and build it this script.

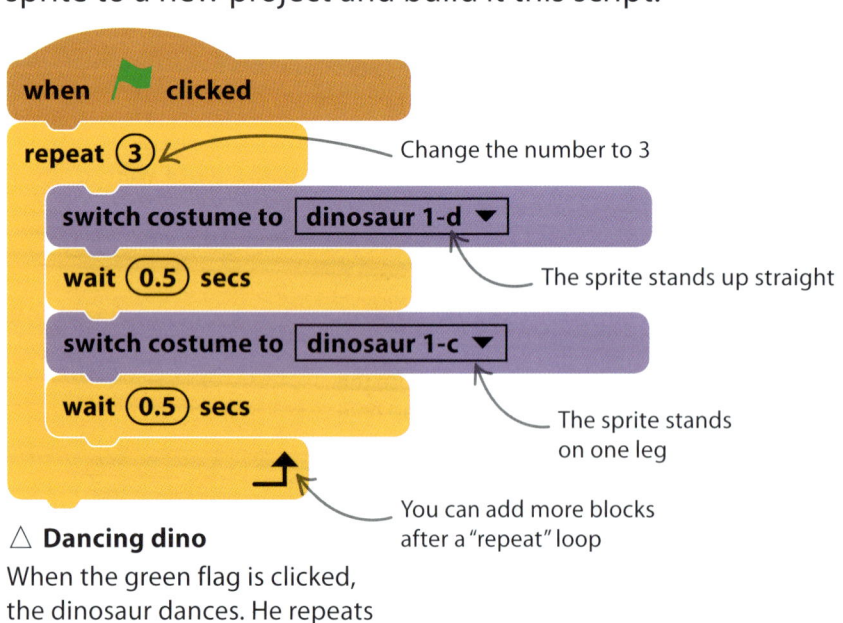

Change the number to 3

The sprite stands up straight

The sprite stands on one leg

You can add more blocks after a "repeat" loop

△ **Dancing dino**
When the green flag is clicked, the dinosaur dances. He repeats his dance moves three times.

> **REMEMBER**
> ### Loop block shape
> The loop blocks are shaped like jaws. Drop the blocks that you want to repeat into the jaws, so the loop wraps around them. As you add more blocks, the jaws stretch to make room for them.

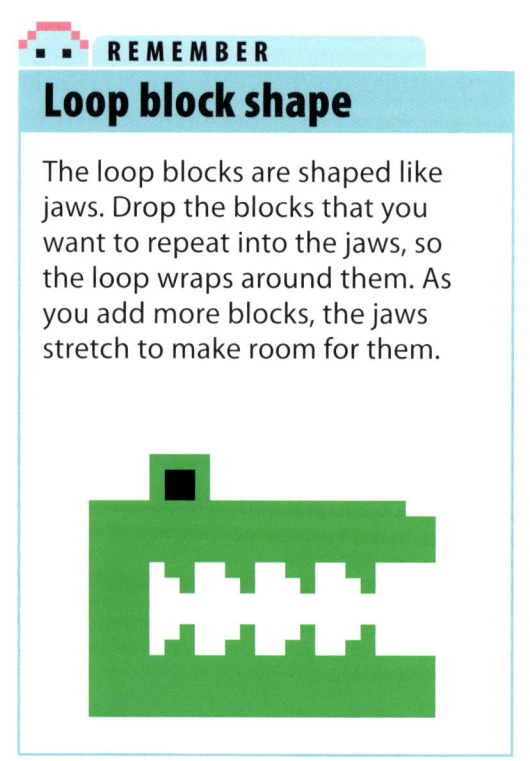

SIMPLE LOOPS 43

Nested loops

Loops can also be "nested", which means they can be put inside each other. In this script, the dinosaur finishes his dance by walking right and left and then thinking for a moment. When he's got his breath back, he dances again and stops only when you click the red stop button.

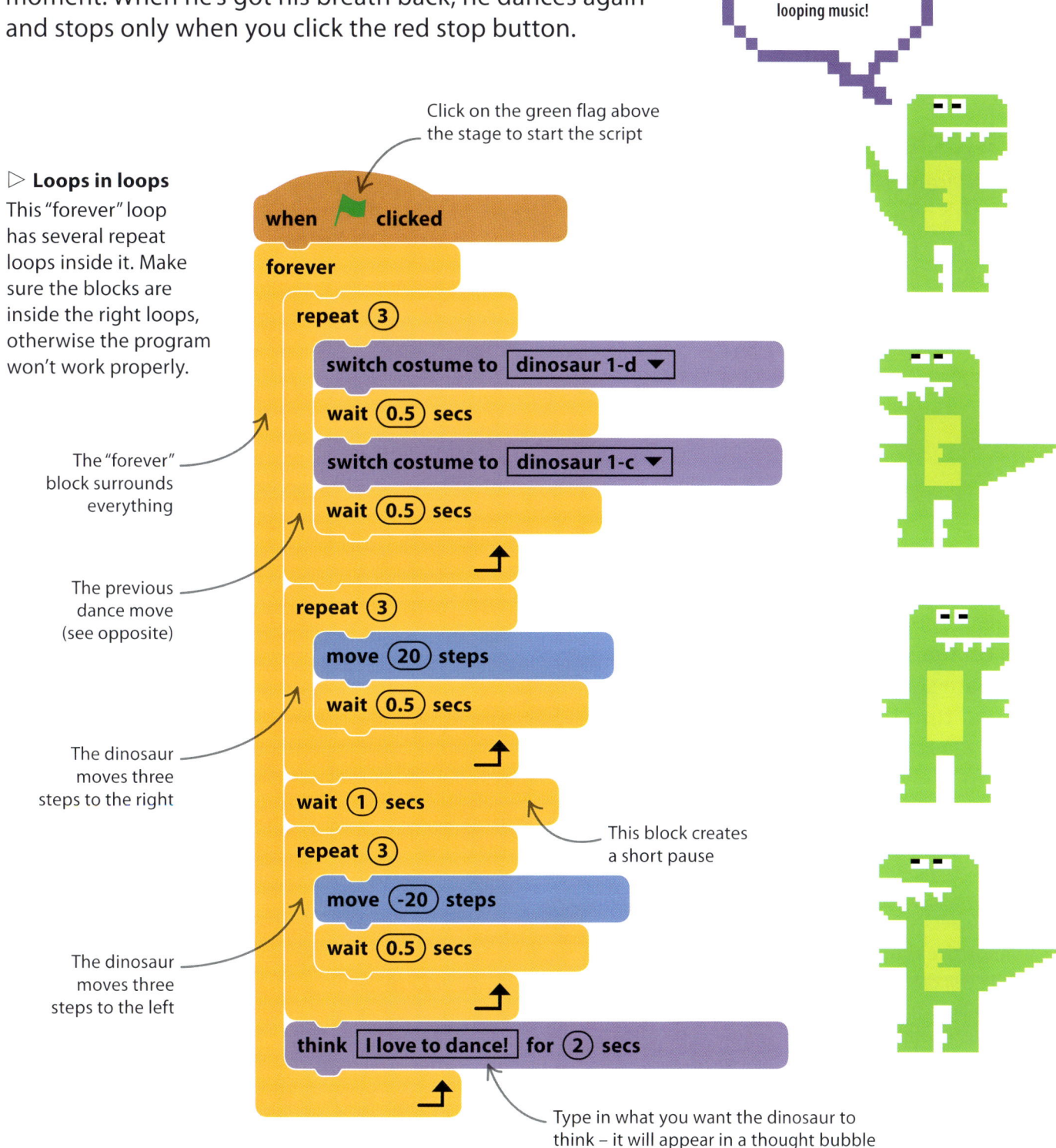

Try giving me some looping music!

▷ **Loops in loops**
This "forever" loop has several repeat loops inside it. Make sure the blocks are inside the right loops, otherwise the program won't work properly.

Click on the green flag above the stage to start the script

The "forever" block surrounds everything

The previous dance move (see opposite)

The dinosaur moves three steps to the right

The dinosaur moves three steps to the left

```
when ▶ clicked
forever
    repeat (3)
        switch costume to [dinosaur 1-d ▼]
        wait (0.5) secs
        switch costume to [dinosaur 1-c ▼]
        wait (0.5) secs
    repeat (3)
        move (20) steps
        wait (0.5) secs
    wait (1) secs
    repeat (3)
        move (-20) steps
        wait (0.5) secs
    think [I love to dance!] for (2) secs
```

This block creates a short pause

Type in what you want the dinosaur to think – it will appear in a thought bubble

Pens and turtles

Each sprite has a pen tool that can draw a line behind it wherever it goes. To create a picture, turn on the pen and then move the sprite across the stage, like moving a pen across paper.

> **SEE ALSO**
> ‹ 40–41 Events
> ‹ 42–43 Simple loops

Pen blocks

The dark green blocks are used to control the pen. Each sprite has its own pen that can be turned on by using the "pen down" block and turned off using the "pen up" block. The size and colour of the pen can also be changed.

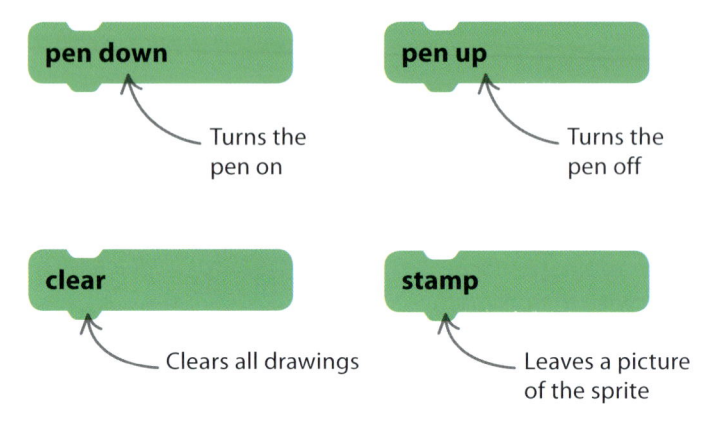

`pen down` — Turns the pen on

`pen up` — Turns the pen off

`clear` — Clears all drawings

`stamp` — Leaves a picture of the sprite

△ **Playing with pens**
Experiment with how you can use the pen blocks to make drawings.

Draw a square

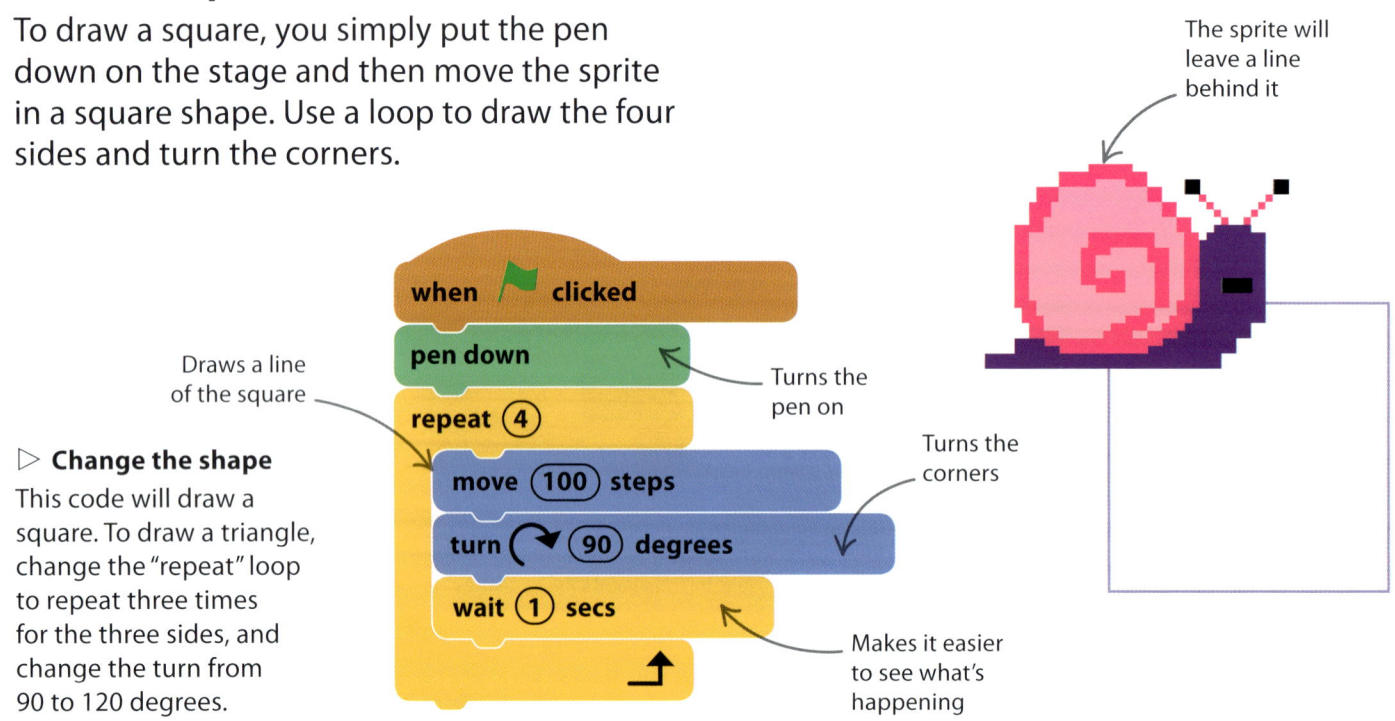

To draw a square, you simply put the pen down on the stage and then move the sprite in a square shape. Use a loop to draw the four sides and turn the corners.

The sprite will leave a line behind it

▷ **Change the shape**
This code will draw a square. To draw a triangle, change the "repeat" loop to repeat three times for the three sides, and change the turn from 90 to 120 degrees.

```
when [flag] clicked
pen down
repeat (4)
    move (100) steps
    turn ↻ (90) degrees
    wait (1) secs
```

- Draws a line of the square
- Turns the pen on
- Turns the corners
- Makes it easier to see what's happening

PENS AND TURTLES   **45**

Skywriting

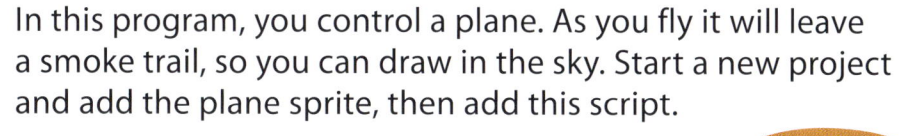

In this program, you control a plane. As you fly it will leave a smoke trail, so you can draw in the sky. Start a new project and add the plane sprite, then add this script.

You can only use colours that appear on the Scratch interface. To select red, click in the square and then click on the red stop button above the stage

▷ **Flying high**
Use the left and right keys to turn the plane. Switch on the smoke with the "a" key and turn it off with the "z" key. Press the spacebar to clear the sky.

```
when [flag] clicked
set size to (20) %
set pen color to [red]
set pen size to (3)
forever
    move (2) steps
    if on edge, bounce
```

Makes the line thicker

Keeps the plane moving

Keeps the plane on the stage

```
when [right arrow ▼] key pressed
turn ↻ (10) degrees
```
Rotates right

```
when [left arrow ▼] key pressed
turn ↺ (10) degrees
```
Rotates left

```
when [a ▼] key pressed
pen down
```
Turns the pen on

```
when [z ▼] key pressed
pen up
```
Turns the pen off

```
when [space ▼] key pressed
clear
```
Clears the pen trail

LINGO
Turtle graphics

Using sprites to draw pictures is called "turtle graphics". That's because there's a type of robot called a turtle that can be moved around the floor to draw pictures. The first programming language to use turtle graphics was called LOGO.

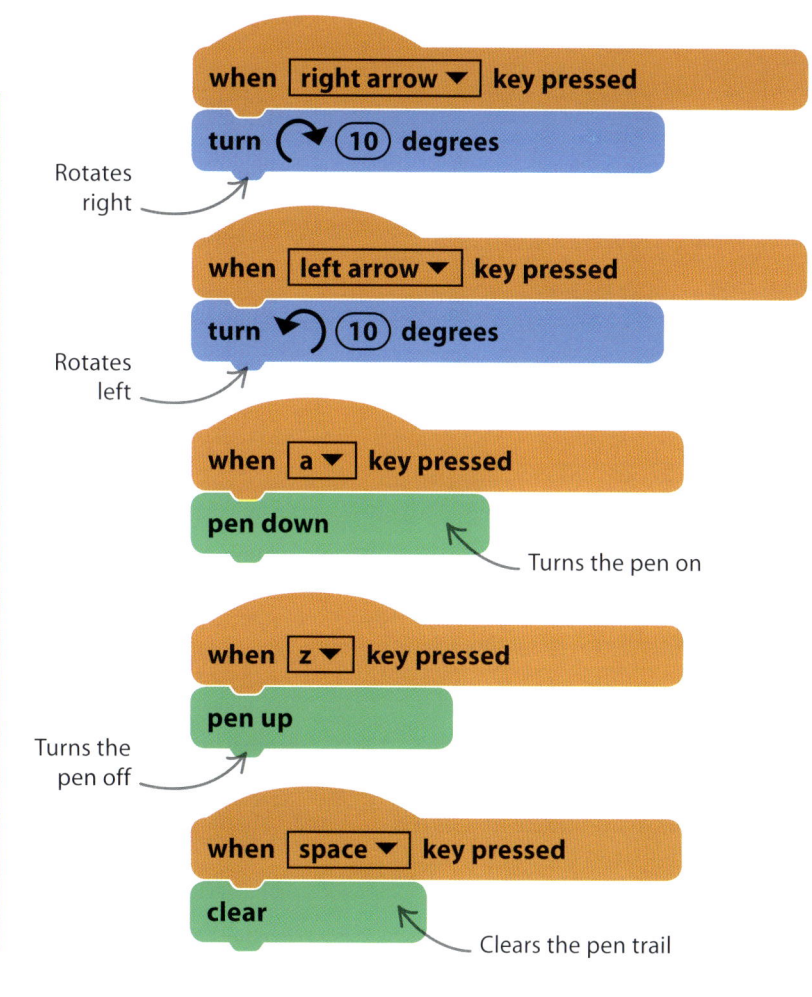

Variables

In coding, a variable is the name for a place where you can store information. They're used to remember things such as the score, a player's name, or a character's speed.

> **SEE ALSO**
> Maths **48–49** 〉
> Variables **104–105** 〉
> in Python

Creating a variable

You can create a variable to use in your program using the "Data" section of the blocks palette. Once a variable has been created, new blocks appear in the blocks palette ready for you to use.

◁ **Storing data**
Variables are like boxes where you can store different bits of information for use in your program.

1 Make a variable
First, click the "Data" button in the blocks palette. Then select the "Make a Variable" button.

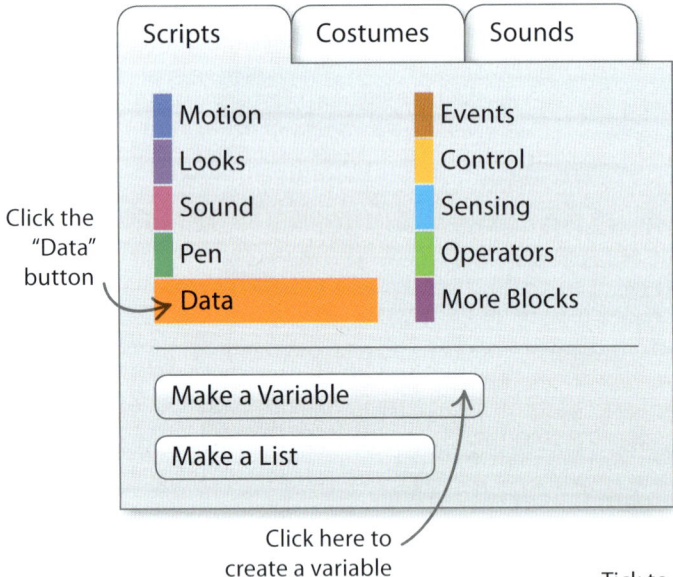

Click the "Data" button

Click here to create a variable

2 Name the new variable
Give the variable a name that will help you to remember what it does. Select which sprites will use the variable, then click "OK".

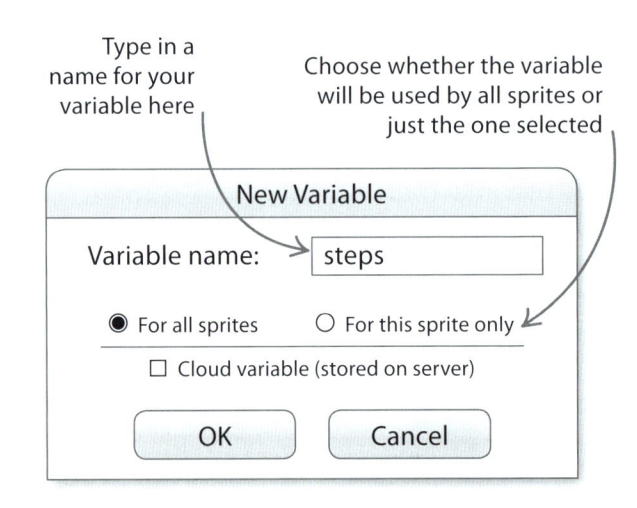

Type in a name for your variable here

Choose whether the variable will be used by all sprites or just the one selected

New Variable
Variable name: steps
● For all sprites   ○ For this sprite only
☐ Cloud variable (stored on server)
OK   Cancel

3 A new variable is created
Once a new variable has been created, new blocks appear in the blocks palette. The menus inside these blocks let you select which variable they apply to, if you have created more than one.

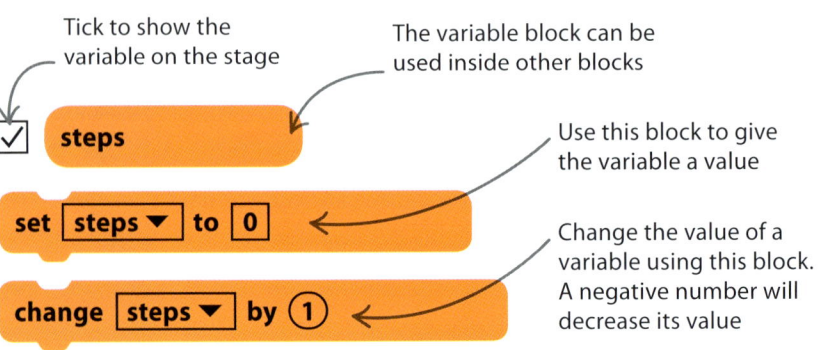

Tick to show the variable on the stage

The variable block can be used inside other blocks

Use this block to give the variable a value

Change the value of a variable using this block. A negative number will decrease its value

VARIABLES **47**

Using a variable

Variables can be used to change a sprite's speed. This simple script shows you how.

1 Set the value of a variable
Create this script. Use the "set steps to 0" block and change the number to 5. Drag the "move 10 steps" block into the script, but drop the "steps" variable block over the "10".

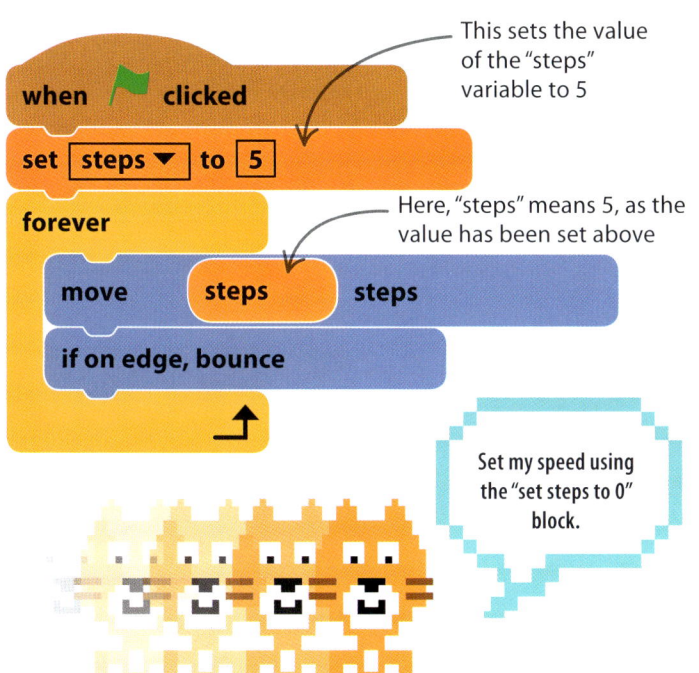

This sets the value of the "steps" variable to 5

```
when ▶ clicked
set steps ▼ to 5
forever
    move steps steps
    if on edge, bounce
```

Here, "steps" means 5, as the value has been set above

Set my speed using the "set steps to 0" block.

2 Changing the value of a variable
Use the "change steps by 1" block to increase the value of the variable "steps" by 1. Put it inside the "forever" block, so the cat keeps on getting faster.

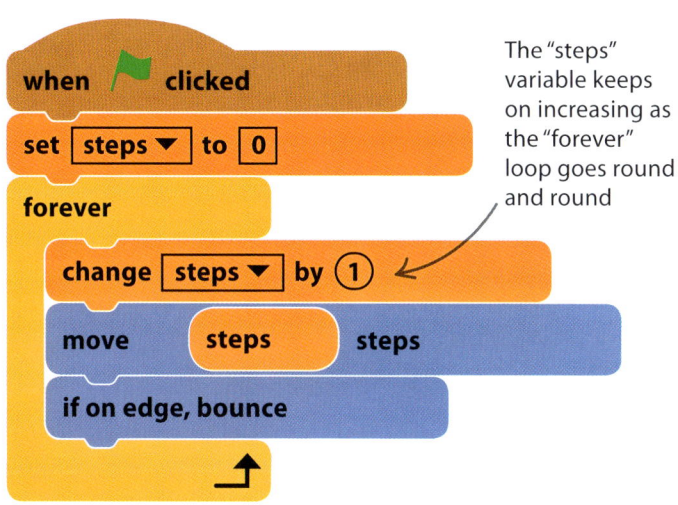

```
when ▶ clicked
set steps ▼ to 0
forever
    change steps ▼ by 1
    move steps steps
    if on edge, bounce
```

The "steps" variable keeps on increasing as the "forever" loop goes round and round

Deleting variables

When you no longer want a variable, right-click on it in the blocks palette and then select "delete variable". You'll lose any information that was in it.

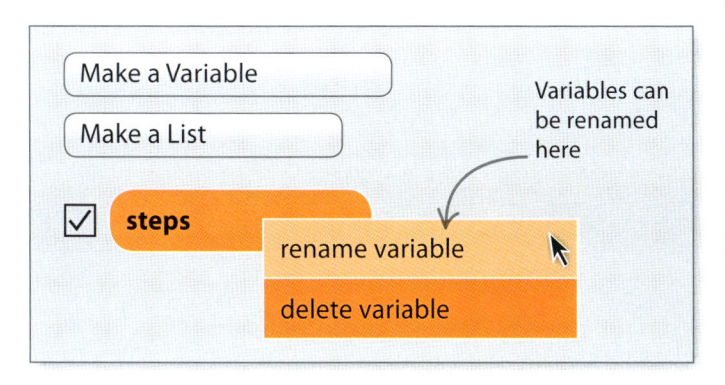

```
Make a Variable
Make a List
☑ steps
    rename variable
    delete variable
```

Variables can be renamed here

▪▪ EXPERT TIPS
Read-only variables

Some variables are set by Scratch and can't be changed. They're still variables though, because their values vary. These blocks are known as sensing blocks.

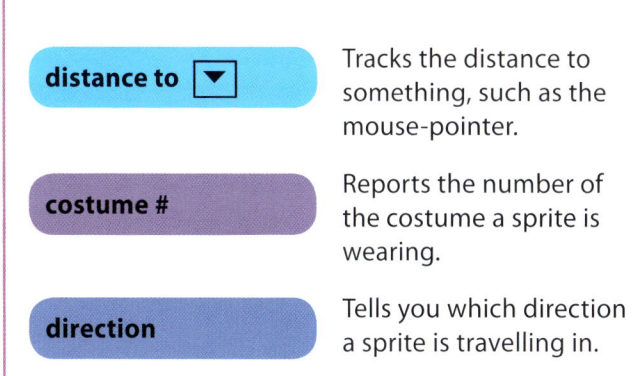

distance to ▼ — Tracks the distance to something, such as the mouse-pointer.

costume # — Reports the number of the costume a sprite is wearing.

direction — Tells you which direction a sprite is travelling in.

Maths

As well as storing numbers in variables (see pp.46–47), Scratch can be used to carry out all sorts of calculations using the "Operator" blocks.

> **SEE ALSO**
> ‹ 46–47 Variables
> Maths 108–109 › in Python

Doing sums

There are four "Operator" blocks that can be used to do simple calculations. These are addition, subtraction, multiplication, and division.

`( 7 ) + ( 22 )`
△ **Addition**
The "+" block adds the two numbers in the block together.

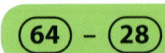

`( 64 ) − ( 28 )`
△ **Subtraction**
The "−" block subtracts the second number from the first.

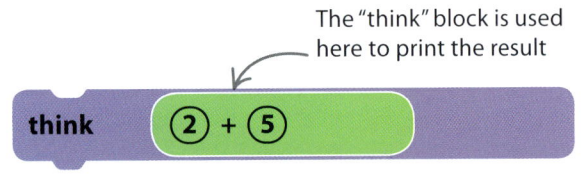

The "think" block is used here to print the result

`think ( 2 ) + ( 5 )`

△ **Printing results**
Drag a "think" block into the scripts area and drop a "+" block inside it. Now add two numbers together and watch your sprite think the answer.

`( 11 ) * ( 10 )`
△ **Multiplication**
Computers use the "*" symbol for multiplication, because "x" looks like a letter.

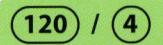

`( 120 ) / ( 4 )`
△ **Division**
There's no division sign on the keyboard, so Scratch uses the "/" symbol instead.

Results in a variable

For more complex calculations, such as fixing the sale price of an item, instead of just using numbers you can use the value of a variable in a sum. The result can be stored in a variable too.

> Variables are useful if you want to repeat the same sum with different values.

1 **Create variables**
Go to the "Data" section of the blocks palette and create two variables – "sale price" and "price".

2 **Set the price**
Select the "set price" block and fix the price of an item to 50.

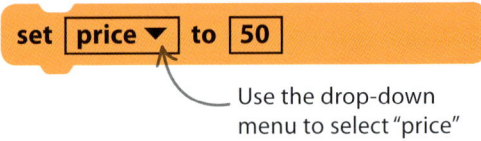

`set price ▼ to 50`

Use the drop-down menu to select "price"

3 **Calculate the sale price**
Use this script to calculate half the price of an item and set it as the sale price.

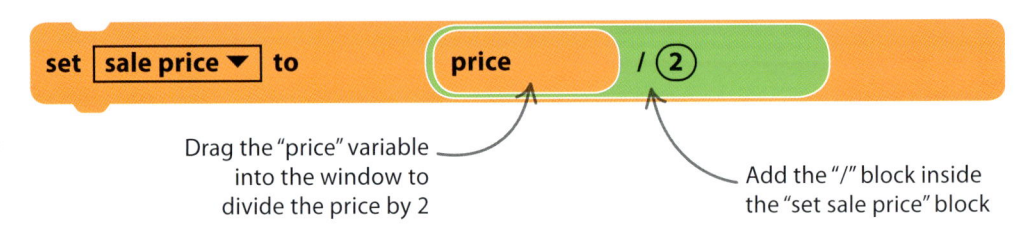

`set sale price ▼ to ( price / 2 )`

Drag the "price" variable into the window to divide the price by 2

Add the "/" block inside the "set sale price" block

MATHS 49

Random numbers

The "pick random" block can be used to select a random number between two values. This block is useful for rolling dice in a game or for when you want to mix up a sprite's costumes.

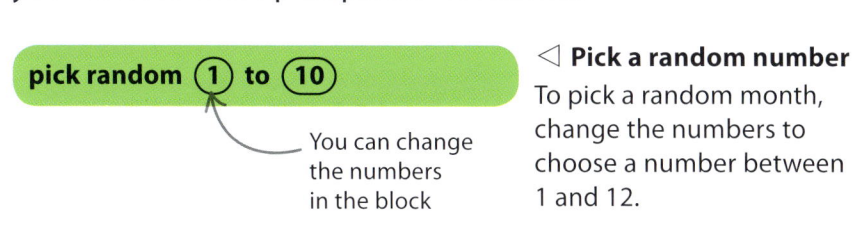

`pick random 1 to 10`

You can change the numbers in the block

◁ **Pick a random number**
To pick a random month, change the numbers to choose a number between 1 and 12.

> **EXPERT TIPS**
> ### Gaming
> Computers often use random numbers to add surprises to games. For example, an alien can be made to appear in a random place, or after a random amount of time. It can be used to select a random value, as if you were rolling a dice, or a random costume for a sprite.

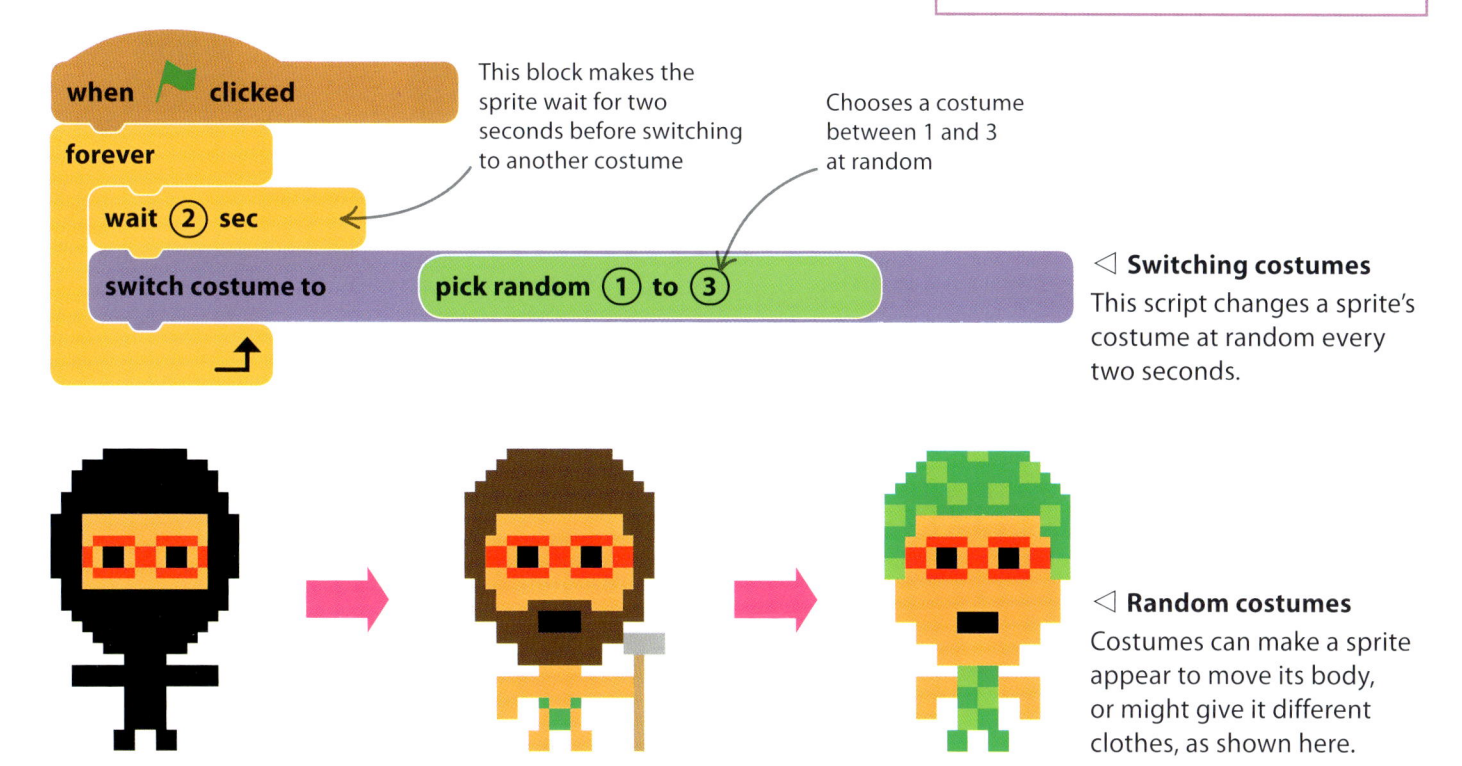

```
when clicked
forever
    wait 2 sec
    switch costume to pick random 1 to 3
```

This block makes the sprite wait for two seconds before switching to another costume

Chooses a costume between 1 and 3 at random

◁ **Switching costumes**
This script changes a sprite's costume at random every two seconds.

◁ **Random costumes**
Costumes can make a sprite appear to move its body, or might give it different clothes, as shown here.

Hard maths

Simple "Operator" blocks can do most calculations, but Scratch can also do more complex maths. The "mod" block divides two numbers and gives the remainder, which is the number that is left over. The "round" block rounds to the nearest whole number, and the "sqrt" block gives the square root of a number.

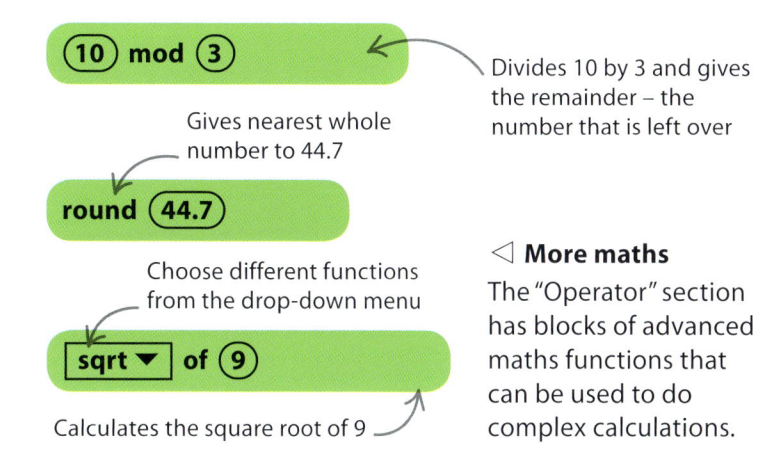

`10 mod 3` — Divides 10 by 3 and gives the remainder – the number that is left over

Gives nearest whole number to 44.7

`round 44.7`

Choose different functions from the drop-down menu

`sqrt of 9`

Calculates the square root of 9

◁ **More maths**
The "Operator" section has blocks of advanced maths functions that can be used to do complex calculations.

Strings and lists

In programming, a sequence of letters and symbols is called a "string". Strings can contain any character on the keyboard (including spaces) and be of any length. Strings can also be grouped together in lists.

> **SEE ALSO**
> ‹ 46–47 Variables
> Strings 110–111 ›
> in Python

Keyboard characters are lined up as if they were hanging from a string

Working with words

Programs often need to remember words, such as a player's name. Variables can be created to remember these words. Scratch programs can also ask the user questions, which they answer by typing into a text box that pops up. The following script asks for the user's name, and then makes a sprite say "Hello" to them.

1 **Create a new variable**
Click the "Data" button in the blocks palette and click the "Make a Variable" button. Create a variable called "greeting".

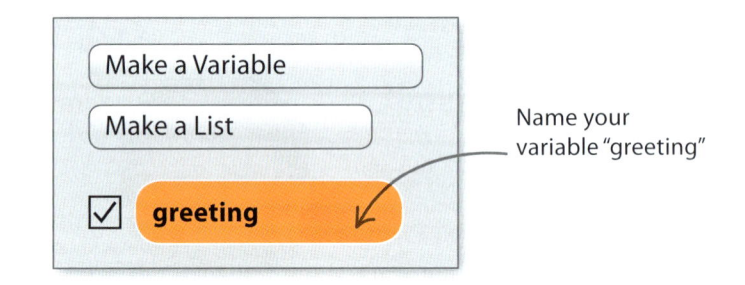

Name your variable "greeting"

2 **Asking a question**
This script makes the sprite ask a question. Whatever the user types into the text box that pops up on the screen is stored in a new variable called "answer". The script then combines the strings contained in the "greeting" and "answer" variables to greet to the user.

This block puts "Hello " into the variable "greeting". Leave a space at the end of "Hello " to make the output of the program neater

The "ask" box (from the "Sensing" section of the blocks palette) makes a text box appear, which the user types their answer into

The "answer" variable (from the "Sensing" section) contains whatever the user typed into the text box

The "say" bubble creates a speech bubble for the sprite

The "greeting" variable holds the string "Hello "

Making lists

Variables are perfect if you just want to remember one thing. To remember lots of similar things, lists can be used instead. Lists can store many items of data (numbers and strings) at the same time – for example, all of the high scores in a game. The following program shows one way of using a list.

1 Create a list
Start a new project. Go into the "Data" section of the blocks palette and click the "Make a List" button. Give your list the name "sentence".

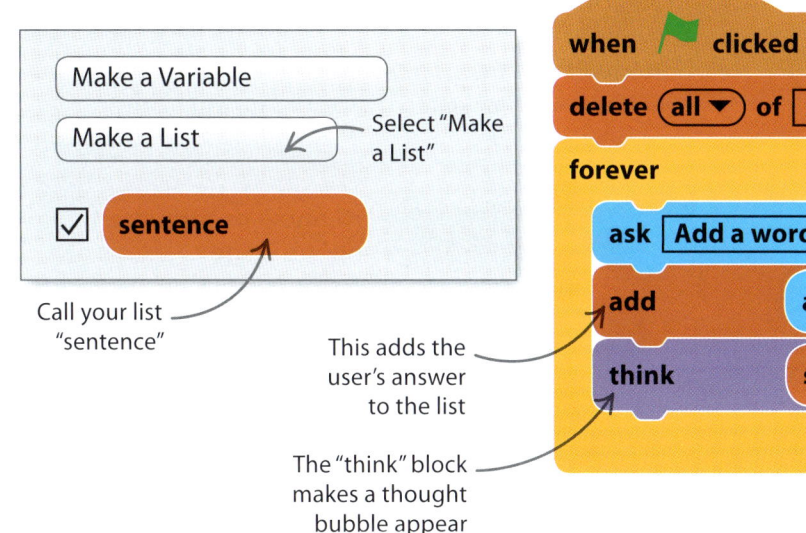

Select "Make a List"

Call your list "sentence"

2 Using your list
This script asks the user to type words into a list. Each word appears in the sprite's speech bubble as it is added to the list.

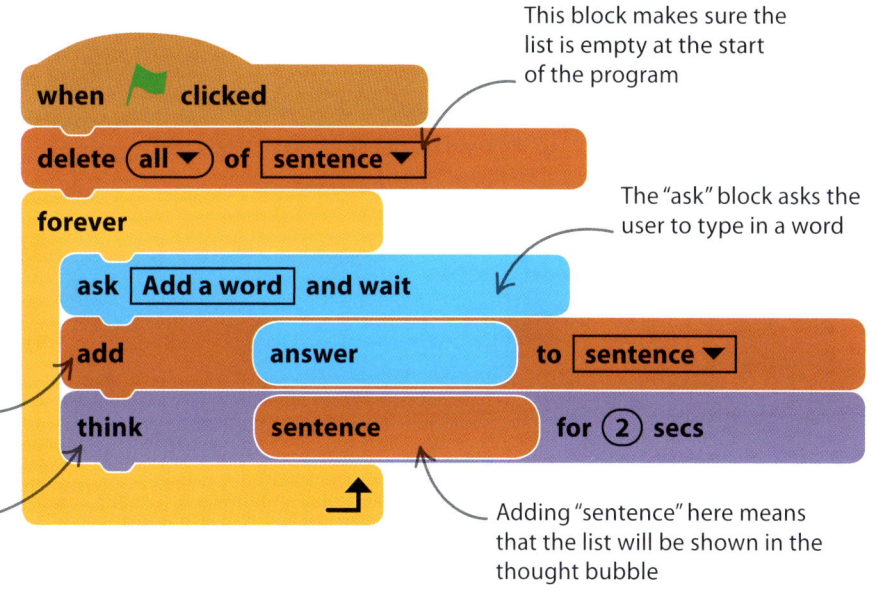

This block makes sure the list is empty at the start of the program

The "ask" block asks the user to type in a word

This adds the user's answer to the list

The "think" block makes a thought bubble appear

Adding "sentence" here means that the list will be shown in the thought bubble

3 Seeing the list
If you tick the box beside the list in the blocks palette, the list is shown on the stage. You can see each new word as it's added to the list.

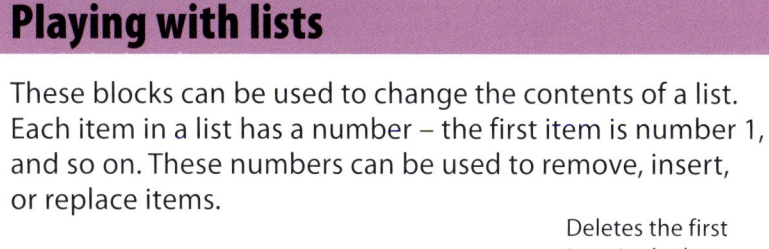

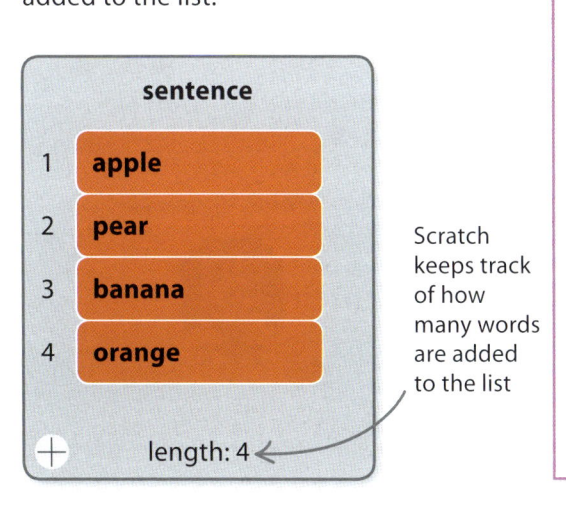

	sentence
1	apple
2	pear
3	banana
4	orange

length: 4

Scratch keeps track of how many words are added to the list

EXPERT TIPS
Playing with lists

These blocks can be used to change the contents of a list. Each item in a list has a number – the first item is number 1, and so on. These numbers can be used to remove, insert, or replace items.

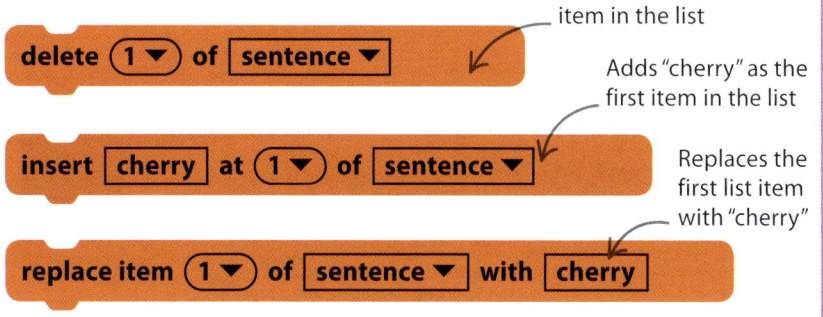

Deletes the first item in the list

Adds "cherry" as the first item in the list

Replaces the first list item with "cherry"

Co-ordinates

To put a sprite in a particular spot, or to find out its exact location, you can use co-ordinates. Co-ordinates are a pair of numbers that pinpoint a sprite's position on the stage using an x and y grid.

> **SEE ALSO**
> ❮ 34–35 Making things move
> ❮ 48–49 Maths

x and y positions

The x and y positions of a sprite and the mouse-pointer are shown on the Scratch interface. It can be helpful to know a sprite's co-ordinates when writing a script.

x: 240   y: 180

△ **Position of the mouse-pointer**
The mouse-pointer's co-ordinates are shown at the bottom right of the stage. Move the mouse-pointer over the stage and watch the co-ordinates change.

◁ **Position of a sprite**
You can see a sprite's current co-ordinates in the top-right corner of the scripts area.

x: -126
y: 96

☑ x position
☑ y position

◁ **Show co-ordinates on the stage**
Tick the boxes beside the "x position" and "y position" blocks to show a sprite's position on the stage.

x and y grid

To pinpoint a spot, count the number of steps left or right, and up or down, from the middle of the stage. Steps to the left or right are called "x". Steps up or down are called "y". Use negative numbers to move left and down.

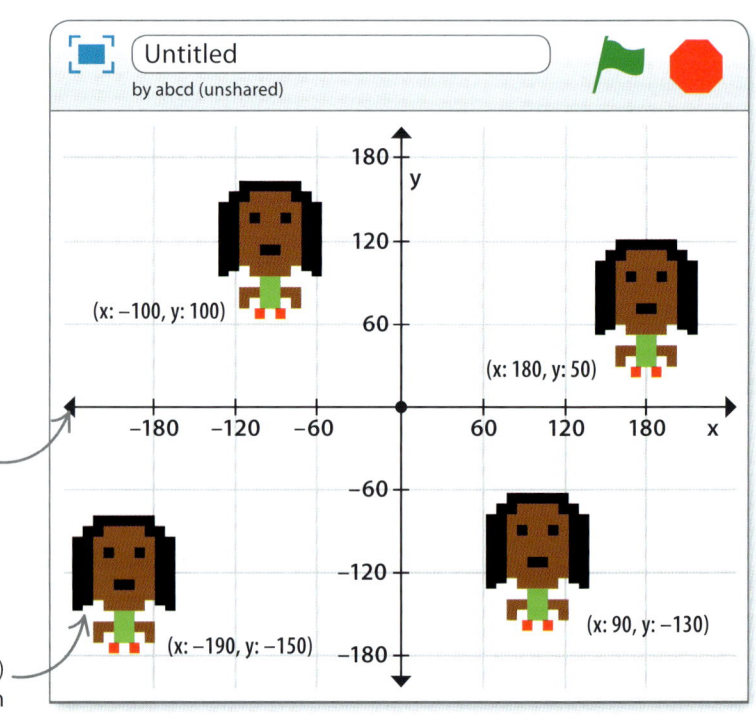

The stage is based upon an x and y grid

(x: –100, y: 100)
(x: 180, y: 50)
(x: –190, y: –150)
(x: 90, y: –130)

This sprite is 190 steps left (–190) and 150 steps down (–150) from the middle of the stage

CO-ORDINATES 53

Moving the sprite

Co-ordinates are used to move a sprite to a particular spot on the stage. It doesn't matter how near or far away the spot is. The "glide 1 secs to x:0 y:0" block from the "Motion" section of the blocks palette makes the sprite glide there smoothly.

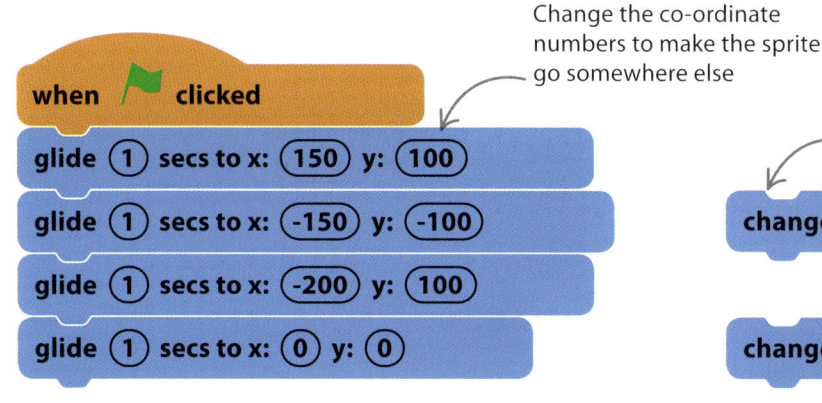

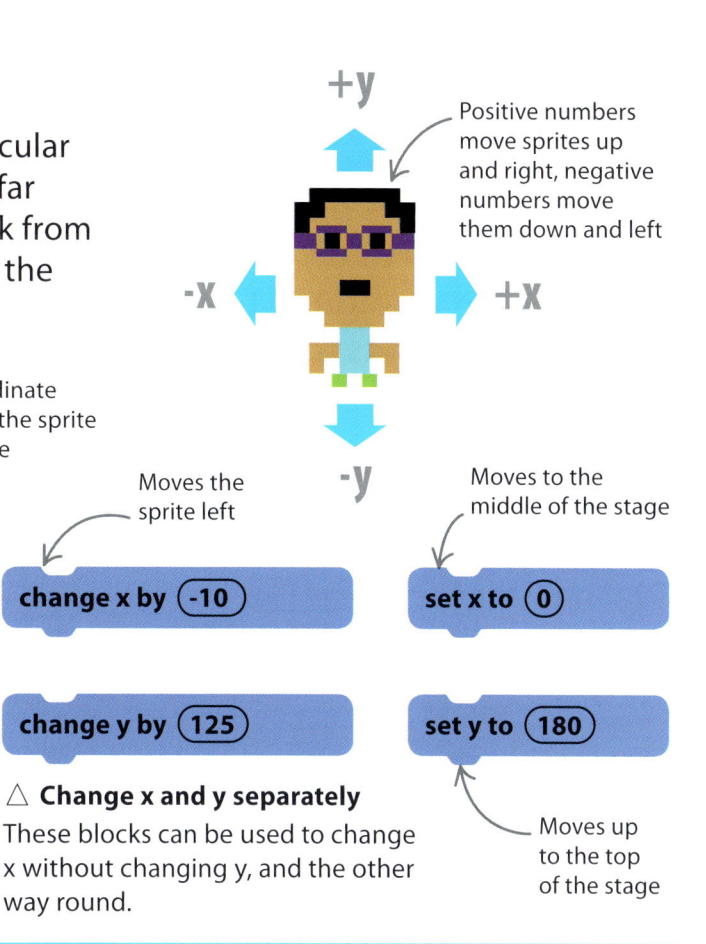

Positive numbers move sprites up and right, negative numbers move them down and left

Change the co-ordinate numbers to make the sprite go somewhere else

```
when ▶ clicked
glide 1 secs to x: 150 y: 100
glide 1 secs to x: -150 y: -100
glide 1 secs to x: -200 y: 100
glide 1 secs to x: 0 y: 0
```

△ **Control the sprite with a script**
Can you work out the path the sprite will take when you run this script? Try it and see!

Moves the sprite left

```
change x by -10
change y by 125
```

△ **Change x and y separately**
These blocks can be used to change x without changing y, and the other way round.

Moves to the middle of the stage

```
set x to 0
set y to 180
```

Moves up to the top of the stage

Crazy horse's trip

Try this fun script to test out co-ordinates. Select the "Horse1" sprite from the sprite list and give it the below script. This program uses the "go to x:0 y:0" block to keep moving the horse to a random position, drawing a line behind it as it goes.

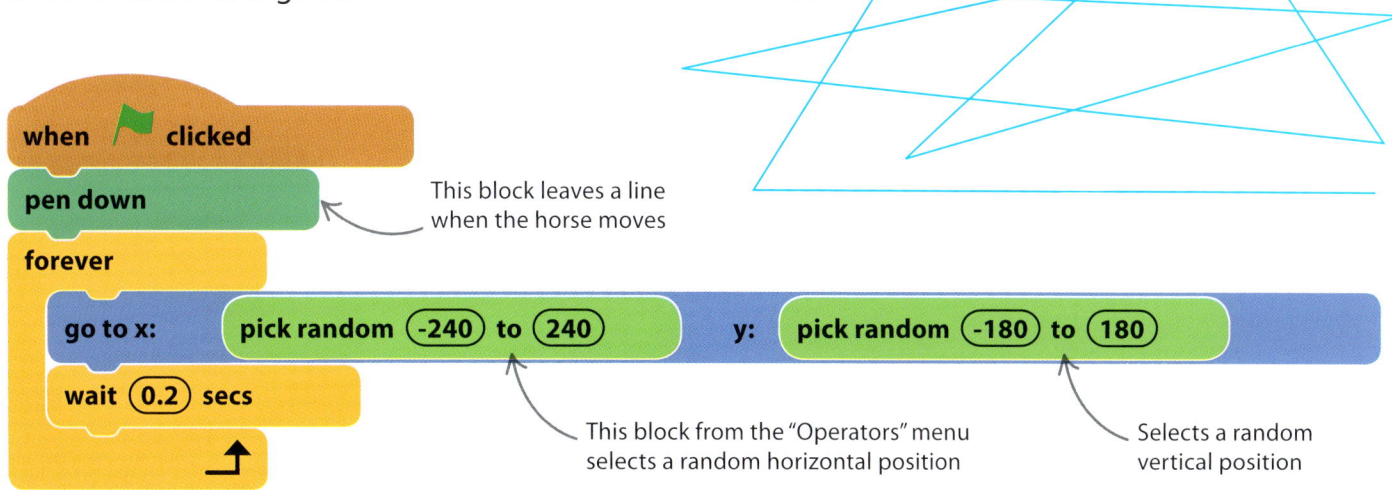

```
when ▶ clicked
pen down
forever
    go to x: pick random -240 to 240  y: pick random -180 to 180
    wait 0.2 secs
```

This block leaves a line when the horse moves

This block from the "Operators" menu selects a random horizontal position

Selects a random vertical position

STARTING FROM SCRATCH

Make some noise!

Scratch programs don't have to be silent. Use the pink "Sound" blocks to try out sound effects and create music. You can also use sound files you already have or record brand new sounds for your program.

> **SEE ALSO**
> Sensing **62–63** ⟩
> and detecting
>
> Monkey **70–77** ⟩
> mayhem

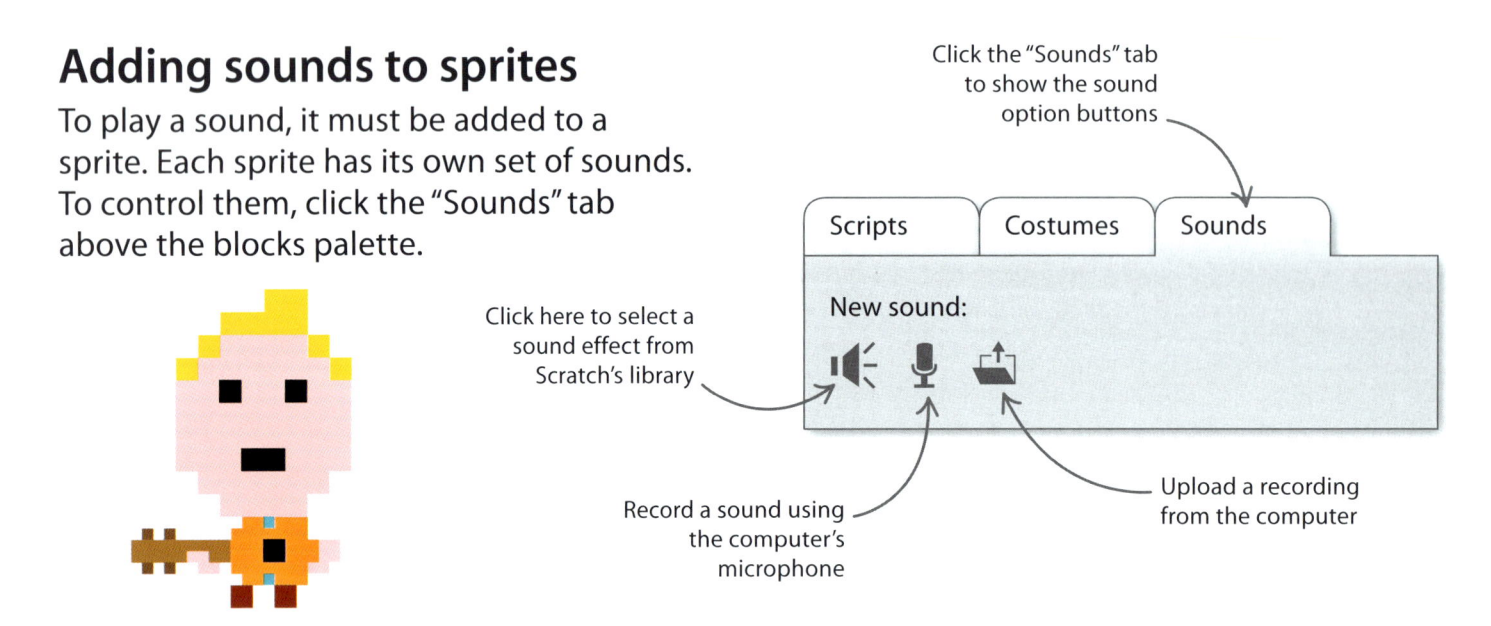

Adding sounds to sprites

To play a sound, it must be added to a sprite. Each sprite has its own set of sounds. To control them, click the "Sounds" tab above the blocks palette.

Click the "Sounds" tab to show the sound option buttons

Click here to select a sound effect from Scratch's library

New sound:

Record a sound using the computer's microphone

Upload a recording from the computer

Playing a sound

There are two blocks that play sounds: "play sound" and "play sound until done". "Until done" makes the program wait until the sound has finished before it moves on.

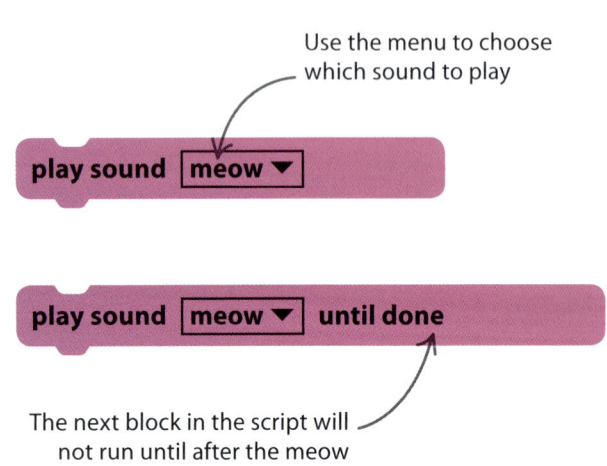

Use the menu to choose which sound to play

`play sound meow ▼`

`play sound meow ▼ until done`

The next block in the script will not run until after the meow sound has finished playing

Turn up the volume

Each sprite has its own volume control, which is set using numbers. 0 is silent and 100 is the loudest.

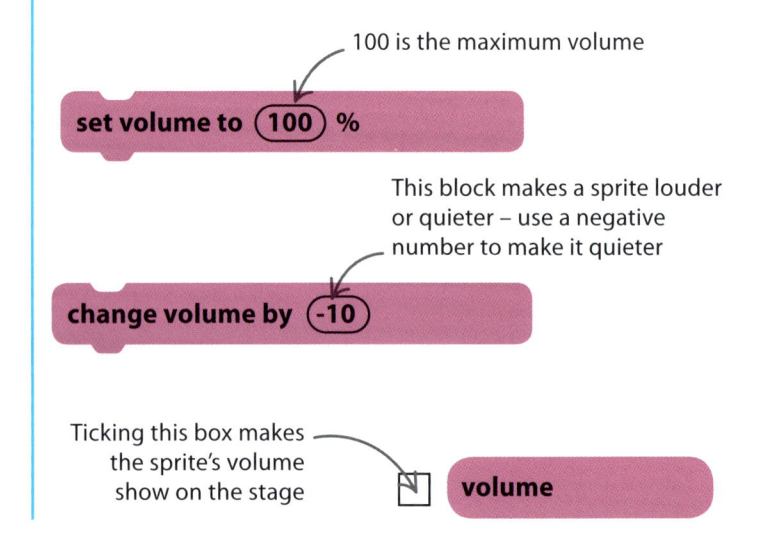

100 is the maximum volume

`set volume to 100 %`

This block makes a sprite louder or quieter – use a negative number to make it quieter

`change volume by -10`

Ticking this box makes the sprite's volume show on the stage

☐ `volume`

MAKE SOME NOISE! 55

Making your own music

Scratch has blocks that can be used to invent musical sounds. You have a whole orchestra of instruments to conduct, as well as a full drum kit. The length of each note is measured in beats.

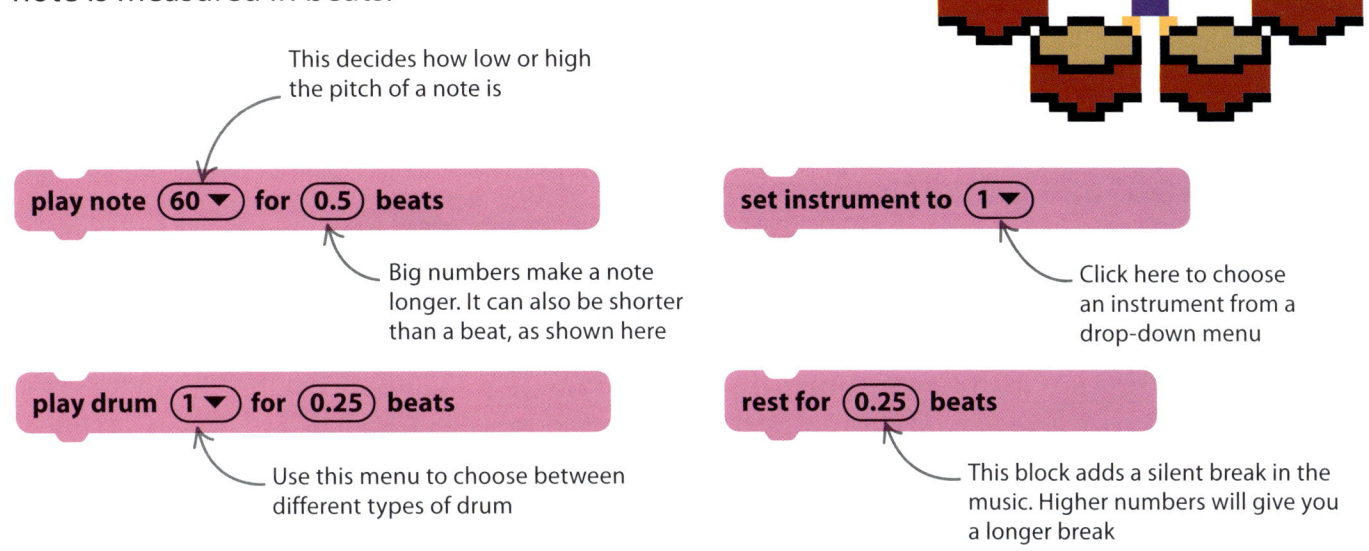

`play note 60 for 0.5 beats`
- This decides how low or high the pitch of a note is
- Big numbers make a note longer. It can also be shorter than a beat, as shown here

`play drum 1 for 0.25 beats`
- Use this menu to choose between different types of drum

`set instrument to 1`
- Click here to choose an instrument from a drop-down menu

`rest for 0.25 beats`
- This block adds a silent break in the music. Higher numbers will give you a longer break

Playing music

Connecting notes together makes a tune. Create a new variable called "note" (see pages 46–47), and then add the script below to any sprite to create a piece of music.

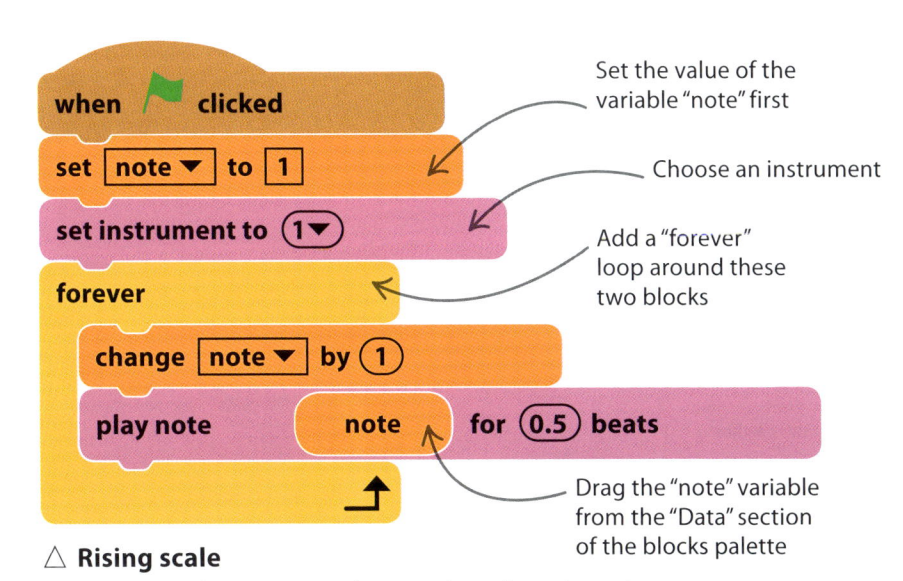

```
when [flag] clicked
set note to 1
set instrument to 1
forever
    change note by 1
    play note note for 0.5 beats
```

- Set the value of the variable "note" first
- Choose an instrument
- Add a "forever" loop around these two blocks
- Drag the "note" variable from the "Data" section of the blocks palette

△ **Rising scale**
This script makes a series of notes that play when the green flag is clicked. The pitch of each note gets higher one step at a time, and each note plays for half a beat.

EXPERT TIPS
Tempo

The speed of music is called its tempo. The tempo decides how long a beat is within a piece of music. There are three blocks for managing the tempo.

`set tempo to 60 bpm`

The tempo is measured in beats per minute, or "bpm".

`change tempo by 60`

Increase the tempo to make your music faster, or use a negative number to make it slower.

☐ `tempo`

Ticking this box makes the sprite's tempo show on the stage.

56 STARTING FROM SCRATCH

▸ PROJECT 2

Roll the dice

Simple programs can be both useful and fun. This program creates a dice that can be rolled. Play it to see who can get the highest number, or use it instead of a real dice when you play a board game.

> **SEE ALSO**
> ‹ **36–37** Costumes
> ‹ **42–43** Simple loops
> ‹ **46–47** Variables
> ‹ **48–49** Maths

How to create a rolling dice

The dice in this program uses six costumes. Each costume shows a face of the dice with a different number on it – from one to six.

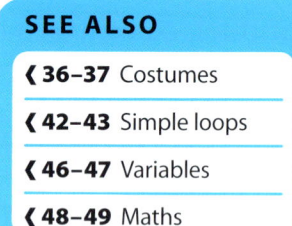

1 Select the paintbrush button under the stage to draw a new sprite.

Draws a new sprite

2 Click the rectangle button on the left of the painting area. To make your dice colourful, select a solid colour from the palette (see box below). Then in the painting area hold down the "shift" key, press the left mouse button, and then drag the mouse-pointer to make a square in the middle.

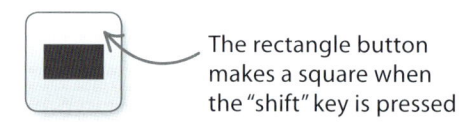

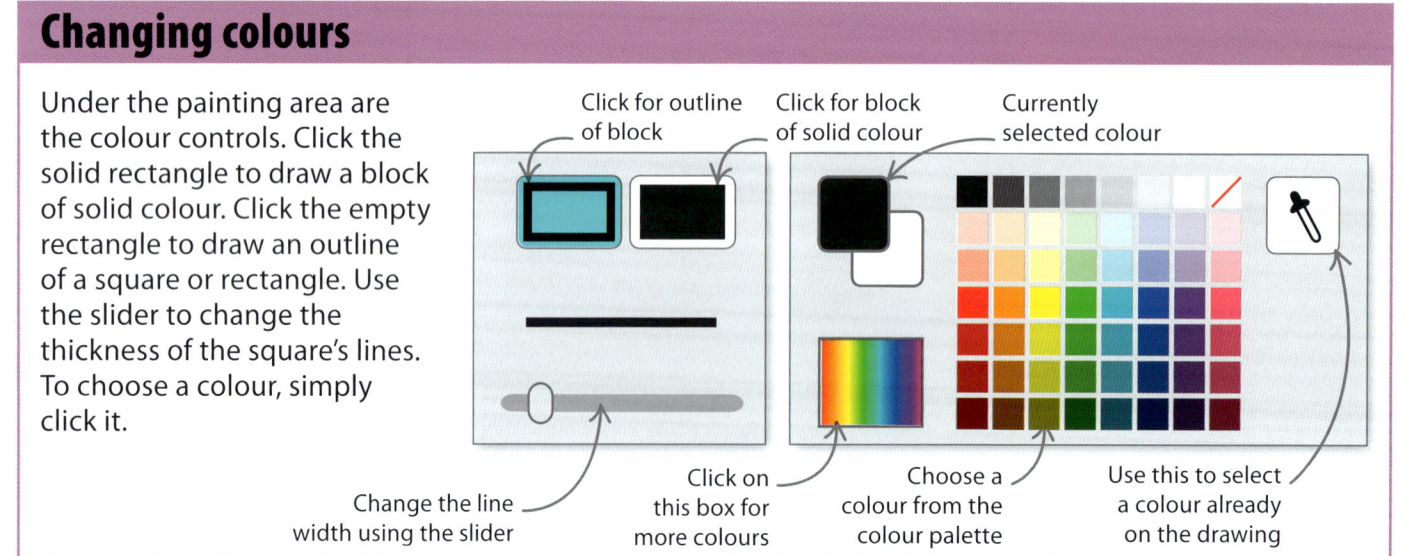

The rectangle button makes a square when the "shift" key is pressed

▪▪ EXPERT TIPS
Changing colours

Under the painting area are the colour controls. Click the solid rectangle to draw a block of solid colour. Click the empty rectangle to draw an outline of a square or rectangle. Use the slider to change the thickness of the square's lines. To choose a colour, simply click it.

- Click for outline of block
- Click for block of solid colour
- Currently selected colour
- Change the line width using the slider
- Click on this box for more colours
- Choose a colour from the colour palette
- Use this to select a colour already on the drawing

ROLL THE DICE 57

3 ▸ Right-click on your costume to the left of the painting area, and choose "duplicate". Repeat this step until you have six costumes.

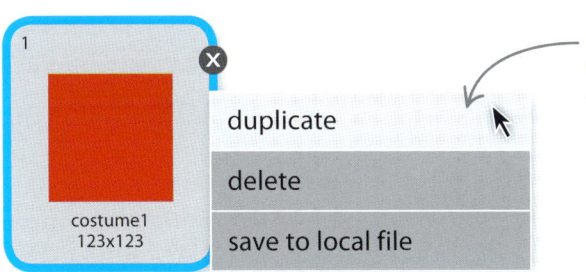

- Use the menu to duplicate the dice costume

EXPERT TIPS
Rotation tool

To make the dice appear to roll when the script is run, you can rotate each costume to a different angle. Click on the "Convert to vector" button in the bottom right-hand corner. When you click back on to the painting area, a rotation tool will appear.

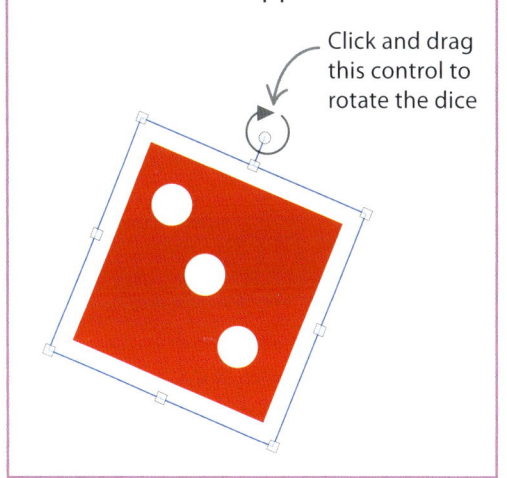

- Click and drag this control to rotate the dice

4 ▸ Select a costume. Click the circle button on the painting area and chose a solid white colour from the palette. Add spots to each of the six costumes until you have made all six sides of a dice.

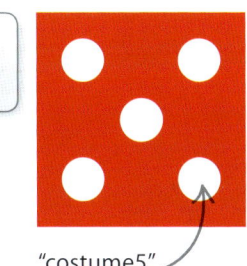

- The circle button makes a perfect circle when the "shift" key is pressed
- "costume5" has 5 spots

5 ▸ Add the script below to the dice sprite. Press the spacebar to roll the dice. Try it a few times to check you can see all of the costumes.

- Clicking the spacebar rolls the dice

```
when [space ▼] key pressed
switch costume to ( pick random (1) to (6) )
```

- This block selects a random costume

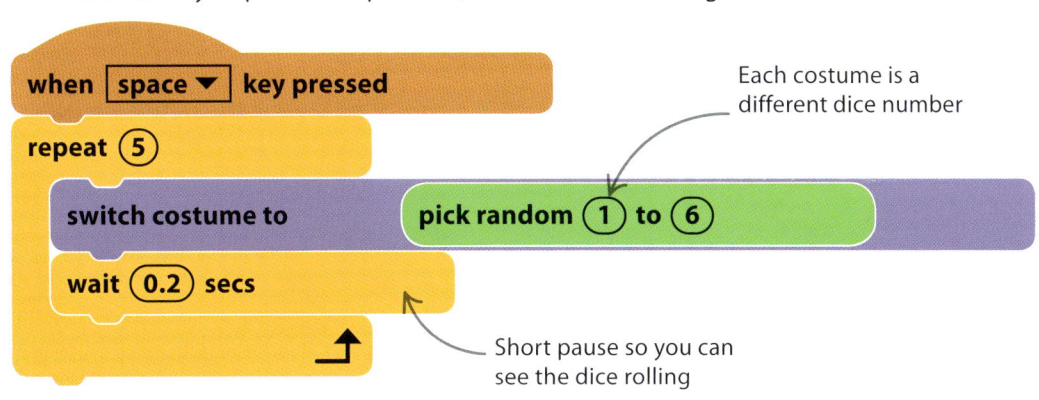

6 ▸ Sometimes you'll roll the same number twice, and it looks like the program isn't working because the image doesn't change. This script makes the dice change costumes five times before it stops. Each time you press the spacebar, it looks like it's rolling.

```
when [space ▼] key pressed
repeat (5)
    switch costume to ( pick random (1) to (6) )
    wait (0.2) secs
```

- Each costume is a different dice number
- Short pause so you can see the dice rolling

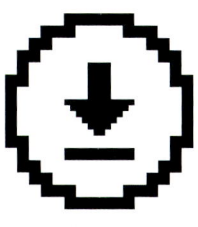

Don't forget to save your work

58 STARTING FROM SCRATCH

True or false?

Computers decide what to do by asking questions and determining whether the answers are true or false. Questions that only have two possible answers are called "Boolean expressions".

> **SEE ALSO**
> Decisions and branches **60–61 〉**
> Making decisions **114–115 〉**

Comparing numbers

You can compare numbers using the "=" block from the "Operators" section of the blocks palette.

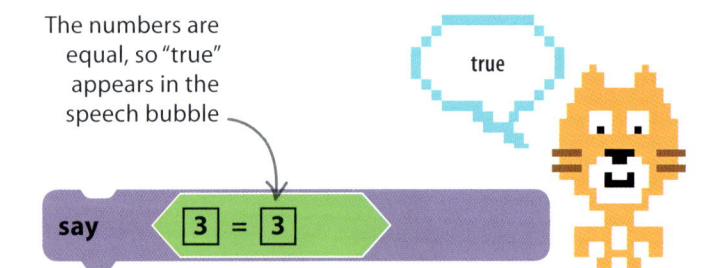

◁ **The "=" block**
This block will give one of two answers – "true" if the two numbers in the boxes are equal, and "false" if they aren't.

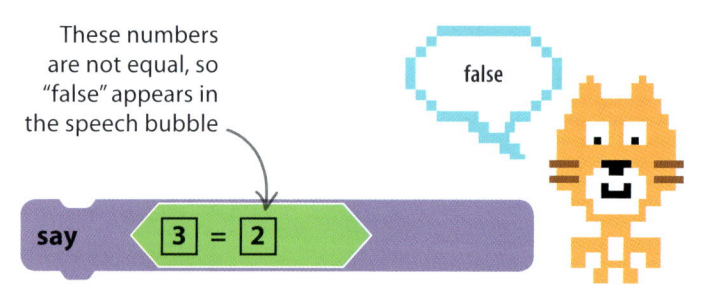

The numbers are equal, so "true" appears in the speech bubble

say 3 = 3

△ **True answer**
Using an "=" block inside a speech block will make "true" or "false" appear in a sprite's speech bubble.

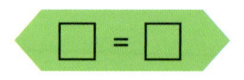

These numbers are not equal, so "false" appears in the speech bubble

say 3 = 2

△ **False answer**
If the numbers in the block are different, the sprite's speech bubble will contain the word "false".

Comparing variables

You can use variables inside comparison blocks. It's not worth comparing fixed numbers because the result will always be the same, whereas the value of variables can change.

set age to 10

△ **Create a variable**
Click the "Data" button in the blocks palette and create a new variable called "age". Set its value to 10 (click on the block to make sure the value has changed). Drag the "age" variable into the comparison blocks.

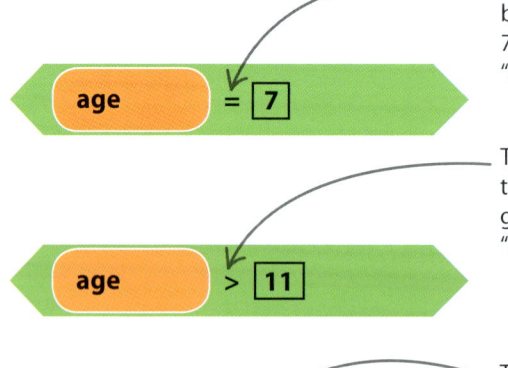

age = 7

This sign means "equals", so the block is asking if "age" is equal to 7. The answer here is "false", as "age" is 10

age > 11

This sign means "more than", so the block is asking if "age" is greater than 11. The answer is "false", as 10 is not bigger than 11

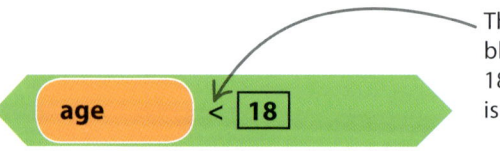

age < 18

This sign means "less than", so the block is asking if "age" is less than 18. The answer will be "true", as 10 is smaller than 18

△ **Comparing numbers**
Find the green comparison blocks in the "Operators" menu. As well as checking whether two numbers are equal, you can check whether one is higher or lower than another.

TRUE OR FALSE? 59

EXPERT TIPS
Comparing words

The "=" block is not just used for numbers – it can also be used to check whether two strings are the same. It ignores capital letters when comparing strings.

`set name to Lizzie`

△ **Create a variable**
To experiment with comparing strings, create a new variable called "name" and set its value to "Lizzie".

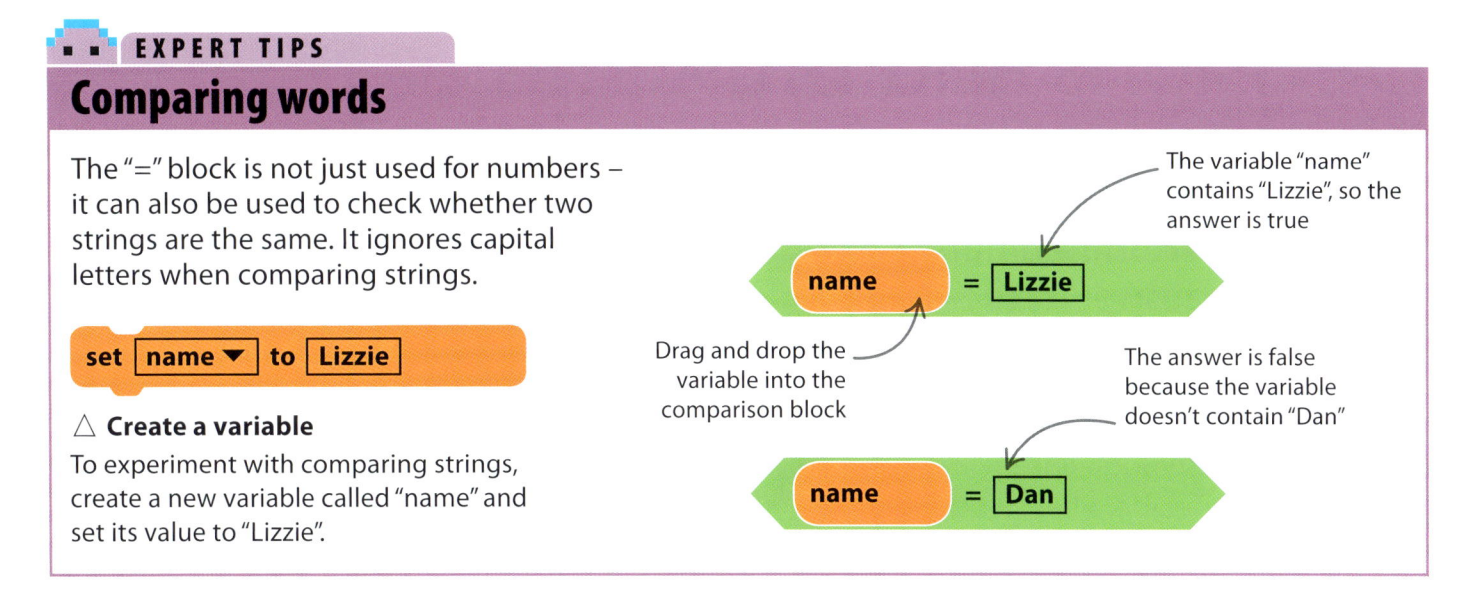

`name = Lizzie`

The variable "name" contains "Lizzie", so the answer is true

Drag and drop the variable into the comparison block

`name = Dan`

The answer is false because the variable doesn't contain "Dan"

Not!

The "not" block can simplify things by reversing the answer of a Boolean expression. For example, it's easier to check if someone's age is not 10 than to check every other possible age.

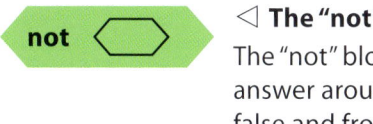

`not ◇`

◁ **The "not" block**
The "not" block changes the answer around, from true to false and from false to true.

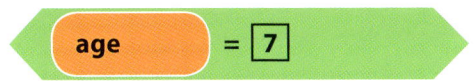

`age = 7`

△ **Without the "not" block**
Here, 10 isn't equal to 7, so the answer is false.

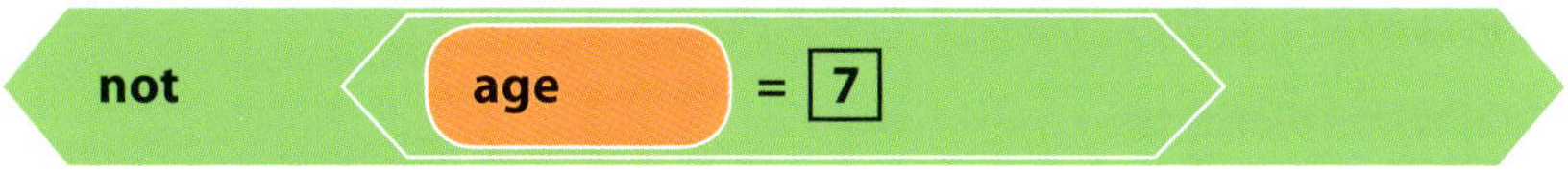

`not age = 7`

△ **With the "not" block**
Adding the "not" block to the same question changes the answer. As 7 does not equal 10, the answer is now true.

Combining questions

To ask more complicated questions, you can combine comparison blocks and ask more than one question at the same time.

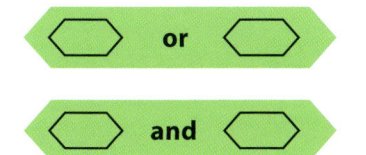

`◇ or ◇`

`◇ and ◇`

△ **Comparison blocks**
The "or" and "and" blocks are used to combine Boolean expressions in different ways.

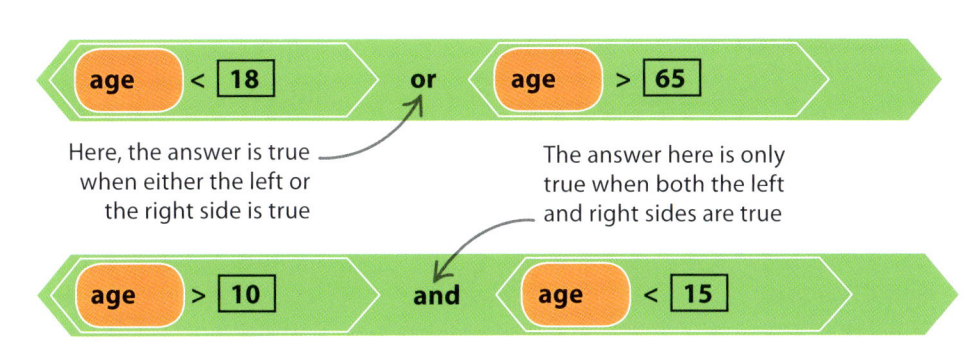

`age < 18 or age > 65`

Here, the answer is true when either the left or the right side is true

The answer here is only true when both the left and right sides are true

`age > 10 and age < 15`

◁ **In practice**
The top block checks whether someone is younger than 18 or older than 65. The bottom block checks if they are aged 11, 12, 13, or 14.

60 STARTING FROM SCRATCH

Decisions and branches

By testing whether something is true or false you can use this information to tell the computer what to do next. It will perform a different action depending on whether the answer is true or false.

> **SEE ALSO**
> ⟨ **58–59** True or false?
> Sensing and **62–63** ⟩ detecting

Making decisions

The "if" blocks use Boolean expressions to decide what to do next. To use them, put other blocks inside their "jaws". The blocks inside the "if" blocks will only run if the answer to the Boolean expression is true.

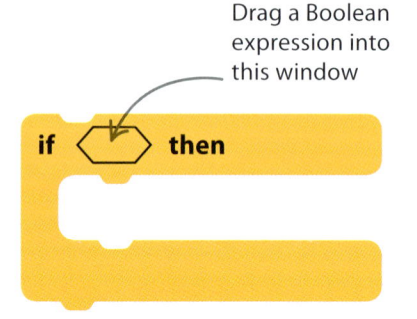

Drag a Boolean expression into this window

△ **"if-then" block**
If a Boolean expression is true, the blocks between the "if-then" block's jaws will run.

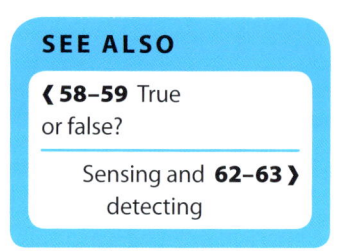

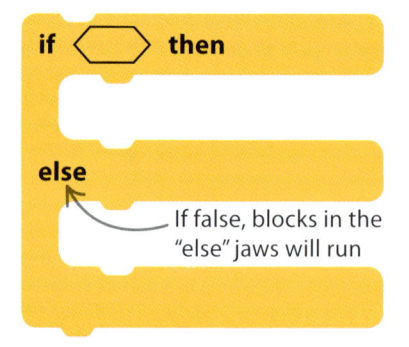

△ **"if-then-else" block**
If the Boolean expression is true, the first set of blocks runs. If not, the second set runs.

If false, blocks in the "else" jaws will run

Using the "if-then" block

The "if-then" block lets you choose whether or not to run part of a script depending on the answer to a Boolean expression. Attach this script to the cat sprite to try it out.

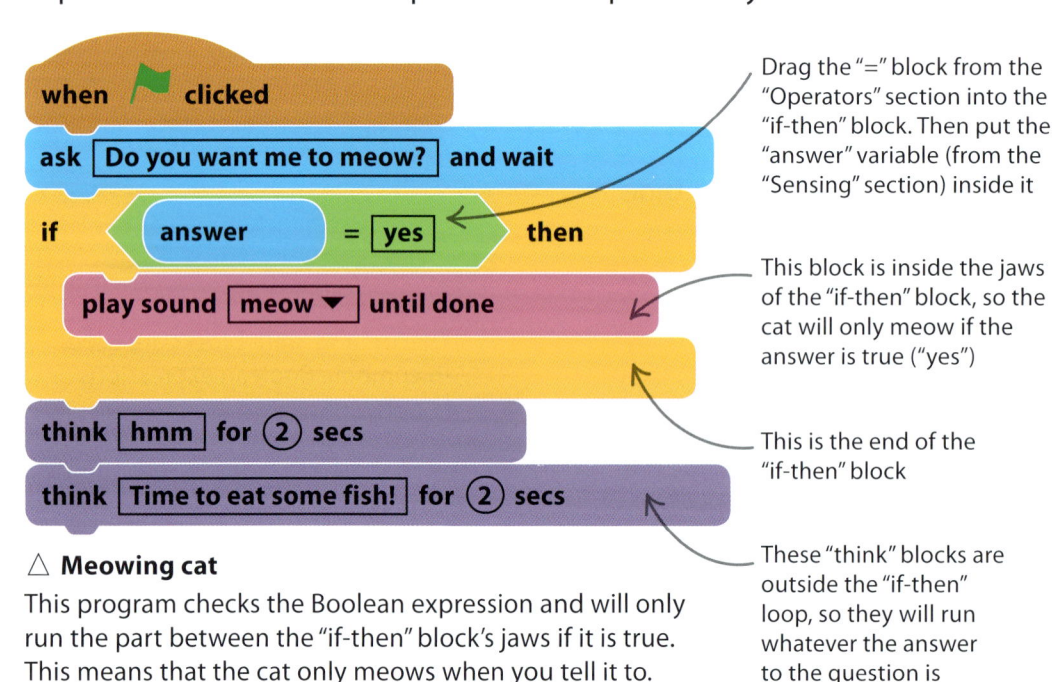

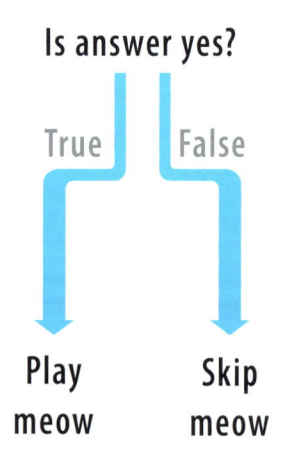

Drag the "=" block from the "Operators" section into the "if-then" block. Then put the "answer" variable (from the "Sensing" section) inside it

This block is inside the jaws of the "if-then" block, so the cat will only meow if the answer is true ("yes")

This is the end of the "if-then" block

These "think" blocks are outside the "if-then" loop, so they will run whatever the answer to the question is

△ **Meowing cat**
This program checks the Boolean expression and will only run the part between the "if-then" block's jaws if it is true. This means that the cat only meows when you tell it to.

Is answer yes?

True → Play meow

False → Skip meow

△ **How it works**
The program checks whether the Boolean expression is true. If it is, it runs the blocks inside the "if-then" block's jaws.

Branching instructions

Often you want a program to do one thing if a condition is true, and something else if it is not. The "if-then-else" block gives a program two possible routes, called "branches". Only one branch will run, depending on the answer to the Boolean expression.

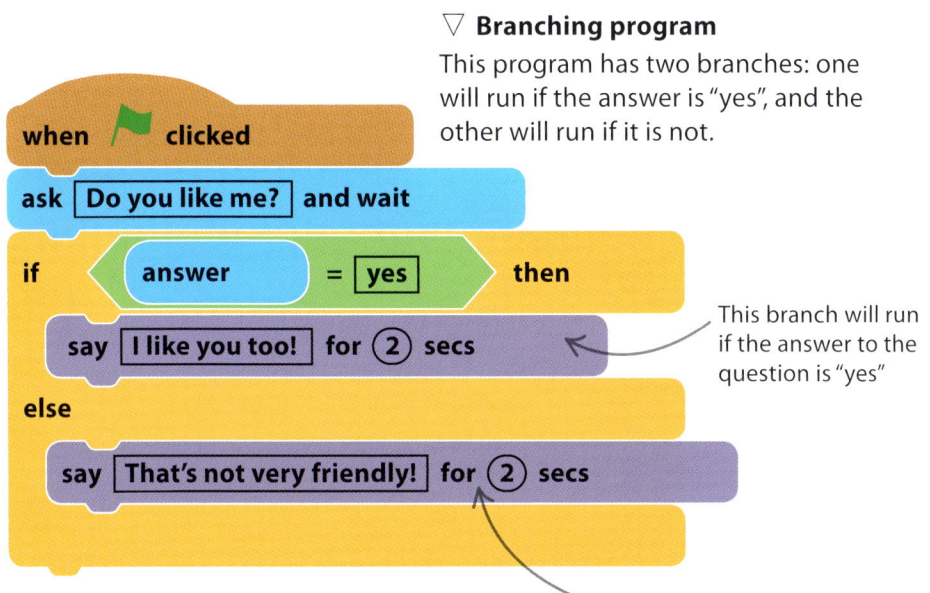

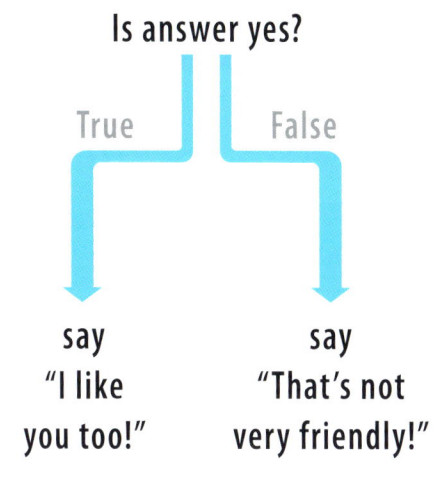

▽ **Branching program**
This program has two branches: one will run if the answer is "yes", and the other will run if it is not.

```
when ▶ clicked
ask  Do you like me?  and wait
if  < answer = yes >  then
    say  I like you too!  for 2 secs
else
    say  That's not very friendly!  for 2 secs
```

This branch will run if the answer to the question is "yes"

This branch will run if the answer to the question is anything except "yes"

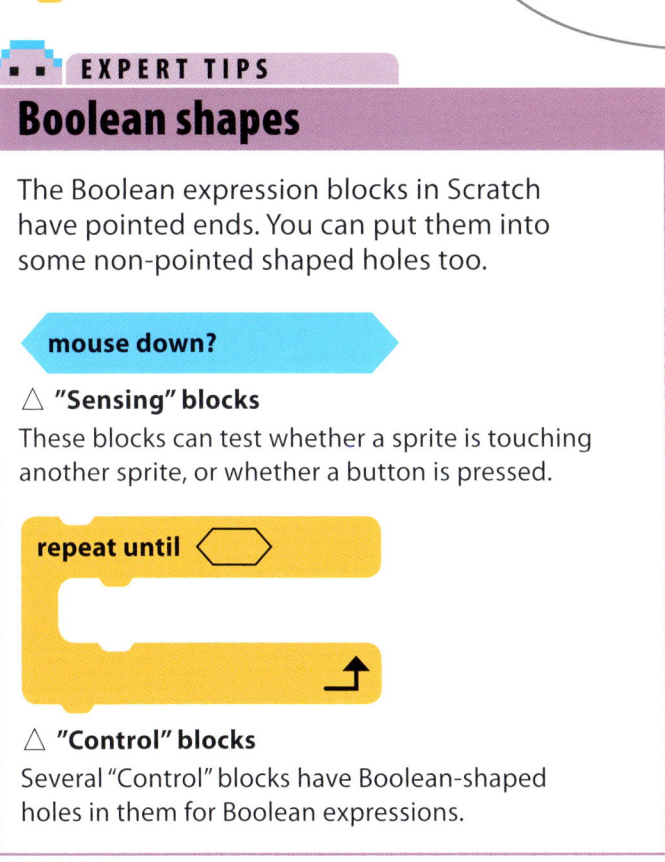

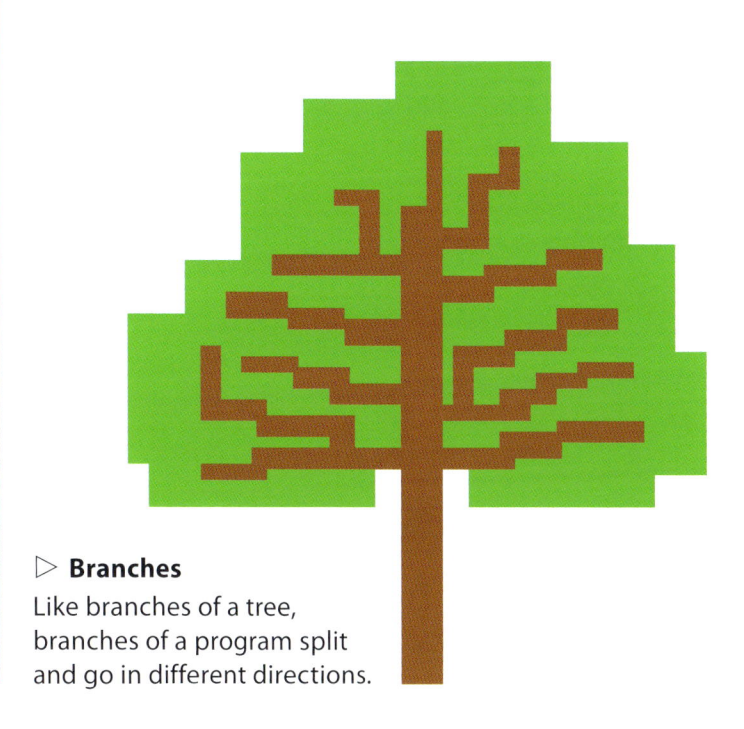

Is answer yes?

True → say "I like you too!"

False → say "That's not very friendly!"

△ **How it works**
The program checks whether you typed in "yes". If so, it shows the first message. If not, it shows the second.

EXPERT TIPS
Boolean shapes

The Boolean expression blocks in Scratch have pointed ends. You can put them into some non-pointed shaped holes too.

`mouse down?`

△ **"Sensing" blocks**
These blocks can test whether a sprite is touching another sprite, or whether a button is pressed.

`repeat until < >`

△ **"Control" blocks**
Several "Control" blocks have Boolean-shaped holes in them for Boolean expressions.

▷ **Branches**
Like branches of a tree, branches of a program split and go in different directions.

Sensing and detecting

The "Sensing" blocks enable a script to see what is happening on your computer. They can detect keyboard controls, and let sprites react when they touch each other.

SEE ALSO
⟨ 36–37 Costumes
⟨ 52–53 Co-ordinates

Keyboard controls

Using "Sensing" blocks with "if-then" blocks allows you to move a sprite around the screen using the keyboard. The "key pressed?" block has a menu of most of the keys on the keyboard, so a sprite can be programmed to react to any key. You can also link actions to the click of a mouse button.

This block checks if a key is being pressed. You can choose which key to check for

`key [space ▼] pressed?`

This block checks if the mouse button is being pressed

`mouse down?`

△ **"Sensing" blocks**
Adding these blocks into an "if-then" block allows the program to detect if a mouse button or key is being pressed.

Putting everything inside a "forever" block means the script repeatedly checks for key presses

The script checks to see if the up arrow is pressed. If it is, the sprite moves upwards on the screen

```
when [flag] clicked
forever
    if  key [up arrow ▼] pressed?  then
        change y by (10)
    if  key [down arrow ▼] pressed?  then
        change y by (-10)
    if  key [left arrow ▼] pressed?  then
        change x by (-10)
    if  key [right arrow ▼] pressed?  then
        change x by (10)
```

△ **Controlling sprites**
Keyboard controls give you precise control over your sprites, which is especially useful in games.

◁ **Movement script**
This script lets you move sprites up, down, left, or right using the arrow keys on the keyboard.

SENSING AND DETECTING 63

Sprite collisions

It can be useful to know when one sprite touches another – in games, for example. Use "Sensing" blocks to make things happen when sprites touch each other, or when a sprite crosses an area that is a certain colour.

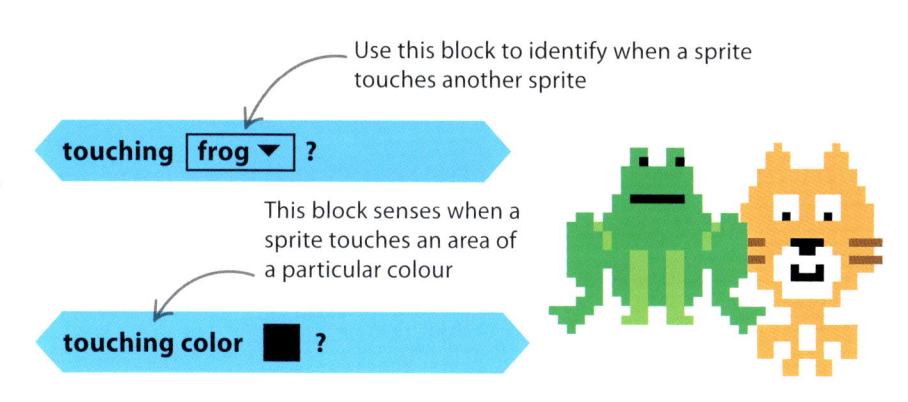

Use this block to identify when a sprite touches another sprite

`touching [ frog ▼ ] ?`

This block senses when a sprite touches an area of a particular colour

`touching color [ ■ ] ?`

Using "Sensing" blocks

Use the "Sensing" blocks to turn your controllable cat into a game. Start by adding the movement script created on the opposite page to the cat sprite, then add the "room1" backdrop and the elephant sprite. Using the "Sounds" tab, add the "trumpet2" sound effect to the elephant, then build it the script below.

▽ **Find the elephant**

This script uses "Sensing" blocks to control the relationship between the cat and the elephant. As the cat gets nearer, the elephant grows. When the cat touches it, the elephant switches costume, makes a sound, and hides somewhere else.

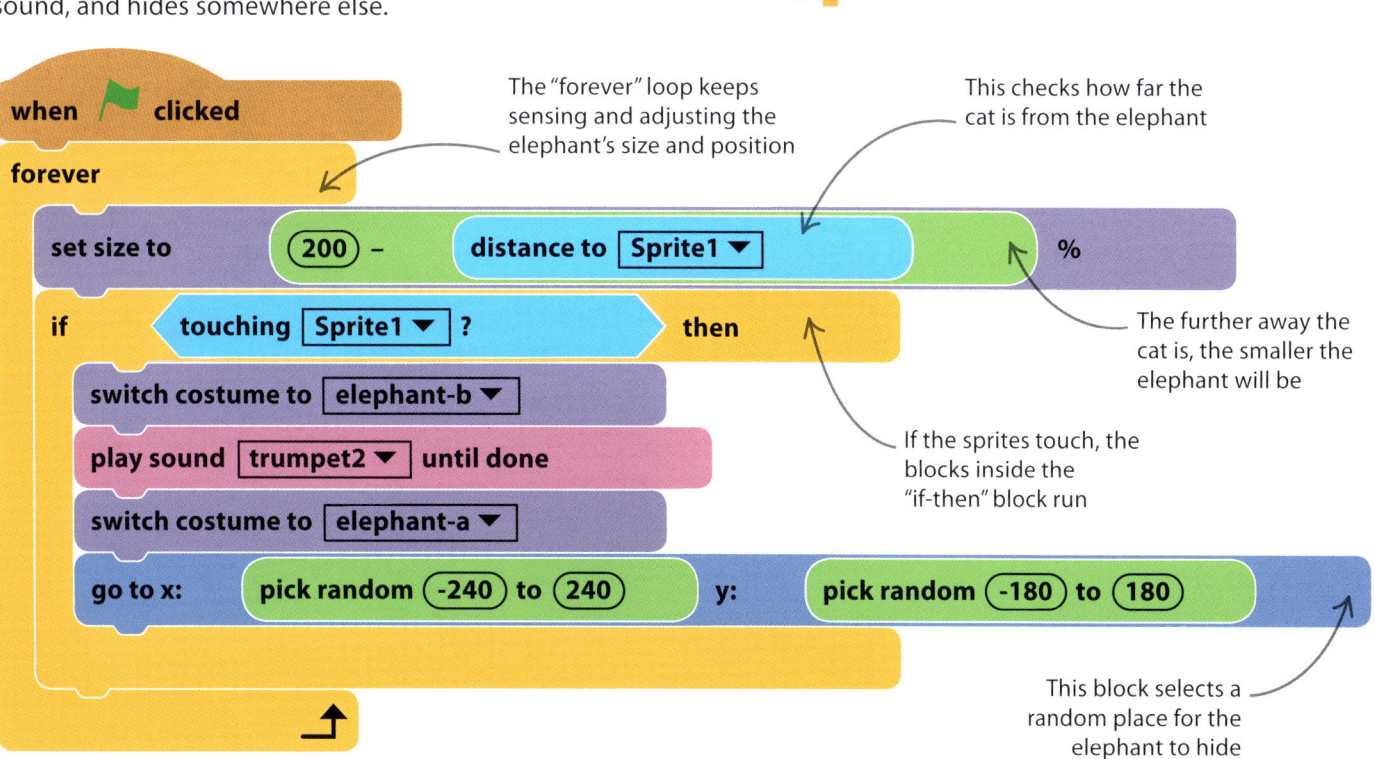

```
when ⚑ clicked
forever
    set size to ( 200 - distance to [ Sprite1 ▼ ] ) %
    if < touching [ Sprite1 ▼ ] ? > then
        switch costume to [ elephant-b ▼ ]
        play sound [ trumpet2 ▼ ] until done
        switch costume to [ elephant-a ▼ ]
        go to x: ( pick random -240 to 240 ) y: ( pick random -180 to 180 )
```

The "forever" loop keeps sensing and adjusting the elephant's size and position

This checks how far the cat is from the elephant

The further away the cat is, the smaller the elephant will be

If the sprites touch, the blocks inside the "if-then" block run

This block selects a random place for the elephant to hide

STARTING FROM SCRATCH

Complex loops

Simple loops are used to repeat parts of a program forever, or a certain number of times. Other, cleverer loops can be used to write programs that decide exactly when to repeat instructions.

> **SEE ALSO**
> ‹ 42–43 Simple loops
> ‹ 58–59 True or false?

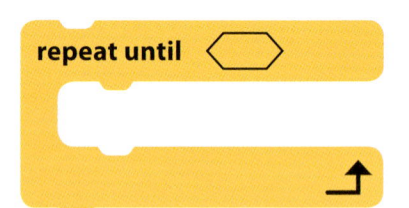

Looping until something happens

Add the "Dog1" sprite to a project, and then give the below script to the cat sprite. When you run the script, the "repeat until" block makes sure the cat keeps moving until it touches the dog. It will then stop and say "Ouch!"

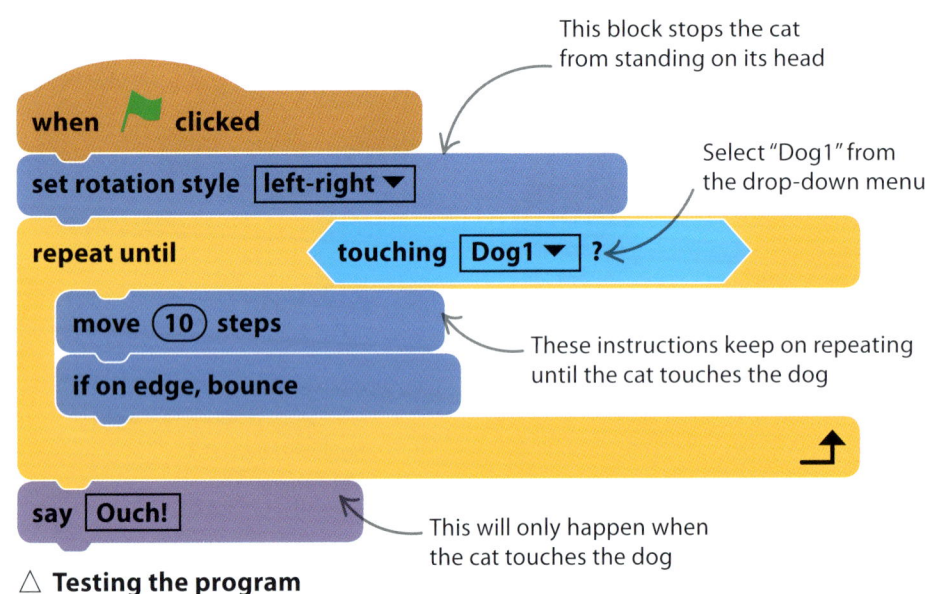

```
when [flag] clicked
set rotation style [left-right ▼]
repeat until <touching [Dog1 ▼] ?>
    move (10) steps
    if on edge, bounce
say [Ouch!]
```

- This block stops the cat from standing on its head
- Select "Dog1" from the drop-down menu
- These instructions keep on repeating until the cat touches the dog
- This will only happen when the cat touches the dog

△ **Testing the program**
Move the dog out of the cat's way and run the program. Then drag and drop the dog into the cat's path to see what happens.

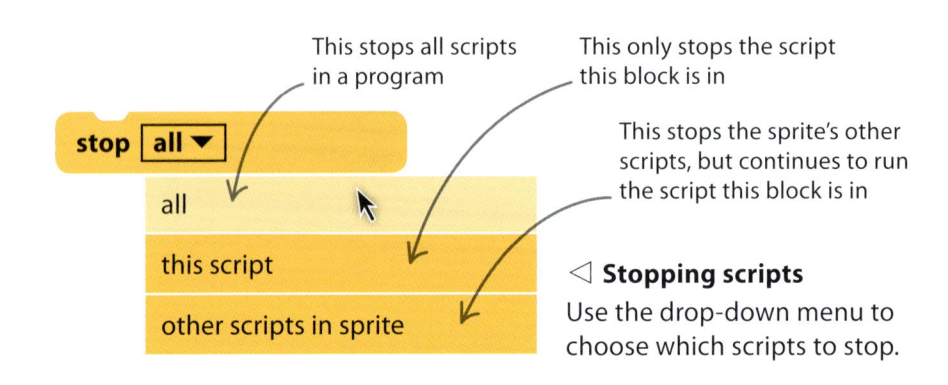

```
repeat until <  >
```

△ **"Repeat until" block**
The blocks inside the "repeat until" block keep repeating until the condition is true (the cat touches the dog).

Ouch!

Stop!

Another useful "Control" block is the "stop all" block, which can stop scripts from running. It's useful if you want to stop sprites moving at the end of a game.

```
stop [all ▼]
    all
    this script
    other scripts in sprite
```

- This stops all scripts in a program
- This only stops the script this block is in
- This stops the sprite's other scripts, but continues to run the script this block is in

◁ **Stopping scripts**
Use the drop-down menu to choose which scripts to stop.

COMPLEX LOOPS 65

Waiting

It's easier to play a game or see what's going on in a program if you can make a script pause for a moment. Different blocks can make a script wait a number of seconds or until something is true.

◁ **Waiting blocks**
The "wait secs" block waits a set amount of time. The "wait until" block responds to what's happening in the program.

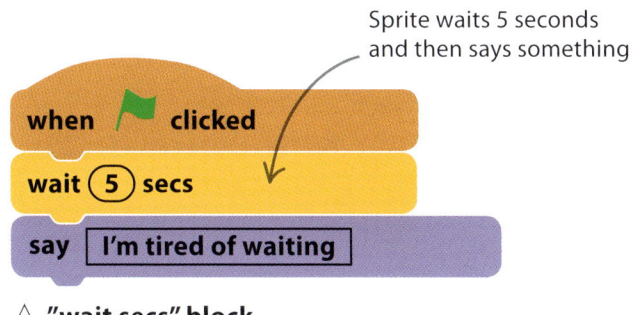

Sprite waits 5 seconds and then says something

△ **"wait secs" block**
With the "wait secs" block you can enter the number of seconds you want a sprite to wait.

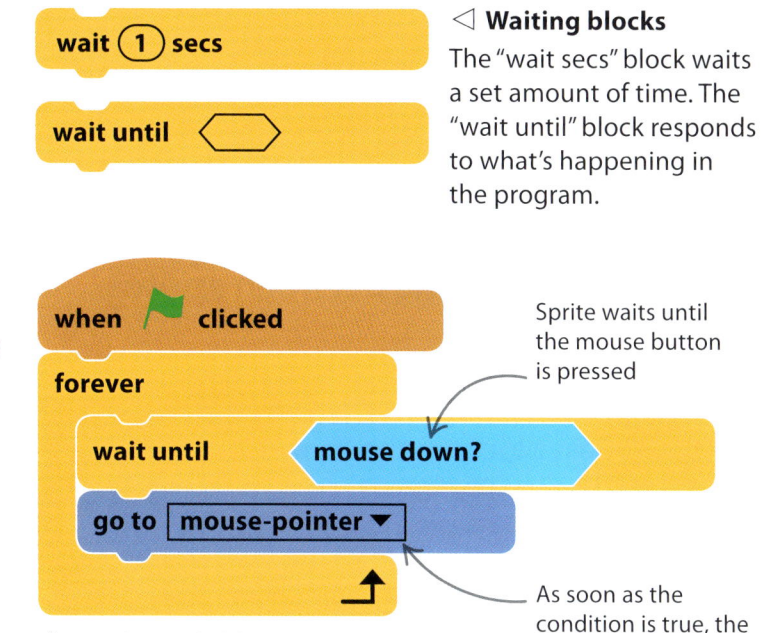

Sprite waits until the mouse button is pressed

△ **"wait until" block**
This block waits until the Boolean expression in it is true.

As soon as the condition is true, the sprite moves to the mouse-pointer

Magnetic mouse

Different loops can be used together to make programs. This program starts once the mouse button is pressed. The sprite follows the mouse-pointer until the mouse button is released. It then jumps up and down five times. The whole thing then repeats itself because it's all inside a "forever" loop.

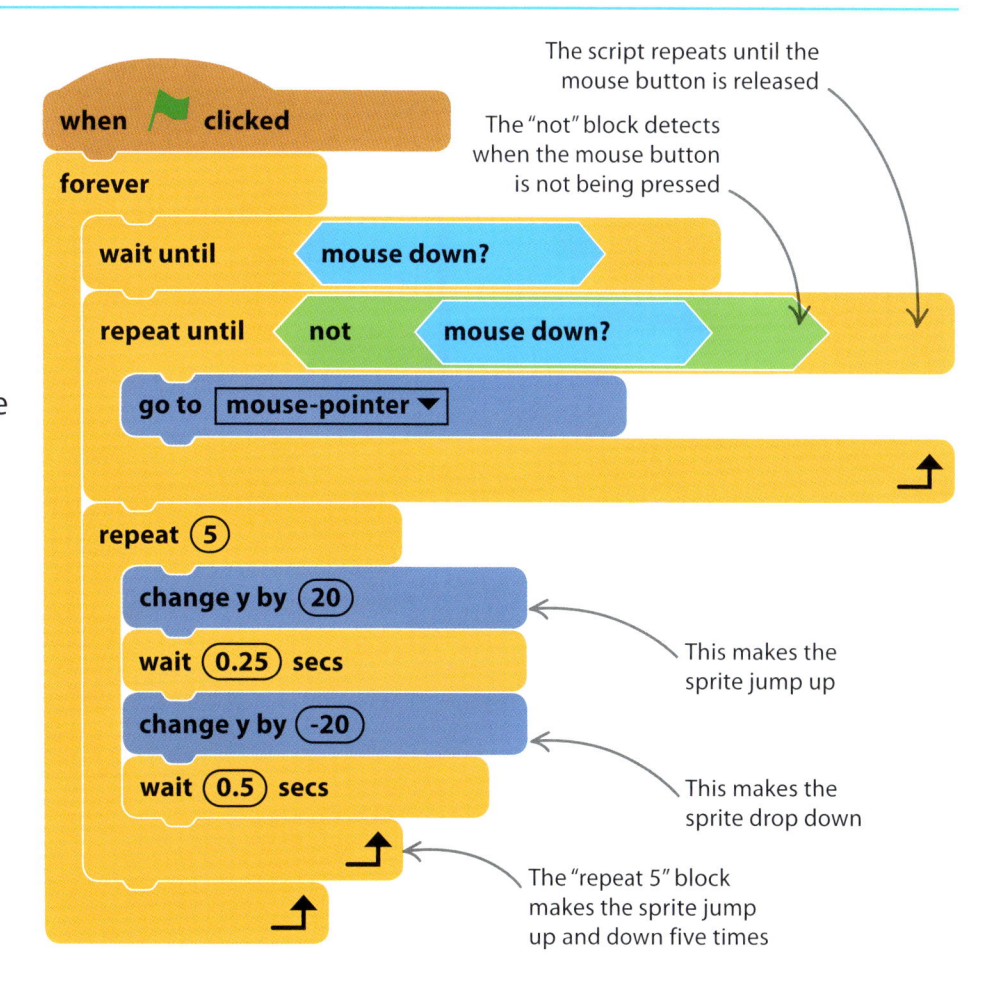

The script repeats until the mouse button is released

The "not" block detects when the mouse button is not being pressed

This makes the sprite jump up

This makes the sprite drop down

The "repeat 5" block makes the sprite jump up and down five times

▷ **Nested loops**
Pay careful attention to how the loops are nested inside the "forever" block.

Sending messages

Sometimes it's useful for sprites to communicate with each other. Sprites can use messages to tell other sprites what to do. Scratch also lets you create conversations between sprites.

> **SEE ALSO**
> ‹ 34–35 Making things move
> ‹ 36–37 Costumes
> ‹ 40–41 Events

Broadcasting

The broadcast blocks in the "Events" menu enable sprites to send and receive messages. Messages don't contain any information other than a name, but can be used to fine-tune a sprite's actions. Sprites only react to messages that they are programmed to respond to – they ignore any other messages.

This "Events" block lets a sprite send a message to all the other sprites

`broadcast message1 ▼`

This block starts a script when a sprite receives a message

`when I receive message1 ▼`

△ **Broadcast blocks**
One type of broadcast block lets a sprite send a message. The other tells the sprite to receive a message. Choose an existing message or create a new one.

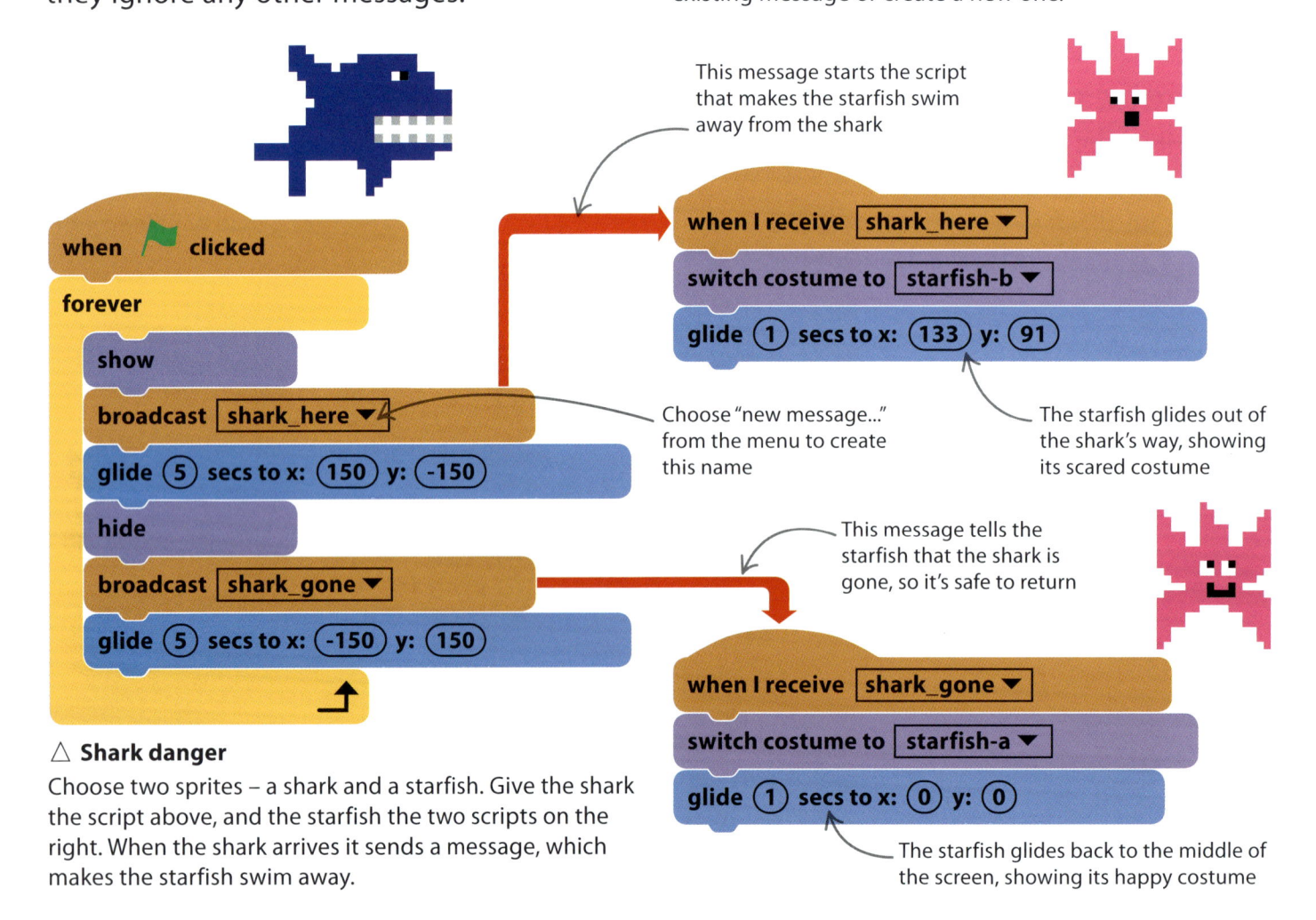

This message starts the script that makes the starfish swim away from the shark

```
when ⚑ clicked
forever
    show
    broadcast shark_here ▼
    glide 5 secs to x: 150 y: -150
    hide
    broadcast shark_gone ▼
    glide 5 secs to x: -150 y: 150
```

Choose "new message…" from the menu to create this name

```
when I receive shark_here ▼
switch costume to starfish-b ▼
glide 1 secs to x: 133 y: 91
```

The starfish glides out of the shark's way, showing its scared costume

This message tells the starfish that the shark is gone, so it's safe to return

```
when I receive shark_gone ▼
switch costume to starfish-a ▼
glide 1 secs to x: 0 y: 0
```

The starfish glides back to the middle of the screen, showing its happy costume

△ **Shark danger**
Choose two sprites – a shark and a starfish. Give the shark the script above, and the starfish the two scripts on the right. When the shark arrives it sends a message, which makes the starfish swim away.

SENDING MESSAGES

Conversations

To create a conversation between sprites use "broadcast message and wait" blocks with "say" blocks, which make your sprites talk using speech bubbles. Start a new project and add two monkey sprites to it. Give the script on the left to one monkey, and the two scripts on the right to the other.

`broadcast [message1 ▼] and wait`

△ **Waiting blocks**
This block sends a message, then waits for all the scripts that react to the message to finish before the program continues.

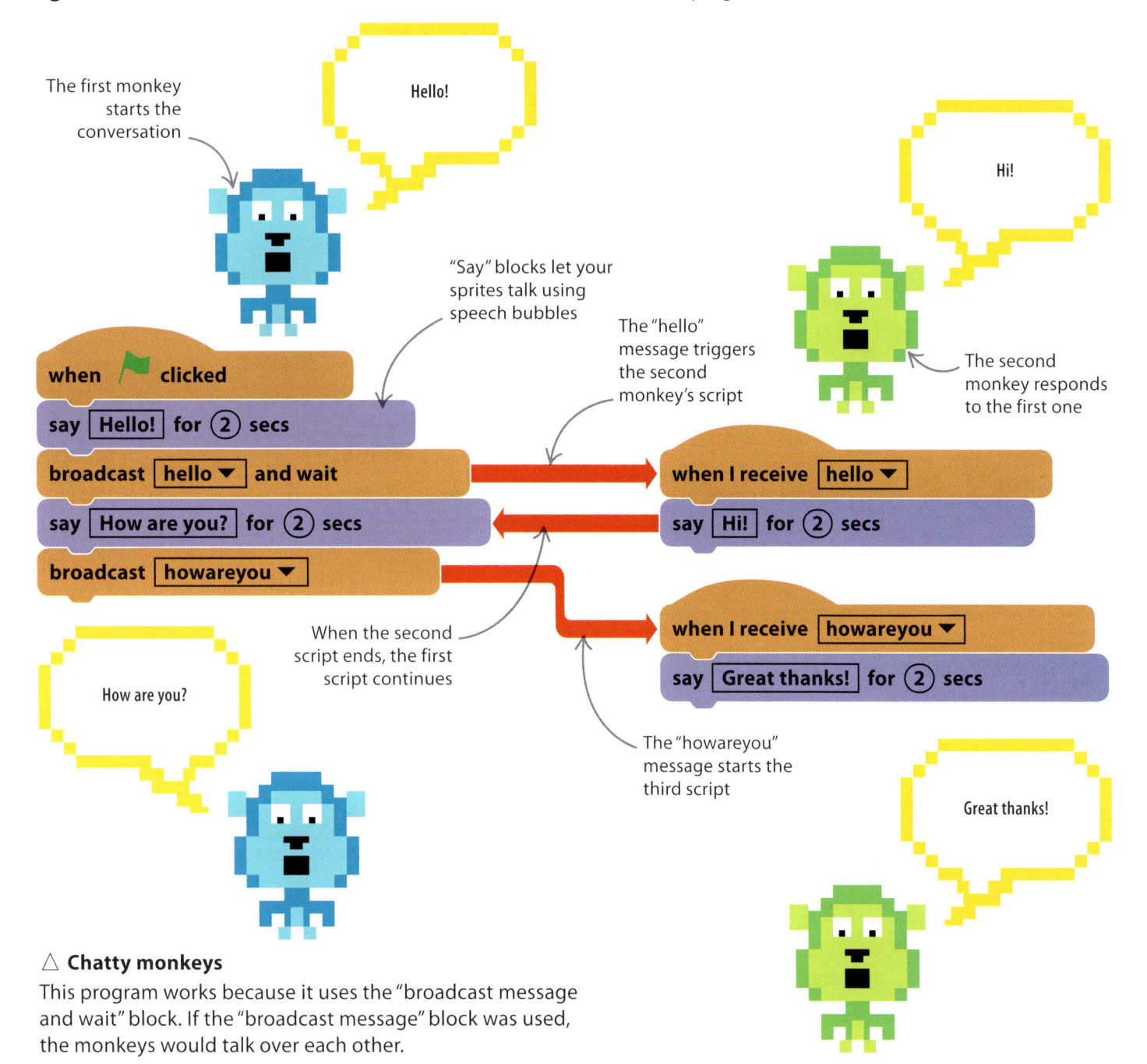

The first monkey starts the conversation

Hello!

"Say" blocks let your sprites talk using speech bubbles

The "hello" message triggers the second monkey's script

Hi!

The second monkey responds to the first one

```
when ⚑ clicked
say [Hello!] for (2) secs
broadcast [hello ▼] and wait
say [How are you?] for (2) secs
broadcast [howareyou ▼]
```

```
when I receive [hello ▼]
say [Hi!] for (2) secs
```

When the second script ends, the first script continues

How are you?

```
when I receive [howareyou ▼]
say [Great thanks!] for (2) secs
```

The "howareyou" message starts the third script

Great thanks!

△ **Chatty monkeys**
This program works because it uses the "broadcast message and wait" block. If the "broadcast message" block was used, the monkeys would talk over each other.

Creating blocks

To avoid repeating the same set of blocks over and over again, it's possible to take a shortcut by creating new blocks. Each new block can contain several different instructions.

SEE ALSO

⟨ **46–47** Variables
Time to **78–79** ⟩
experiment

Making your own block

You can make your own blocks in Scratch that run a script when they're used. Try this example to see how they work. Programmers call these reusable pieces of code "subprograms" or "functions".

1 Create a new block
Click on the "More Blocks" button, and then select "Make a Block". Type the word "jump" and click "OK".

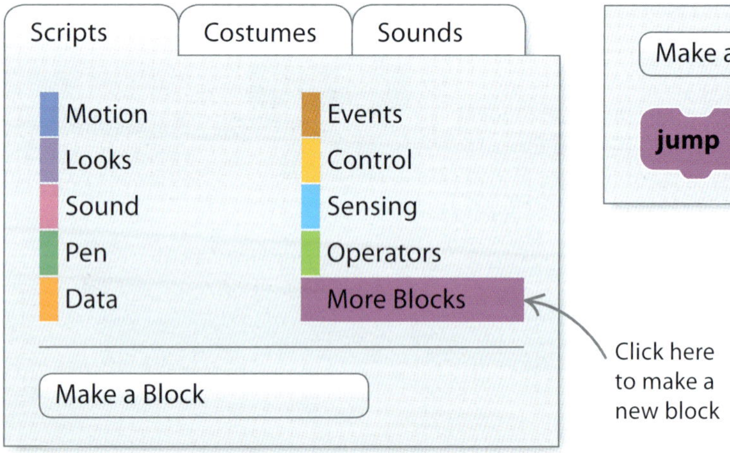

Scripts | Costumes | Sounds

- Motion
- Looks
- Sound
- Pen
- Data
- Events
- Control
- Sensing
- Operators
- More Blocks

Make a Block

Click here to make a new block

2 New block appears
Your new block "jump" appears in the blocks palette, and a "define" block appears in the scripts area.

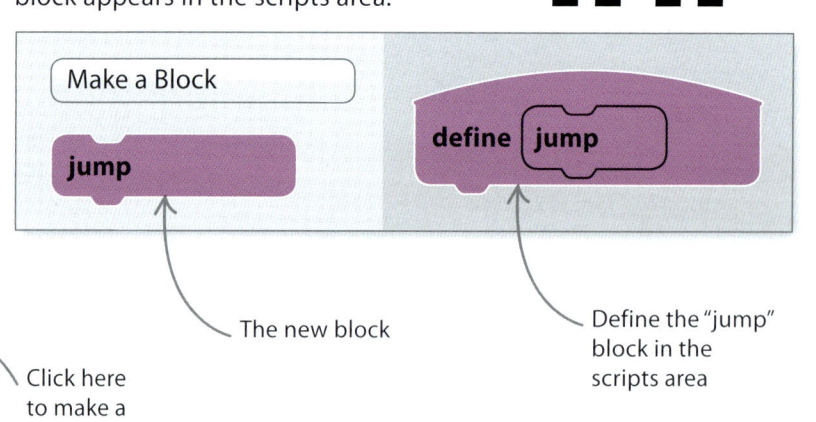

Make a Block

jump   define jump

The new block

Define the "jump" block in the scripts area

3 Define the block
The "define" block tells Scratch which blocks to run when using the new block. Add this script to define the block.

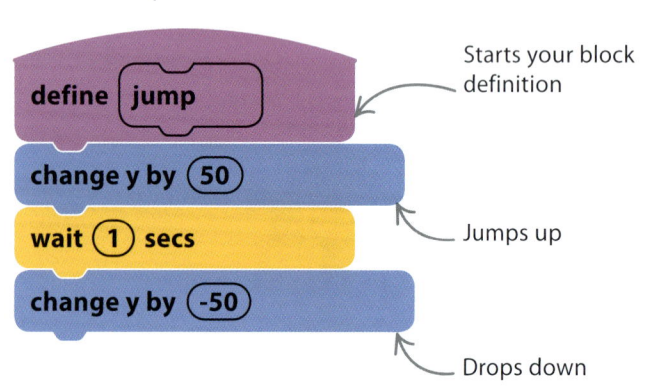

define jump — Starts your block definition
change y by 50 — Jumps up
wait 1 secs
change y by -50 — Drops down

4 Use the block in a script
The new block can now be used in any script. It's as if those jumping blocks were in the script individually.

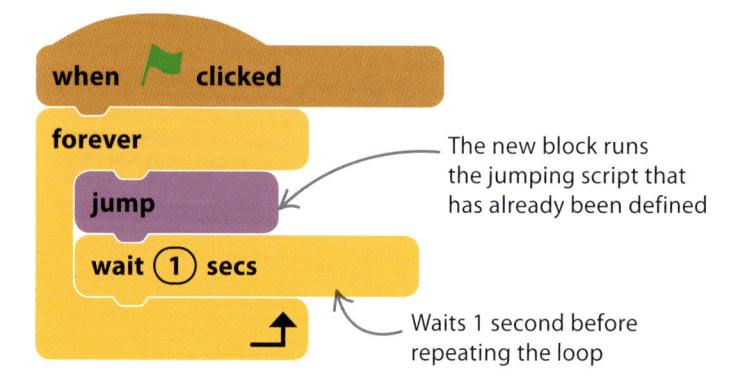

when ⚑ clicked
forever
  jump — The new block runs the jumping script that has already been defined
  wait 1 secs — Waits 1 second before repeating the loop

CREATING BLOCKS 69

Blocks with inputs

Windows in a new block can be used to give it numbers and words to work with. These holes can be used to change how far the block moves a sprite.

New Block

slide (steps) and shout [greeting]

▼ Options

Add number input:
Add string input:
Add boolean input:
Add label text: text
☐ Run without screen refresh

OK   Cancel

Click here to see all of the options

1 Make a new block
Make a new block called "slide" and then click on "Options". Now select "Add number input" and type "steps". Select "Add label text" and change it to "and shout". Click "Add string input" and call it "greeting". Then click "OK".

2 Define the block
In the "define" block, the holes are replaced with variables called "steps" and "greeting". Drag these variables from the "define" block into the script wherever you need them. Add this script to your sprite.

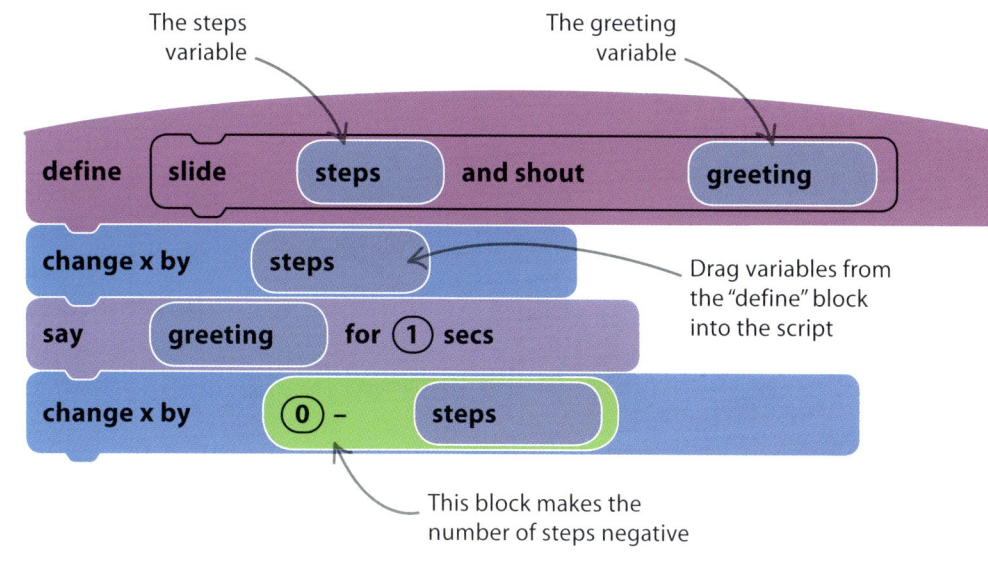

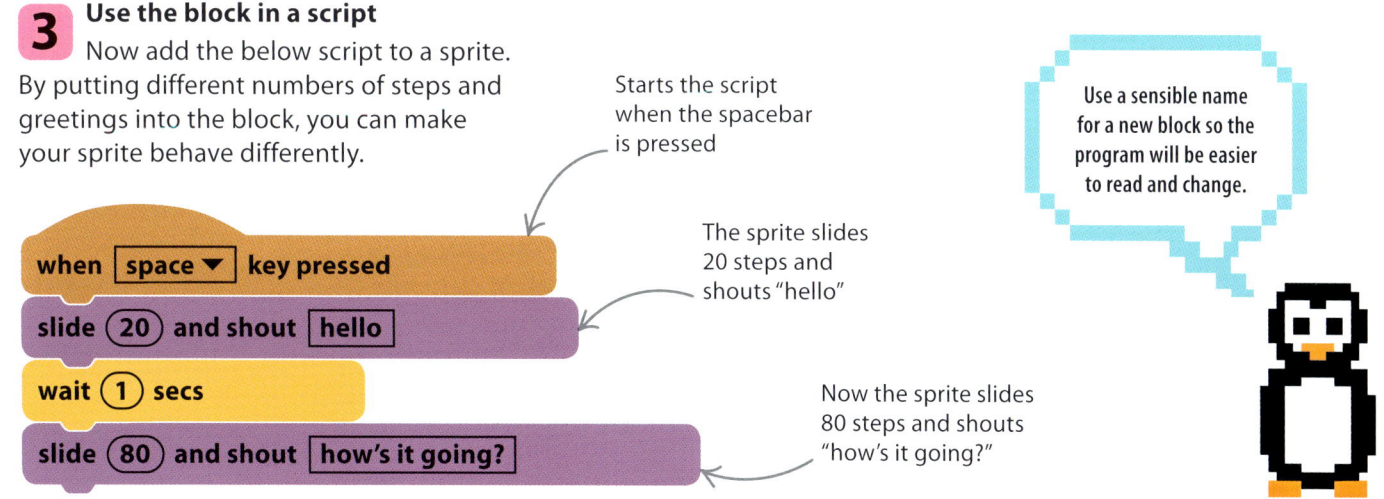

The steps variable

The greeting variable

define slide (steps) and shout (greeting)
change x by (steps)
say (greeting) for (1) secs
change x by ((0) – (steps))

Drag variables from the "define" block into the script

This block makes the number of steps negative

3 Use the block in a script
Now add the below script to a sprite. By putting different numbers of steps and greetings into the block, you can make your sprite behave differently.

when [space ▼] key pressed
slide (20) and shout [hello]
wait (1) secs
slide (80) and shout [how's it going?]

Starts the script when the spacebar is pressed

The sprite slides 20 steps and shouts "hello"

Now the sprite slides 80 steps and shouts "how's it going?"

Use a sensible name for a new block so the program will be easier to read and change.

STARTING FROM SCRATCH

PROJECT 3

Monkey mayhem

This exciting, fast-paced game brings together all of the Scratch skills you've learned so far. Follow these steps to create your very own "Monkey mayhem" and see if you can hit the bat with the bananas!

> **SEE ALSO**
>
> ‹ 36–37 Costumes
> ‹ 34–35 Making things move
> ‹ 62–63 Sensing and detecting

Getting started

Start a new Scratch project. The cat sprite isn't needed for this project. To remove it, right-click on it in the sprite list and then click "delete" in the menu. This will leave you a blank project to work on.

> **EXPERT TIPS**
>
> ## Avoiding errors
>
> This is the biggest Scratch program you've tried so far, so you might find that the game doesn't always work as you expect it to. Here are some tips to help things run smoothly:
>
> **Make sure you add scripts** to the correct sprite.
>
> **Follow the instructions** carefully. Remember to make a variable before using it.
>
> **Check that all the numbers** in the blocks are correct.

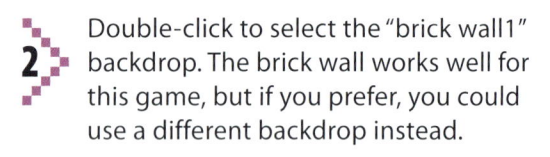

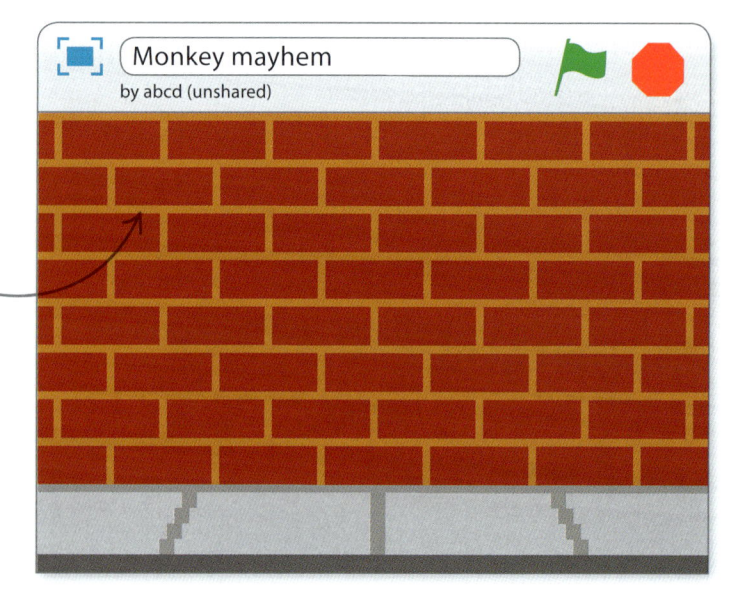

1 Add a new backdrop from the backdrop library. This button is found to the left of the sprite list.

Stage
1 backdrop

New backdrop:

Click here to add a new backdrop from the backdrop library

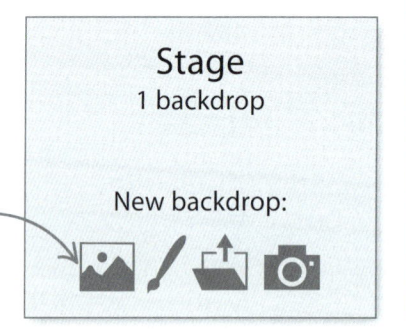

2 Double-click to select the "brick wall1" backdrop. The brick wall works well for this game, but if you prefer, you could use a different backdrop instead.

Monkey mayhem
by abcd (unshared)

Double-click on a backdrop in the backdrop library to make it appear on the stage

MONKEY MAYHEM **71**

3 Go to the sprite library to add a new sprite to the game. Select "Monkey1" from the "Animals" section. The user will control this sprite in the game.

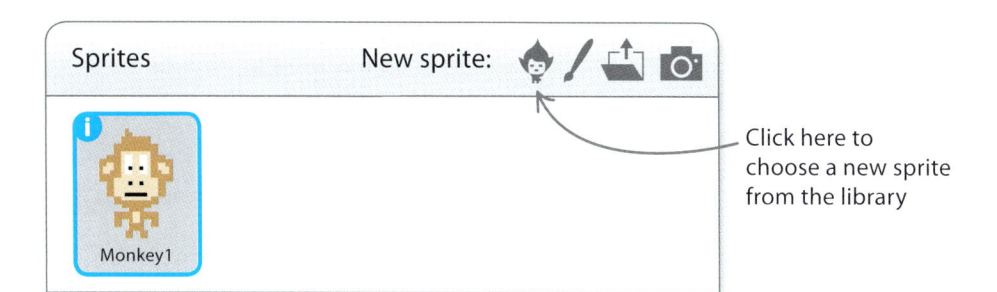

Click here to choose a new sprite from the library

4 Give the monkey the script below. Remember – all of the different blocks can be found in the blocks palette, organized by colour. In this script, "Sensing" blocks are used to move the monkey around the stage using the keyboard arrow keys. Run the script when you've finished to check it works.

The arrow keys on the keyboard will make the monkey run left and right

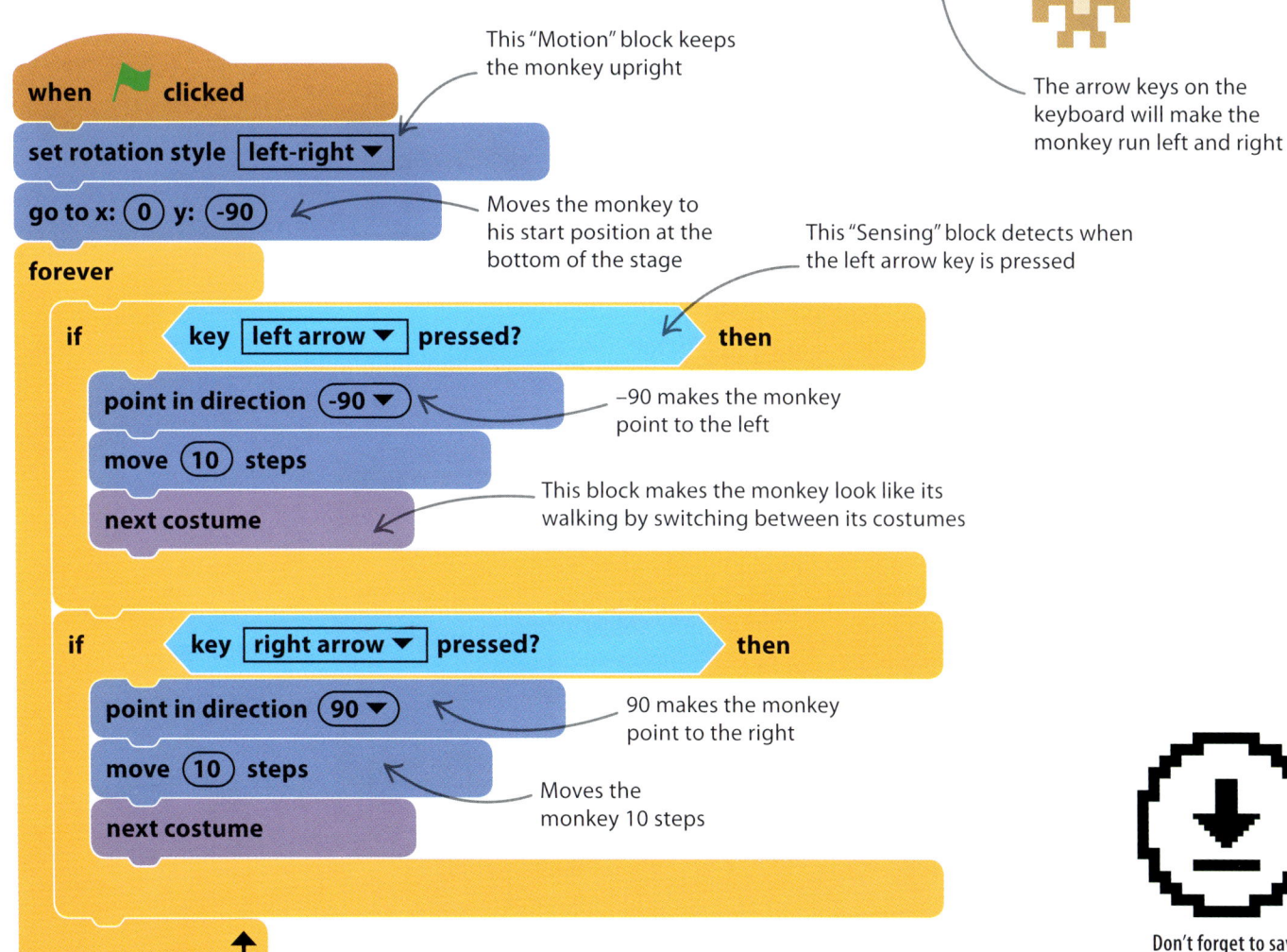

This "Motion" block keeps the monkey upright

```
when [flag] clicked
set rotation style [left-right ▼]
go to x: (0) y: (-90)
forever
    if < key [left arrow ▼] pressed? > then
        point in direction (-90 ▼)
        move (10) steps
        next costume
    if < key [right arrow ▼] pressed? > then
        point in direction (90 ▼)
        move (10) steps
        next costume
```

Moves the monkey to his start position at the bottom of the stage

This "Sensing" block detects when the left arrow key is pressed

−90 makes the monkey point to the left

This block makes the monkey look like its walking by switching between its costumes

90 makes the monkey point to the right

Moves the monkey 10 steps

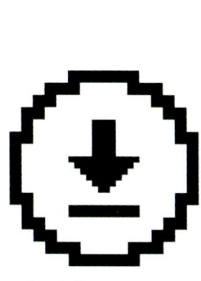

Don't forget to save your work

MONKEY MAYHEM

Adding more sprites

The monkey can now be moved across the stage using the left and right arrow keys. To make the game more interesting, add some more sprites. Give the monkey some bananas to throw, and a bat to throw them at!

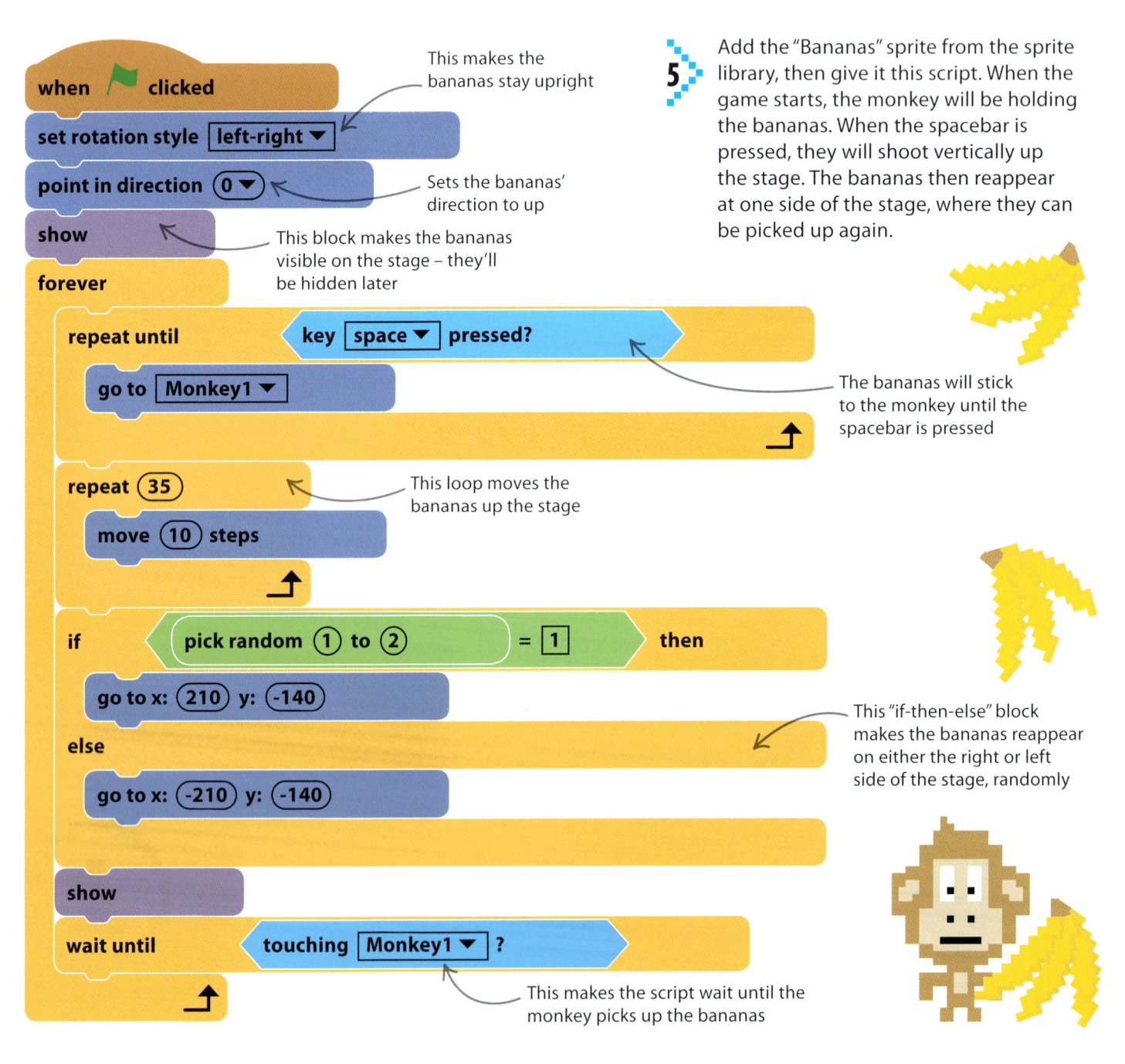

5 Add the "Bananas" sprite from the sprite library, then give it this script. When the game starts, the monkey will be holding the bananas. When the spacebar is pressed, they will shoot vertically up the stage. The bananas then reappear at one side of the stage, where they can be picked up again.

```
when [flag] clicked
set rotation style [left-right]         ← This makes the bananas stay upright
point in direction (0)                  ← Sets the bananas' direction to up
show                                    ← This block makes the bananas visible on the stage – they'll be hidden later
forever
    repeat until <key [space] pressed?>
        go to [Monkey1]                 ← The bananas will stick to the monkey until the spacebar is pressed
    repeat (35)                         ← This loop moves the bananas up the stage
        move (10) steps
    if <(pick random (1) to (2)) = (1)> then
        go to x: (210) y: (-140)
    else                                ← This "if-then-else" block makes the bananas reappear on either the right or left side of the stage, randomly
        go to x: (-210) y: (-140)
    show
    wait until <touching [Monkey1]?>    ← This makes the script wait until the monkey picks up the bananas
```

MONKEY MAYHEM 73

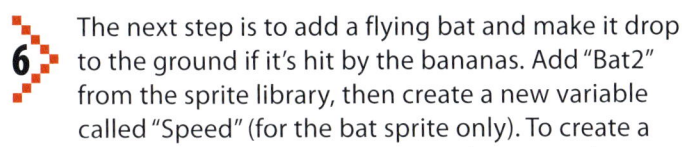

6 The next step is to add a flying bat and make it drop to the ground if it's hit by the bananas. Add "Bat2" from the sprite library, then create a new variable called "Speed" (for the bat sprite only). To create a new variable, first click the "Data" button in the blocks palette, and then select the "Make a Variable" button. Untick the box by the "Speed" variable in the "Data" section so it doesn't appear on the screen.

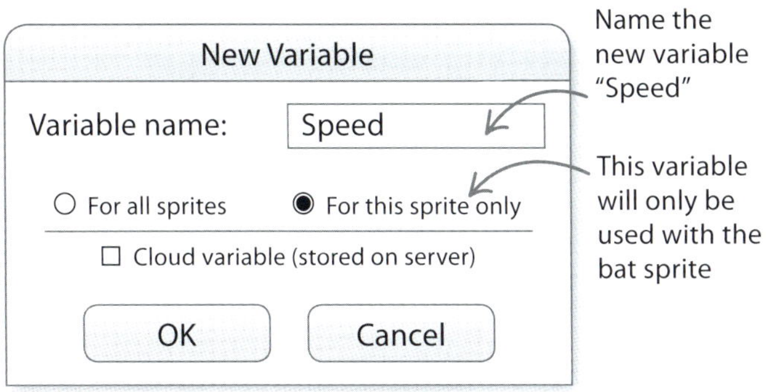

New Variable

Variable name: Speed

○ For all sprites   ● For this sprite only

☐ Cloud variable (stored on server)

OK   Cancel

Name the new variable "Speed"

This variable will only be used with the bat sprite

7 Add the below script to the bat. In the main "forever" loop, the bat moves to a random position on the left of the stage, chooses a random speed, then moves backwards and forwards across the stage until the bananas hit it. When the bat is hit, it drops to the ground.

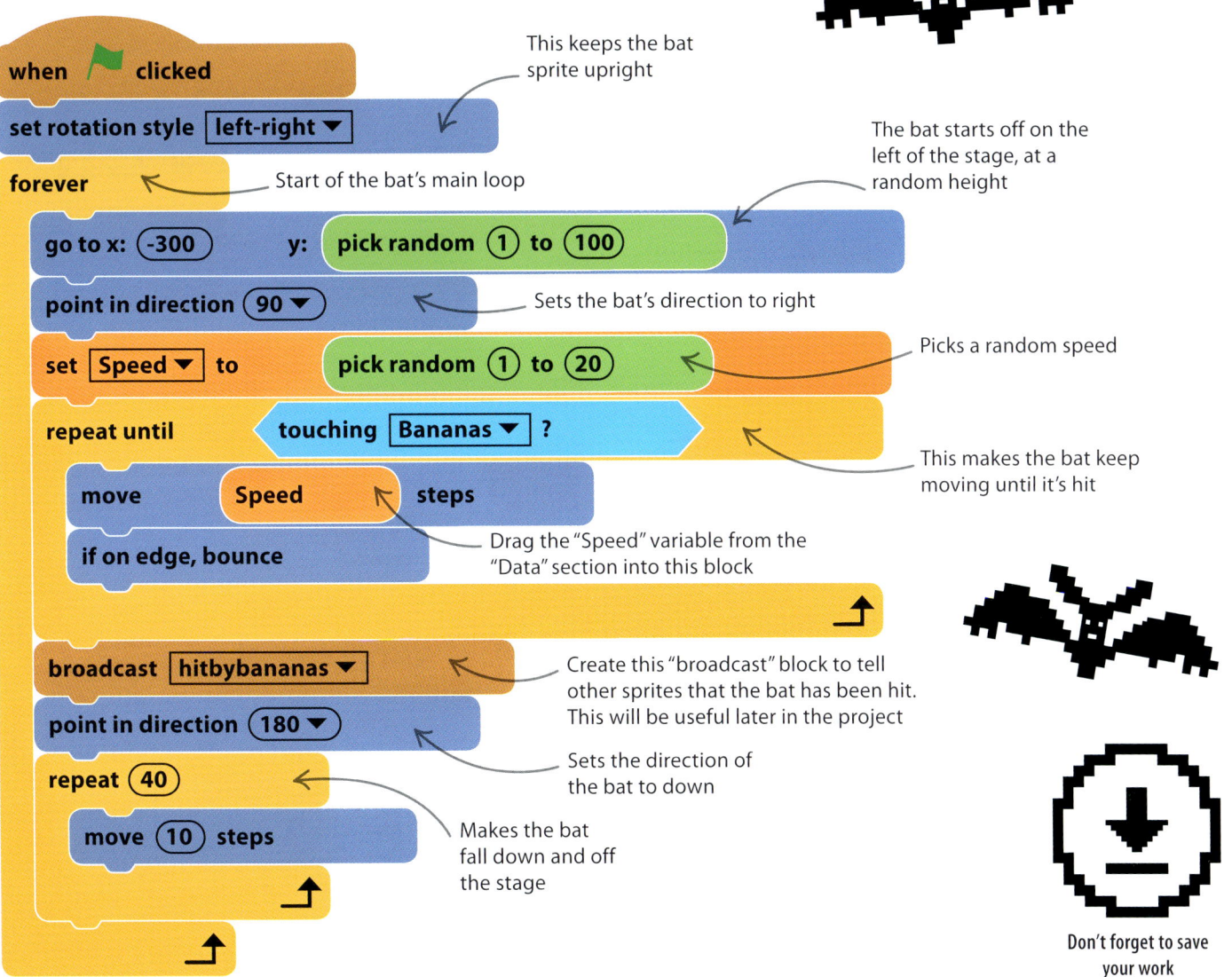

```
when [flag] clicked
set rotation style [left-right ▼]      ← This keeps the bat sprite upright
forever                                 ← Start of the bat's main loop
    go to x: (-300) y: (pick random (1) to (100))   ← The bat starts off on the left of the stage, at a random height
    point in direction (90 ▼)           ← Sets the bat's direction to right
    set [Speed ▼] to (pick random (1) to (20))      ← Picks a random speed
    repeat until <touching [Bananas ▼]?>            ← This makes the bat keep moving until it's hit
        move (Speed) steps
        if on edge, bounce
                                        ← Drag the "Speed" variable from the "Data" section into this block
    broadcast [hitbybananas ▼]          ← Create this "broadcast" block to tell other sprites that the bat has been hit. This will be useful later in the project
    point in direction (180 ▼)          ← Sets the direction of the bat to down
    repeat (40)                         ← Makes the bat fall down and off the stage
        move (10) steps
```

Don't forget to save your work

MONKEY MAYHEM

The finishing touches
To make the game even more exciting, you can add a timer, use a variable to keep score of how many bats the player hits, and add a game over screen that appears once the player is out of time.

8 ▷ Create a new variable called "Time". Make sure it's available for all sprites in the game by selecting the "For all sprites" option. Check that the box next to the variable in the blocks palette is ticked, so that players can see the time displayed on the stage.

☑ Time

9 ▷ Click on the small picture of the stage in the stage list, then select the "Backdrops" tab above the blocks palette. Right-click the existing backdrop and duplicate it. Add the words "GAME OVER" to the new backdrop.

Use the text tool to write on the duplicate backdrop

Your game over screen will look something like this

10 ▷ Click the "Scripts" tab and add this script to the stage to set up the timer. When the timer begins, it starts a count-down loop. When the loop finishes, the "GAME OVER" screen is shown and the game ends.

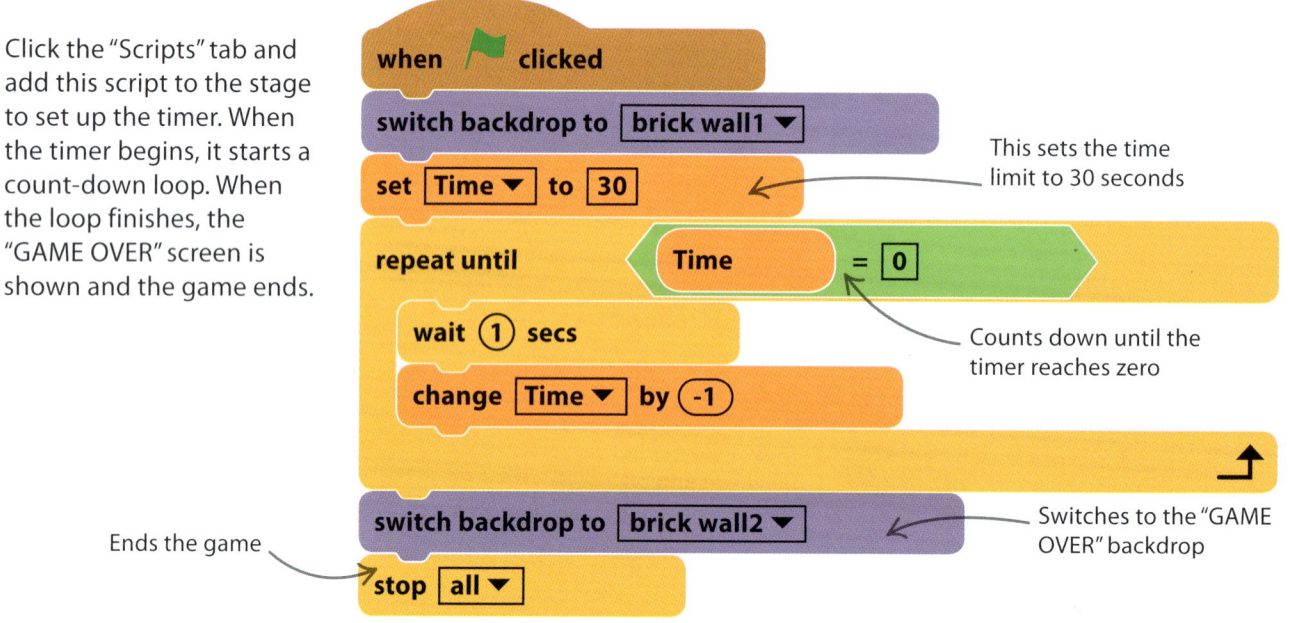

when ⚑ clicked
switch backdrop to brick wall1
set Time to 30 — This sets the time limit to 30 seconds
repeat until Time = 0
  wait 1 secs
  change Time by -1
— Counts down until the timer reaches zero
switch backdrop to brick wall2 — Switches to the "GAME OVER" backdrop
stop all — Ends the game

MONKEY MAYHEM   75

11 ▸ Click the bananas sprite in the sprite list. Create a new variable called "Score" and make it available for all sprites. Move the score to the top right of the stage by dragging it.

Tick the box to show the score on the stage

☑ Score

12 ▸ Add this short script to the bananas sprite. It sets the score to 0 at the beginning of the game.

```
when ⚑ clicked
set Score ▾ to 0
```

This resets the score

13 ▸ Add this script to the bananas sprite too. When the bananas hit the bat, it plays a sound, increases the score by 10, and hides the bananas.

Makes the bananas disappear

```
when I receive hitbybananas ▾
hide
play sound pop ▾
change Score ▾ by 10
```

Add the "pop" sound from the sound library to the banana sprite (see pp.54–55)

Each time the bat is hit the player scores 10 points

14 ▸ Next add some music to the game. Click on the stage and select the "Sounds" tab above the blocks palette. Load the "eggs" music from the sound library.

2
eggs
00:15.2

Add the "eggs" music from the "Sounds" tab

15 ▸ Add the script below to the stage. It plays the "eggs" music on a loop, but will stop when the "stop all" block ends the game.

```
when ⚑ clicked
forever
  play sound eggs ▾ until done
```

The background music is repeated in an endless loop

Don't forget to save your work

▪▪ REMEMBER
Achievements

Congratulations – you've built a complete Scratch game. Here are some of the things you have achieved so far:

Made a sprite throw objects at another sprite.

Made a sprite fall off the stage once hit.

Added a time limit to your game.

Added background music that plays as long as the game continues.

Added a game over screen that appears at the end of the game.

MONKEY MAYHEM

Time to play

Now the game is ready to play. Click the green flag to start and see how many times you can hit the bat with the bananas before the time runs out.

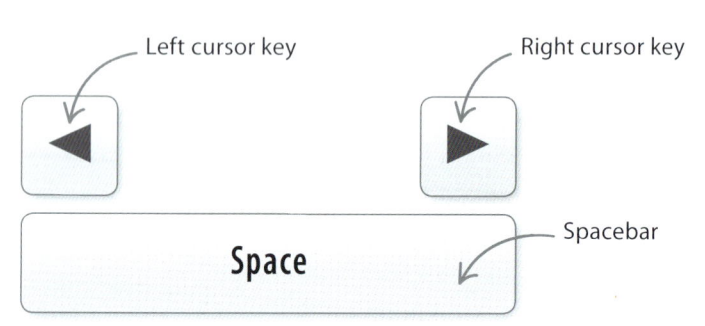

Left cursor key

Right cursor key

Spacebar

△ **Controls**
Steer the monkey left and right with the keyboard cursor keys. Tap the spacebar to fire bananas at the bat.

Make up a new title for the game and type it in

To make the game last longer, try increasing the time limit

Untitled
by abcd (unshared)

Time 30

To make the game harder, make the bat move faster

EXPERT TIPS
Adding more sprites

To add more bats to aim at, right-click the bat in the sprite list and select "duplicate". A new bat will appear with all the same scripts as the first one. Try adding some other flying sprites:

1. Add a sprite from the sprite library. The flying hippo ("Hippo1") is great for this game.

2. Click on the bat in the sprite list.

3. Click the bat's script and hold the mouse button down.

4. Drag the bat's script on to the new sprite in the sprite list.

5. The script will copy across to the new sprite.

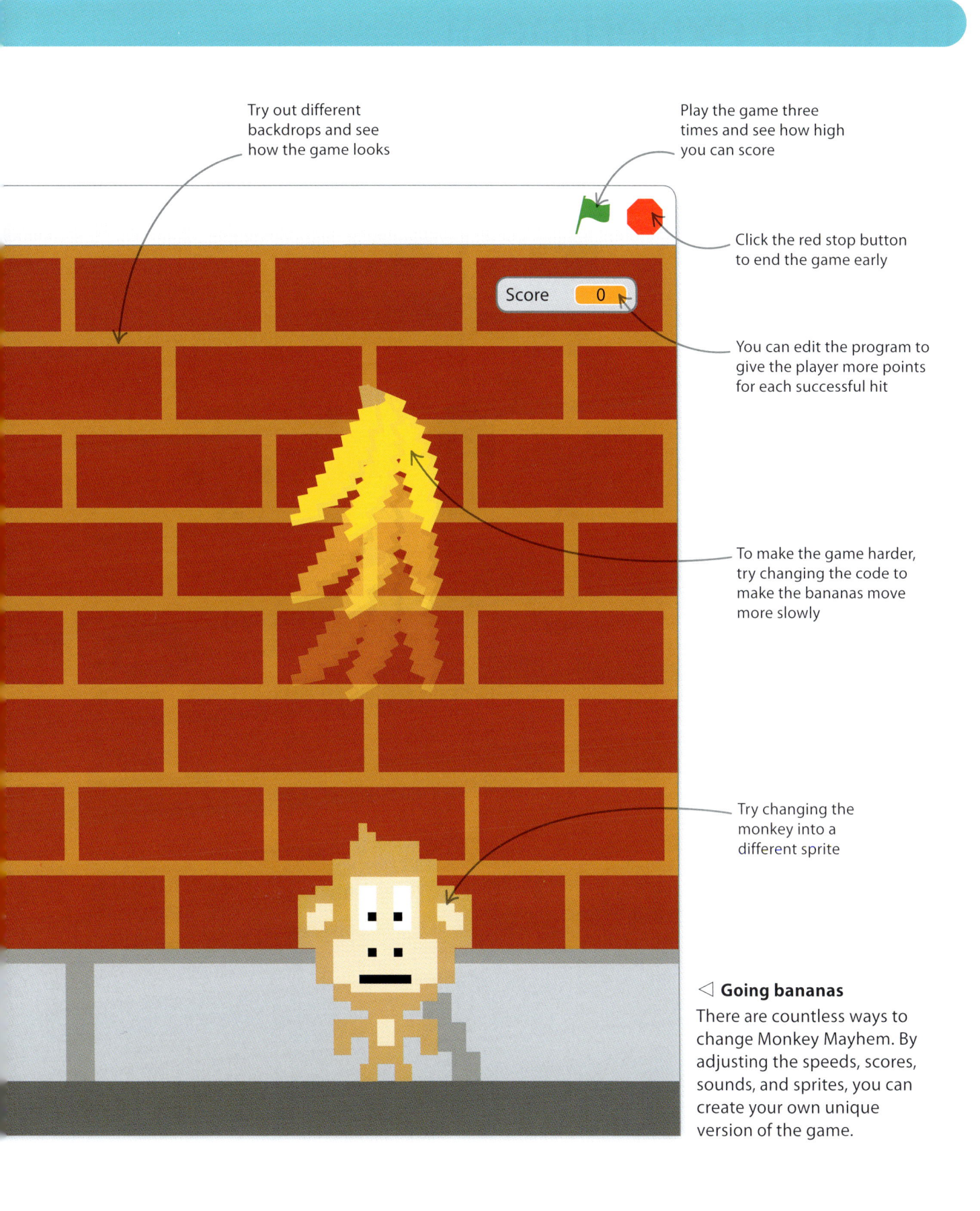

MONKEY MAYHEM 77

Try out different backdrops and see how the game looks

Play the game three times and see how high you can score

Click the red stop button to end the game early

Score 0

You can edit the program to give the player more points for each successful hit

To make the game harder, try changing the code to make the bananas move more slowly

Try changing the monkey into a different sprite

◁ **Going bananas**
There are countless ways to change Monkey Mayhem. By adjusting the speeds, scores, sounds, and sprites, you can create your own unique version of the game.

Time to experiment

Now you've learned the basics of Scratch, you can experiment with some of its more advanced features. The more you practise, the better your coding will become.

> **SEE ALSO**
> What is Python? **82–83 >**
> Simple commands **98–99 >**

Things to try

Not sure what to do next with Scratch? Here are a few ideas. If you don't feel ready to write a whole program on your own yet, you can start with one that has already been written and change parts of it.

◁ **Join a coding club**
Is there a coding club in your school or local area? They're great places to meet other Scratch users and share ideas.

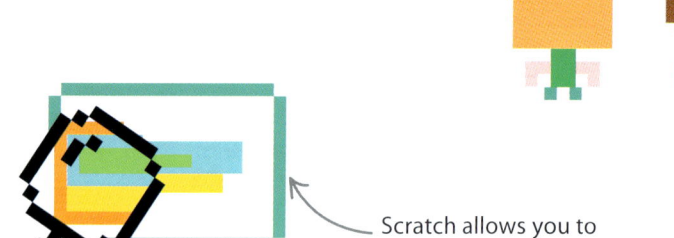

Scratch allows you to look at the coding of all projects on its website

△ **Look at code**
Looking at other programs is a great way to learn. Go through projects shared on the Scratch website. What can you learn from them?

▷ **Remix existing projects**
Can you improve the projects on the Scratch website? Scratch lets you add new features and then share your version.

Backpack

The backpack enables you to store useful scripts, sprites, sounds, and costumes and move them from project to project. It's found at the bottom of the Scratch screen.

Drag and drop to copy a script or sprite into the backpack

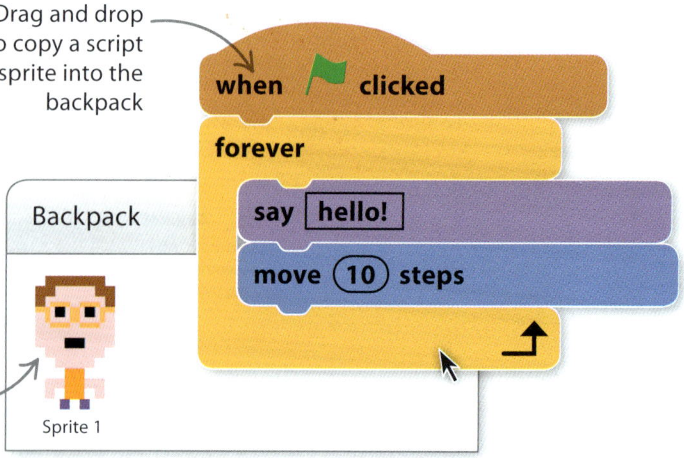

A sprite in the backpack

▷ **Drag and drop**
You can drag sprites and scripts into your backpack, then add them to other projects.

TIME TO EXPERIMENT   79

Help!
It can be hard to write a program if you don't know about some of the blocks you could use. Scratch has a help menu to make sure you understand every block.

1 Block help
To find out more about a particular block, click the "block help" button on the cursor tools bar at the top of the screen.

This is the "block help" button

2 Ask a question
The cursor will turn into a question mark. Use this to click on the block you want to know about.

The cursor becomes a question mark

3 Help window
The help window opens to tell you how the block works, with tips on how it can be used.

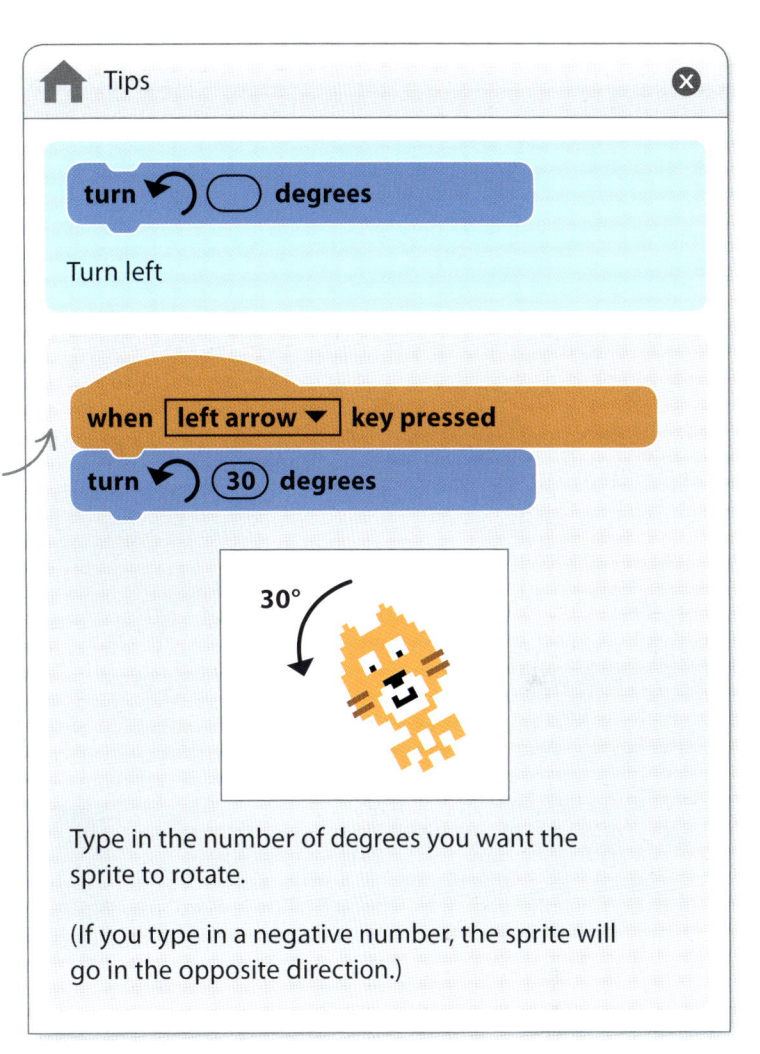

Tips

turn ↺ ◯ degrees
Turn left

The help window explains every block

when [left arrow ▼] key pressed
turn ↺ (30) degrees

30°

Type in the number of degrees you want the sprite to rotate.

(If you type in a negative number, the sprite will go in the opposite direction.)

Learn another language
You're now on your way to mastering your first programming language. Learning other languages will enable you to write different types of programs. Why not try Python next? What you've already learned about Scratch will help you to pick up Python quickly.

▷ **Similar to Scratch**
Python uses loops, variables, and branches too. Use your Scratch knowledge to start learning Python!

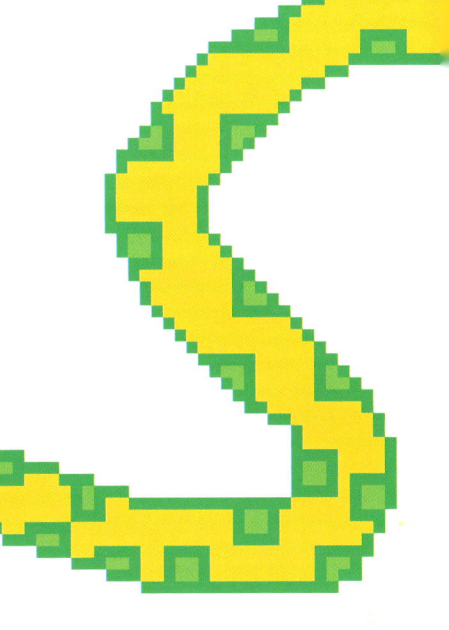

3

Playing with Python

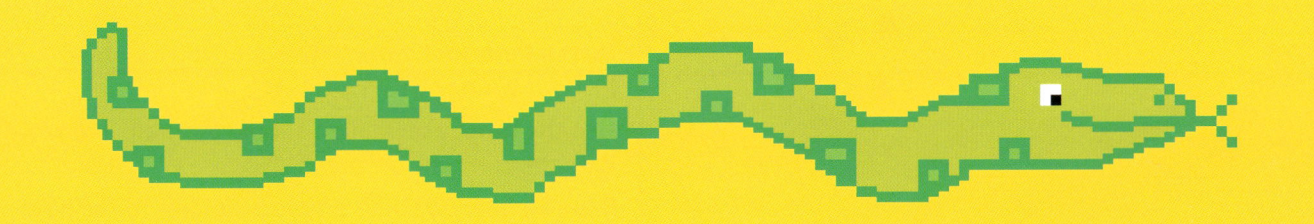

What is Python?

Python is a text-based programming language. It takes a bit longer to learn than Scratch, but can be used to do much more.

SEE ALSO

Installing Python **84–87 ›**

Simple commands **98–99 ›**

Harder commands **100–101 ›**

A useful language

Python is a versatile language that can be used to make many different types of programs, from word processing to web browsers. Here are a few great reasons to learn Python.

1 Easy to learn and use
Python programs are written in a simple language. The code is quite easy to read and write, compared to many other programming languages.

2 Contains ready-to-use code
Python contains libraries of preprogrammed code that you can use in your programs. It makes it easier to write complex programs quickly.

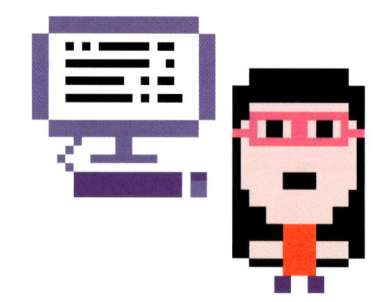

Python contains lots of programs you can use and build on

3 Useful for big organizations
Python is powerful. It can be used to write real-world programs. It is used by Google, NASA, and Pixar, among others.

EXPERT TIPS
Getting started

Before learning how to program in Python, it's useful to get familiar with how it works. The next few pages will teach you how to:

Install Python: Python is free, but you'll have to install it yourself (see pp.84–87).

Use the interface: Make a simple program and save it on the computer.

Experiment: Try some simple programs to see how they work.

WHAT IS PYTHON? **83**

Scratch and Python

Lots of elements that are used in Scratch are also used in Python – they just look different. Here are a few similarities between the two languages.

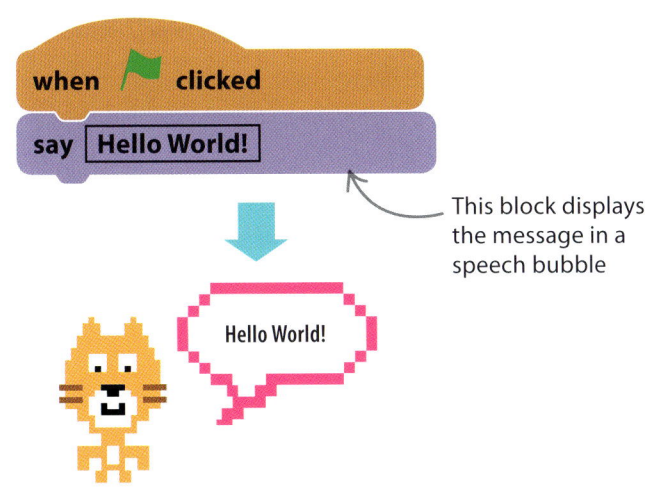

```
when clicked
say Hello World!
```

This block displays the message in a speech bubble

Hello World!

```
print('Hello World!')
```
Type the message you want here

The message appears on screen like this

```
Hello World!
```

△ **Print in Scratch**
In Scratch, the "say" block is used to show something on the screen.

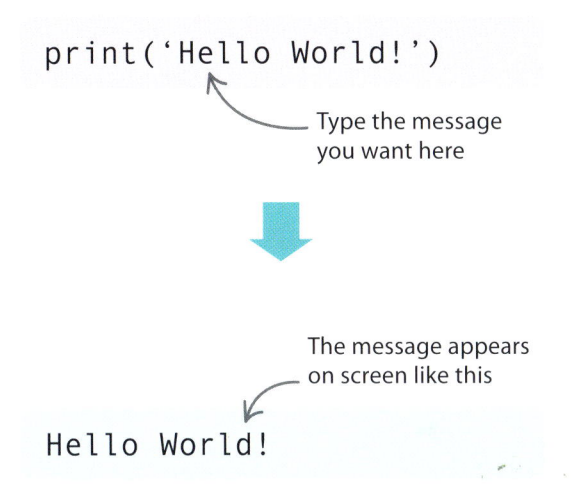

△ **Print in Python**
In Python, a command called "print" displays text on the screen.

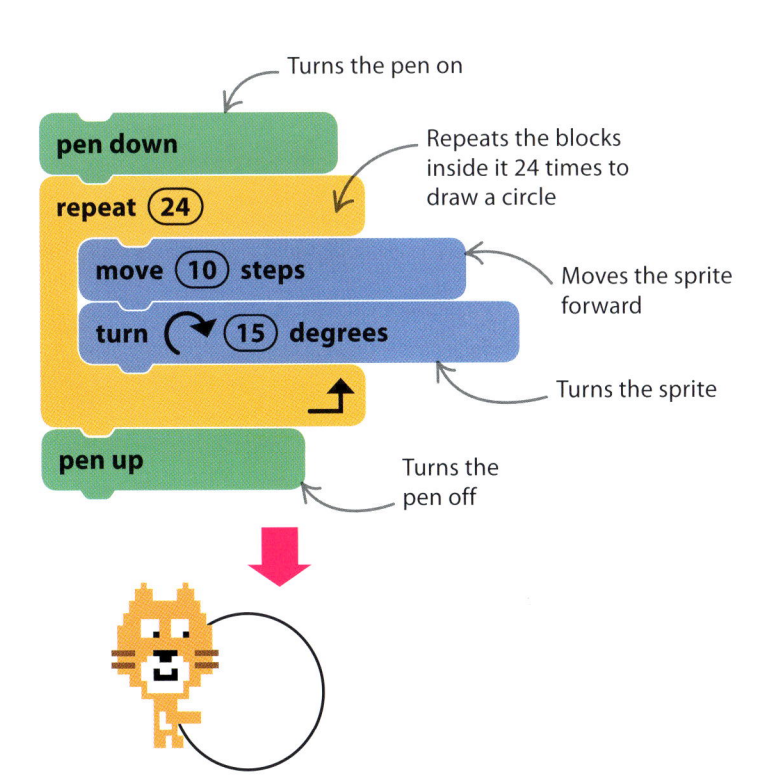

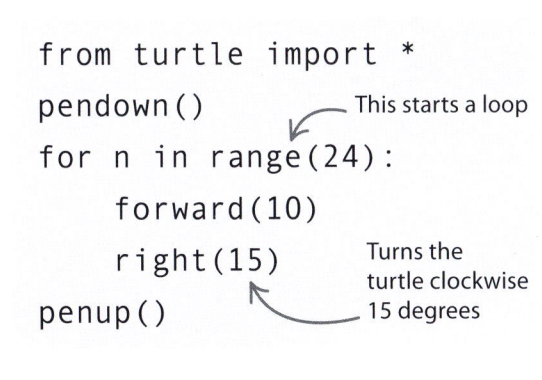

Turns the pen on

```
pen down
repeat 24
    move 10 steps
    turn 15 degrees
pen up
```

Repeats the blocks inside it 24 times to draw a circle

Moves the sprite forward

Turns the sprite

Turns the pen off

```
from turtle import *
pendown()
for n in range(24):
    forward(10)
    right(15)
penup()
```

This starts a loop

Turns the turtle clockwise 15 degrees

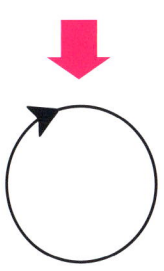

△ **Turtle graphics in Scratch**
The script above uses the "pen down" block to move the cat sprite and draw a circle.

△ **Turtle graphics in Python**
There's also a turtle in Python. The code above can be used to draw a circle.

Installing Python

Before you can use the Python programming language, you need to download and install it on your computer. Python 3 is free, easy to install, and works on Windows PCs, Macs, and Linux operating systems such as Ubuntu.

What is IDLE?

When you install Python 3, you'll also get a free program called IDLE (Integrated DeveLopment Environment). Designed for beginners, IDLE includes a basic text editor that allows you to write and edit Python code.

> **EXPERT TIPS**
> ### Saving code
> When saving work in Python, you will need to use the "File > Save As…" menu command so you can name your files. First create a folder to keep all your files in. Give the folder a clear name, like "PythonCode", and agree with the person who owns the computer where to keep it.

WINDOWS

△ **Windows**
Before you download Python, check what kind of operating system your computer has. If you have Windows, find out whether it's the 32-bit or 64-bit version. Click the "Start" button, right-click "Computer", and left-click "Properties". Then choose "System" if the option appears.

MAC

△ **Mac**
If you use an Apple Mac, find out which operating system it has before you install Python. Click the apple icon in the top left and choose "About This Mac".

UBUNTU

△ **Ubuntu**
Ubuntu is a free operating system that works just like Windows and Macs. To find out how to install Python on Ubuntu, turn over to page 87.

INSTALLING PYTHON   85

Python 3 on Windows

Before you install Python 3 on a Windows PC, make sure you get permission from the computer's owner. You may also need to ask the owner to provide an admin password during installation.

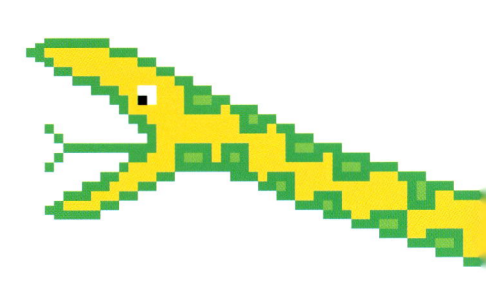

1 Go to the Python website
Type the address below into your Internet browser to open the Python website. Click on "Download" to open the download page.

> http://www.python.org

This is the URL (web address) for Python

2 Download Python
Click on the latest version of Python for Windows, beginning with the number 3, which will be near the top of the list.

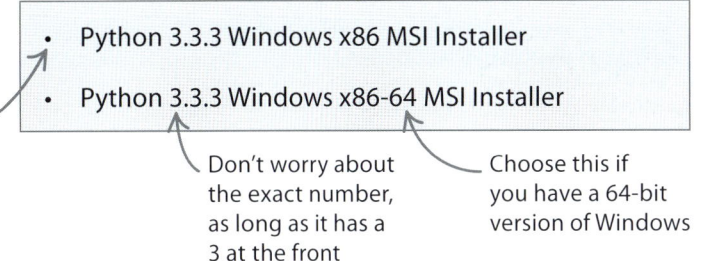

- Python 3.3.3 Windows x86 MSI Installer
- Python 3.3.3 Windows x86-64 MSI Installer

Choose this if you have a 32-bit version of Windows

Don't worry about the exact number, as long as it has a 3 at the front

Choose this if you have a 64-bit version of Windows

3 Install
The installer file will download automatically. When it finishes, double-click it to install Python. Choose "install for all users" and click "next" at each prompt, without changing the default settings.

The Windows installer icon appears while Python is installing

4 Run IDLE
Now check that the program installed correctly. Open the Windows "Start" menu, click on "All Programs", "Python", and then choose "IDLE".

Python 3.3
IDLE (Python GUI)
Module Docs
Python (command line)
Python Manuals
Uninstall Python

Make sure you select Python 3

5 A Python window opens
A window like the one below should open up. You can now start coding – just type into the window after the angle brackets (>>>).

IDLE	File	Edit	Shell	Debug	Window	Help
Untitled

```
Python 3.3.3 (v3.3.3:c3896275c0f6, Nov 18 2013, 21:19:30) [MSC v.1600
64 bit (AMD64)] on win32
Type "copyright", "credits" or "license()" for more information.
>>>
```

Begin typing code here

Python 3 on a Mac

Before you install Python 3 on a Mac, make sure you get permission from the computer's owner. You may also need to ask the owner to provide an admin password during installation.

1 Go to the Python link
Type the address below into your web browser to open the Python website. Click on "Download" in the navigation panel to go to the download page.

🔍 http://www.python.org

Don't worry about the exact number, as long as it has a 3 at the front

2 Download Python
Check which operating system your Mac has (see page 88) and click on the matching version of Python 3. You'll be prompted to save a .dmg file. Save it on your Mac desktop.

- Python 3.3.3 Mac OS X 64-bit... (for Mac OS X 10.6 and later) — This version is for newer Macs
- Python 3.3.3 Mac OS X 32-bit... (for Mac OS X 10.5 and later) — This version runs on most Macs

3 Install
Double-click the .dmg file. A window will open with several files in it, including the Python installer file "Python.mpkg". Double-click it to start the installation.

Python installer file

Python.mpkg

4 Run IDLE
During installation, click "next" at each prompt to accept the default settings. After installation ends, open the "Applications" folder on your Mac and open the "Python" folder (make sure you select Python 3, not Python 2). Double-click "IDLE" to check the installation worked.

IDLE icon

5 A Python window opens
A window like the one below should open. You can now start coding – just type into the window after the angle brackets.

```
IDLE    File   Edit   Shell   Debug   Window   Help
Untitled

Python 3.3.3 (v3.3.3:c3896275c0f6, Nov 16 2013, 23:39:35)
[GCC 4.2.1 (Apple Inc. build 5666) (dot 3)] on darwin
Type "copyright", "credits" or "license()" for more information.
>>>
```

INSTALLING PYTHON **87**

Python 3 on Ubuntu

If you use the Linux operating system Ubuntu, you can download Python 3 without having to use a browser – just follow the steps below. If you have a different version of Linux, ask the computer's owner to install Python 3 for you.

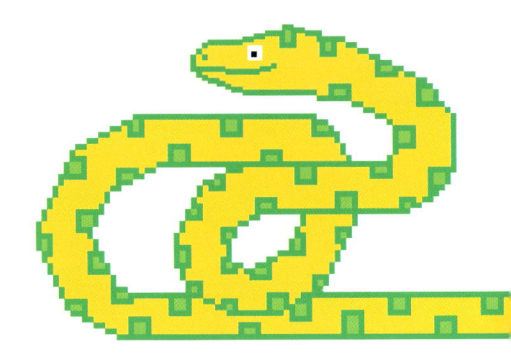

1 **Go to Ubuntu Software Center**
Find the Ubuntu Software Centre icon in the Dock or the Dash and double-click it.

2 **Enter "Python" into the search bar**
You will see a search box in the top right. Type "Python" in the box and press enter.

🔍 Python

Look for version 3

IDLE (using Python-3.3)   ★★★★☆   (17)
Integrated Development Environment for Python (using Python-3.3)

More info   Install

3 **Select IDLE and click "Install"**
Look for "IDLE (using Python)". Highlight the version beginning with the number 3 and click "Install".

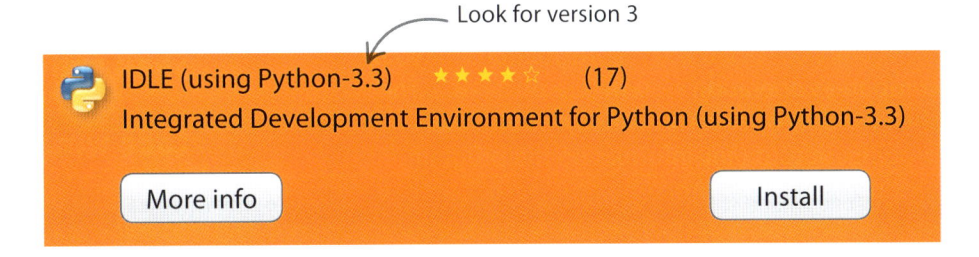

4 **Select Dash**
After installation finishes, check the program works. First, select the Dash icon in the top right.

Dash icon

5 **Run IDLE**
Enter "IDLE" into the search bar and double-click on the blue-and-yellow "IDLE (using Python 3)" icon.

IDLE icon

6 **A Python window opens**
A window like the one below should open. You can now start coding – just type into the window after the angle brackets.

IDLE	File	Edit	Shell	Debug	Window	Help

Untitled

```
Python 3.2.3 (default, Sep 25 2013, 18:25:56)
[GCC 4.6.3] on linux2
Type "copyright", "credits" or "license()" for more information.
>>>
```

88 PLAYING WITH PYTHON

Introducing IDLE

IDLE helps you write and run programs in Python. See how it works by creating this simple program that writes a message on the screen.

SEE ALSO
⟨ 84–87 Installing Python
Which window? 102–103 ⟩

Working in IDLE

Follow these steps to make a Python program using IDLE. It will teach you how to enter, save, and run programs.

EXPERT TIPS
Different windows

Python uses two different windows – the "shell" window and the "code" window (see pages 102–103). We've given them different colours to tell them apart.

Shell window

Code window

1 Start IDLE
Start up IDLE using the instructions for your computer's operating system (see pp.84–87). The shell window opens. This window shows the program output (any information the program produces) and any errors.

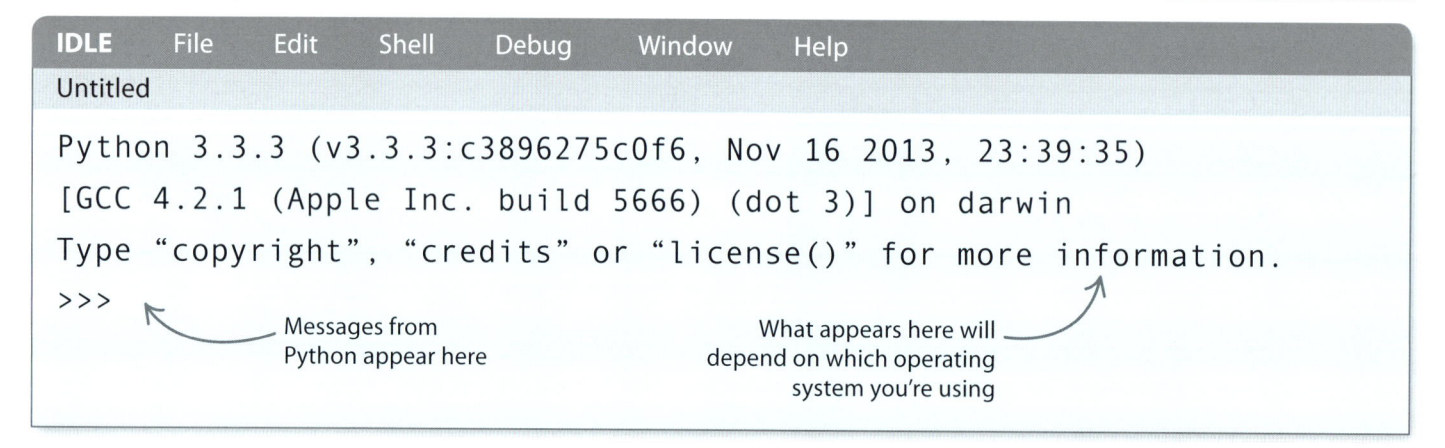

```
Python 3.3.3 (v3.3.3:c3896275c0f6, Nov 16 2013, 23:39:35)
[GCC 4.2.1 (Apple Inc. build 5666) (dot 3)] on darwin
Type "copyright", "credits" or "license()" for more information.
>>>
```

Messages from Python appear here

What appears here will depend on which operating system you're using

2 Open a new window
Click the "File" menu at the top of the shell window and select "New Window". This opens the code window.

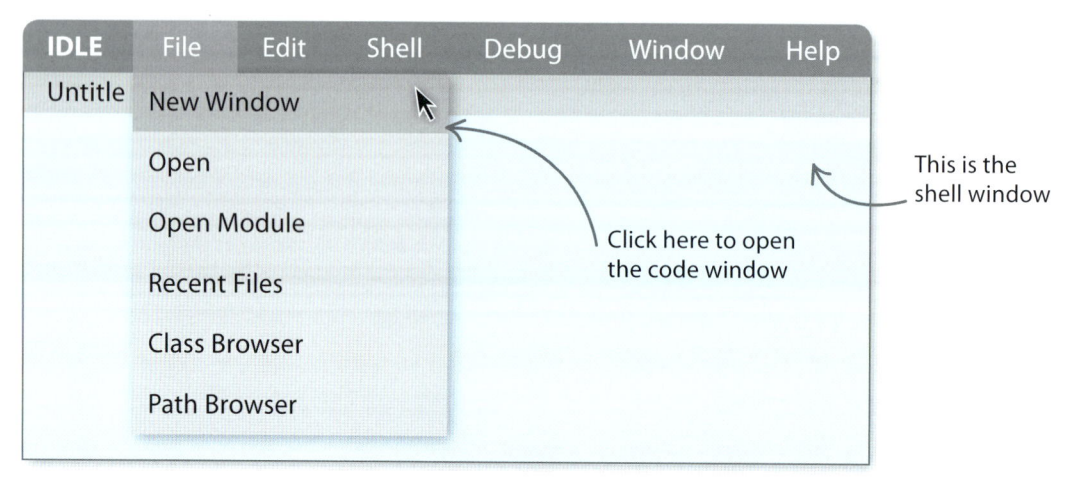

New Window
Open
Open Module
Recent Files
Class Browser
Path Browser

This is the shell window

Click here to open the code window

INTRODUCING IDLE   89

3 Enter the code
In the new code window, type in this text. It's an instruction to write the words "Hello World!"

```
print('Hello World!')
```
Use single quote marks

4 Save the code window
Click the "File" menu and select "Save As". Enter the file name "HelloWorld" and click "Save".

If you get an error message, check your code carefully to make sure you haven't made any mistakes.

Click here to save the file

5 Run the program
In the code window, click the "Run" menu and select "Run Module". This will run the program in the shell window.

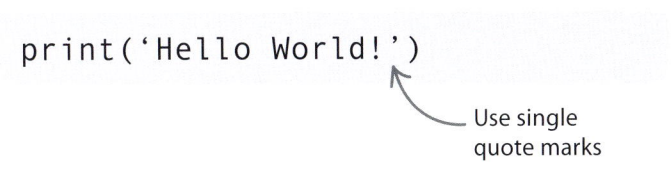

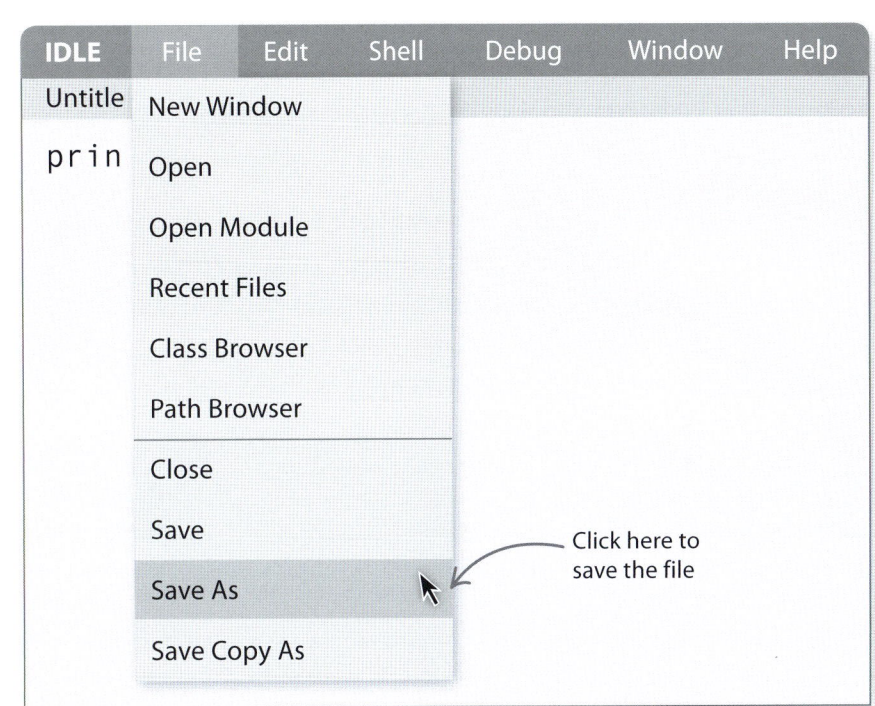

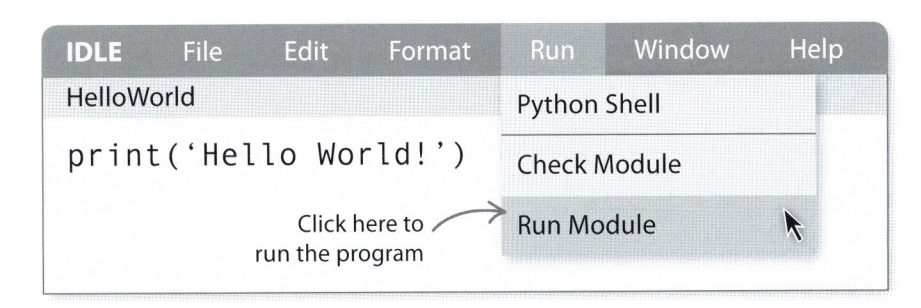

Click here to run the program

6 Output in the shell window
Look at the shell window. The "Hello World!" message should appear when the program runs. You've now created your first bit of code in Python!

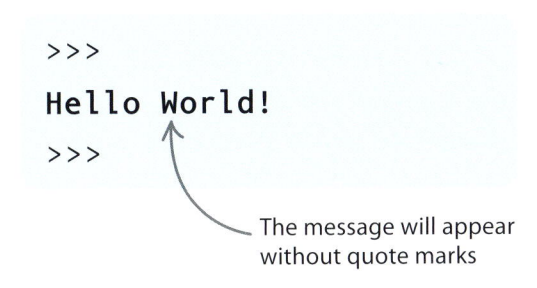

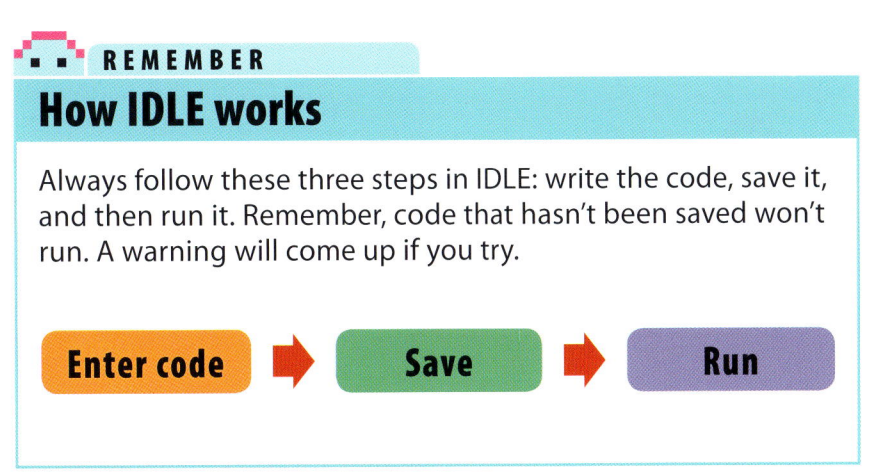

```
>>>
Hello World!
>>>
```
The message will appear without quote marks

▪▪▪ REMEMBER
How IDLE works

Always follow these three steps in IDLE: write the code, save it, and then run it. Remember, code that hasn't been saved won't run. A warning will come up if you try.

Enter code ➡ **Save** ➡ **Run**

Errors

Sometimes programs don't work the first time, but they can always be fixed. When code for a program isn't entered correctly, Python will display an error message telling you what has gone wrong.

> **SEE ALSO**
> Bugs and debugging **144–145 ›**
> What next? **172–173 ›**

Errors in the code window

When trying to run a program in the code window, you might see a pop-up window appear with an error message (such as "SyntaxError") in it. These errors stop the program from running and need to be fixed.

1 Syntax error
If a pop-up window appears with a "SyntaxError" message, it often means there's a spelling mistake or typing error in the code.

SyntaxError
❌ invalid syntax
OK

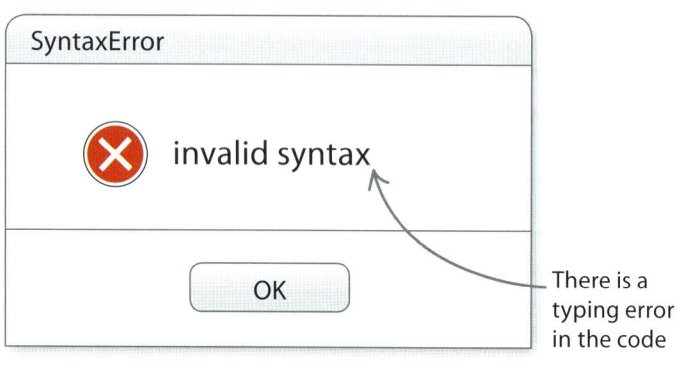

There is a typing error in the code

SyntaxError
❌ unexpected indent
OK

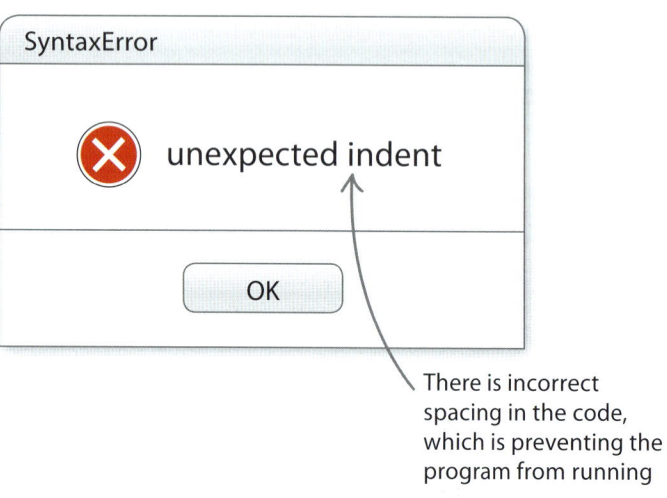

There is incorrect spacing in the code, which is preventing the program from running

2 Error highlighted
Click "OK" in the pop-up window and you'll go back to your program. There will be a red highlight on or near the error. Check that line for mistakes carefully.

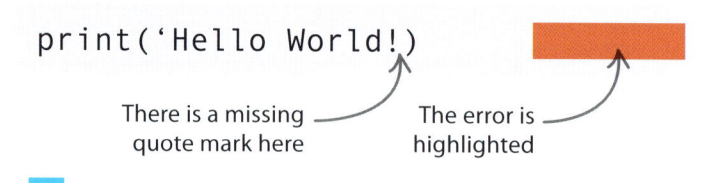

```
print('Hello World!)
```

There is a missing quote mark here   *The error is highlighted*

EXPERT TIPS
Classic errors

Some mistakes are particularly easy to make. Keep an eye out for these common problems:

Upper vs lower case: The case has to match exactly. If you write "Print" instead of "print", Python won't understand the instruction.

Single and double quotes: Don't mix up single and double quotes. All opening quotes need a matching closing quote.

Minus and underscore: Don't confuse the minus sign (-) with the underscore sign (_).

Different brackets: Different-shaped brackets, such as (), {} and [], are used for different things. Use the correct ones, and check there's a complete pair.

ERRORS

Errors in the shell window

Sometimes, an error message will appear in red text in the shell window. This will also stop the program from working.

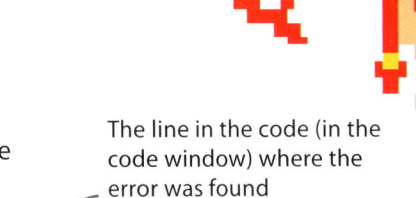

1 Name error
If the error message "NameError" appears, it means Python can't understand one of the words that has been used. If the error is in code entered in the code window, right-click on the error message in the shell window and select "Go to file/line".

Red text means there's something wrong!

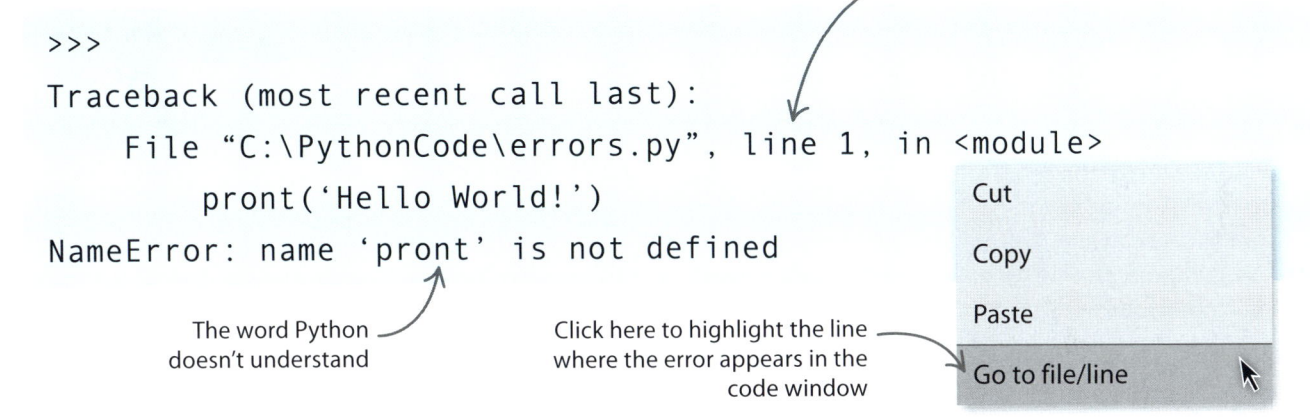

The line in the code (in the code window) where the error was found

```
>>>
Traceback (most recent call last):
    File "C:\PythonCode\errors.py", line 1, in <module>
        pront('Hello World!')
NameError: name 'pront' is not defined
```

The word Python doesn't understand

Click here to highlight the line where the error appears in the code window

Cut
Copy
Paste
Go to file/line

2 Fix the error
The line with the error is highlighted in the code window. The word "pront" has been typed instead of "print". You can then edit the code to fix the error.

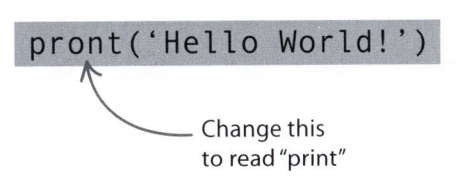

```
pront('Hello World!')
```

Change this to read "print"

Spotting errors

Use the tips on these two pages to find the line in the code where the errors appear, then double-check that line. Go through the check list on the right to help you find out what has gone wrong.

▷ **When things go wrong**
There are some methods you can use to find errors more easily. Here's a handy check list.

ERROR BUSTING	
Check your code for the following points	✓
Have you copied exactly what you were asked to enter?	✓
Have you spelled everything correctly?	✓
Are there two quote marks (') around the expression you want to print?	✓
Do you have extra spaces at the beginning of the line? Spacing is very important in Python.	✓
Have you checked the lines above and below the highlighted line? Sometimes that's where the problem is.	✓
Have you asked someone else to check the code against the book? They might spot something you have missed.	✓
Are you using Python 3 not Python 2? Programs for Python 3 don't always work in Python 2.	✓

PROJECT 4

Ghost game

This simple game highlights some of the things to watch out for when writing programs in Python. Once the code has been typed in, run the program to play the game. Can you escape the haunted house?

SEE ALSO
Ghost game **94–95** decoded
Program **96–97** flow

1 Start IDLE, and use the "File" menu to open a new window. Save the game as "ghostgame". Arrange the windows so you can see them both, then type this into the code window.

```python
# Ghost Game
from random import randint
print('Ghost Game')
feeling_brave = True
score = 0
while feeling_brave:
    ghost_door = randint(1, 3)
    print('Three doors ahead...')
    print('A ghost behind one.')
    print('Which door do you open?')
    door = input('1, 2, or 3?')
    door_num = int(door)
    if door_num == ghost_door:
        print('GHOST!')
        feeling_brave = False
    else:
        print('No ghost!')
        print('You enter the next room.')
        score = score + 1
print('Run away!')
print('Game over! You scored', score)
```

- Use single quotes
- Only use capital letters where they are shown
- Make sure to add a colon here
- These must be underscores, not minus signs
- This section needs to be indented by four spaces. If this doesn't happen automatically, check there is a colon after "feeling_brave"
- This indent will start at eight spaces and needs to be reduced to just four spaces
- Use two equals signs here
- Delete all indents here
- There should be no quotes around "score" here

GHOST GAME | 93

2 ▸ Once the code has been carefully typed in, use the "Run" menu to select "Run Module". You must save the program first.

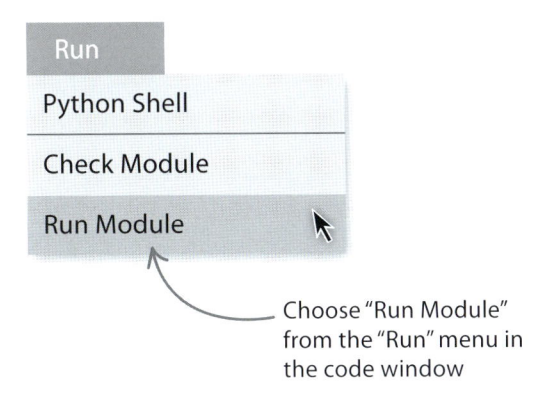

```
Run
Python Shell
Check Module
Run Module
```

Choose "Run Module" from the "Run" menu in the code window

3 ▸ The game begins in the shell window. The ghost is hiding behind one of three doors. Which one will you pick? Type 1, 2, or 3 then press "Enter".

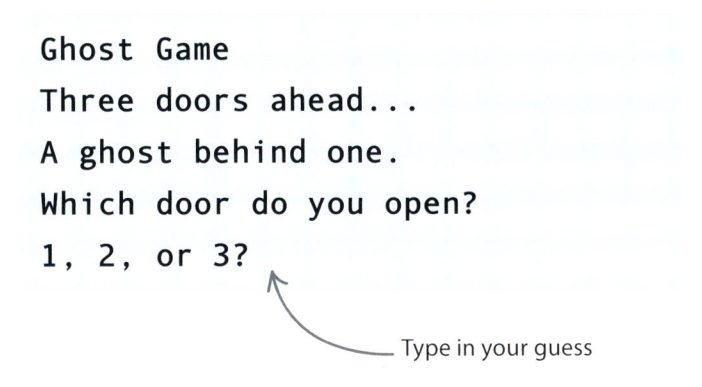

```
Ghost Game
Three doors ahead...
A ghost behind one.
Which door do you open?
1, 2, or 3?
```

Type in your guess

4 ▸ The aim of the game is to pick a door with no ghost behind it. If this happens, you'll move to the next room and keep playing the game.

```
Ghost Game
Three doors ahead...
A ghost behind one.
Which door do you open?
1, 2, or 3?3
No ghost!
```

The number you type in appears here

This is what you'll see if there is no ghost behind the door you choose

5 ▸ If you're unlucky you'll pick a door with a ghost behind it, and the game ends. Run the program again to see if you can beat your last score.

```
Ghost Game
Three doors ahead...
A ghost behind one.
Which door do you open?
1, 2, or 3?2
GHOST!
Run away!
Game over! You scored 0
```

This is what appears if the ghost is behind your door

The score shows how many rooms you survived

Ghost game decoded

The ghost game displays some of the key features of Python. You can break down the code to see how the program is structured and what the different parts of it do.

> **SEE ALSO**
> ‹ **92–93** Ghost game
> Program **96–97** ›
> flow

Code structure

Python uses spaces at the start of lines to work out which instructions belong together. These spaces are called "indents". For example, the code after "while feeling_brave" is indented by four spaces to show it's all part of the main loop.

```
# Ghost Game
from random import randint
print('Ghost Game')
feeling_brave = True
score = 0
while feeling_brave:
    ghost_door = randint(1, 3)
    print('Three doors ahead...')
    print('A ghost behind one.')
    print('Which door do you open?')
    door = input('1, 2 or 3?')
    door_num = int(door)
    if door_num == ghost_door:
        print('GHOST!')
        feeling_brave = False
    else:
        print('No ghost!')
        print('You enter the next room.')
        score = score + 1
print('Run away!')
print('Game over! You scored', score)
```

1 — Game set-up
2 — The main loop
3 — Branching part
4 — Game ending

◁ **Code key**
This diagram shows the structure of the ghost game. The numbered parts are explained in more detail below.

This is a "comment". It's not shown when the game is run

1 Game set-up
These instructions only run once – at the beginning of the game. They set up the title, variables, and the "randint" command.

```
# Ghost Game
from random import randint
print('Ghost Game')
feeling_brave = True
score = 0
```

This sets up the "randint" command, which generates random numbers

The "print" command displays text when the game is run

This resets the score to 0

EXPERT TIPS
Type carefully

When using Python, enter the code very carefully. If you miss out a colon, quote mark, or bracket, the program won't work properly. You need to match the use of capital letters and spaces exactly too.

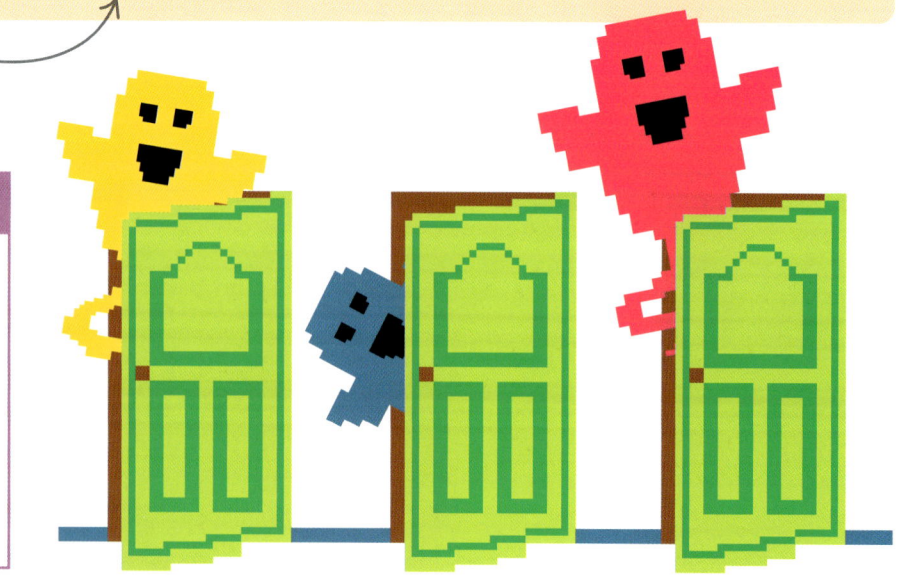

2 The main loop
This loop tells the story and receives the player's guess. It keeps on going as long as there isn't a ghost behind the door that's picked. When a ghost appears, the "feeling_brave" variable changes to "False" and the loop stops repeating.

3 Branching part
The program takes a different path depending on whether or not there was a ghost behind the door that was picked. If there was a ghost, the "feeling_brave" variable is set to "False". If there wasn't a ghost, the player's score increases by one.

```python
while feeling_brave:
    ghost_door = randint(1, 3)
    print('Three doors ahead...')
    print('A ghost behind one.')
    print('Which door do you open?')
    door = input('1, 2 or 3?')
    door_num = int(door)
    if door_num == ghost_door:
        print('GHOST!')
        feeling_brave = False
    else:
        print('No ghost!')
        print('You enter the next room.')
        score = score + 1
```

- This selects a random number between 1 and 3
- The "print" command displays the text onscreen
- This line asks for the player's answer
- This branch runs if there's a ghost behind the door the player picks
- If there's no ghost, the player sees this message
- The score increases by one each time the player enters a room without meeting a ghost

4 Game ending
This runs just once, when you meet the ghost and the loop ends. Python knows this isn't part of the loop because it's not indented.

- This shows a message telling the player to run away from the ghost

```python
print('Run away!')
print('Game over! You scored', score)
```

- The score is a variable – it will change depending on how many rooms the player gets through

REMEMBER

Achievements

Congratulations – you've created your first Python game! You'll learn more about these commands later in the book, but you've already achieved a lot:

Entered a program: You've typed a program into Python and saved it.

Run a program: You've learned how to run a Python program.

Structured a program: You've used indents to structure a program.

Used variables: You've used variables to store the score.

Displayed text: You've displayed messages on the screen.

Program flow

Before learning more about Python, it's important to understand how programs work. The programming basics learned in Scratch can also be applied to Python.

> **SEE ALSO**
> ⟨ **26–27** Coloured blocks and scripts
> Simple **98–99** ⟩ commands
> Harder **100–101** ⟩ commands

From input to output

A program takes input (information in), processes it (or changes it), and then gives back the results (output). It's a bit like a chef taking ingredients, turning them into cakes, and then giving you the cakes to eat.

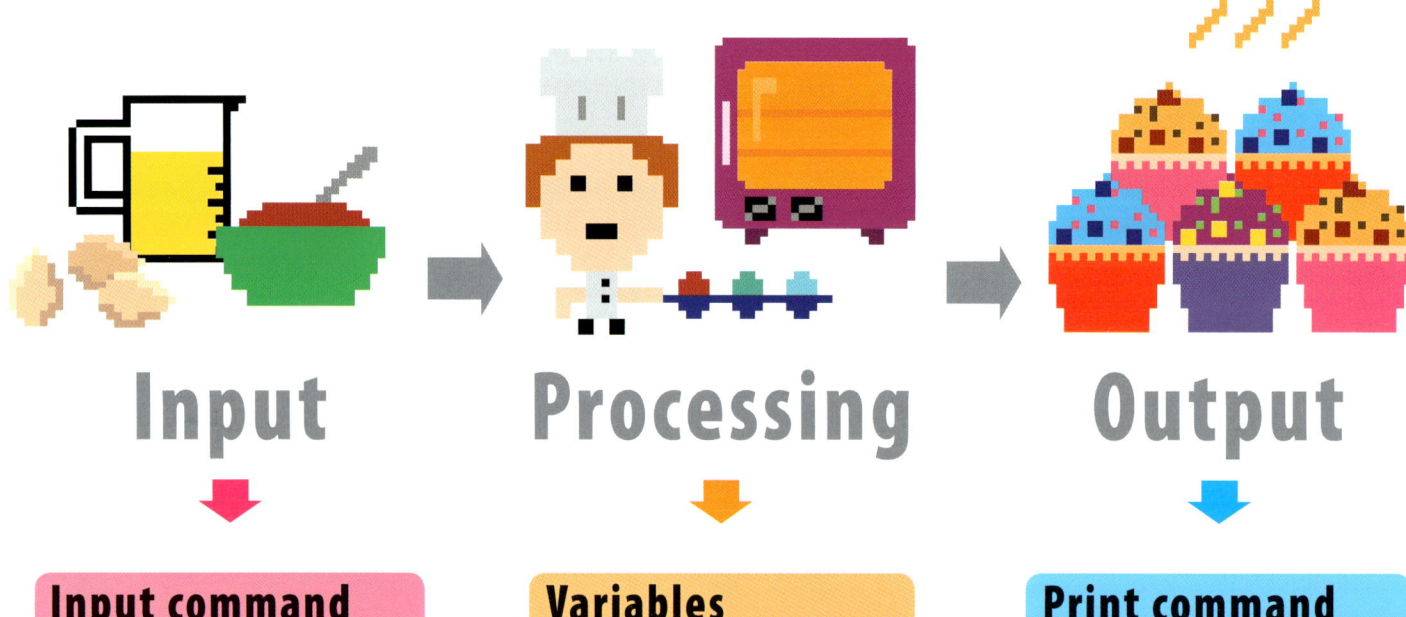

Input
- Input command
- Keyboard
- Mouse

Processing
- Variables
- Maths
- Loops
- Branches
- Functions

Output
- Print command
- Screen
- Graphics

△ **Program flow in Python**
In Python, the keyboard and mouse are used to input information, which is processed using elements such as loops, branches, and variables. The output is then displayed on the screen.

PROGRAM FLOW 97

Looking at the Ghost game through Scratch goggles

Program flow works the same in most programming languages. Here are some examples of input, processing, and output in Python's Ghost game – and what they might look like in Scratch.

> **EXPERT TIPS**
> ### One script at a time
> There's an important difference between Scratch and Python. In Scratch, lots of scripts can run at the same time. In Python, however, the program is made up of only one script.

Python and Scratch are more similar than they appear.

1 Input
In Python, the "input()" function takes an input from the keyboard. It's similar to the "ask and wait" block in Scratch.

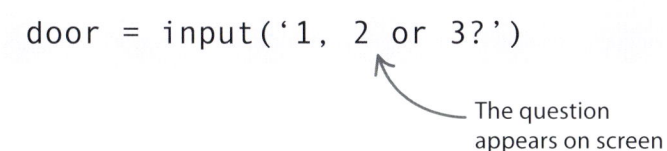

```
door = input('1, 2 or 3?')
```

The question appears on screen

The question in the Scratch block

`ask | 1, 2 or 3? | and wait`

"ask and wait" Scratch block

2 Processing
Variables are used to keep track of the score and the function "randint" picks a random door. Different blocks are used to do these things in Scratch.

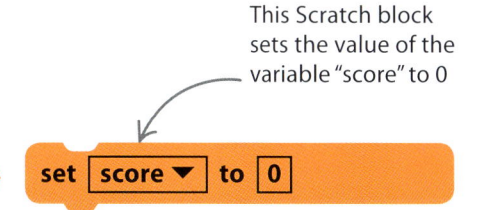

```
score = 0
```

Sets the variable "score" to 0

This Scratch block sets the value of the variable "score" to 0

`set | score ▼ | to | 0 |`

"set score to 0" Scratch block

```
ghost_door = randint(1, 3)
```

Selects a random whole number between 1 and 3

`pick random | 1 | to | 3 |`

"pick random" Scratch block

This Scratch block selects a random number

3 Output
The "print()" function is used to output things in Python, while the "say" block does the same thing in Scratch.

```
print('Ghost game')
```

Displays "Ghost game" on the screen

Shows a speech bubble containing the words "Ghost game"

`say | Ghost game |`

"say" Scratch block

Simple commands

At first glance, Python can look quite scary, especially when compared to Scratch. However, the two languages aren't actually as different as they seem. Here is a guide to the similarities between basic commands in Python and Scratch.

> **SEE ALSO**
> ‹ 82–83 What is Python?
> Harder 100–101 › commands

Command	Python 3	Scratch 2.0
Run program	"Run" menu or press "F5" (in code window)	🚩
Stop program	Press "CTRL-C" (in shell window)	🛑
Write text to screen	`print('Hello!')`	say [Hello!]
Set a variable to a number	`magic_number = 42`	set [magic_number ▼] to [42]
Set a variable to a text string	`word = 'dragon'`	set [word ▼] to [dragon]
Read text from keyboard into variable	`age = input('age?')` `print('I am ' + age)`	ask [age?] and wait say join [I am] (answer)

Add a number to a variable	`cats = cats + 1`
	or
	`cats += 1`
		change [cats ▼] by (1)

Add	`a + 2`	(a) + (2)
Subtract	`a - 2`	(a) - (2)
Multiply	`a * 2`	(a) * (2)
Divide	`a / 2`	(a) / (2)

SIMPLE COMMANDS

Command	Python 3	Scratch 2.0
Forever loop	`while True:` `    jump()`	forever / jump
Loop 10 times	`for i in range (10):` `    jump()`	repeat 10 / jump
Is equal to?	`a == 2`	a = 2
Is less than?	`a < 2`	a < 2
Is more than?	`a > 2`	a > 2
NOT	`not`	not
OR	`or`	or
AND	`and`	and
If then	`if a == 2:` `    print('Hello!')`	if a = 2 then / say Hello!

If then else	`if a == 2:`
	`    print('Hello!')`
	`else:`
	`    print('Goodbye!')`
		if a = 2 then / say Hello! / else / say Goodbye!

Harder commands

Python can also be used to do some of the more complicated things that are possible in Scratch: for example, creating complex loops, playing with strings and lists, and drawing pictures with turtle graphics.

> **SEE ALSO**
> ‹ 82–83 What is Python?
> ‹ 98–99 Simple commands

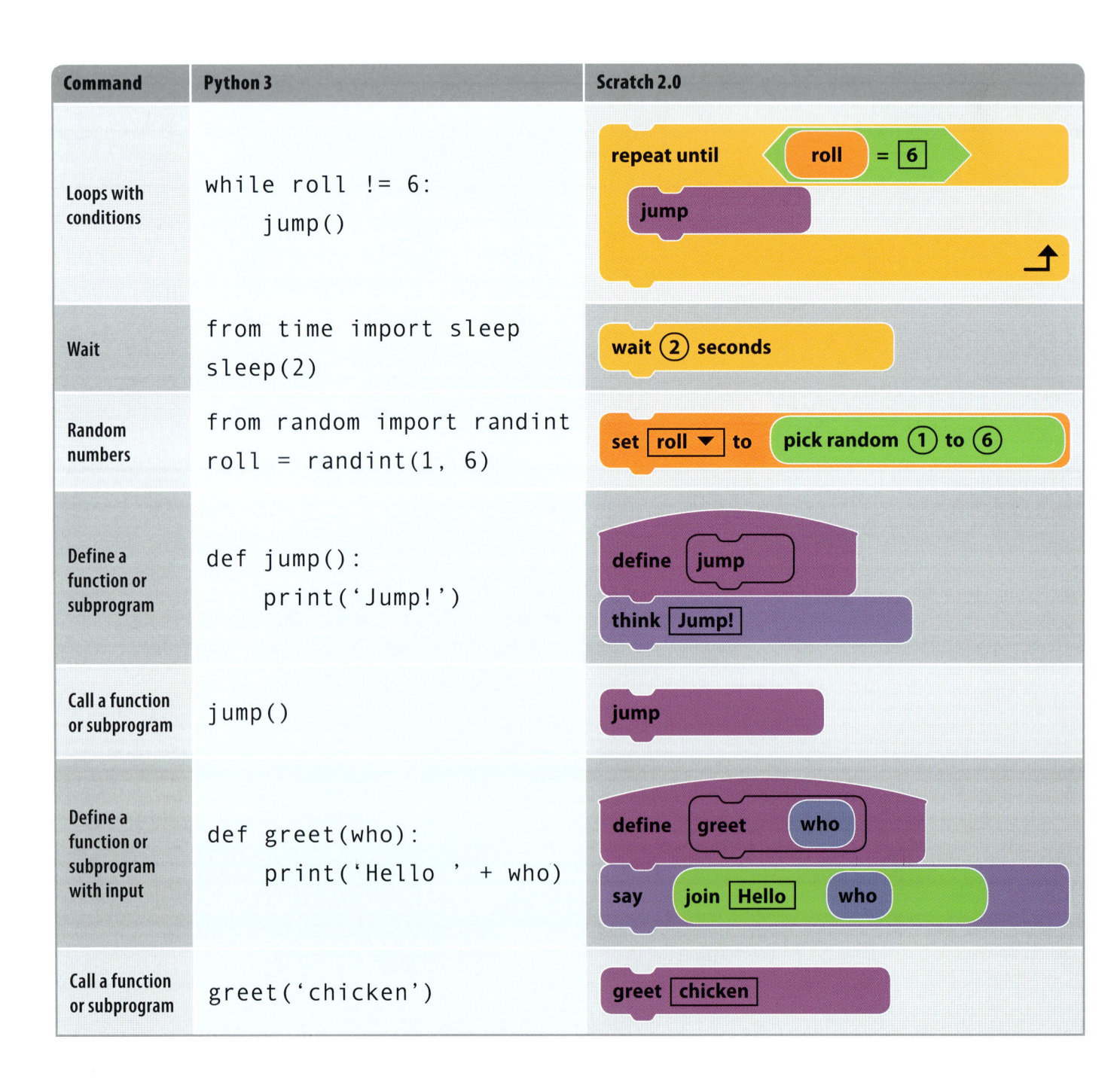

Command	Python 3	Scratch 2.0
Loops with conditions	`while roll != 6:` `    jump()`	repeat until roll = 6 / jump
Wait	`from time import sleep` `sleep(2)`	wait 2 seconds
Random numbers	`from random import randint` `roll = randint(1, 6)`	set roll to pick random 1 to 6
Define a function or subprogram	`def jump():` `    print('Jump!')`	define jump / think Jump!
Call a function or subprogram	`jump()`	jump
Define a function or subprogram with input	`def greet(who):` `    print('Hello ' + who)`	define greet who / say join Hello who
Call a function or subprogram	`greet('chicken')`	greet chicken

HARDER COMMANDS

Command	Python 3	Scratch 2.0

Turtle graphics	`from turtle import *`
	`clear()`
	`pendown()`
	`forward(100)`
	`right(90)`
	`penup()`
		clear / pen down / move 100 steps / turn 90 degrees / pen up

Join strings	`print(greeting + name)`	say join greeting name
Get one letter of a string	`name[0]`	letter 1 of name
Length of a string	`len(name)`	length of name
Create an empty list	`menu = list()`	Make a List
Add an item to end of list	`menu.append(thing)`	add thing to menu
How many items on list?	`len(menu)`	length of menu
Value of 5th item on list	`menu[4]`	say item 5 of menu
Delete 2nd item on list	`del menu[1]`	delete 2 of menu
Is item on list?	`if 'olives' in menu:` `    print('Oh no!')`	if menu contains olives then say Oh no!

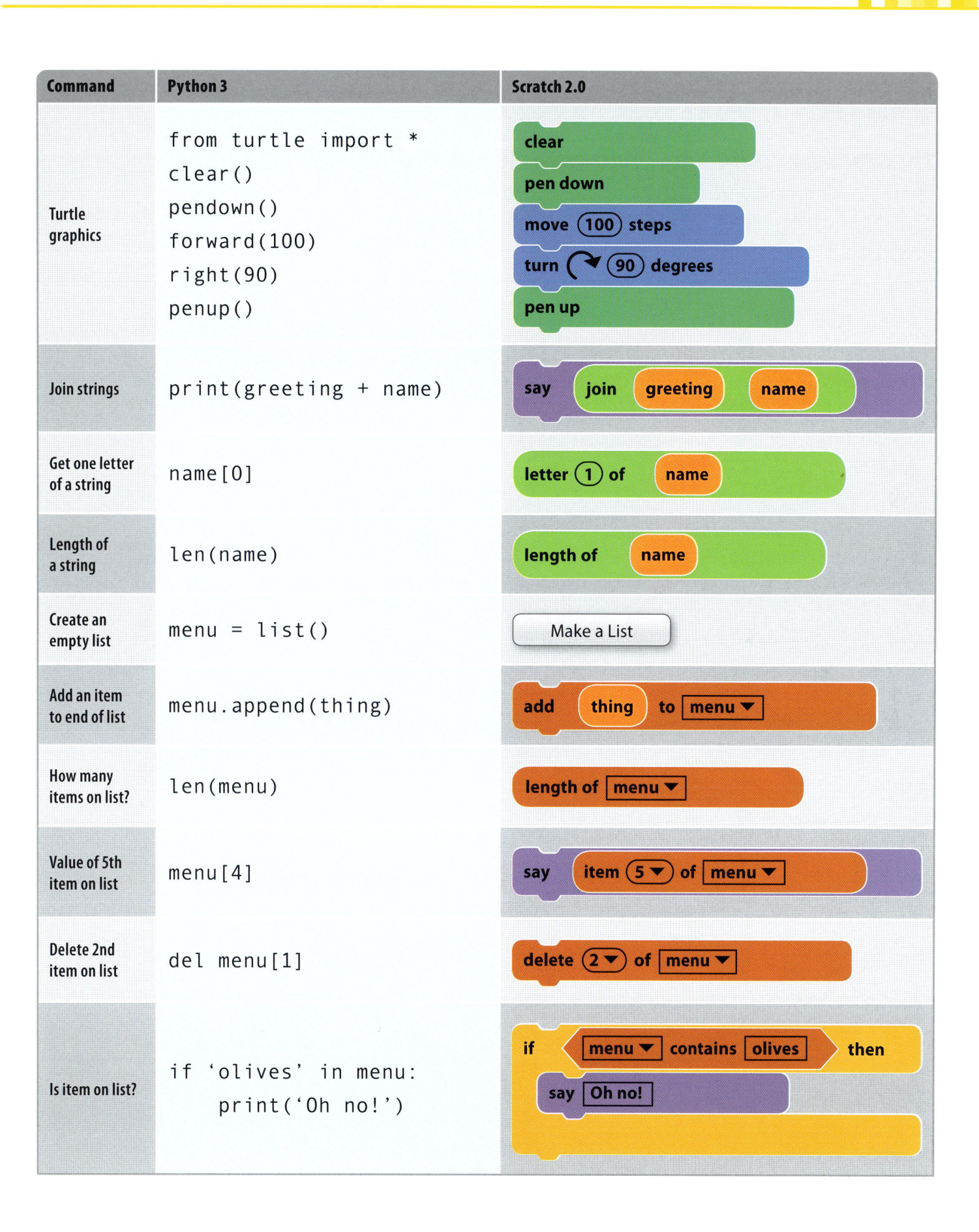

Which window?

There are two different windows to choose from in IDLE. The code window can be used to write and save programs, while the shell window runs Python instructions straight away.

> **SEE ALSO**
> ‹ **88–89** Introducing IDLE
> ‹ **92–93** Ghost game

The code window

So far in this book, the code window has been used to write programs. You enter the program, save it, run it, and the output appears in the shell window.

▽ **Running programs**
This process is used for running Python programs. Programs always have to be saved before running them.

| Enter code | → | Save | → | Run module | → | Output |

1 Enter a program in the code window
Enter this code in the code window, save it, and then click on "Run module" in the "Run" menu to run the program.

```
a = 10
b = 4
print(a + b)
print(a - b)
```

Give "a" the value 10
Give "b" the value 4
The "print" command shows the answers to these sums

2 Output in the shell window
When the program runs, its output (the results of the program) is shown in the shell window.

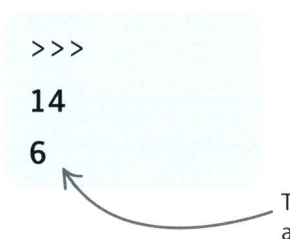

```
>>>
14
6
```

The answers to the sums appear in the shell window

The shell window

Python can also understand commands that are typed in the shell window. They run as soon as they are typed in, and the result is shown straight away.

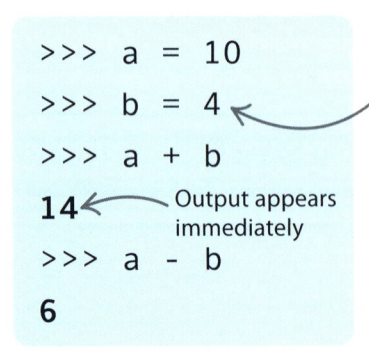

```
>>> a = 10
>>> b = 4
>>> a + b
14
>>> a - b
6
```

The first two commands have no output because they are just assigning values to "a" and "b"

Output appears immediately

◁ **Code and output together**
The shell window shows the code and the output together. It's easier to tell which answer belongs to which sum when the commands are typed in the shell window.

△ **Test your ideas**
The shell window gives you an immediate response, which makes it ideal for testing instructions and exploring what they can do.

Python playground

The shell window can be used to try out all sorts of Python commands, including drawing. The turtle is used to draw on screen in the same way that the pen is used in Scratch.

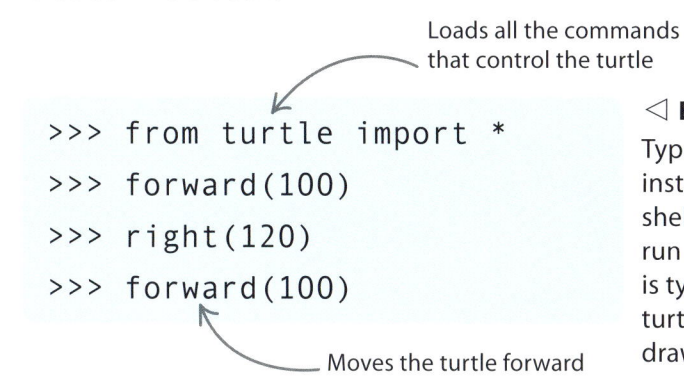

Loads all the commands that control the turtle

```
>>> from turtle import *
>>> forward(100)
>>> right(120)
>>> forward(100)
```

Moves the turtle forward

◁ **Enter the code**
Type these instructions in the shell window. They run after each one is typed. As the turtle moves, it draws a line.

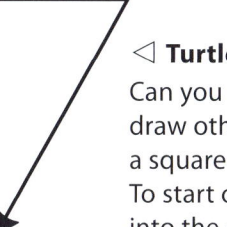

◁ **Turtle graphic**
Can you work out how to draw other shapes, such as a square or a pentagon? To start over, type "clear()" into the shell window.

Which window should you use?

Should you use the code window or the shell window? It depends on the type of program you're writing, and whether it has to be repeated.

EXPERT TIPS
Colours in the code

IDLE colour-codes the text. The colours give you some clues about what Python thinks each piece of text is.

◁ **Built-in functions**
Commands in Python, such as "print", are shown in purple.

◁ **Strings in quotes**
Green indicates strings. If the brackets are green too, there's a missing quote mark.

◁ **Most symbols and names**
Most code is shown in black.

◁ **Output**
Python's output in the shell window is shown in blue.

◁ **Keywords**
Keywords, such as "if" and "else", are orange. Python won't let you use keywords as variable names.

◁ **Errors**
Python uses red to alert you to any error messages in the shell window.

Code vs Shell

▷ **Code window**
The code window is ideal for longer pieces of code because they can be saved and edited. It's easier than retyping all the instructions if you want to do the same thing again or try something similar. It needs to be saved and run each time, though.

◁ **Shell window**
The shell window is perfect for quick experiments, such as checking how a command works. It's also a handy calculator. It doesn't save the instructions though, so if you're trying something you might want to repeat, consider using the code window instead.

Variables in Python

Variables are used to remember pieces of information in a program. They are like boxes where data can be stored and labelled.

> **SEE ALSO**
> Types of data 106–107 ❯
> Maths in Python 108–109 ❯
> Strings in Python 110–111 ❯
> Input and output 112–113 ❯
> Functions 126–127 ❯

Creating a variable

When a number or string is put into a variable it's called assigning a value to the variable. You use an "=" sign to do this. Try this code in the shell window.

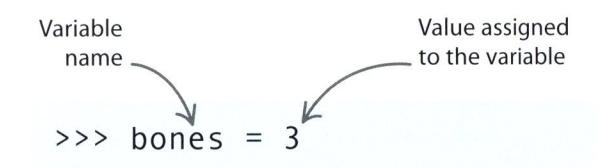

Variable name → `>>> bones = 3` ← Value assigned to the variable

△ **Assign a number**
To assign a number, type in the variable name, an equals sign, and then the number.

Variable name → `>>> dogs_name = 'Bruno'` ← String assigned to the variable

△ **Assign a string**
To assign a string, type in the variable name, an equals sign, and then the string in quote marks.

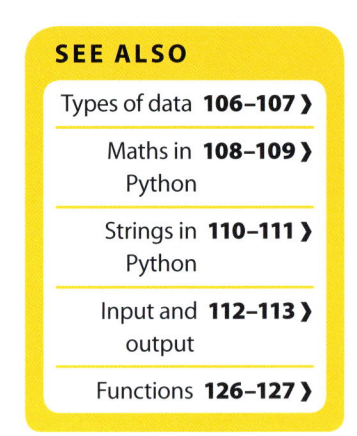

> ## REMEMBER
> ### Variables in Scratch
>
> The command to assign a variable in Python does the same job as this Scratch block. However, in Python you don't have to click a button to create a variable. Python creates the variable as soon as you assign a value to it.
>
> `set bones ▼ to 3`
>
> Scratch block for giving a value to a variable

Printing a variable

The "print" command is used to show something on the screen. It has nothing to do with the printer. You can use it to show the value of a variable.

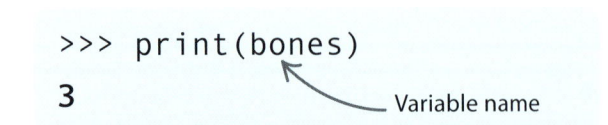

```
>>> print(bones)
3
```
← Variable name

△ **Number output**
The variable "bones" contains the number 3, so that's what the shell window prints.

```
>>> print(dogs_name)
Bruno
```
← No quote marks here

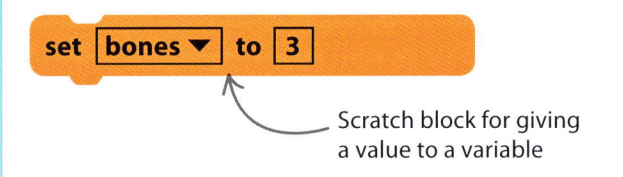

△ **String output**
The variable "dogs_name" contains a string, so the string is printed. No quote marks are shown when you print a string.

VARIABLES IN PYTHON 105

Changing the contents of a variable

To change the value of a variable, simply assign a new value to it. Here, the variable "gifts" has the value 2. It changes to 3 when it's assigned a new value.

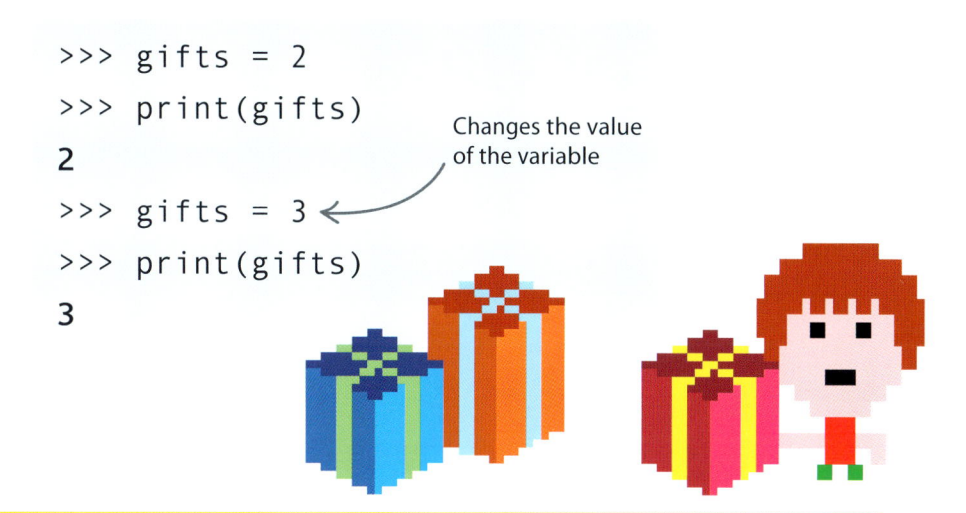

```
>>> gifts = 2
>>> print(gifts)
2
>>> gifts = 3
>>> print(gifts)
3
```

◁ Changes the value of the variable

Using variables

The value of one variable can be assigned to another one using the "=" sign. For example, if the variable "rabbits" contains the number of rabbits, we can use it to assign the same value to the variable "hats", so that each rabbit has a hat.

1 Assign the variables
This code assigns the number 5 to the variable "rabbits". It then assigns the same value to the variable "hats".

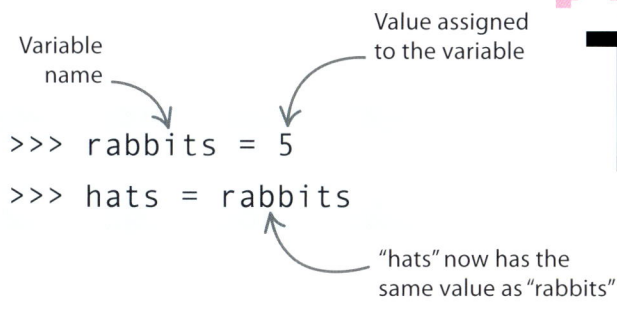

Variable name ↓   Value assigned to the variable ↓
```
>>> rabbits = 5
>>> hats = rabbits
```
↑ "hats" now has the same value as "rabbits"

2 Print the values
To print two variables, put them both in brackets after the "print" command, and put a comma between them. Both "hats" and "rabbits" contain the value 5.

```
>>> print(rabbits, hats)
5 5
```
↑ Leave a space after the comma

EXPERT TIPS
Naming variables

There are some rules you have to follow when naming your variables:

All letters and numbers can be used.
You can't start with a number.
Symbols such as -, /, #, or @ can't be used.
Spaces can't be used.
An underscore (_) can be used instead of a space.
Uppercase and lowercase letters are different. Python treats "Dogs" and "dogs" as two different variables.
Don't use words Python uses as a command, such as "print".

3 Change the value of "rabbits"
If you change the value of "rabbits", it doesn't affect the value of "hats". The "hats" variable only changes when you assign it a new value.

```
>>> rabbits = 10
>>> print(rabbits, hats)
10 5
```
◁ Give "rabbits" a new value
◁ Value for "hats" remains the same

Types of data

There are several different types of data in Python. Most of the time, Python will work out what type is being used, but sometimes you'll need to change data from one type to another.

> **SEE ALSO**
> Maths in **108–109**
> Python
> Strings in **110–111**
> Python
> Making **114–115**
> decisions
> Lists **124–125**

Numbers

Python has two data types for numbers. "Integers" are whole numbers, (numbers without a decimal point). "Floats" are numbers with a decimal point. An integer can be used to count things such as sheep, while a float can be used to measure things such as weight.

```
>>> sheep = 1
>>> print(sheep)
1
```

An integer is a whole number

△ **Integers**
An integer is a number without a decimal point, such as the 1 in the variable "sheep".

```
>>> sheep = 1.5
>>> print(sheep)
1.5
```

1.5 is a float

△ **Floats**
A float is a number with a decimal point, such as 1.5. They aren't normally used to count whole objects.

Strings

Just like in Scratch, a piece of text in Python is called a "string". Strings can include letters, numbers, spaces, and symbols such as full stops and commas. They are usually put inside single quote marks.

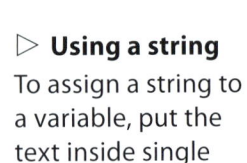

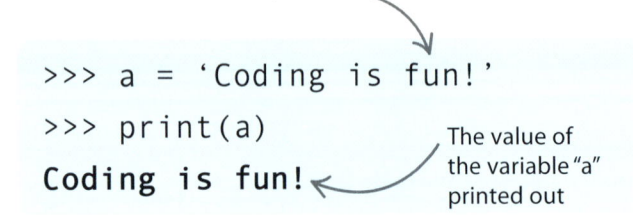

▷ **Using a string**
To assign a string to a variable, put the text inside single quote marks.

```
>>> a = 'Coding is fun!'
>>> print(a)
Coding is fun!
```

The string in quotes

The value of the variable "a" printed out

> Always remember that strings need quote marks at the start and the end.

TYPES OF DATA

Booleans

In Python, a Boolean always has a value that is either "True" or "False". In both cases, the word begins with a capital letter.

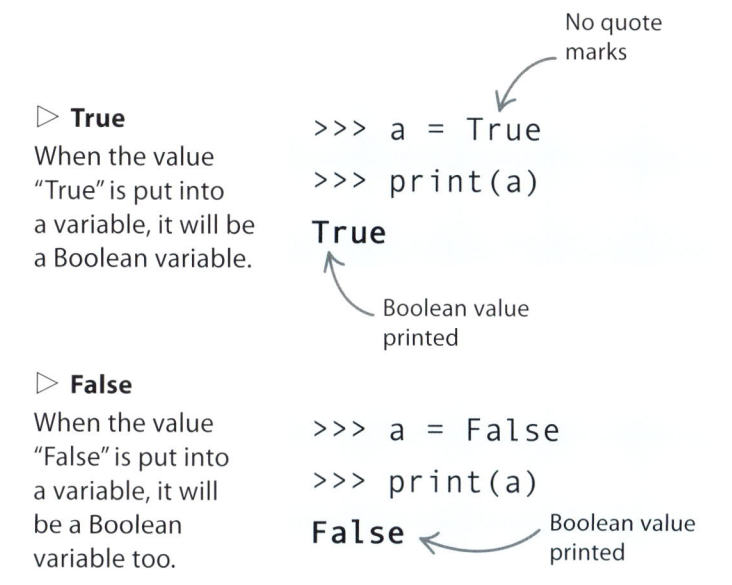

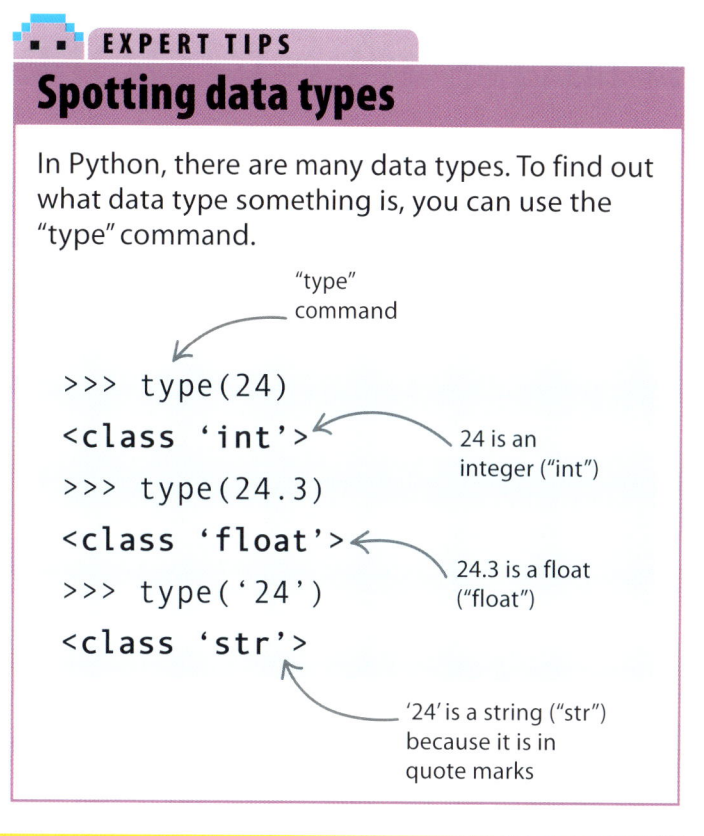

▷ **True**
When the value "True" is put into a variable, it will be a Boolean variable.

```
>>> a = True
>>> print(a)
True
```
No quote marks
Boolean value printed

▷ **False**
When the value "False" is put into a variable, it will be a Boolean variable too.

```
>>> a = False
>>> print(a)
False
```
Boolean value printed

EXPERT TIPS
Spotting data types

In Python, there are many data types. To find out what data type something is, you can use the "type" command.

```
>>> type(24)
<class 'int'>
>>> type(24.3)
<class 'float'>
>>> type('24')
<class 'str'>
```
"type" command
24 is an integer ("int")
24.3 is a float ("float")
'24' is a string ("str") because it is in quote marks

Converting data types

Variables can contain any type of data. Problems occur if you try to mix types together. Data types sometimes have to be converted, otherwise an error message will appear.

▷ **Mixed type**
The "input" command always gives a string, even if a number is entered. In this example, since "apple" actually contains a string, an error message is displayed.

```
>>> apple = input('Enter number of apples ')
Enter number of apples 2
>>> print(apple + 1)
TypeError
```
Variable name
String in quote marks shown on screen
Tries to add the number 1 to the variable "apple"
The program gives an error message as Python doesn't know how to add a number to a string

▷ **Converting data types**
To convert the string into a number, the "int()" command is used to turn it into an integer.

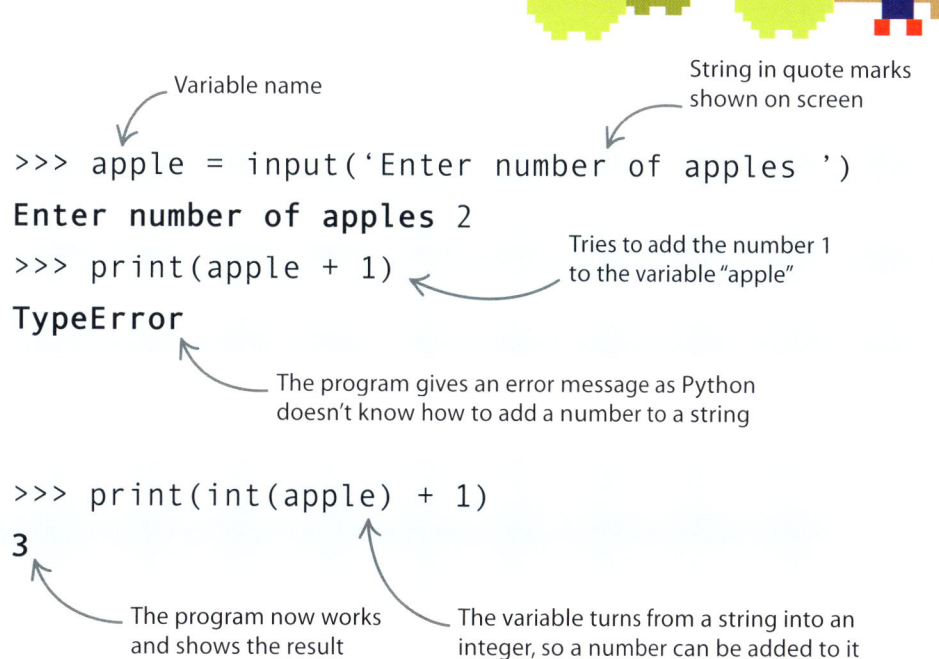

```
>>> print(int(apple) + 1)
3
```
The program now works and shows the result
The variable turns from a string into an integer, so a number can be added to it

Maths in Python

Python can be used to solve all sorts of mathematical problems, including addition, subtraction, multiplication, and division. Variables can also be used in sums.

> **SEE ALSO**
> ❮ **48–49** Maths
> ❮ **104–105** Variables in Python

Simple calculations

In Python, simple calculations can be made by typing them into the shell window. The "print()" function is not needed for this – Python gives the answer straight away. Try these examples in the shell window:

You can't divide by zero, so you'll always get an error if you try to do so.

```
>>> 12 + 4
16
```
Use the shell window to get instant results

△ **Addition**
Use the "+" symbol to add numbers together.

The answer appears when you press "Enter"

```
>>> 12 - 4
8
```

△ **Subtraction**
Use the "-" symbol to subtract the second number from the first one.

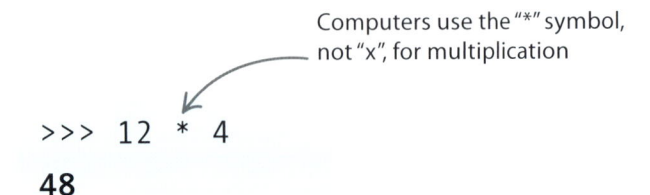

Computers use the "" symbol, not "x", for multiplication*

```
>>> 12 * 4
48
```

△ **Multiplication**
Use the "*" symbol to multiply two numbers together.

```
>>> 12 / 4
3.0
```

Division in Python gives an answer as a float (a number with a decimal point)

△ **Division**
Use the "/" symbol to divide the first number by the second one.

Using brackets

Brackets can be used to instruct Python which part of a sum to do first. Python will always work out the value of the sum in the bracket, before solving the rest of the problem.

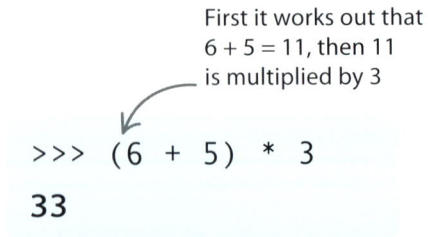

First it works out that 6 + 5 = 11, then 11 is multiplied by 3

```
>>> (6 + 5) * 3
33
```

△ **Addition first**
In this sum, brackets are used to instruct Python to do the addition first.

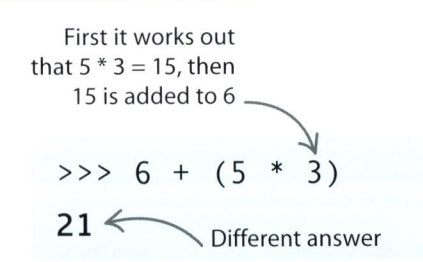

*First it works out that 5 * 3 = 15, then 15 is added to 6*

```
>>> 6 + (5 * 3)
21
```
Different answer

△ **Multiplication first**
Brackets here are used to do the multiplication first, in order to end up with the correct answer.

MATHS IN PYTHON

Putting answers in variables

If variables are assigned number values, you can use them within sums. When a sum is assigned to a variable, the answer goes into the variable, but not the sum.

1. Do a simple addition
This program adds together the variables "ants" and "spiders", and puts the answer into the variable "bugs".

```
>>> ants = 22
>>> spiders = 35
>>> bugs = ants + spiders
>>> print(bugs)
57
```
Adds the values of the two variables together
Prints the value in "bugs"

2. Change the value of a variable
Change the value of the "ants" or "spiders" variable. Add the variables together again and put the answer in the variable "bugs".

```
>>> ants = 22
>>> spiders = 18
>>> bugs = ants + spiders
>>> print(bugs)
40
```
Change the value in "spiders"
Add the variables together again
The answer changes

3. Skipping the assignment
If the sum is not assigned to the variable "bugs", even if the value of "ants" and "spiders" changes, the value of "bugs" won't.

```
>>> ants = 11
>>> spiders = 17
>>> print(bugs)
40
```
Prints the value in "bugs"
The answer hasn't changed (it's still 18 + 22)

Random numbers

To pick a random number, you first need to load the "randint" function into Python. To do this, use the "import" command. The "randint()" function is already programmed with code to pick a random integer (whole number).

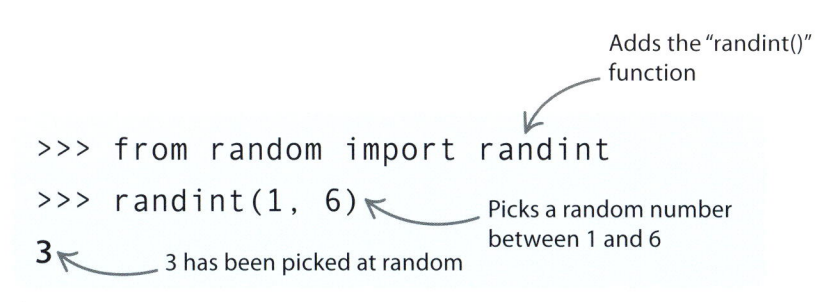

```
>>> from random import randint
>>> randint(1, 6)
3
```
Adds the "randint()" function
Picks a random number between 1 and 6
3 has been picked at random

△ **Roll the dice**
The "randint()" function picks a random number between the two numbers in the brackets. In this program, "randint(1, 6)" picks a value between 1 and 6.

> **REMEMBER**
> ### Random block
> The "randint()" function works like the "pick random" block in Scratch. In Scratch, the lowest and highest possible numbers are typed into the windows in the block. In Python, the numbers are put in brackets, separated by a comma.
>
> **pick random (1) to (6)**
>
> △ **Whole numbers**
> Both the Python "randint()" function and the Scratch block pick a random whole number – the result is never in decimals.

Strings in Python

Python is excellent for using words and sentences within programs. Different strings (sequences of characters) can be joined together, or individual parts of them can be selected and pulled out.

> **SEE ALSO**
> ❮ **50–51** Strings and lists
> ❮ **106–107** Types of data

Creating a string

A string might include letters, numbers, symbols, or spaces. These are all called characters. Strings can be placed in variables.

▷ **Strings in variables**
Variables can store strings. Type these two strings into the variables "a" and "b".

```
>>> a = 'Run! '
>>> b = 'Aliens are coming.'
```

The quote marks indicate the variable contains a string

Adding strings

Adding two numbers together creates a new number. In the same way, when two strings are added together, one string simply joins on to the other one.

```
>>> c = a + b
>>> print(c)
Run! Aliens are coming.
```

The variables "a" and "b" combine to become variable "c"

△ **Adding strings together**
The "+" symbol joins one string to another. and the answer becomes the variable "c".

A new string is added to variable "c"

```
>>> c = b + ' Watch out! ' + a
>>> print(c)
Aliens are coming. Watch out! Run!
```

△ **Adding another string in between**
A new string can also be added between two strings. Try the example above.

The new string appears in the middle of the message

> **EXPERT TIPS**
> ## Length of a string
>
> The "len()" function is used to find out the length of a string. Python counts all of the characters, including spaces, to give the total number of characters in a string.
>
> Calculates the length of the string in variable "a" ("Run! ")
>
> ```
> >>> len(a)
> 4
> >>> len(b)
> 18
> ```
>
> The string in variable "b" ("Aliens are coming.") is 18 characters long

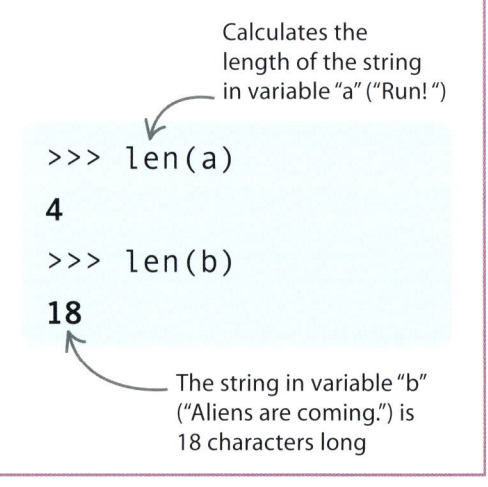

STRINGS IN PYTHON 111

Numbering the characters

Each character in a string is allocated a number according to its position. This position number can be used to look at individual letters or symbols, or to pull them out of a string.

1 Count begins from zero
When counting the positions, Python starts at 0. The second character is in position 1, the third in position 2, and so on.

```
>>> a = 'FLAMINGO'
```

The sixth letter, "N", is in position 5

F L A M I N G O
0 1 2 3 4 5 6 7

The first character, "F", is in position 0

The last character, "O", is in position 7

2 Counting the characters
The position number is called an "index". It can be used to pull out a particular letter from a string.

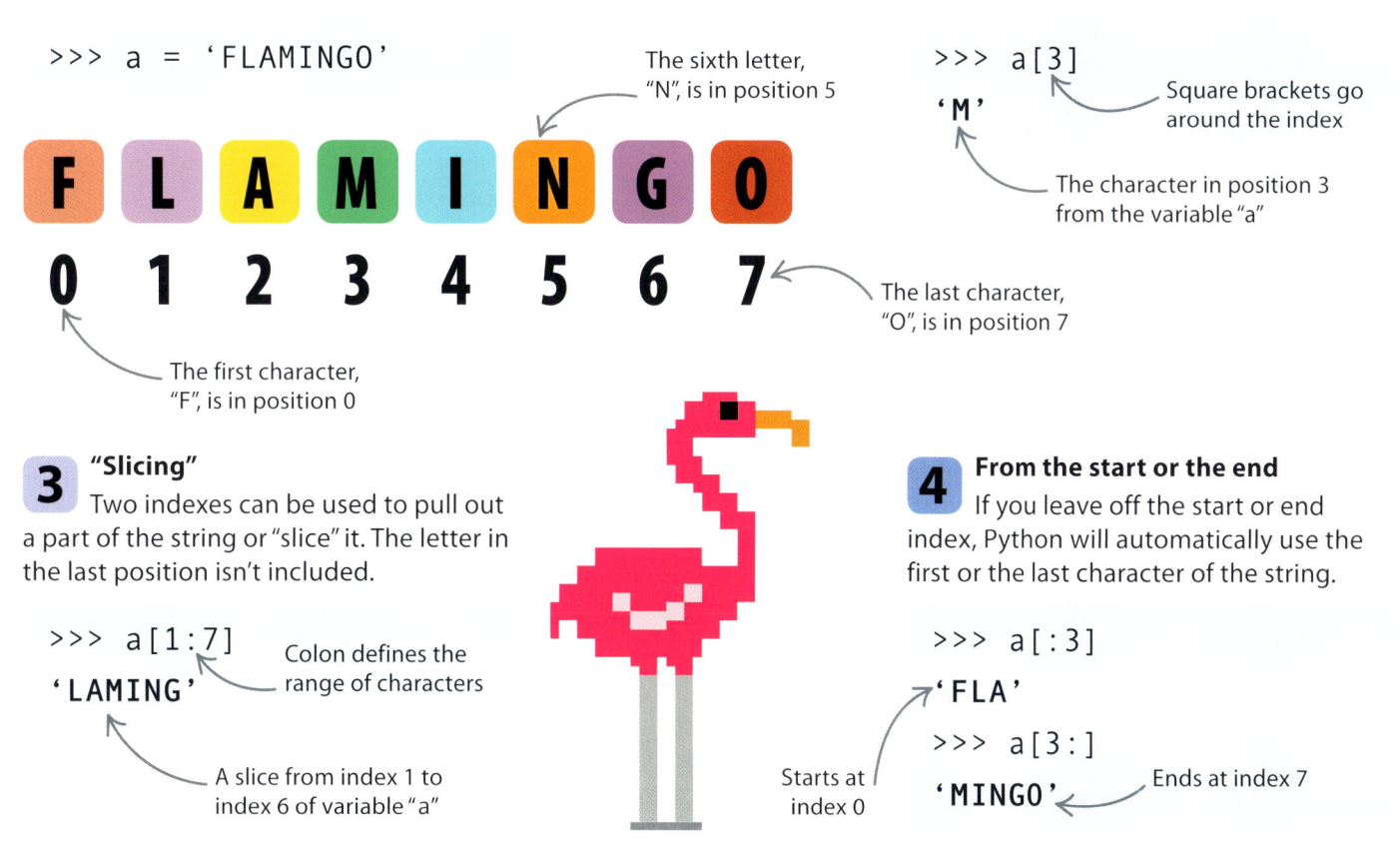

```
>>> a[3]
'M'
```

Square brackets go around the index

The character in position 3 from the variable "a"

3 "Slicing"
Two indexes can be used to pull out a part of the string or "slice" it. The letter in the last position isn't included.

```
>>> a[1:7]
'LAMING'
```

Colon defines the range of characters

A slice from index 1 to index 6 of variable "a"

4 From the start or the end
If you leave off the start or end index, Python will automatically use the first or the last character of the string.

```
>>> a[:3]
'FLA'
>>> a[3:]
'MINGO'
```

Starts at index 0

Ends at index 7

Apostrophes

Strings can go in single quotes or double quotes. However, the string should start and end with the same type of quote mark. This book uses single quotes. But what happens if you want to use an apostrophe in your string?

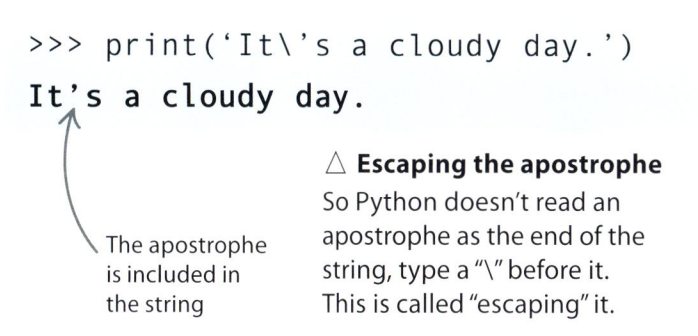

```
>>> print('It\'s a cloudy day.')
It's a cloudy day.
```

The apostrophe is included in the string

△ **Escaping the apostrophe**
So Python doesn't read an apostrophe as the end of the string, type a "\" before it. This is called "escaping" it.

PLAYING WITH PYTHON

Input and output

Programs interact with users through input and output. Information can be input into a program using a keyboard. Output is shown as information printed on the screen.

> **SEE ALSO**
> ‹ **96–97** Program flow
> ‹ **106–107** Types of data
> Loops **118–119** ›
> in Python

Input

The "input()" function is used to accept input from the keyboard into a program. It waits until the user finishes typing and presses the "return" or "Enter" key.

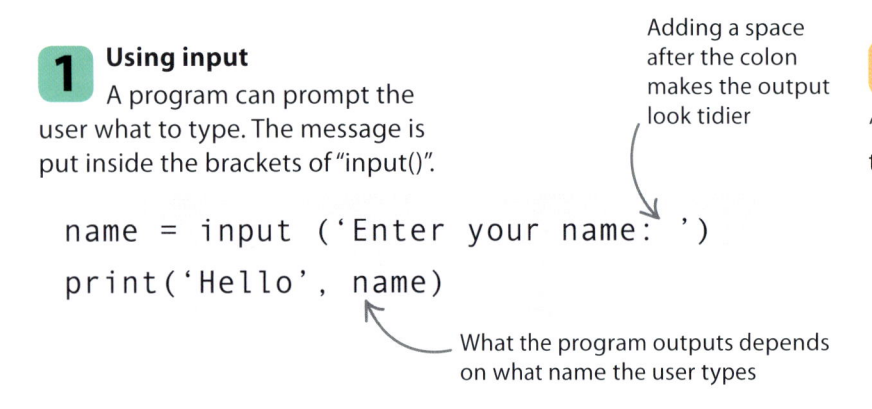

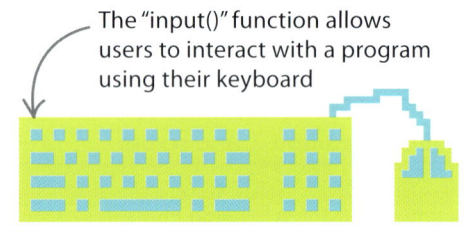

The "input()" function allows users to interact with a program using their keyboard

1 Using input
A program can prompt the user what to type. The message is put inside the brackets of "input()".

Adding a space after the colon makes the output look tidier

```
name = input ('Enter your name: ')
print('Hello', name)
```

What the program outputs depends on what name the user types

2 Output in the shell window
When the program is run, the message "Enter your name: " and its response appear in the shell window.

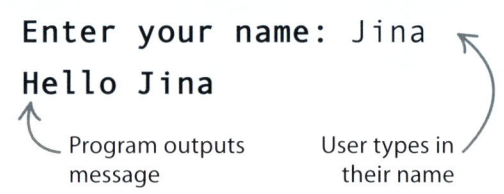

```
Enter your name: Jina
Hello Jina
```

Program outputs message

User types in their name

Output

The "print()" function is used to display characters in the shell window. It can be used to show a combination of text and variables.

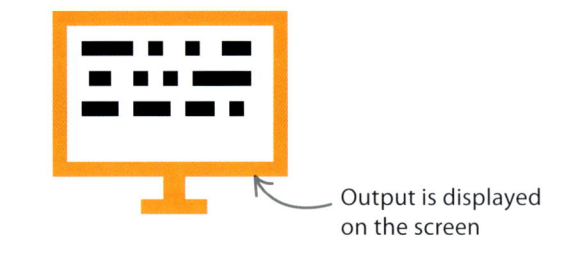

Output is displayed on the screen

1 Create some variables
Set up three variables for this simple experiment. Two are strings and one is an integer (whole number).

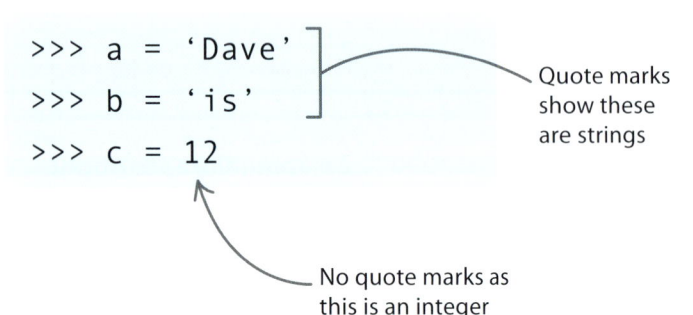

```
>>> a = 'Dave'
>>> b = 'is'
>>> c = 12
```

Quote marks show these are strings

No quote marks as this is an integer

2 Using the "print()" function
You can put several items inside the brackets of the "print()" function. You can combine variables of different types, and even combine strings and variables.

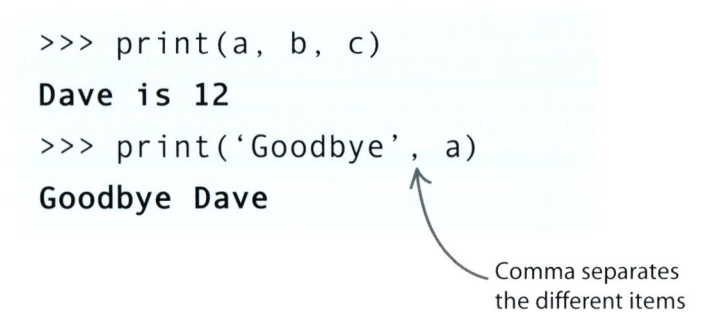

```
>>> print(a, b, c)
Dave is 12
>>> print('Goodbye', a)
Goodbye Dave
```

Comma separates the different items

INPUT AND OUTPUT   113

Two ways to separate strings

So far, the output has been printed on one line with a space between the items. Here are two other ways of separating strings.

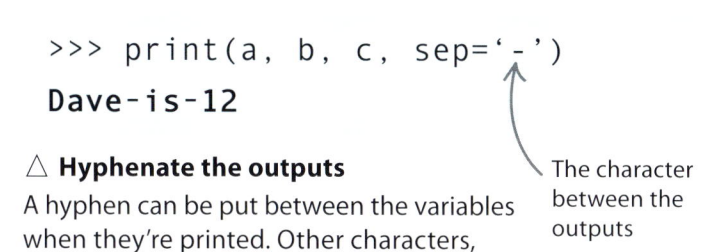

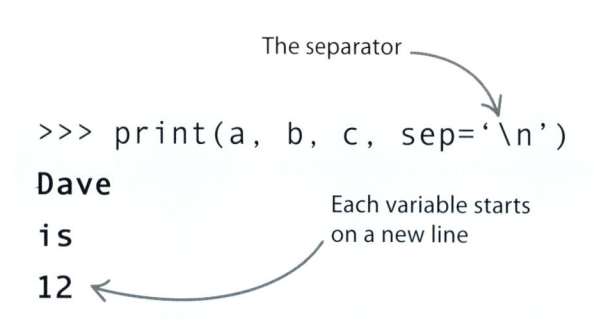

```
>>> print(a, b, c, sep='-')
Dave-is-12
```

△ **Hyphenate the outputs**
A hyphen can be put between the variables when they're printed. Other characters, such as "+" or "*", can be used too.

The character between the outputs

The separator

```
>>> print(a, b, c, sep='\n')
Dave
is
12
```

Each variable starts on a new line

△ **Outputs on new lines**
The space or character between the outputs is called a "separator" ("sep"). Using "\n" prints each output on a new line.

Three ways to end output

There are several different ways you can signal the end of the output of a "print" function.

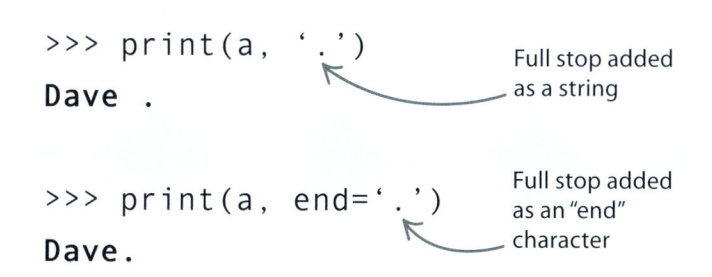

```
>>> print(a, '.')
Dave .
```
Full stop added as a string

```
>>> print(a, end='.')
Dave.
```
Full stop added as an "end" character

△ **Add a full stop to the output**
A full stop can be added as another string to be printed, but it will print with a space before it. To avoid this, use "end='.'" instead.

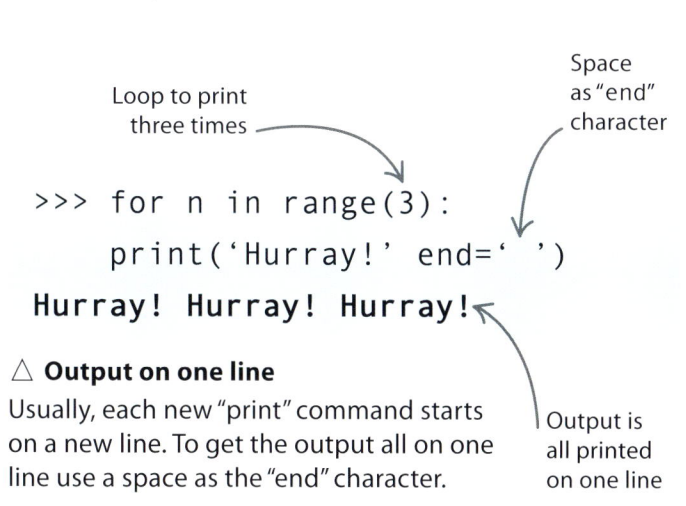

> **EXPERT TIPS**
> ### Options at the end
> The "end" and "sep" labels tell Python that the next item in the program isn't just another string. Remember to use them, otherwise the program will not work correctly.
>
> end   sep

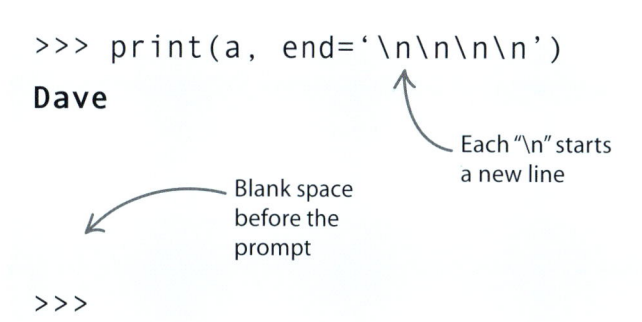

```
>>> for n in range(3):
        print('Hurray!' end=' ')
Hurray! Hurray! Hurray!
```
Loop to print three times
Space as "end" character
Output is all printed on one line

△ **Output on one line**
Usually, each new "print" command starts on a new line. To get the output all on one line use a space as the "end" character.

```
>>> print(a, end='\n\n\n\n')
Dave



>>>
```
Each "\n" starts a new line
Blank space before the prompt

△ **Blank lines at the end**
Using "\n" starts each output from a new line. Several of them can be used together to add blank lines at the end of a program.

Making decisions

Programs make decisions about what to do by comparing variables, numbers, and strings using Boolean expressions. These give an answer of either "True" or "False".

> **SEE ALSO**
> ‹ 58–59 True or false?
> ‹ 104–105 Variables in Python

Logical operators

Logical operators are used to compare variables against numbers or strings, or even against other variables. The resulting answer is either "True" or "False".

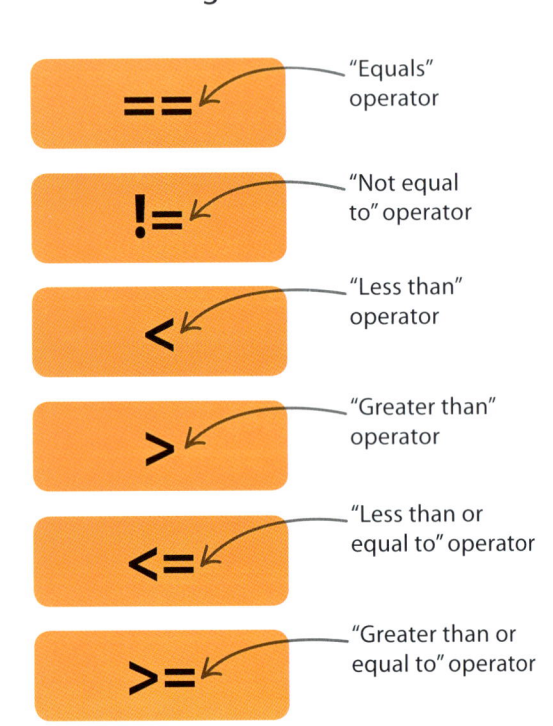

- `==` — "Equals" operator
- `!=` — "Not equal to" operator
- `<` — "Less than" operator
- `>` — "Greater than" operator
- `<=` — "Less than or equal to" operator
- `>=` — "Greater than or equal to" operator

△ **Types of comparison operators**
There are six comparison operators. Python uses two equals signs to compare if two things are the same. (A single equals sign is used to assign a value to a variable.)

▷ **Use the shell to check**
Logical operators also work in the shell window. Use this example to try out several logical operators, including "not", "or", and "and".

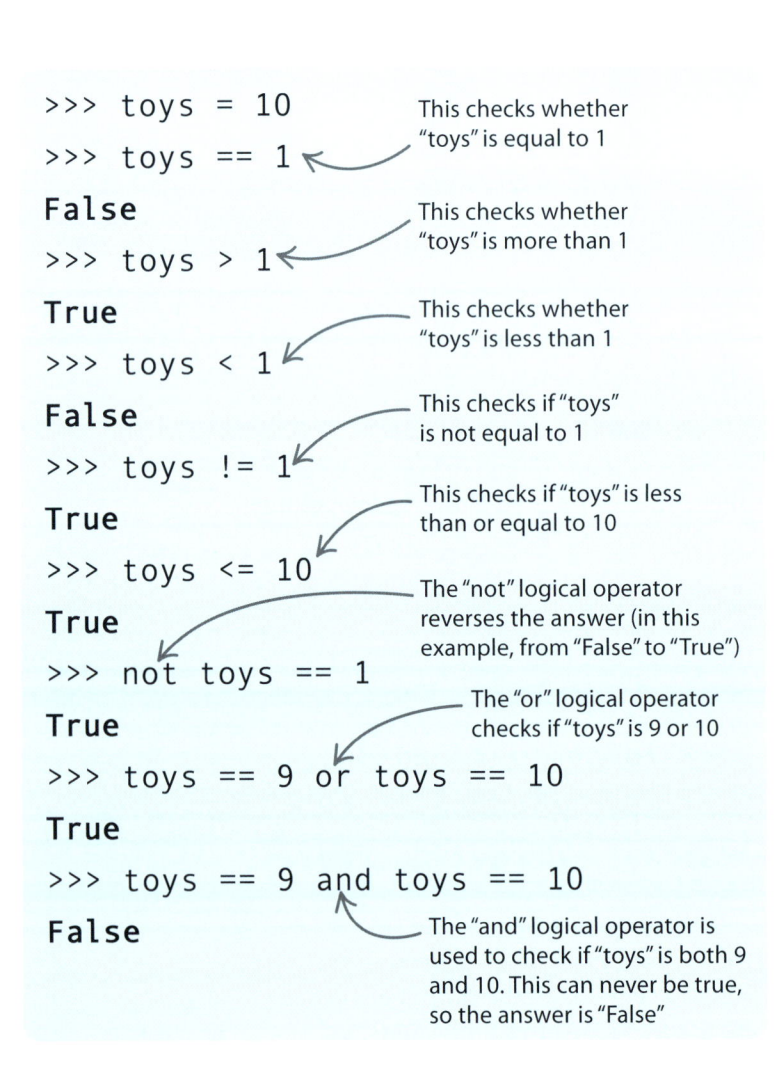

```
>>> toys = 10
>>> toys == 1
False
>>> toys > 1
True
>>> toys < 1
False
>>> toys != 1
True
>>> toys <= 10
True
>>> not toys == 1
True
>>> toys == 9 or toys == 10
True
>>> toys == 9 and toys == 10
False
```

- This checks whether "toys" is equal to 1
- This checks whether "toys" is more than 1
- This checks whether "toys" is less than 1
- This checks if "toys" is not equal to 1
- This checks if "toys" is less than or equal to 10
- The "not" logical operator reverses the answer (in this example, from "False" to "True")
- The "or" logical operator checks if "toys" is 9 or 10
- The "and" logical operator is used to check if "toys" is both 9 and 10. This can never be true, so the answer is "False"

Is it Ella's birthday?

Ella's birthday is the 28th of July. This program takes a day and a month and uses logical operators to check whether it's Ella's birthday.

1 Check for the birthday
Create variables for a day and a month. Use the "and" logical operator to check whether it is the 28th of July.

```
>>> day = 28
>>> month = 7
>>> day == 28 and month == 7
True
```

The "and" operator checks to see if both conditions are true

Remember to use two equals signs

It's Ella's birthday!

2 Not the birthday detector
You can reverse the answer using the "not" logical operator. You will get the answer "True" on every day, except for Ella's birthday.

```
>>> day = 28
>>> month = 7
>>> not (day == 28 and \
         month == 7)
False
```

This character is used to make code go over two lines

It's Ella's birthday, so the answer is "False"

3 Birthday or New Year's Day?
Use the "or" logical operator to check whether it's Ella's birthday or New Year's Day. Use brackets to combine the correct days and months.

```
>>> day = 28
>>> month = 7
>>> (day == 28 and month == 7) \
    or (day == 1 and month == 1)
True
```

Checks for the 28th of July

The answer will be "True" if it's Ella's birthday or New Year's Day

Strings

Two strings can be compared using the "==" operator or the "!=" operator. Strings have to match exactly to get a "True" output.

```
>>> dog = 'Woof woof'
>>> dog == 'Woof woof'
True
>>> dog == 'woof woof'
False
>>> dog == 'Woof woof '
False
```

The strings match exactly, so the answer is "True"

The strings don't match because there isn't a capital "W"

The strings don't match because there's extra space before the quote mark

△ **Exactly the same**
Strings must match for them to be equal. That means they must use capital letters, spaces, and symbols in exactly the same way.

EXPERT TIPS
Operator for strings

The "in" operator can be used to see whether one string is inside another string. Use it to check if a string contains a particular letter or a group of letters.

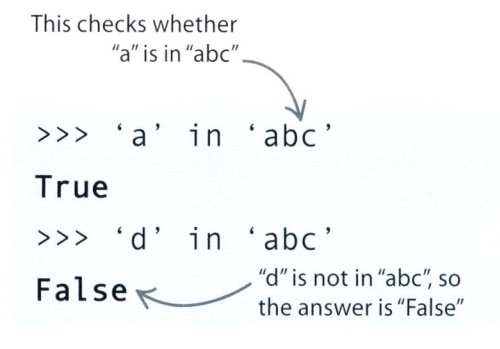

This checks whether "a" is in "abc"

```
>>> 'a' in 'abc'
True
>>> 'd' in 'abc'
False
```

"d" is not in "abc", so the answer is "False"

PLAYING WITH PYTHON

Branching

Boolean expressions can be used to determine which route a program should follow, depending on whether the answer to the expression is "True" or "False". This is known as "branching".

> **SEE ALSO**
> ‹ 60–61 Decisions and branches
> ‹ 114–115 Making decisions

Do or do not

The "if" command means that if a condition is "True", then the program runs a block of commands. If the condition isn't "True", the block is skipped. The block after the "if" command is always indented by four spaces.

1 **"if" condition**
This code asks the user if it's their birthday. It checks whether the answer is "y". If so, a birthday message is printed.

```
ans = input('Is it your birthday? (y/n)')
if ans == 'y':
    print('Happy Birthday!')
```

- Prompts users what to type in
- This part of the program only runs if the user types "y"
- Indented by four spaces

2 **Output if condition is "True"**
Run the program and enter "y". The message is printed. It doesn't appear if anything else is entered.

```
Is it your birthday? (y/n)y
Happy Birthday!
```

- Type in "y"
- The message appears

Do this or that

The "if" command can be combined with an "else" command. This combination means that if something is "True", one thing happens, and if not, something else happens.

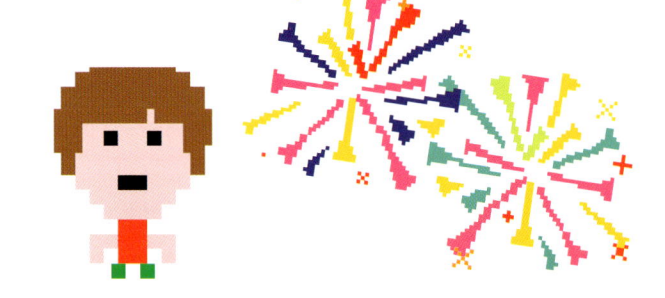

1 **"if-else" condition**
If "y" is entered, the program prints a special message for New Year. It shows a different message if anything else is entered.

```
ans = input('Is it New Year? (y/n)')
if ans == 'y':
    print('Happy New Year!')
    print('Time for Fireworks.')
else:
    print('Not yet!')
```

- Remember the colon
- This message only appears if the user enters "y"
- Remember to put a colon here too
- Only runs if user does not enter "y"

BRANCHING 117

2. Output if condition is "True"
Run the program and type in "y". The program shows your New Year message. It doesn't show the other message.

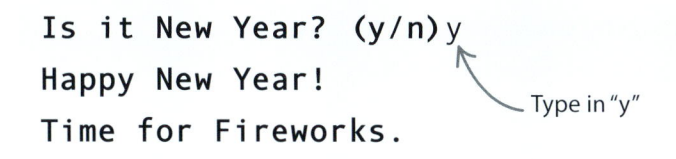

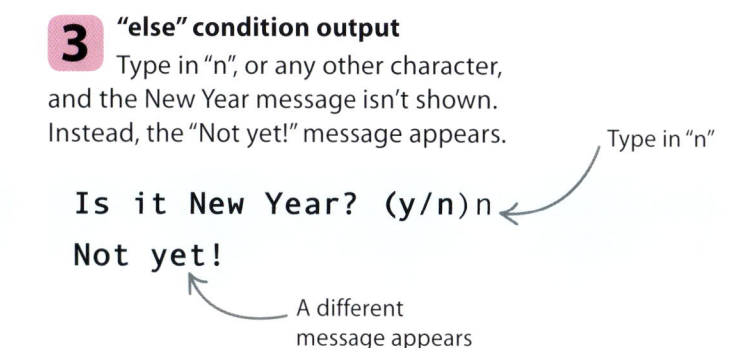

```
Is it New Year? (y/n)y
Happy New Year!
Time for Fireworks.
```
Type in "y"

3. "else" condition output
Type in "n", or any other character, and the New Year message isn't shown. Instead, the "Not yet!" message appears.

```
Is it New Year? (y/n)n
Not yet!
```
Type in "n"

A different message appears

Do one of these things
The "elif" command is short for "else-if". It means that if something is "True", do one thing, otherwise check if something else is "True" and do something else if it is. The following calculator program uses the "elif" command.

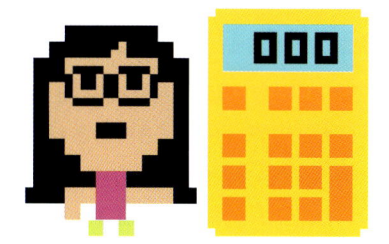

1. "if-elif-else" condition
This program checks what is typed in. If it's "add", "sub", "mul", or "div", the result of the sum is shown.

Asks the user to input a number

Remember to add quote marks and brackets

```
a = int(input('a = '))
b = int(input('b = '))
op = input('add/sub/mul/div:')
if op == 'add':
    c = a + b
elif op == 'sub':
    c = a - b
elif op == 'mul':
    c = a * b
elif op == 'div':
    c = a / b
else:
    c = 'Error'
print('Answer = ',c)
```

Type "add" to add the variables together

Type "div" to divide the variables

Shows an error message in "c" if something else is typed in

Shows the answer or error message

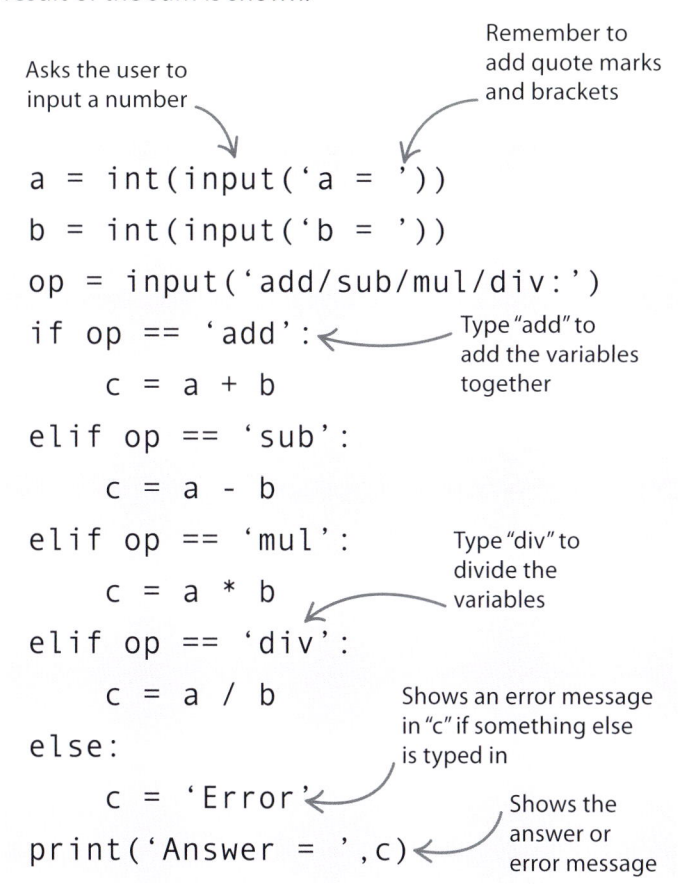

2. Output for the condition that's "True"
Test the program. Enter two numbers and type in "sub". The answer will be the first number minus the second number.

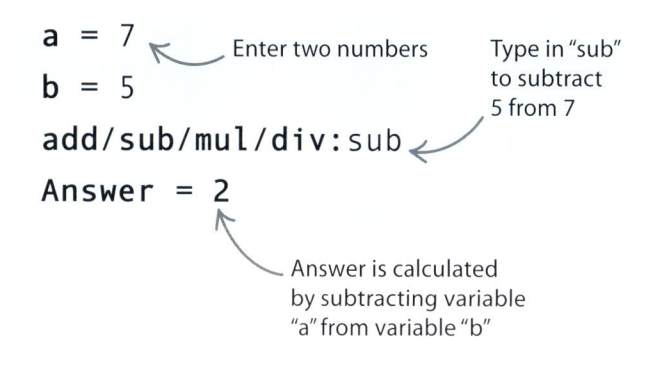

```
a = 7
b = 5
add/sub/mul/div:sub
Answer = 2
```

Enter two numbers

Type in "sub" to subtract 5 from 7

Answer is calculated by subtracting variable "a" from variable "b"

3. "else" condition output
The "else" condition runs if something other than "add", "sub", "mul", or "div" is typed in, and an error message is displayed.

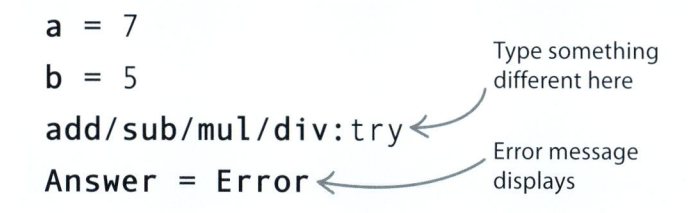

```
a = 7
b = 5
add/sub/mul/div:try
Answer = Error
```

Type something different here

Error message displays

Loops in Python

Programs that contain repeating lines of code can be time-consuming to type in and difficult to understand. A clearer way of writing them is by using a loop command. The simplest loops are ones that repeat a certain number of times, such as "for" loops.

> **SEE ALSO**
> ⟨ **44–45** Pens and turtles
> While loops **120–121** ⟩
> Escaping loops **122–123** ⟩

Repeating things

A "for" loop repeats the code without having to type it in again. It can be used to repeat something a certain number of times. For example, if you want to print the names of a class of 30 students.

1 Program the turtle
A "for" loop can also be used to shorten the code. This program allows the user to control a turtle that draws a line as it moves around the screen. The user can draw shapes on the screen, such as a triangle, by directing the turtle's movements.

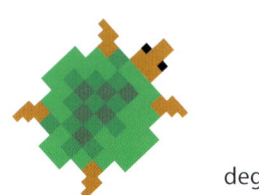

```
from turtle import *
forward(100)
right(120)
forward(100)
right(120)
forward(100)
right(120)
```

- Loads all the commands that control the turtle
- This command moves the turtle forward
- This makes the turtle turn 120 degrees to the right

2 The turtle draws a triangle
The program tells the turtle how to draw a triangle by giving it the length of the three sides and the angles between them. The turtle will appear in a separate window when you run the program.

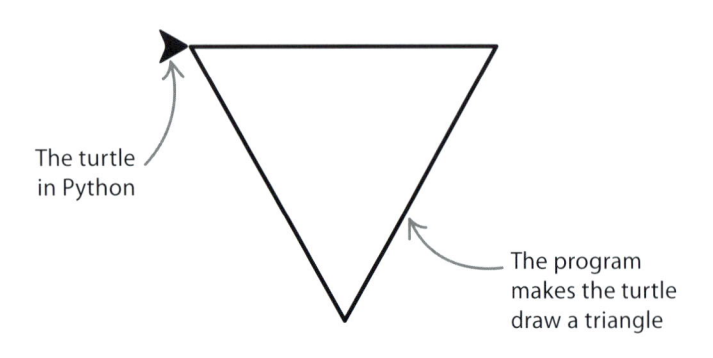

- The turtle in Python
- The program makes the turtle draw a triangle

3 Use a "for" loop
The program above gives the turtle the same two commands, "forward(100)" and "right(120)", three times – once for each side of the triangle. An alternative to this is to use these two commands inside a "for" loop. Try drawing a triangle simply using the code shown below.

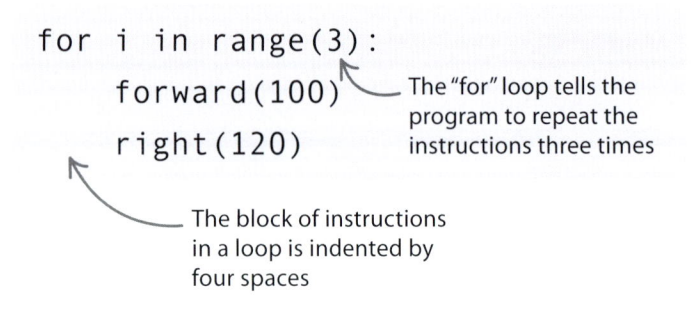

```
for i in range(3):
    forward(100)
    right(120)
```

- The "for" loop tells the program to repeat the instructions three times
- The block of instructions in a loop is indented by four spaces

LOOPS IN PYTHON   119

Loop variables

A loop variable counts the number of times a loop has repeated itself. It starts at the first value in the range (0) and stops one before the last value.

The loop variable — The loop repeats ten times

```
for i in range(10):
    print(i, end=' ')
```

Python stops counting one before the last value

```
>>> 0 1 2 3 4 5 6 7 8 9
```

△ **Simple loop variable**
Here, the loop's range doesn't state what the starting value should be. So Python starts counting from 0, the same way as it does with strings.

This tells the program to count in twos

```
for i in range(2, 11, 2):
    print(i, end=' ')
```

This tells the program to count backwards

```
for i in range(10, 0, -1):
    print(i, end=' ')
```

```
>>> 2 4 6 8 10
```
The output appears in twos

```
>>> 10 9 8 7 6 5 4 3 2 1
```

△ **Counting in twos**
This loop has a third value in its range, which tells the loop to count in twos. It stops at 10, which is one loop before the loop variable gets to 11.

△ **Counting backwards**
This time the program counts backwards from 10, like in a rocket launch. The loop variable starts at 10 and takes steps of -1 until it reaches 1.

Nested Loops

Loops inside a loop are called "nested loops". In nested loops, the outer loop only repeats after the inner loop has gone round its required number of times.

To make the loops repeat "n" number of times, the last number in the range must be "n + 1"

```
n = 3
for a in range(1, n + 1):
    for b in range(1, n + 1):
        print(b, 'x', a, '=', b * a)
```

The value of "b"   Outer loop   Inner loop

This sum will be printed nine times

```
>>>
1 x 1 = 1
2 x 1 = 2
3 x 1 = 3
1 x 2 = 2
2 x 2 = 4
3 x 2 = 6
1 x 3 = 3
2 x 3 = 6
3 x 3 = 9
```

The value of "a"

First time round the outer loop (the inner loop repeats three times)

Second time round the outer loop

Third time round the outer loop

△ **Loops inside a loop**
In this example, each time the outer loop goes round once, the inner loop goes round three times. So in total, the outer loop is executed three times and the inner loop is executed nine times.

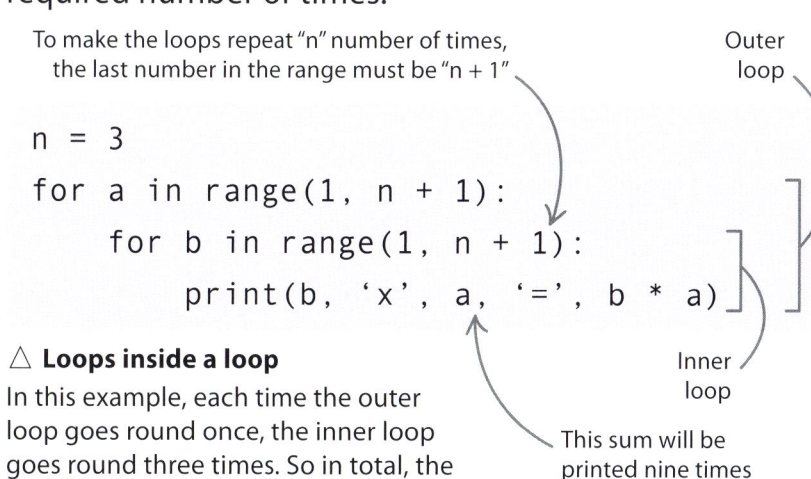

△ **What happens**
The nested loops print the first three lines of the 1, 2, and 3 times tables. The value of "a" only changes when the outer loop repeats. The value of "b" counts from 1 to 3 for each value of "a".

While loops

"For" loops are useful when you know how many times a task needs to be repeated. But sometimes you'll need a loop to keep repeating until something changes. A "while" loop keeps on going round as many times as it needs to.

SEE ALSO

❮ 114–115 Making decisions
❮ 118–119 Loops in Python
Escaping loops 122–123 ❯

While loops

A while loop keeps repeating as long as a certain condition is true. This condition is called the "loop condition" and is either true or false.

▷ **How it works**
A while loop checks if the condition is true. If it is, it goes round the loop again. If it's not, it skips the loop.

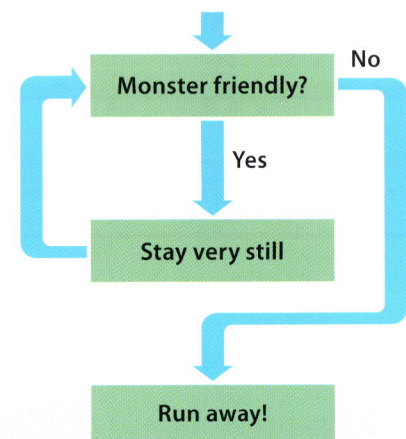

Monster friendly? — No → **Run away!**
Yes ↓
Stay very still
↓ (loops back)

1 Create a while loop
Set the starting value of the "answer" variable in the loop condition. The loop condition has to be true to start with or the program will never run the loop.

The code inside the loop must be indented four spaces

```
answer = 'y'
while answer == 'y':
    print('Stay very still')
    answer = input('Is the monster friendly? (y/n)')
print('Run away!')
```

The "answer" variable is set to "y"

The while loop only runs if the condition is true

If the condition is false, unindented code after the loop runs and a different message appears

2 What the program looks like
The value entered is stored in the variable "answer". The loop condition is "answer == 'y'". If you type "y", the loop keeps going. If you type "n", the loop stops.

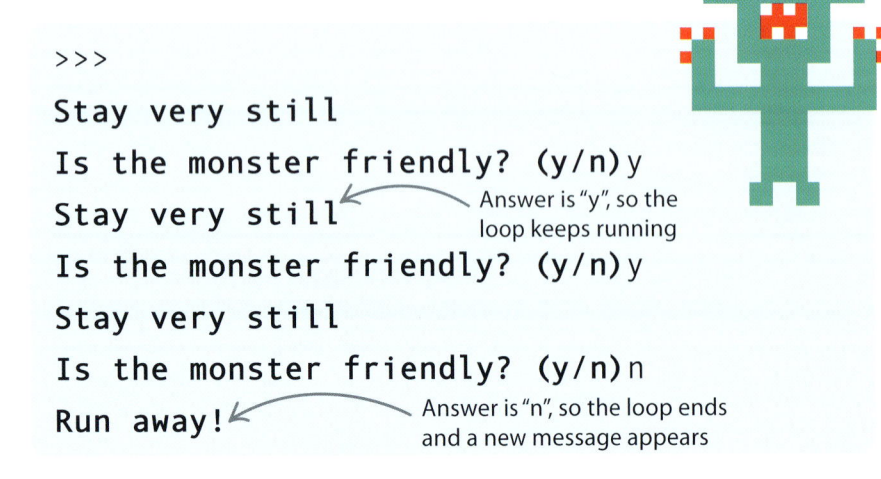

```
>>>
Stay very still
Is the monster friendly? (y/n)y
Stay very still
Is the monster friendly? (y/n)y
Stay very still
Is the monster friendly? (y/n)n
Run away!
```

Answer is "y", so the loop keeps running

Answer is "n", so the loop ends and a new message appears

REMEMBER
"repeat until" block

Python's "while" loop is similar to the "repeat until" block in Scratch. Both keep on repeating until something different happens in the program.

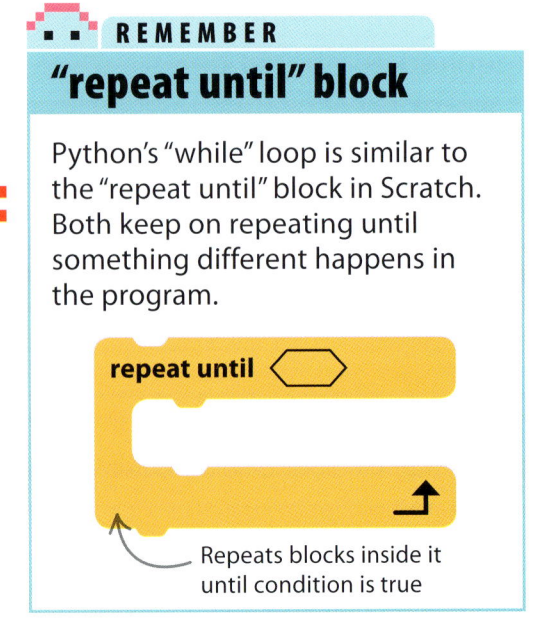

repeat until ⬡

Repeats blocks inside it until condition is true

WHILE LOOPS

Forever loops

Some loops run forever. If you set the condition in a "while" loop to be "True", it can never be false and the loop will never end. This can either be useful or very annoying.

1. Create a forever loop
The loop condition here is set to "True". Nothing that happens inside the loop will make "True" equal anything but "True", so the loop runs forever.

```
while True:
    answer = input('Type a word and press enter: ')
    print('Please do not type \'' + answer + '\' again.')
```

The loop is always "True" so will never end

The typed word is stored in the variable "answer"

△ **Going loopy**
A loop with the condition "True" is called an "infinite" loop. If something is infinite it has no end.

2. What the program looks like
On the opposite page the monster program's loop condition checked to see what the user's answer was. If the answer isn't "y", the loop will stop. The loop shown above doesn't check the answer, so the user can't make it stop.

```
>>>
Type a word and press enter: tree
Please do not type 'tree' again
Type a word and press enter: hippo
Please do not type 'hippo' again
Type a word and press enter: water
Please do not type 'water': again
Type a word and press enter
```

No matter what is typed, this loop just keeps on going

REMEMBER
"forever" block

Remember the "forever" block in Scratch? It repeats the code inside it until the red stop button is clicked. A "while True" loop does exactly the same thing. It can be used to make a program keep doing something, such as asking questions or printing a number, as long as the program is running.

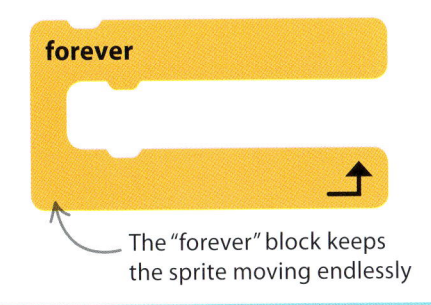

forever

The "forever" block keeps the sprite moving endlessly

EXPERT TIPS
Stop the loop

If you get stuck in an infinite loop, you can stop it from IDLE. Click in the Python shell window, then hold down the "CTRL" key and press the "C" key. This asks IDLE to stop the program. You might have to press "CTRL-C" a few times. This is similar to clicking the red stop button in Scratch.

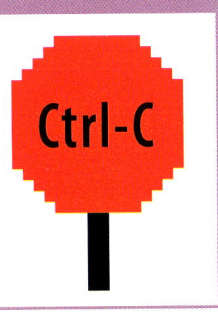

Ctrl-C

Escaping loops

Programs can get stuck in a loop, but there are ways to escape. The word "break" leaves a loop (even a "forever" loop), and the word "continue" skips back to the start of the next loop.

> **SEE ALSO**
> ❰ **118–119** Loops in Python
> ❰ **120–121** While loops

Inserting breaks

Putting a break into a loop makes the program jump out of the loop at once – even if the loop condition is true. Any commands inside the loop that come after the break are ignored.

```
table = 7
for i in range(1, 13):
    print('What\'s', i, 'x', table, '?')
    guess = input()
    ans = i * table
    if int(guess) == ans:
        print('Correct!')
    else:
        print('No, it\'s', ans)
print('Finished')
```

- The variable "i" will count from 1 to 12
- "i" is the loop variable
- The backslash ("\") tells Python the next quote mark is an apostrophe, not the end of the string

1 Write a simple program
This program tests the user on the 7 times table. The program continues looping until all 12 questions are answered. Write this program in the code window, as it will be edited later.

2 Insert a "break"
A "break" can be added so the user can escape the loop. The program executes a break if the user types "stop".

If "guess" equals "stop", the program skips the rest of the loop and prints "Finished"

```
table = 7
for i in range(1,13):
    print('What\'s', i, 'x', table, '?')
    guess = input()
    if guess == 'stop':
        break
    ans = i * table
    if int(guess) == ans:
        print('Correct!')
    else:
        print('No, it\'s', ans)
print('Finished')
```

The "ans" variable holds the correct answer to the question

ESCAPING LOOPS   123

```
>>>
What's 1 x 7 ?
1
No, it's 7
What's 2 x 7 ?
14
Correct!
What's 3 x 7 ?
stop
Finished
```

- The first time around the loop "i" is equal to 1
- The value of "i" changes to 2 next time around the loop
- This executes the break command and the program exits the loop

3 How it works
If the user decides not to carry on after the third question and types "stop", the break command is executed and the program leaves the loop.

Skipping

The "continue" keyword can be used to skip a question without leaving the loop. It tells the program to ignore the rest of the code inside the loop and skip straight to the start of the next loop.

```
table = 7
for i in range(1,13):
    print('What\'s', i, 'x', table, '?')
    guess = input()
    if guess == 'stop':
        break
    if guess == 'skip':
        print('Skipping')
        continue
    ans = i * table
    if int(guess) == ans:
        print('Correct!')
    else:
        print('No, it\'s', ans)
print('Finished')
```

- Asks the question "What's 1 x 7?" first time around the loop
- Skips straight to the next loop

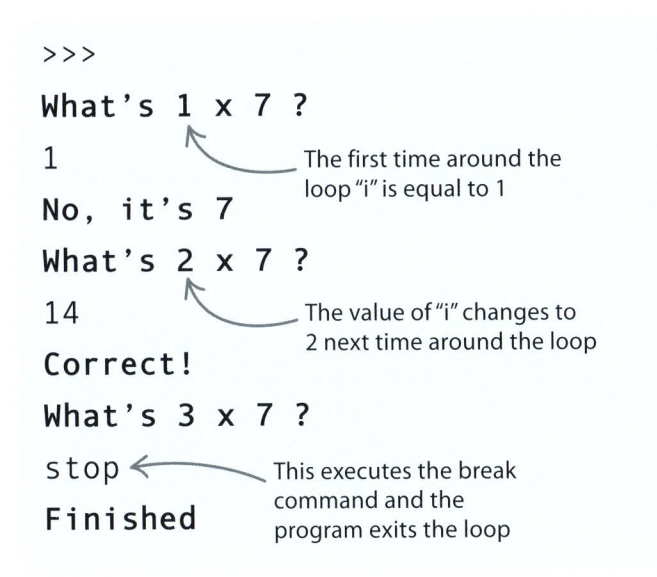

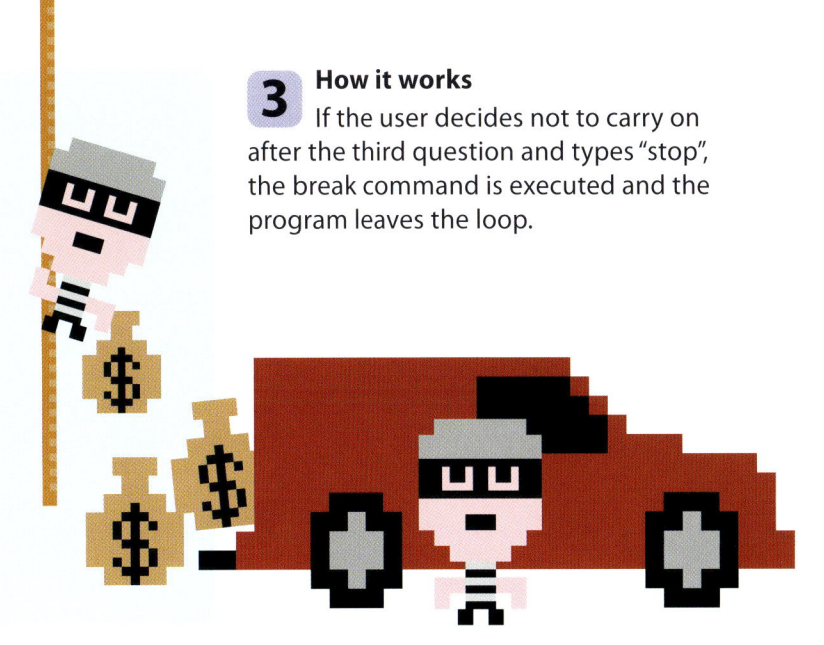

4 Insert a continue
Add an "if" statement inside the loop to see if the user answered "skip". If so, the program will print "Skipping" and execute a "continue" to skip to the next go around the loop.

5 What happens
If the user doesn't want to answer a question, they can type "skip" and continue to the next question.

```
>>>
What's 1 x 7 ?
skip
Skipping
What's 2 x 7 ?
14
Correct!
What's 3 x 7 ?
```

- Type "skip" to go to the next question
- The loop goes around again as normal when the answer is correct

# Lists

If you need to keep lots of data in one place, then you can put it in a list. Lists can contain numbers, strings, other lists, or a combination of all these things.

> **SEE ALSO**
> ⟨ **50–51** Strings and lists
> Silly **128–129** ⟩ sentences

What is a list?

A list is a structure in Python where items are kept in order. Each entry is given a number that you can use to refer back to it. You can change, delete, or add to the items in a list at any point.

▽ **Looking at lists**
Each item in a list sits inside single quote marks, and is separated from the next item by a comma. The whole list sits inside a pair of square brackets.

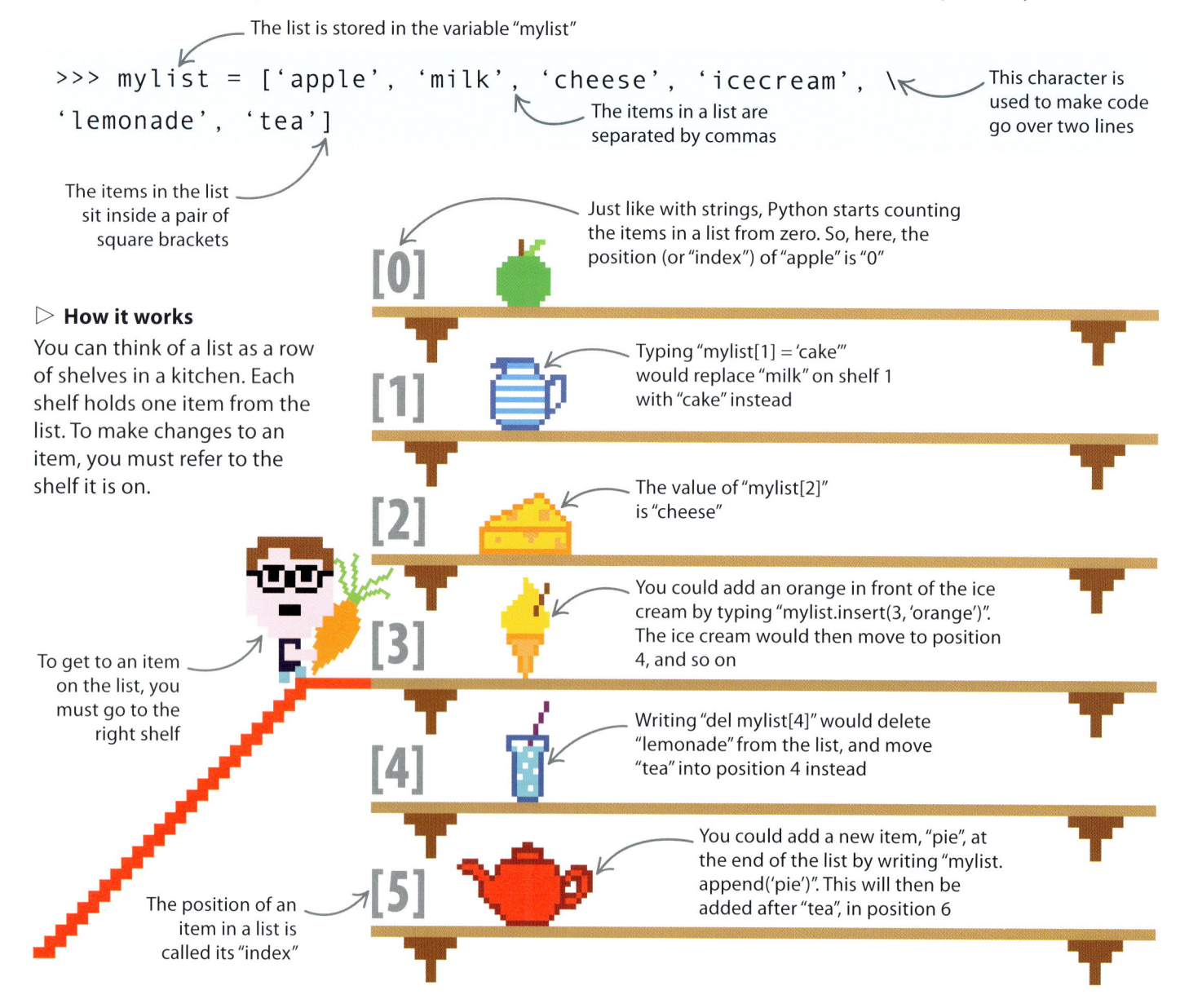

The list is stored in the variable "mylist"

```
>>> mylist = ['apple', 'milk', 'cheese', 'icecream', \
'lemonade', 'tea']
```

The items in a list are separated by commas

The items in the list sit inside a pair of square brackets

This character is used to make code go over two lines

▷ **How it works**
You can think of a list as a row of shelves in a kitchen. Each shelf holds one item from the list. To make changes to an item, you must refer to the shelf it is on.

To get to an item on the list, you must go to the right shelf

The position of an item in a list is called its "index"

[0] Just like with strings, Python starts counting the items in a list from zero. So, here, the position (or "index") of "apple" is "0"

[1] Typing "mylist[1] = 'cake'" would replace "milk" on shelf 1 with "cake" instead

[2] The value of "mylist[2]" is "cheese"

[3] You could add an orange in front of the ice cream by typing "mylist.insert(3, 'orange')". The ice cream would then move to position 4, and so on

[4] Writing "del mylist[4]" would delete "lemonade" from the list, and move "tea" into position 4 instead

[5] You could add a new item, "pie", at the end of the list by writing "mylist. append('pie')". This will then be added after "tea", in position 6

Using lists

Once a list has been created, you can write programs to manipulate the data inside it – in a loop, for example. You can also combine lists to make new lists.

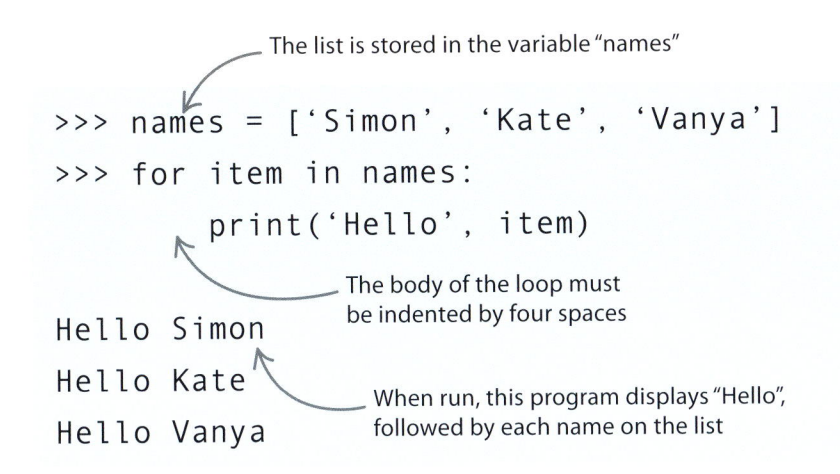

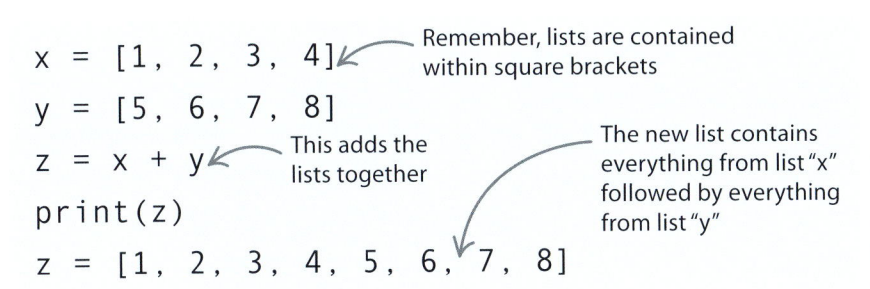

> LINGO
> ## Mutable objects
> Lists in Python are "mutable". This means that they can change. You can add or delete items, or switch around their order. Other functions in Python, such as tuples (see pp.130–131), can't be altered once you create them. These are called "immutable".

The list is stored in the variable "names"

```
>>> names = ['Simon', 'Kate', 'Vanya']
>>> for item in names:
        print('Hello', item)
```

The body of the loop must be indented by four spaces

```
Hello Simon
Hello Kate
Hello Vanya
```

When run, this program displays "Hello", followed by each name on the list

◁ **Lists in loops**
You can use a loop to work through every item in a list. This program says "Hello" to a series of names, one after the other.

```
x = [1, 2, 3, 4]
y = [5, 6, 7, 8]
z = x + y
print(z)
z = [1, 2, 3, 4, 5, 6, 7, 8]
```

Remember, lists are contained within square brackets
This adds the lists together
The new list contains everything from list "x" followed by everything from list "y"

◁ **Adding lists**
Two lists can be added together. The new list will contain the items from both of the old lists.

▽ **Lists in lists**
The items in a list can be lists themselves. The "suitcase" list below contains two lists of clothes – it is like a suitcase shared by two people, where they each pack three items.

As the list is inside square brackets, it becomes an individual item within the "suitcase" list – "suitcase[0]"   *"suitcase[1]"*

```
>>> suitcase=[['hat', 'tie', 'sock'],['bag', 'shoe', 'shirt']]
>>> print(suitcase)
[['hat', 'tie', 'sock'],['bag', 'shoe', 'shirt']]
>>> print(suitcase[1])
['bag', 'shoe', 'shirt']
>>> print(suitcase[1][2])
shirt
```

This will print the whole suitcase list

This will print everything in the second list, "suitcase[1]"

This prints the item at index 2 in "suitcase[1]" – remember, Python starts counting the items from zero

Functions

A function is a piece of code that performs a specific task. It bundles up the code, gives it a name, and can be used any time by "calling" it. A function can be used to avoid entering the same lines of code more than once.

> **SEE ALSO**
> Silly sentences **128–129 ›**
> Variables and functions **134–135 ›**

Useful functions

Python contains lots of useful functions for performing certain tasks. When a function is called, Python retrieves the code for that function and then runs it. When the function is finished, the program returns to the line of code that called it and runs the next command.

print()

△ **"print()" function**
This function lets the program send output to the user by printing instructions or results on the screen.

input()

△ **"input()" function**
This function is the opposite of the "print()" function. It lets the user give instructions or data to the program by typing them in.

randint()

△ **"randint()" function**
This function gives a random number (like throwing a dice). It can be used to add an element of chance to programs.

Making and calling functions

The functions that come with Python aren't the only ones that can be used. To make a new function, collect the code you want to use in a special "wrapper" and give it a name. This name allows the function to be called whenever it is needed.

1 Define a function
The definition of a function will always have the keyword "def" and the function's name at the beginning of the code.

```
def greeting():
    print('Hello!')
```

A colon marks the end of the function's name and the start of the code it contains

This is the code within the function

2 Call the function
Typing the function name followed by brackets into the shell window calls the function and shows the output.

```
>>> greeting()
Hello!
```

The "greeting" function is called and the output is displayed

Brackets show that this is a function call and not a variable

FUNCTIONS 127

Passing data to functions

A function has to be told which values to work with. For example, in "print(a, b, c)", the function "print()" is being passed the values "a", "b", and "c". In "height(1, 45)", the values 1 and 45 are being passed to the function "height".

1 Add parameters to the function
Values passed to a function are called "parameters". Parameters are put inside the brackets next to the function's name in its definition.

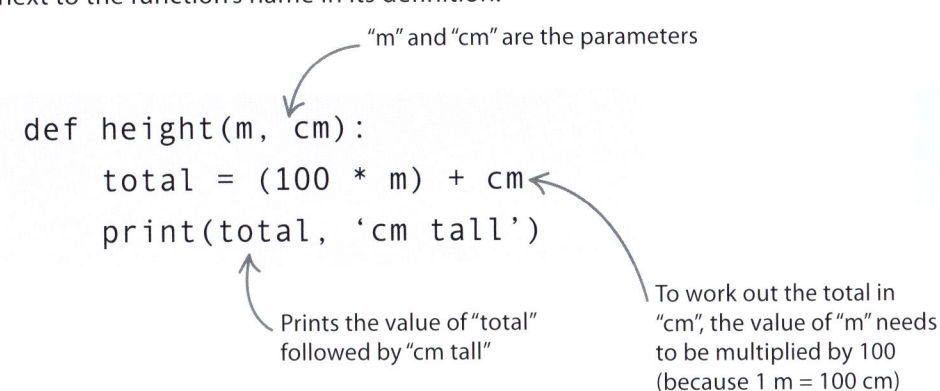

"m" and "cm" are the parameters

```
def height(m, cm):
    total = (100 * m) + cm
    print(total, 'cm tall')
```

Prints the value of "total" followed by "cm tall"

To work out the total in "cm", the value of "m" needs to be multiplied by 100 (because 1 m = 100 cm)

2 Values are defined
The code inside the function uses the values that are passed to it.

Calls the function to give the answer when "m" = 1 and "cm" = 45

```
>>> height(1, 45)
145 cm tall
```

Shows that 1 m 45 cm is equal to 145 cm

Getting data back from functions

Functions are most useful when they send some data back to the program – a return value. To make a function return a value, add "return" followed by the value to be sent back.

1 Define a function that returns a number
Python's "input()" function always returns a string, even if a number is entered. The new function below gives back a number instead.

```
def num_input(prompt):
    typed = input(prompt)
    num = int(typed)
    return num
a = num_input('Enter a')
b = num_input('Enter b')
print('a + b =', a + b)
```

The number is stored as a string in the variable "typed"

Returns the value stored in the variable

This converts the string into a number and stores it in the variable "num"

2 Number as output
If the program used the function "input", "a + b" would put the strings "10" and "7" together to give "107".

```
Enter a 10
Enter b 7
a + b = 17
```

Adding "a + b" outputs "17" because the function "num_input" gives back numbers, not strings

PROJECT 5

Silly sentences

Loops, functions, and lists can be used individually for lots of different tasks. They can also be used together to create interesting programs that can do even more complex tasks.

> **SEE ALSO**
> ‹ 120–121 While loops
> ‹ 124–125 Lists
> ‹ 126–127 Functions

Make silly sentences

This program will make sentences by using three separate lists of words. It will pick one word from each list and put them together randomly in a silly sentence.

> Try using different words to the ones shown here to create your own silly sentences.

1 ▸ Enter the three lists shown below into a new code window. This defines the lists that will be used to make the sentences.

◁ Single quotes show that each item in the list is a string

◁ Square brackets mean that this is a list

```
name = ['Neha', 'Lee', 'Sam']
verb = ['buys', 'rides', 'kicks']
noun = ['lion', 'bicycle', 'plane']
```

2 ▸ Each sentence is made up of words picked at random from the lists you have created. Define a function to do this, as it will be used several times in the program.

◁ This loads the function for generating a random number ("randint")

◁ Finds out how many words are in the list (the function works for lists of any length)

◁ Picks a random number that refers to one of the items in the list

```
from random import randint
def pick(words):
    num_words = len(words)
    num_picked = randint(0, num_words - 1)
    word_picked = words[num_picked]
    return word_picked
```

◁ Stores the random word that has been picked in the variable "word_picked"

SILLY SENTENCES

3 ▸ Print a random silly sentence by running the "pick" function once for each of the three lists. Use the "print" command to show the sentence on the screen.

Add an "a" so that the sentence makes sense (see below)

```
print(pick(name), pick(verb), 'a', pick(noun), end='.\n')
```

This adds a full stop at the end, while the "\n" starts a new line

4 ▸ Save and run the program to get a silly sentence made from the lists of names, verbs, and nouns.

```
Neha kicks a bicycle.
```

The sentence is randomly selected each time the program is run

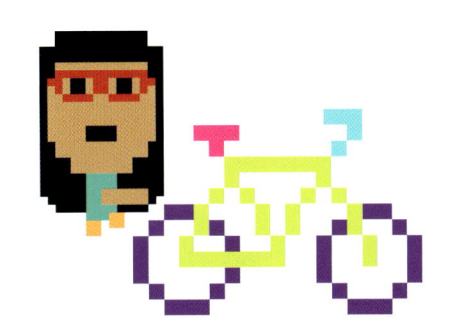

Silly sentences forever!

A forever loop can be added to the silly sentences program to keep it running forever, or until the user presses "Ctrl-C" to escape the loop.

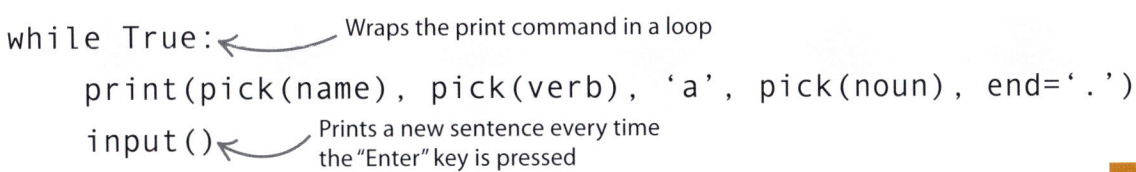

EXPERT TIPS
Readable code

It's very important to write a program that can be easily understood. It makes the program easier to change in the future because you don't have to start by solving the puzzle of how it works!

1 ▸ The program keeps printing silly sentences if the "print" command is wrapped in a "while True" loop.

```
while True:
    print(pick(name), pick(verb), 'a', pick(noun), end='.')
    input()
```

Wraps the print command in a loop

Prints a new sentence every time the "Enter" key is pressed

2 ▸ The "input()" function waits for the user to press the "Enter" key before printing another sentence. Without this it would print them too fast to read.

The program will keep on creating random sentences

```
Sam rides a lion.
Neha kicks a plane.
Lee buys a bicycle.
```

Tuples and dictionaries

Python uses lists for keeping data in order. It also has other data types for storing information called "tuples" and "dictionaries". Data types such as these, which hold lots of items, are called "containers".

SEE ALSO
❰ 106–107 Types of data
❰ 124–125 Lists

Tuples

Tuples are a bit like lists, but the items inside them can't be changed. Once a tuple is set up it always stays the same.

Tuples are surrounded by brackets

```
>>> dragonA = ('Sam', 15, 1.70)
>>> dragonB = ('Fiona', 16, 1.68)
```

The items in a tuple are separated by commas

◁ **What is a tuple?**
A tuple contains items separated by commas and surrounded by brackets. Tuples are useful for collecting several bits of data together, such as a dragons' name, age, and height.

▷ **Grabbing an item from a tuple**
To get an item from a tuple, use its position in the tuple (its index). Tuples count from zero, just like lists and strings.

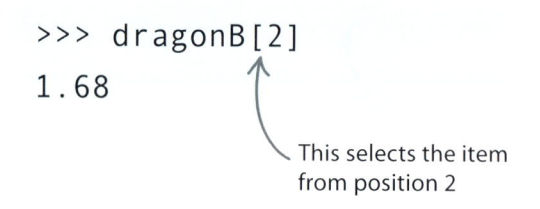

```
>>> dragonB[2]
1.68
```

This selects the item from position 2

```
>>> name, age, height = dragonA
>>> print(name, age, height)
Sam 15 1.7
```

The items that make up the tuple "dragonA" are displayed separately

◁ **Splitting a tuple into variables**
Assign three variables to the tuple "dragonA" – "name", "age", and "height". Python splits the tuple into three items, putting one in each variable.

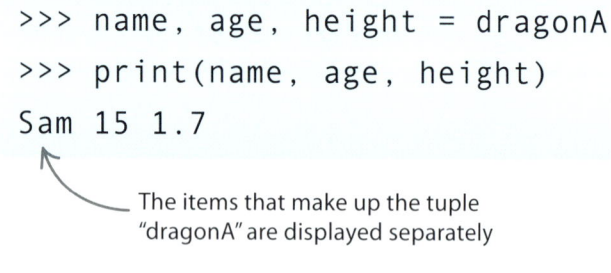

▷ **Putting tuples in a list**
Tuples can be put into a list because containers can go inside each other. Use this code to create a list of tuples.

Create a list of tuples called "dragons"

Lists go in square brackets

```
>>> dragons = [dragonA, dragonB]
>>> print(dragons)
[('Sam', 15, 1.7), ('Fiona', 16, 1.68)]
```

Each tuple is surrounded by round brackets inside the list's square brackets

Python displays all the items that are in the list, not just the names of the tuples

Dictionaries

Dictionaries are like lists but they have labels. These labels, called "keys", identify items instead of index numbers. Every item in a dictionary has a key and a value. Items in a dictionary don't have to stay in a particular order, and the contents of a dictionary can be changed.

▷ **Create a dictionary**
This program creates a dictionary called "age". The key for each item is the name of a person. The value is their age.

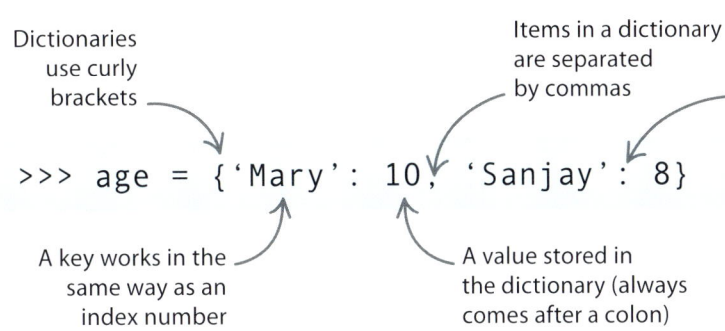

```
>>> age = {'Mary': 10, 'Sanjay': 8}
```

- Dictionaries use curly brackets
- A key works in the same way as an index number
- Items in a dictionary are separated by commas
- A value stored in the dictionary (always comes after a colon)
- Use a colon between a key and a value

```
>>> print(age)
{'Sanjay': 8, 'Mary': 10}
```

- Name of the dictionary
- The key for this item is 'Sanjay'
- The value of 'Mary' is 10

◁ **Print the dictionary**
The order of the items can change, because the positions of items in a dictionary are not fixed.

▷ **Add a new item**
A new value can be added to the dictionary by labelling it with the new key.

```
>>> age['Owen'] = 11
>>> print(age)
{'Owen': 11, 'Sanjay': 8, 'Mary': 10}
```

- Dictionary name
- New key
- Adds a new item to the dictionary
- The new value is now in the dictionary
- The existing values are still there

```
>>> age['Owen'] = 12
>>> print(age)
{'Owen': 12, 'Sanjay': 8, 'Mary': 10}
```

- Assign a new value to the item labelled 'Owen'
- The value for 'Owen' has changed

◁ **Change a value**
Assign a new value to an existing key to change its value.

▷ **Delete an item**
Deleting an item in a dictionary doesn't affect other items because they are identified by their key, not by their position in the dictionary.

```
>>> del age['Owen']
>>> print(age)
{'Sanjay': 8, 'Mary': 10}
```

- This deletes the item labelled 'Owen'
- The item labelled 'Owen' no longer appears in the dictionary

Lists in variables

There's something about how Python stores lists in variables that might seem a bit odd at first. But take a look at what's going on behind the scenes and it all makes sense.

> **SEE ALSO**
>
> ‹ **104–105** Variables in Python
>
> ‹ **124–125** Lists

Remember how variables only store values?

Variables are like boxes that hold values. The value in one variable can be copied and stored in another. It's like photocopying the value contained in box "a" and storing a copy in box "b".

△ **How variables work**
Each variable is like a box containing a piece of paper with a value written on it.

1 **Assign a value to a variable**
Assign the value 2 to variable "a", then assign the value in "a" to variable "b". The value 2 is copied and stored in "b".

```
>>> a = 2
>>> b = a
>>> print('a =', a, 'b =', b)
a = 2 b = 2
```

This copies the contents of "a" into "b"

Now "a" and "b" both contain the value 2

This prints out the variable names with their values

2 **Change a value**
If you change the value stored in one variable it won't affect the value stored in another variable. In the same way changing what's written on a piece of paper in box "a" won't affect what's on the paper in box "b".

```
>>> a = 100
>>> print('a =', a, 'b =', b)
a = 100 b = 2
```

Change the value in "a" to 100

Now "a" contains 100, but "b" still contains 2

3 **Change a different value**
Change the value in "b" to 22. Variable "a" still contains 100. Even though the value of "b" was copied from "a" at the start, they are now independent – changing "b" doesn't change "a".

```
>>> b = 22
>>> print('a =', a, 'b =', b)
a = 100 b = 22
```

"b" now contains 22, but "a" is still 100

What happens if a list is put in a variable?

Copying the value in a variable creates two independent copies of the value. This works if the value is a number, but what about other types of value? If a variable contains a list it works a bit differently.

1 Copy a list
Store the list [1, 2, 3] in a variable called "listA". Then store the value of "listA" in another variable called "listB". Now both variables contain [1, 2, 3].

Use square brackets to create a list

This prints out the variable names alongside their values to see what's inside them

```
>>> listA = [1, 2, 3]
>>> listB = listA
>>> print('listA =', listA, 'listB =', listB)
listA = [1, 2, 3] listB = [1, 2, 3]
```

"listA" and "listB" both hold the same value

This changes the second item in the list because lists count from zero

2 Change list A
Change the value in "listA[1]" to 1000. "listB[1]" now contains 1000 as well. Changing the original list has changed the copy of the list too.

```
>>> listA[1] = 1000
>>> print('listA =', listA, 'listB =', listB)
listA = [1, 1000, 3] listB = [1, 1000, 3]
```

The second item of both "listA" and "listB" has been changed

This is the third item in the list

3 Change list B
Change the value of "listB[2]" to 75. "listA[2]" is now 75 as well. Changing the copy of the list has changed the original list as well.

```
>>> listB[2] = 75
>>> print('listA =', listA, 'listB =', listB)
listA = [1, 1000, 75] listB = [1, 1000, 75]
```

The third item of both "listA" and "listB" has been changed

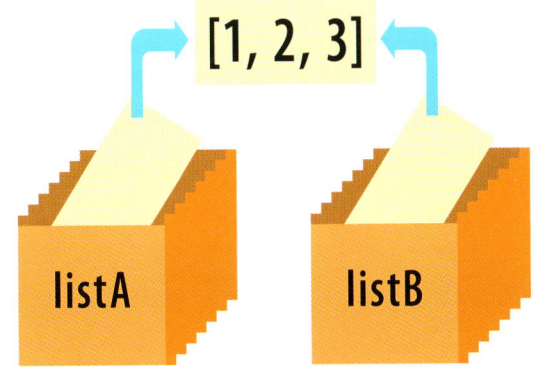

△ **What's going on?**
A variable containing a list doesn't hold the list itself, just a link to it. Copying the value in "listA" copies the link. So both "listA" and "listB" contain a link to the same list.

EXPERT TIPS
Copying lists

To make a separate copy of a list, use the "copy" function. "listC" will contain a link to a completely new list whose values are copies of those in "listA". Changing "listC" won't change "listA", and changing "listA" won't change "listC".

```
>>> listC = listA.copy()
```

Variables and functions

Variables created inside a function (local variables) and variables created in the main program (global variables) work in different ways.

SEE ALSO
‹ 126–127 Functions
Making 154–155 › shapes

Local variables

Local variables only exist inside a single function, so the main program and other functions can't use them. If you try to use a local variable outside of the function, an error message appears.

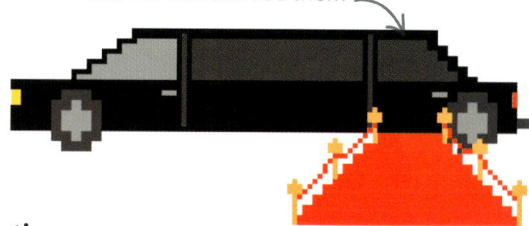

Local variables are like film stars in a car with mirrored windows – they are inside the car (function) but no one can see them

1 Variable inside the function
Create a local variable called "a" inside "func1". Print out the value of "a" by calling "func1" from the main program.

```
>>> def func1():
        a = 10
        print(a)
>>> func1()     Calling "func1"
10              prints the value
                given to "a"
```

2 Variable outside the function
If you try to print "a" directly from the main program, it gives an error. "a" only exists inside "func1".

```
>>> print(a)
Traceback (most recent call last):
  File "<pyshell#6>", line 1, in <module>
    print(a)
NameError: name 'a' is not defined
```

The main program doesn't know what "a" is, so it prints an error message

Global variables

A variable created in the main program is called a global variable. Other functions can read it, but they can't change its value.

1 Variable outside the function
Create a global variable called "b" in the main program. The new function ("func2") can read the value of "b" and print it.

```
>>> b = 1000
>>> def func2():
        print(b)
>>> func2()
1000
```

"func2" can see the value of "b" because "b" is a global variable

Printing "func2" gives you the value stored in "b"

2 Same global variable
We can also print "b" directly from the main program. "b" can be seen everywhere because it wasn't created inside a function.

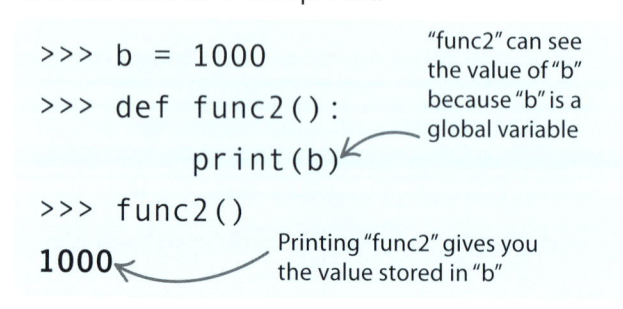

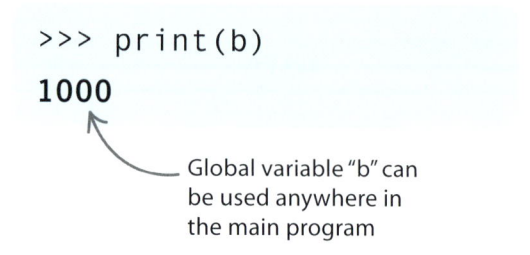

```
>>> print(b)
1000
```

Global variables are like people walking along the street – everyone can see them

Global variable "b" can be used anywhere in the main program

Variables as input to functions

When a variable is used as input to a function its value is copied into a new local variable. So changing the value of this new local variable inside the function doesn't change the value of the original variable.

1 Changing values inside a variable
"func3" uses input "y", which is a local variable. It prints the value of "y", then changes that value to "bread" and prints the new value.

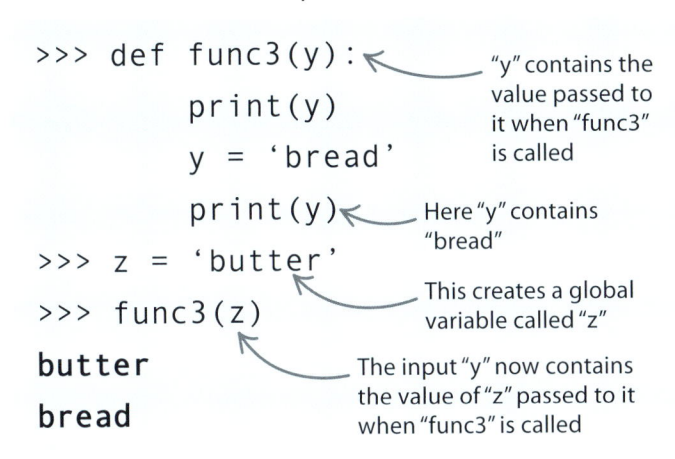

```
>>> def func3(y):
        print(y)
        y = 'bread'
        print(y)
>>> z = 'butter'
>>> func3(z)
butter
bread
```

- "y" contains the value passed to it when "func3" is called
- Here "y" contains "bread"
- This creates a global variable called "z"
- The input "y" now contains the value of "z" passed to it when "func3" is called

2 Print variable
Printing the value of "z" after calling "func3" shows it hasn't changed. Calling "func3" copies the value in "z" ("butter") into local variable "y", but "z" is left unchanged.

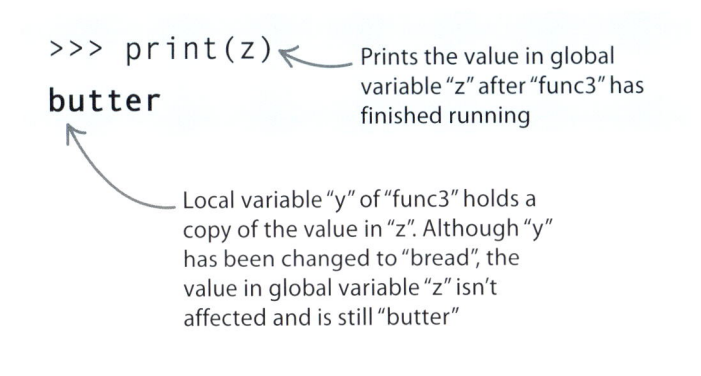

```
>>> print(z)
butter
```

- Prints the value in global variable "z" after "func3" has finished running
- Local variable "y" of "func3" holds a copy of the value in "z". Although "y" has been changed to "bread", the value in global variable "z" isn't affected and is still "butter"

Masking a global variable

A global variable can't be changed by a function. A function trying to change a global variable actually creates a local variable with the same name. It covers up, or "masks", the global variable with a local version.

1 Changing a global variable
Global variable "c" is given the value 12345. "func4" gives "c" the value 555 and prints it out. It looks like our global variable "c" has been changed.

```
>>> c = 12345
>>> def func4():
        c = 555
        print(c)
>>> func4()
555
```

- Initial value in global variable "c"
- Prints the value of "c" inside "func4"

2 Print variable
If we print "c" from outside the function, we see that "c" hasn't changed at all. "func4" only prints the value of its new local variable – also called "c".

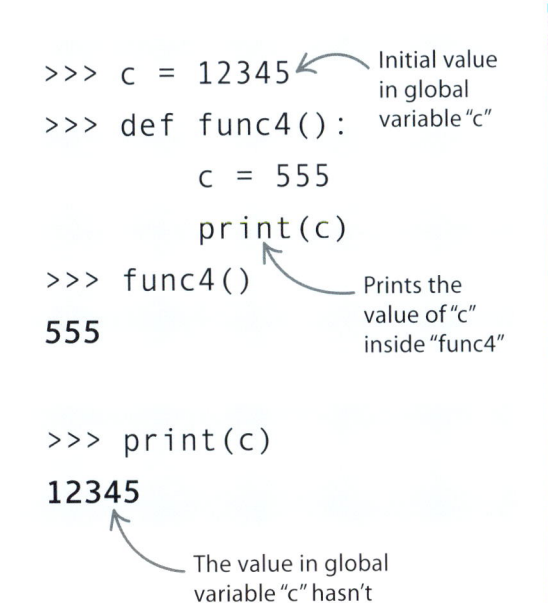

```
>>> print(c)
12345
```

- The value in global variable "c" hasn't been changed

> **EXPERT TIPS**
> ### Calling functions
> There are two different ways of calling functions.
>
> **function(a)**
>
> In Python, items of data are called "objects". Some functions are called by passing them the data object ("a").
>
> **a.function()**
>
> Other functions are called by adding their name at the end of the data object ("a") after a full stop.

PROJECT 6

Drawing machine

It's time to try a more complex project. This program, the drawing machine, turns a string of simple instructions into turtle commands to draw different shapes. The skills used in planning this program are essential for any coder.

> **SEE ALSO**
> ‹ 118–119 Loops in Python
> Libraries 148–149 ›

Choose a test shape

To write a program that can draw any shape, it's useful to choose a shape to start with. Use this house shape as an example to test the program at each stage. By the end of the project it will be possible to draw this house with far less code – by using a single string containing several short drawing commands (for example, "F100").

```
from turtle import *
reset()
left(90)
forward(100)
right(45)
forward(70)
right(90)
forward(70)
right(45)
forward(100)
right(90)
forward(100)
```

- Loads all the commands that control the turtle
- Resets the turtle's position and puts the pen down ready to draw
- Moves the turtle forward by 70
- Makes the turtle turn 90 degrees to the right

▷ **Turtle draws a house**
The arrow shows the final direction and position of the turtle. Starting at the bottom left, it has moved clockwise around the house.

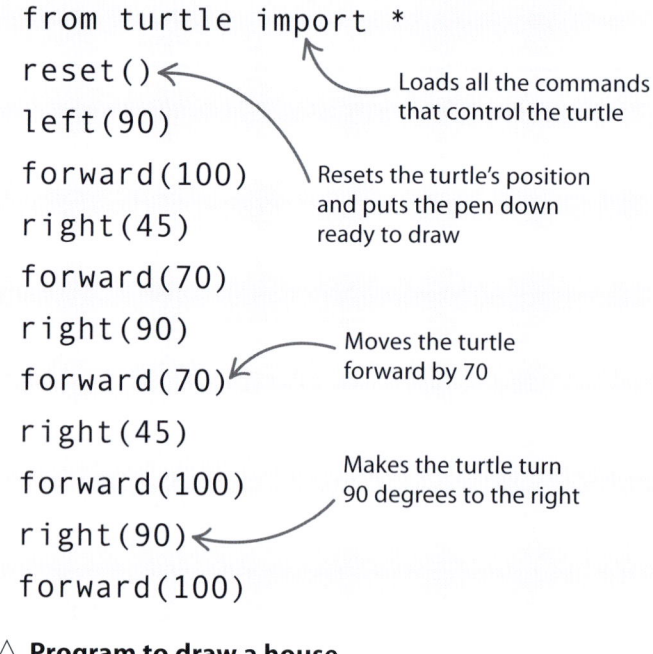

The turtle

△ **Program to draw a house**
This code tells the turtle to draw a house. It requires lots of lines of code for what is actually quite a simple program.

Three parts of the program

The drawing machine will be a large program. To help with the planning, it can be broken down into three parts, each one related to a different task.

Function 1

△ **Turtle controller**
This function takes a simple command from the user and turns it into a turtle command. The user command will come as a single letter and a number.

Function 2

△ **String artist**
In this program, the user enters a string of instructions. This function splits the string into smaller units, which are then fed to the Turtle controller.

Main program

△ **User interface**
The String artist needs to get its input from somewhere. The User interface allows the user to type in a string of commands for the String artist to work on.

DRAWING MACHINE 137

Draw a flowchart

Coders often plan programs on paper, to help them write better code with fewer errors. One way to plan is to draw a flowchart – a diagram of the steps and decisions that the program needs to follow.

1 ▶ This flowchart shows the plan for the Turtle controller function. It takes a letter (input "do") and number (input "val") and turns them into a turtle command. For example, "F" and "100" will be turned into the command "forward(100)". If the function doesn't recognize the letter, it reports an error to the user.

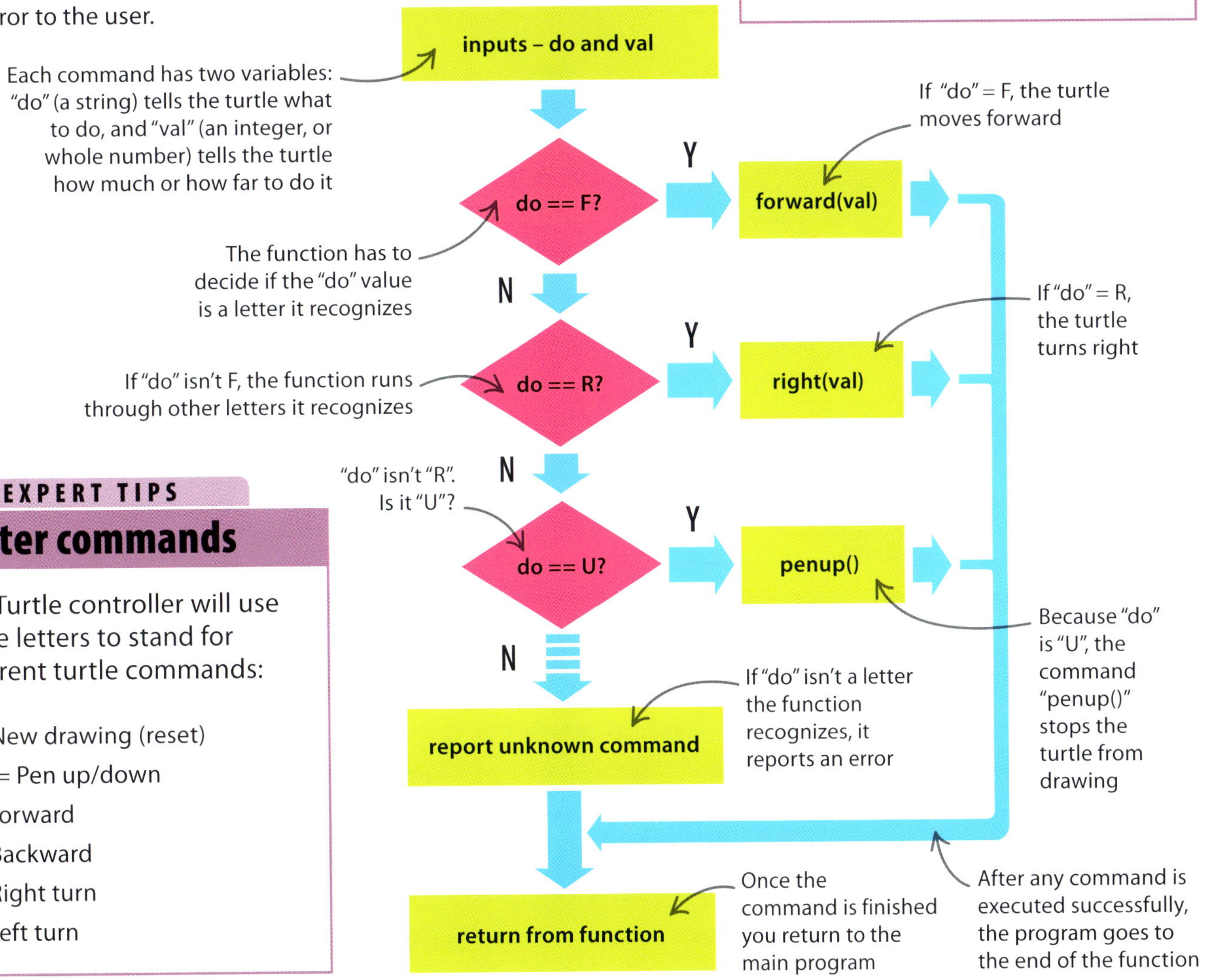

Each command has two variables: "do" (a string) tells the turtle what to do, and "val" (an integer, or whole number) tells the turtle how much or how far to do it

The function has to decide if the "do" value is a letter it recognizes

If "do" isn't F, the function runs through other letters it recognizes

"do" isn't "R". Is it "U"?

EXPERT TIPS
Squares and diamonds

Flowcharts are made up of squares and diamonds. The squares contain actions that the program performs. The diamonds are points where it makes a decision.

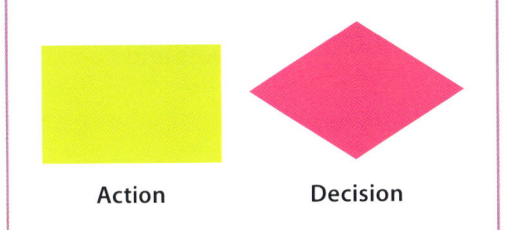

Action   Decision

inputs – do and val

do == F? Y → forward(val)   If "do" = F, the turtle moves forward

N

do == R? Y → right(val)   If "do" = R, the turtle turns right

N

do == U? Y → penup()   Because "do" is "U", the command "penup()" stops the turtle from drawing

N

report unknown command   If "do" isn't a letter the function recognizes, it reports an error

return from function   Once the command is finished you return to the main program

After any command is executed successfully, the program goes to the end of the function

EXPERT TIPS
Letter commands

The Turtle controller will use these letters to stand for different turtle commands:

N = New drawing (reset)
U/D = Pen up/down
F = Forward
B = Backward
R = Right turn
L = Left turn

DRAWING MACHINE

The Turtle controller

The first part of the program is a function that moves the turtle, one command at a time. It is planned out in the flowchart on the previous page. This code enables the turtle to convert the "do" and "val" values into movement commands.

2 ▸ This code creates the Turtle controller function. It turns "do" inputs into directions for the turtle, and "val" inputs into angles and distances.

```python
from turtle import *
def turtle_controller(do, val):
    do = do.upper()
    if do == 'F':
        forward(val)
    elif do == 'B':
        backward(val)
    elif do == 'R':
        right(val)
    elif do == 'L':
        left(val)
    elif do == 'U':
        penup()
    elif do == 'D':
        pendown()
    elif do == 'N':
        reset()
    else:
        print('Unrecognized command')
```

- Loads all the commands that control the turtle
- Defines "do" and "val" as inputs for the function
- This command converts all the letters in "do" to upper case (capital letters)
- This tells the function to turn a "do" value of F into the turtle command "forward"
- As in the flowchart, the function checks the "do" letter against all the letters it understands
- This command tells the turtle to start drawing on the page
- This command instructs the turtle to stop drawing on the page
- This command resets the turtle's position to the centre of the screen
- This message appears if the "do" value is a letter that the function cannot recognise

The starting position of the turtle

3 ▸ Here are some examples of how to use the Turtle controller. Each time it is used, it takes a "do, val" command and turns it into code the turtle can understand.

```
>>> turtle_controller('F', 100)
>>> turtle_controller('R', 90)
>>> turtle_controller('F', 50)
```

- This calls the function using its name
- These "do" and "val" inputs tell the turtle to move 100 steps forward
- This makes the turtle turn right 90 degrees

DRAWING MACHINE   139

Write some pseudocode

Another way to plan a program is to write it in pseudocode. "Pseudo" means fake, so pseudocode isn't real code that you can run. It's rough code where you can write your ideas in the style of the real thing.

4 ▸ It's time to plan the String artist. This function takes a string of several "do" and "val" inputs and breaks it into pairs made up of a letter and a number. It then passes the pairs to the Turtle controller one at a time.

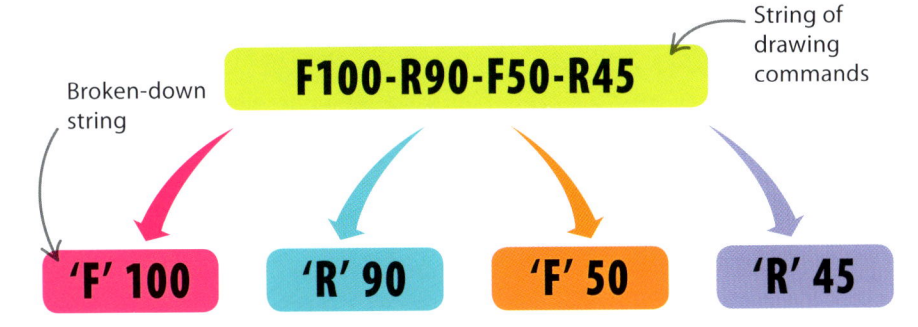

Broken-down string

F100-R90-F50-R45 ← String of drawing commands

'F' 100   'R' 90   'F' 50   'R' 45

5 ▸ This is the String artist written in pseudocode. It lets you organize the ideas and structure of the code without having to think about the details yet.

◦◦ EXPERT TIPS
Clear coding

It's not only computers that need to be able to read your code, it should be clear to people too. So it's important to make your code as easy to understand as possible.

Use functions to break your code into smaller chunks. Each function should do a single task in the program.

Give your variables and functions names that say what they do: "age_in_years" makes more sense than "aiy".

Use plenty of comments (using the "#" symbol) to explain what's happening. This makes it easier to read back over the code.

Don't use symbols that can be confused with others: an upper-case "O" looks like zero, and a lower-case "L" can look like an upper-case "i" or a "1".

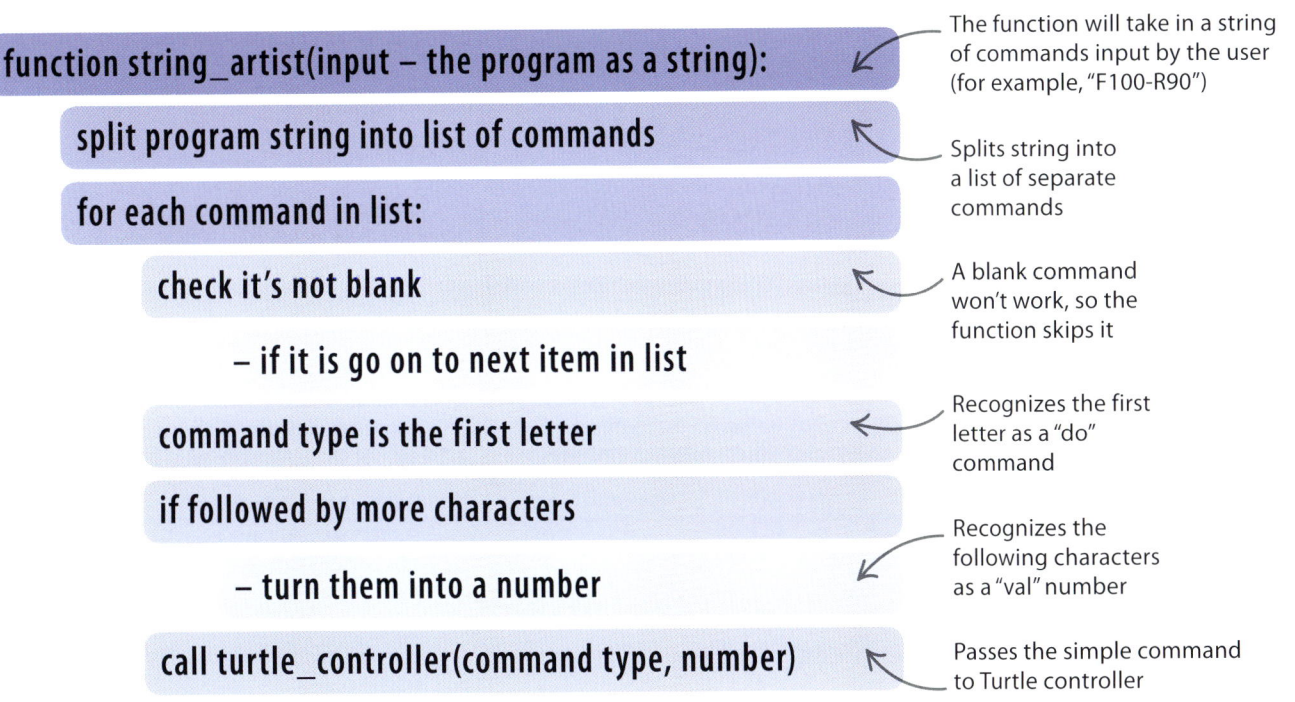

---

function string_artist(input – the program as a string): ← The function will take in a string of commands input by the user (for example, "F100-R90")

   split program string into list of commands ← Splits string into a list of separate commands

   for each command in list:

      check it's not blank ← A blank command won't work, so the function skips it

         – if it is go on to next item in list

      command type is the first letter ← Recognizes the first letter as a "do" command

      if followed by more characters

         – turn them into a number ← Recognizes the following characters as a "val" number

      call turtle_controller(command type, number) ← Passes the simple command to Turtle controller

140 PLAYING WITH PYTHON

▶ DRAWING MACHINE

Creating the String artist

The pseudocode on the previous page plans a function called the String artist, which will turn a string of values into single commands that are sent to the Turtle controller. The next stage is to turn the pseudocode into real Python code, using a function called "split()".

6. The "split()" function splits a string into a list of smaller strings. Each break point is marked by a special character ("-" in this program).

This string lists the commands to create the sample house shape

```
>>> program = 'N-L90-F100-R45-F70-R90-F70-R45-F100-R90-F100'
>>> cmd_list = program.split('-')
>>> cmd_list
['N', 'L90', 'F100', 'R45', 'F70', 'R90', 'F70', 'R45', 'F100', 'R90', 'F100']
```

The "split()" function breaks the string down into a list of separate commands

7. Now write out the pseudocode for the String artist using real Python code. Use the "split()" function to slice up the input string into turtle commands.

Tells the program to split the string wherever it sees a "-" character

This makes the program loop through the list of strings – each item is one command for the turtle

```
def string_artist(program):
    cmd_list = program.split('-')
    for command in cmd_list:
        cmd_len = len(command)
        if cmd_len == 0:
            continue
        cmd_type = command[0]
        num = 0
        if cmd_len > 1:
            num_string = command[1:]
            num = int(num_string)
        print(command, ':', cmd_type, num)
        turtle_controller(cmd_type, num)
```

If the length of the command is 0 (so the command is blank), the function skips it and moves to the next one

Gets the length of the command string

Takes the first character of the command (remember, strings start at 0) and sets it as the command type ("F", "U", etc.)

Checks if the command is followed by more characters (the number)

This takes all the remaining characters from the command by cutting off the first one

Converts the characters from strings into numbers

Prints the command on the screen so you can see what the code is doing

Passes the command to the turtle

DRAWING MACHINE | **141**

8 When the string representing the instructions for the house shape is passed into the String artist, it shows this output in the shell window.

```
>>> string_artist('N-L90-F100-R45-F70-R90-F70-R45-F100-R90-F100')
N : N 0
L90 : L 90
F100 : F 100
R45 : R 45
F70 : F 70
R90 : R 90
F70 : F 70
R45 : R 45
F100 : F 100
R90 : R 90
F100 : F 100
```

- N : N 0 — Resets the screen and puts the turtle back at the centre
- The turtle commands are all separated by a "-"
- For command "F100", the command type is "F" and "num" is "100"
- This makes the turtle turn 45 degrees before drawing the roof
- This command makes the turtle draw the right-hand side of the roof
- The turtle turns 90 degrees right, ready to draw the bottom of the house

9 Each command in the string that is passed to the "string_artist" function is extracted, identified, and executed. A picture of a house is drawn in the turtle graphics window.

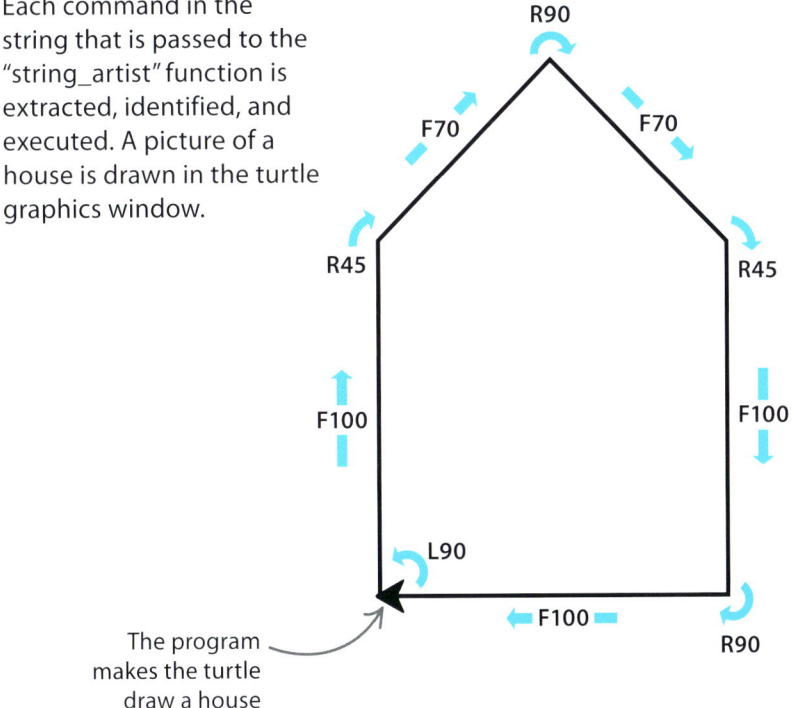

Diagram labels: R90, F70, F70, R45, R45, F100, F100, L90, F100, R90

The program makes the turtle draw a house

REMEMBER
Commands

Here's a reminder of the turtle commands in this program. Some of these are only one letter long, while others include a number telling the turtle how far to travel or turn. Each time you activate "string_artist", it adds to the drawing, until "N" clears the screen.

N = New drawing
U/D = Pen Up/Down
F100 = Forward 100
B50 = Backwards 50
R90 = Right turn 90 deg
L45 = Left turn 45 deg

DRAWING MACHINE

Finish off the code with a user interface

The drawing machine needs an interface to make it easier to use. This will let the user enter a string from the keyboard to tell the machine what to draw.

10 ▸ This code creates a pop-up window where the user can input instructions. A "while True" loop lets them keep entering new strings.

The triple quote (''') tells Python that everything until the next triple quote is part of the same string, including the line breaks

```
instructions = '''Enter a program for the turtle:
eg F100-R45-U-F100-L45-D-F100-R90-B50
N = New drawing
U/D = Pen Up/Down
F100 = Forward 100
B50 = Backwards 50
R90 = Right turn 90 deg
L45 = Left turn 45 deg'''
screen = getscreen()
while True:
    t_program = screen.textinput('Drawing Machine', instructions)
    print(t_program)
    if t_program == None or t_program.upper() == 'END':
        break
    string_artist(t_program)
```

Tells the user what letters to use for different turtle commands

End of the string

Gets the data needed to create the pop-up window

This line tells the program what to show in the pop-up window

Stops the program if the user types "END" or presses the "Cancel" button

Passes the string to the String artist function

11 ▸ This window pops up over the turtle window ready for the user to type a drawing machine program string.

Drawing Machine
Enter a program for the turtle:
eg F100-R45-U-F100-L45-D-F100-R90-B50
N = New drawing
U/D = Pen Up/Down
F100 = Forward 100
B50 = Backwards 50
R90 = Right turn 90 deg
L45 = Left turn 45 deg

[OK]   [Cancel]

Type the program string here and then click "OK" to run the program

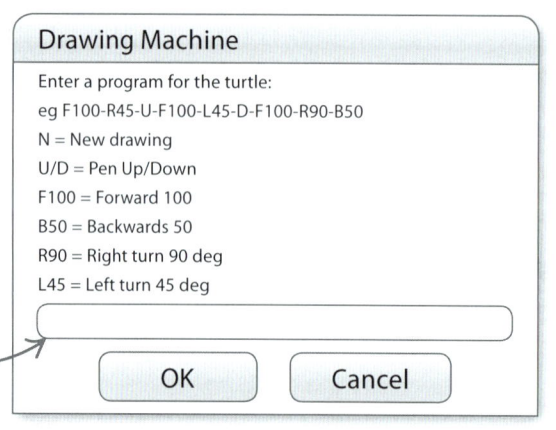

△ **Turtle control**
Using this program, the turtle is easier to control, and you don't have to restart the program to draw another picture.

DRAWING MACHINE 143

12 ▸ The drawing machine can be used to create more than just outlines. By lifting up the turtle's pen while moving to a new position, it's possible to fill in details inside a shape. Run the program and try entering the string below.

N-L90-F100-R45-F70-R90-F70-R45-F100-R90-F100-
B10-U-R90-F10-D-F30-R90-F30-R90-F30-R90-F30

Lifts up the turtle's pen so it moves without leaving a line

Puts the pen down to draw a window

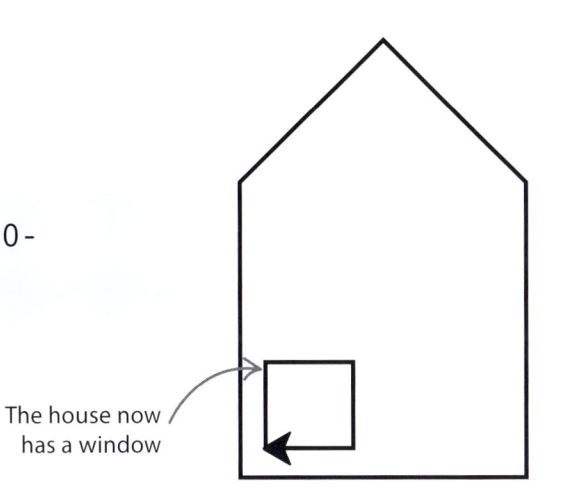

The house now has a window

Time for something different

Now you know how to add details, you can really have fun with the drawing machine. Try drawing this owl face using the string of instructions below.

N-F100-L90-F200-L90-F50-R60-F30-L120-F30-R60-F40-
R60-F30-L120-F30-R60-F50-L90-F200-L90-F100-L90-U-
F150-L90-F20-D-F30-L90-F30-L90-F30-L90-F30-R90-U-
F40-D-F30-R90-F30-R90-F30-R90-F30-L180-U-F60-R90-
D-F40-L120-F40-L120-F40

The string lifts the pen three times to draw the eyes and nose separately

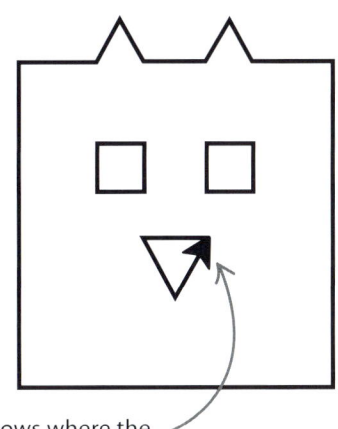

The arrow shows where the turtle stopped. This means that the owl's nose was drawn last

REMEMBER
Achievements

You created the drawing machine program by achieving several smaller targets:

Used a flowchart to plan a function by working out the decision points and the resulting actions.

Wrote pseudocode to plan out a function before writing out the real code.

Created the function "turtle_controller" that works out what turtle command to execute from the letter and number it's been given.

Created the function "string_artist" that produced a turtle drawing from a string of instructions.

Made an interface that allows the user to tell the program what to draw from the keyboard.

Bugs and debugging

Programmers aren't perfect, and most programs contain errors at first. These errors are known as "bugs" and tracking them down is called "debugging".

> **SEE ALSO**
> ‹ **90–91** Errors
> ‹ **118–119** Loops in Python
> What next? **172–173** ›

Types of bugs

Three main types of bugs can turn up in programs – syntax, runtime, and logic errors. Some are quite easy to spot, while others are more difficult, but there are ways of finding and fixing them all.

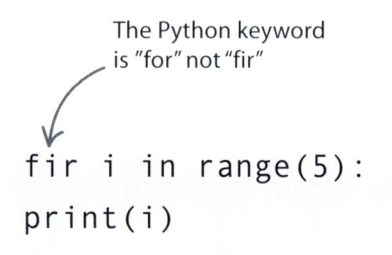

The Python keyword is "for" not "fir"

```
fir i in range(5):
    print(i)
```

This will cause an error as no number can be divided by 0

```
a = 0
print(10 / a)
```

Age cannot be less than 5 and greater than 8 at the same time, so no free tickets

```
if age < 5 and age > 8:
    print('Free ticket!')
```

△ **Easy to spot**
A syntax error is a mistake in the program's words or symbols, such as misspelled keywords, missing brackets, or incorrect indents.

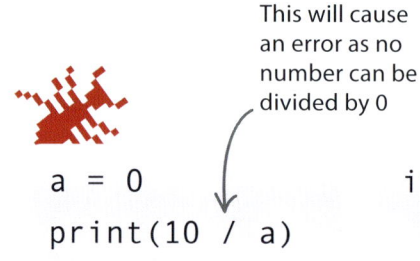

△ **Harder to spot**
Runtime errors appear only when the program is running. Adding numbers to strings or dividing by 0 can cause them.

△ **Hardest to spot**
Logic errors are mistakes in a program's thinking. Using "<" instead of ">", for example, or adding when you should be subtracting result in these errors.

Find and fix a bug

Syntax errors are easy to spot as IDLE highlights them in red when you run the program. Finding runtime and logic errors takes a bit more work.

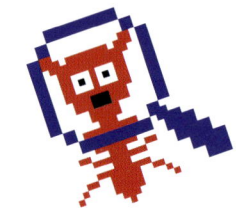

1 Problem program
This program aims to add all the numbers from 1 up to the value stored in the variable "top_num". It then prints the total.

```
top_num = 5
total = 0
for n in range(top_num):
    total = total + n
print('Sum of numbers 1 to', top_num, 'is', total)
```

The highest number in the series of numbers being added

This command prints a sentence to let the user know the result

2 Output
The answer for the program should be (1 + 2 + 3 + 4 + 5), but it shows the answer as "10". You need to find out why.

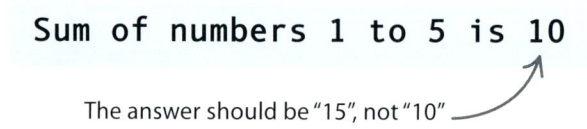

```
Sum of numbers 1 to 5 is 10
```

The answer should be "15", not "10"

BUGS AND DEBUGGING | **145**

3. Add a "print" and "input()"

The program doesn't show what it's doing at each step. Adding a "print" command here will let you see what's happening. The "input()" command waits for the "return" or "Enter" key to be pressed before looping.

```
top_num = 5
total = 0
for n in range(top_num):
    total = total + n
    print('DEBUG: n=', n, 'total=', total)
    input()
print('Sum of numbers 1 to', top_num, 'is', total)
```

This command prints the current value of the loop variable and the total so far

4. New output

The loop is only adding the numbers from 0 up to 4, and not 1 to 5. This is because a "for" loop always starts counting from 0 (unless told otherwise), and always stops 1 before the end of the range.

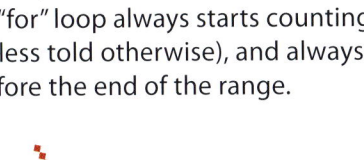

```
DEBUG: n= 0 total= 0
DEBUG: n= 1 total= 1
DEBUG: n= 2 total= 3
DEBUG: n= 3 total= 6
DEBUG: n= 4 total= 10
Sum of numbers 1 to 5 is 10
```

This is actually the sum of the numbers from 0 to 4, not 1 to 5

5. Fix the faulty line

The range should go from 1 up to "top_num + 1", so that the loop adds up the numbers from 1 to "top_num" (5).

```
top_num = 5
total = 0
for n in range(1, top_num + 1):
    total = total + n
    print('DEBUG: n=', n, 'total=', total)
    input()
print('Sum of numbers 1 to', top_num, 'is', total)
```

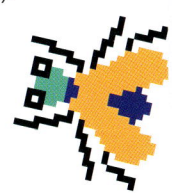

The new range will count from 1 and stop at "top_num" (1 less than "top_num + 1")

6. Correct output

The "print" command shows that the program is adding the numbers from 1 to 5 and getting the correct answer. The bug has now been fixed!

```
DEBUG: n= 1 total= 1
DEBUG: n= 2 total= 3
DEBUG: n= 3 total= 6
DEBUG: n= 4 total= 10
DEBUG: n= 5 total= 15
Sum of numbers 1 to 5 is 15
```

When "n= 3", the total is (1 + 2 + 3)

The correct answer is now printed

Algorithms

An algorithm is a set of instructions for performing a task. Some algorithms are more efficient than others and take less time or effort. Different types of algorithms can be used for simple tasks such as sorting a list of numbers.

> **SEE ALSO**
> ‹ 12–13 Think like a computer
> Libraries 148–149 ›

Insertion sort

Imagine you've been given your class's exam papers to put in order from the lowest to the highest mark. "Insertion sort" creates a sorted section at the top of the pile and then inserts each unsorted paper into the correct position.

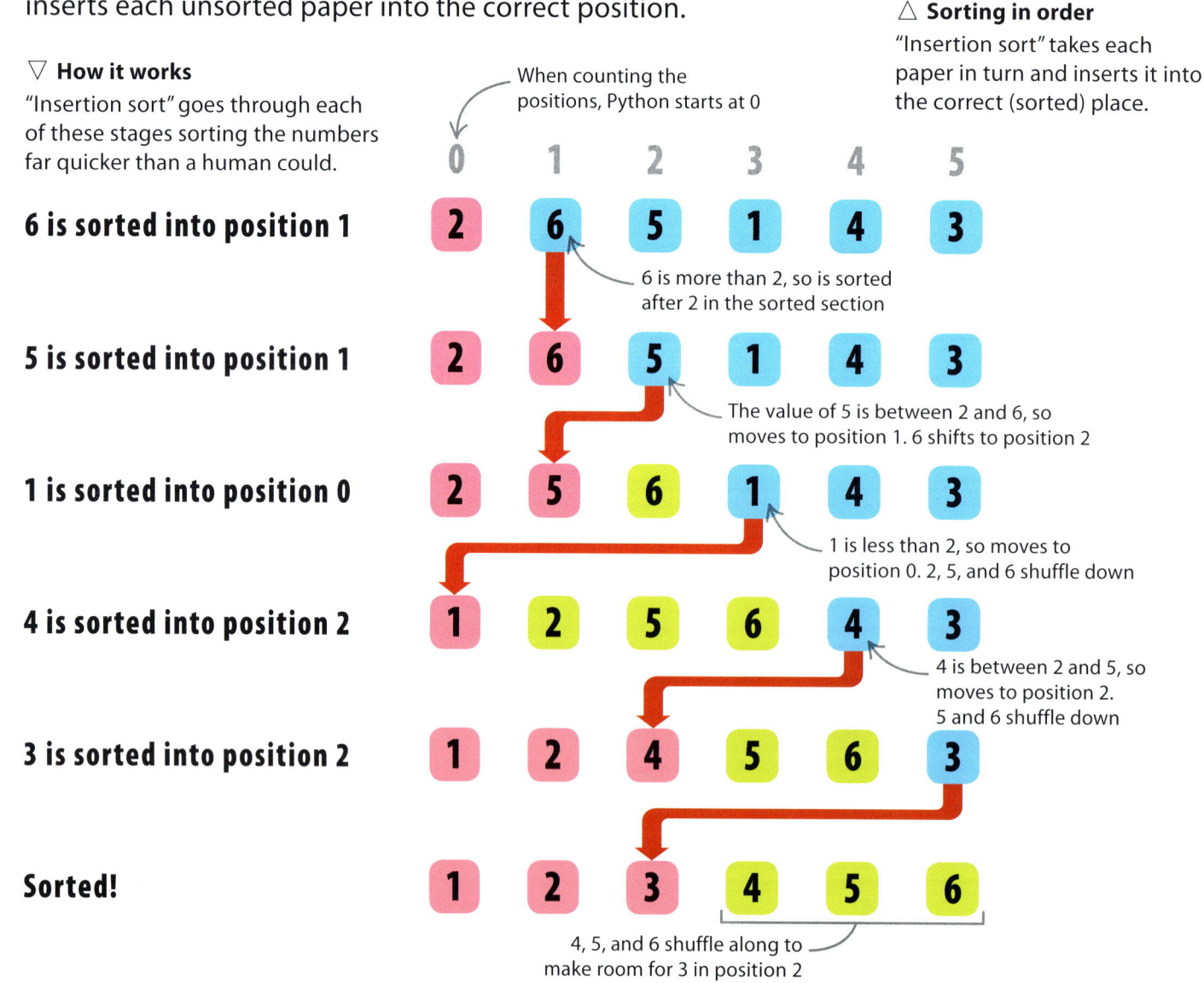

△ **Sorting in order**
"Insertion sort" takes each paper in turn and inserts it into the correct (sorted) place.

▽ **How it works**
"Insertion sort" goes through each of these stages sorting the numbers far quicker than a human could.

When counting the positions, Python starts at 0

0 1 2 3 4 5

6 is sorted into position 1
2 6 5 1 4 3
6 is more than 2, so is sorted after 2 in the sorted section

5 is sorted into position 1
2 6 5 1 4 3
The value of 5 is between 2 and 6, so moves to position 1. 6 shifts to position 2

1 is sorted into position 0
2 5 6 1 4 3
1 is less than 2, so moves to position 0. 2, 5, and 6 shuffle down

4 is sorted into position 2
1 2 5 6 4 3
4 is between 2 and 5, so moves to position 2. 5 and 6 shuffle down

3 is sorted into position 2
1 2 4 5 6 3

Sorted!
1 2 3 4 5 6
4, 5, and 6 shuffle along to make room for 3 in position 2

ALGORITHMS **147**

Selection sort

"Selection sort" works differently to "insertion sort". It swaps pairs of items rather than constantly shifting all of the items. Each swap moves one number to its final (sorted) position.

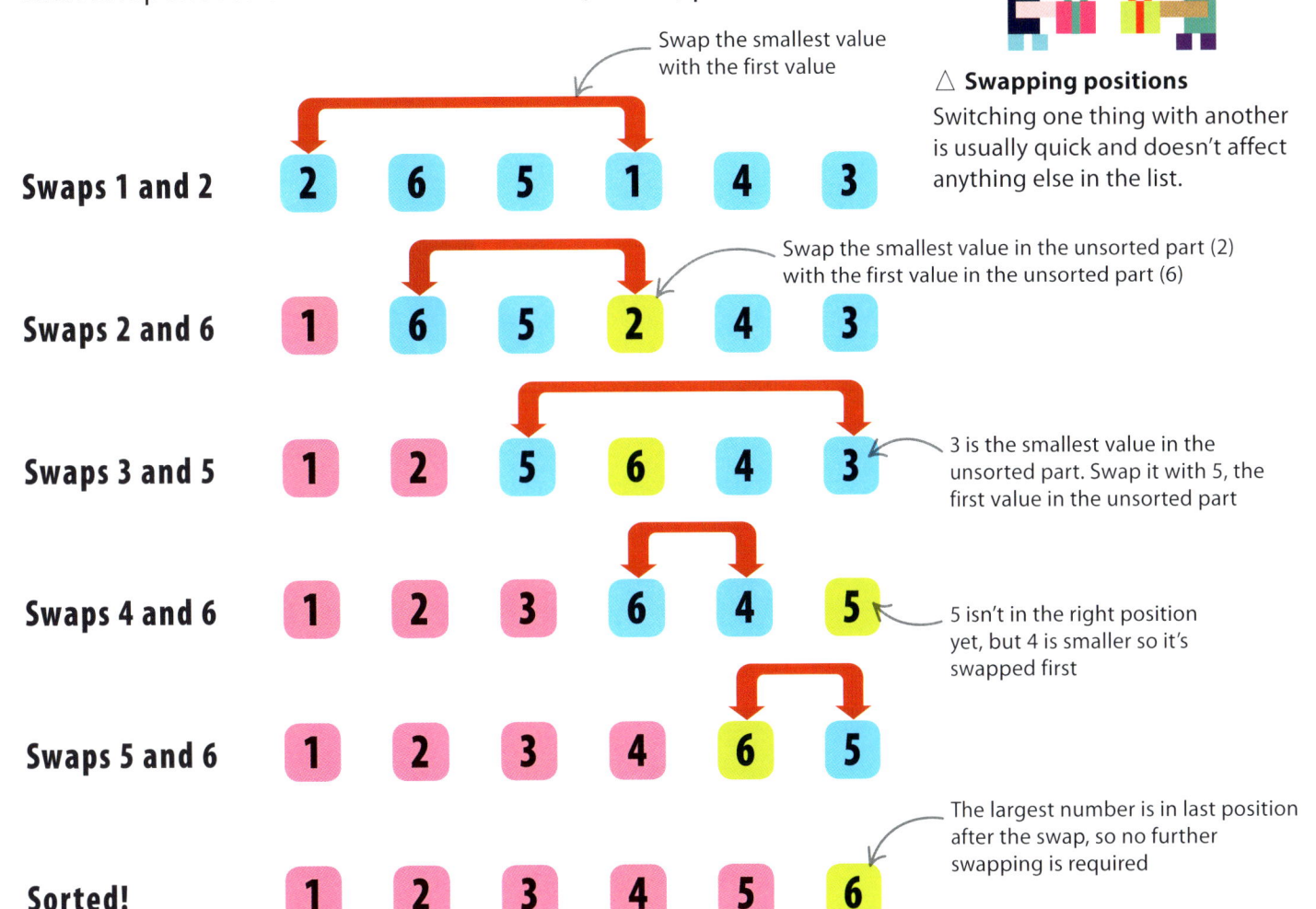

Swap the smallest value with the first value

△ **Swapping positions**
Switching one thing with another is usually quick and doesn't affect anything else in the list.

Swaps 1 and 2   2 6 5 1 4 3

Swap the smallest value in the unsorted part (2) with the first value in the unsorted part (6)

Swaps 2 and 6   1 6 5 2 4 3

Swaps 3 and 5   1 2 5 6 4 3

3 is the smallest value in the unsorted part. Swap it with 5, the first value in the unsorted part

Swaps 4 and 6   1 2 3 6 4 5

5 isn't in the right position yet, but 4 is smaller so it's swapped first

Swaps 5 and 6   1 2 3 4 6 5

The largest number is in last position after the swap, so no further swapping is required

Sorted!   1 2 3 4 5 6

EXPERT TIPS
Sorting in Python

There are lots of different sorting algorithms, each with different strengths and weaknesses. Python's "sort()" function uses an algorithm called "Timsort", named after its designer, Tim Peters. It's based on two sorting algorithms: "Insertion sort" and "Merge sort". Type in this code to see how it works.

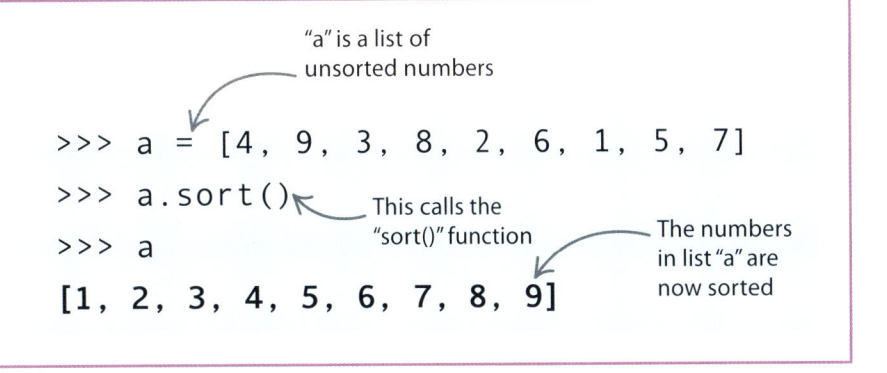

"a" is a list of unsorted numbers

```
>>> a = [4, 9, 3, 8, 2, 6, 1, 5, 7]
>>> a.sort()
>>> a
[1, 2, 3, 4, 5, 6, 7, 8, 9]
```

This calls the "sort()" function

The numbers in list "a" are now sorted

Libraries

Writing new code takes time, so it's useful to be able to reuse bits of other programs. These snippets of code can be shared in packages called "libraries".

> **SEE ALSO**
> Making **150–151** ❯
> windows
> Colour and **152–153** ❯
> co-ordinates

Standard Library modules

Python comes with a "Standard Library" that has lots of useful bits of code ready to use. Stand-alone sections of a library called "modules" can be added to Python to make it even more powerful.

◁ **Batteries included**
Python's motto is "batteries are included". This means it comes with lots of ready-to-use code.

◁ **Random**
This module can pick a random number, or shuffle a list into a random order.

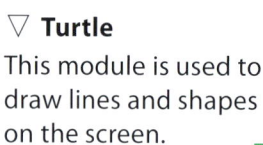

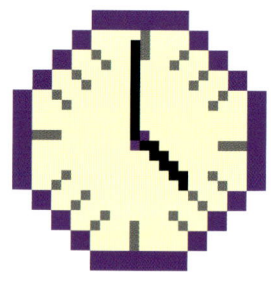

▽ **Turtle**
This module is used to draw lines and shapes on the screen.

△ **Time**
The Time module gives the current time and date, and can calculate dates – for instance, what day will it be in three days' time?

▽ **Tkinter**
Tkinter is used to make buttons, windows, and other graphics that help users interact with programs.

△ **Socket**
The code in this module helps computers connect to each other over networks and the Internet.

▷ **Math**
Use the Math module to work with complex mathematical calculations.

LIBRARIES 149

Importing modules

Before using a module, you have to tell the computer to import it so it can be used by your program. This allows the bits of code it contains to be available to you. Importing modules is done using the "import" command. Python can import modules in a few different ways.

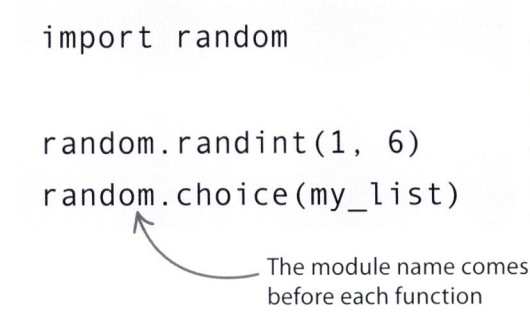

```
import random

random.randint(1, 6)
random.choice(my_list)
```

◁ **"import random"**
This way of importing requires you to type the module name at the start of the code. It makes it easier to read because you know which module it came from.

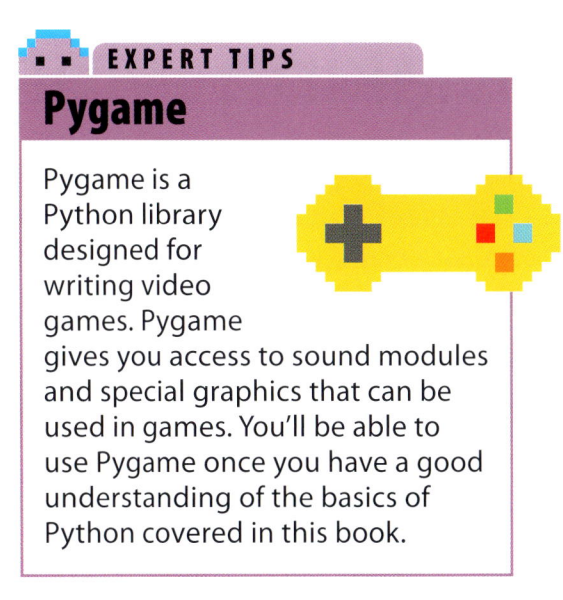

The module name comes before each function

> **EXPERT TIPS**
> ### Pygame
> Pygame is a Python library designed for writing video games. Pygame gives you access to sound modules and special graphics that can be used in games. You'll be able to use Pygame once you have a good understanding of the basics of Python covered in this book.

▷ **"from random import *"**
Importing a module like this works well for small programs. But it can get confusing with bigger programs, as it isn't clear which module the function belongs to.

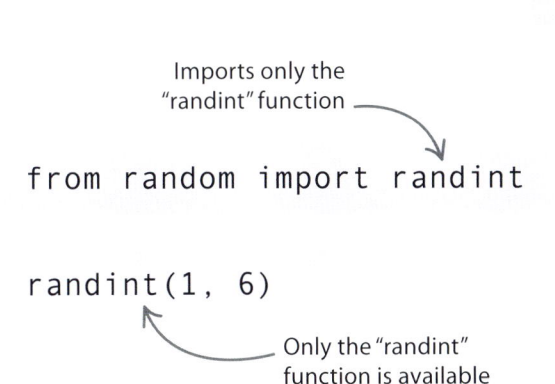

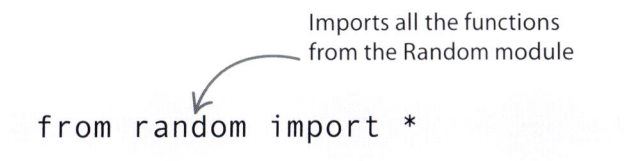

Imports all the functions from the Random module

```
from random import *

randint(1, 6)
choice(my_list)
```

This code doesn't show which module the function came from

Imports only the "randint" function

```
from random import randint

randint(1, 6)
```

Only the "randint" function is available

◁ **"from random import randint"**
You can import a single function from the module. This can be more efficient than importing the whole module if it's the only function you want to use.

Help and documentation

Not sure how to use a module or what functions are available? The Python Library Reference has all the details. Simply click on the library you want to learn more about. It's a good idea to get to know the libraries, modules, and functions that are available, so you don't waste time writing code that already exists.

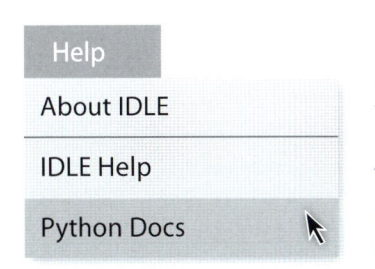

Help
About IDLE
IDLE Help
Python Docs

◁ **Help!**
At the top of any IDLE window, click "Help" and choose "Python Docs". This brings up a window with lots of useful information.

Making windows

Many programs have windows and buttons that can be used to control them. These make up the "graphical user interface", or "GUI" (pronounced "gooey").

> **SEE ALSO**
> Colour and **152–153** ›
> co-ordinates
> Making **154–155** ›
> shapes
> Changing **156–157** ›
> things

Make a simple window

The first step in creating a GUI is to make the window that will hold everything else inside it. Tkinter (from Python's Standard Library) can be used to create a simple one.

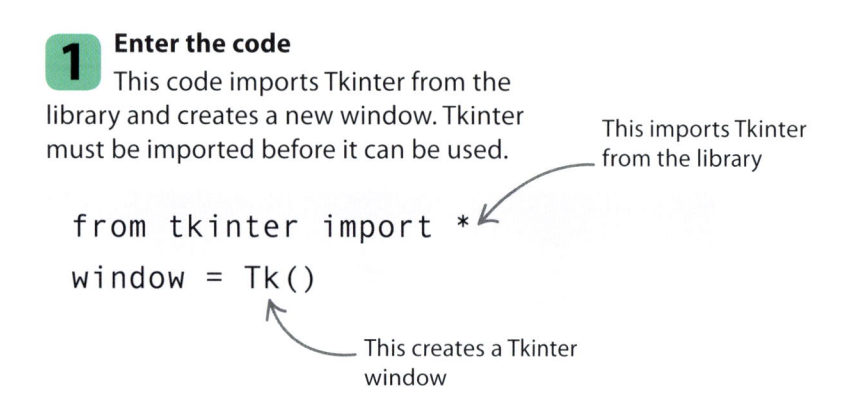

1 Enter the code
This code imports Tkinter from the library and creates a new window. Tkinter must be imported before it can be used.

```
from tkinter import *
window = Tk()
```

This imports Tkinter from the library

This creates a Tkinter window

2 A Tkinter window appears
Run the code and a window appears. It looks a bit dull for now, but this is only the first part of your GUI.

Add buttons to the window

Make the GUI more interactive by adding buttons. A different message will be displayed when the user clicks each button.

1 Create two buttons
Write this code to create a simple window with two buttons.

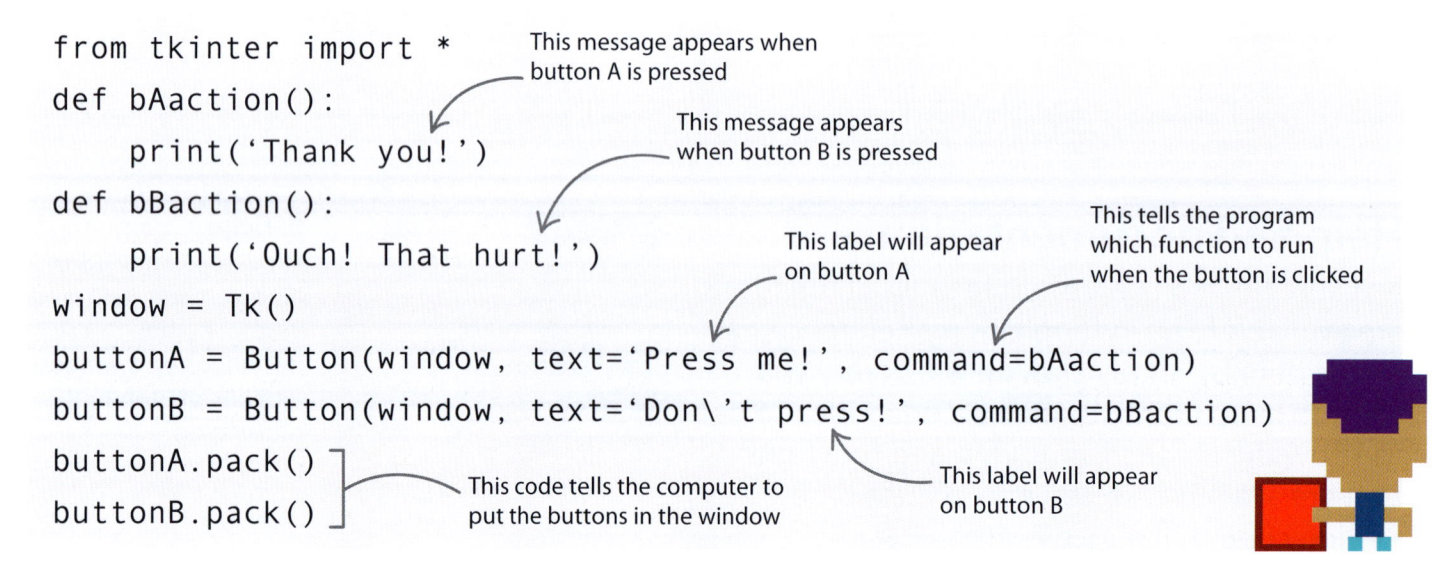

```
from tkinter import *
def bAaction():
    print('Thank you!')
def bBaction():
    print('Ouch! That hurt!')
window = Tk()
buttonA = Button(window, text='Press me!', command=bAaction)
buttonB = Button(window, text='Don\'t press!', command=bBaction)
buttonA.pack()
buttonB.pack()
```

This message appears when button A is pressed

This message appears when button B is pressed

This label will appear on button A

This tells the program which function to run when the button is clicked

This label will appear on button B

This code tells the computer to put the buttons in the window

MAKING WINDOWS **151**

2 Click the buttons to print messages

When the program is run, a window with two buttons appears. Click the buttons and different messages will appear in the shell. You've now made an interactive GUI that responds to the user's commands.

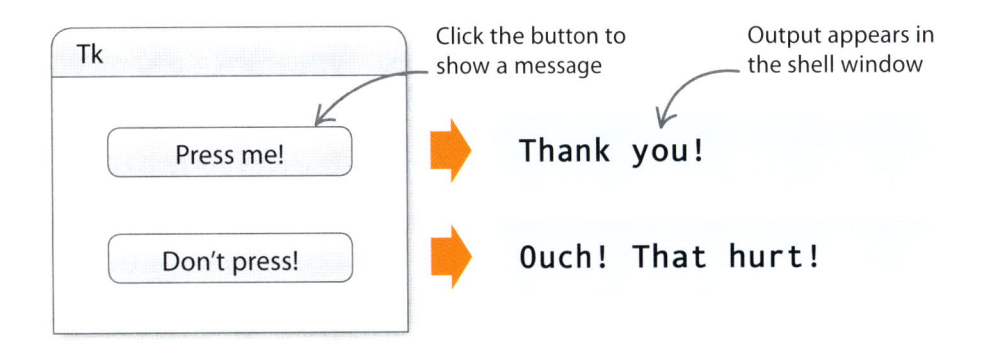

```
Tk
    Press me!         →    Thank you!
    Don't press!      →    Ouch! That hurt!
```

Click the button to show a message
Output appears in the shell window

Roll the dice

Tkinter can be used to build a GUI for a simple application. The code below creates a program that simulates rolling a six-sided dice.

1 Create a dice simulator
This program creates a button that, when pressed, tells the function "roll()" to display a random number between 1 and 6.

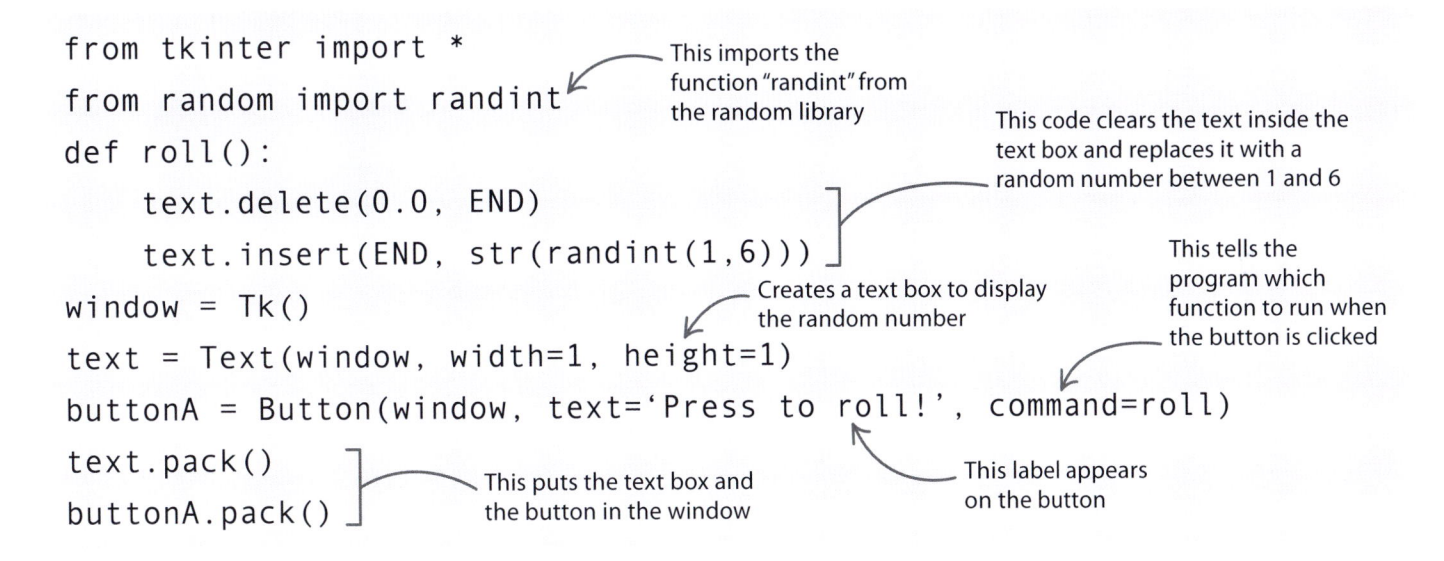

```
from tkinter import *
from random import randint
def roll():
    text.delete(0.0, END)
    text.insert(END, str(randint(1,6)))
window = Tk()
text = Text(window, width=1, height=1)
buttonA = Button(window, text='Press to roll!', command=roll)
text.pack()
buttonA.pack()
```

This imports the function "randint" from the random library

This code clears the text inside the text box and replaces it with a random number between 1 and 6

Creates a text box to display the random number

This tells the program which function to run when the button is clicked

This label appears on the button

This puts the text box and the button in the window

2 Press the button to roll the dice

Run the program, then click the button to roll the dice and see the result. This program can be simply changed so that it simulates a 12-sided dice, or a coin being tossed.

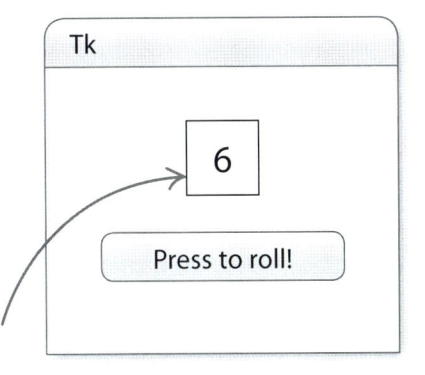

A new number appears here each time the button is clicked

```
Tk
       6
  Press to roll!
```

EXPERT TIPS
Clear and simple

When you're designing a GUI, try not to confuse the user by filling the screen with too many buttons. Label each button with a sensible name to make the application easy to understand.

Colour and co-ordinates

Pictures and graphics on a computer screen are made up of tiny coloured dots called pixels. To create graphics in a program, the computer needs to be told exactly what colour each pixel should be.

> **SEE ALSO**
> ‹ 150–151 Making windows
> Making shapes 154–155 ›
> Changing things 156–157 ›

Selecting colours

It's important to describe colours in a way that computers can understand. Tkinter includes a useful tool to help you do this.

1 Launch the colour selection tool
Type the following code into the shell window to launch the Tkinter tool for selecting colours.

This imports all of the Tkinter functions

```
>>> from tkinter import *
>>> t = Tk()
>>> colorchooser.askcolor()
```

Use the American spelling of colour

EXPERT TIPS
Mixing colours

Each pixel can give out red, green, and blue light. By mixing these colours together, you can make any colour imaginable.

- Red and green make yellow
- Red and blue make purple
- Mixing all three makes white

Select the colour you want by clicking on it

2 Choose a colour
The "color chooser" window will appear. Pick the colour you want and then click the "OK" button.

This window makes it easy to pick the exact colour you want

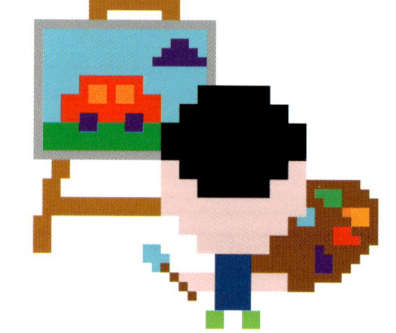

3 Colour values
When a colour is selected, a list of numbers will appear in the shell window. These numbers are the values of red, green, and blue that have been mixed to make the chosen colour.

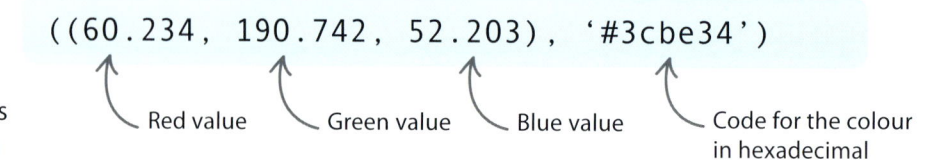

```
((60.234, 190.742, 52.203), '#3cbe34')
```

- Red value
- Green value
- Blue value
- Code for the colour in hexadecimal

COLOUR AND CO-ORDINATES

Drawing on a canvas

To create graphics using Python, you need to make a blank area to draw on. This is known as a canvas. You can use x and y co-ordinates to tell Python exactly where to draw on the canvas.

EXPERT TIPS
Co-ordinates

In Tkinter, x co-ordinates get larger moving to the right, and y co-ordinates get larger moving downwards. (0,0) is in the top-left corner.

- (0,0)
- (300,50)
- (50,100)
- (250,200)

1 Create a graphics program
Use this code to create a window and put a canvas inside it. It will then draw random circles on the canvas.

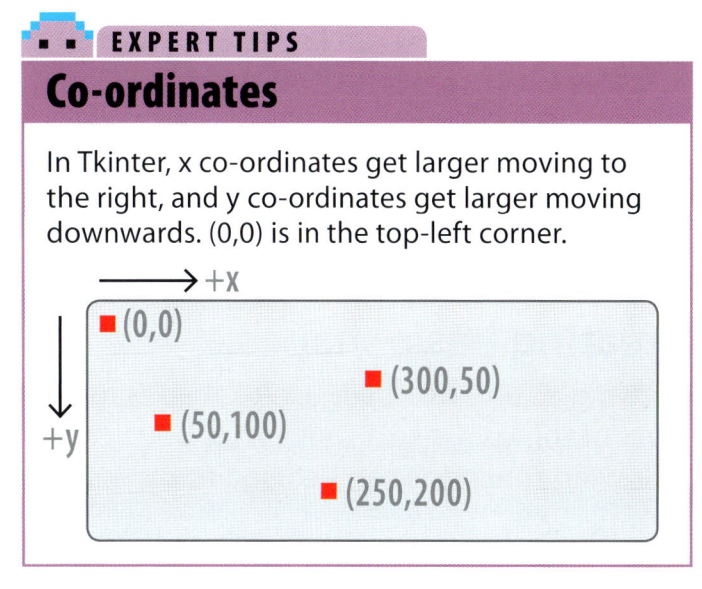

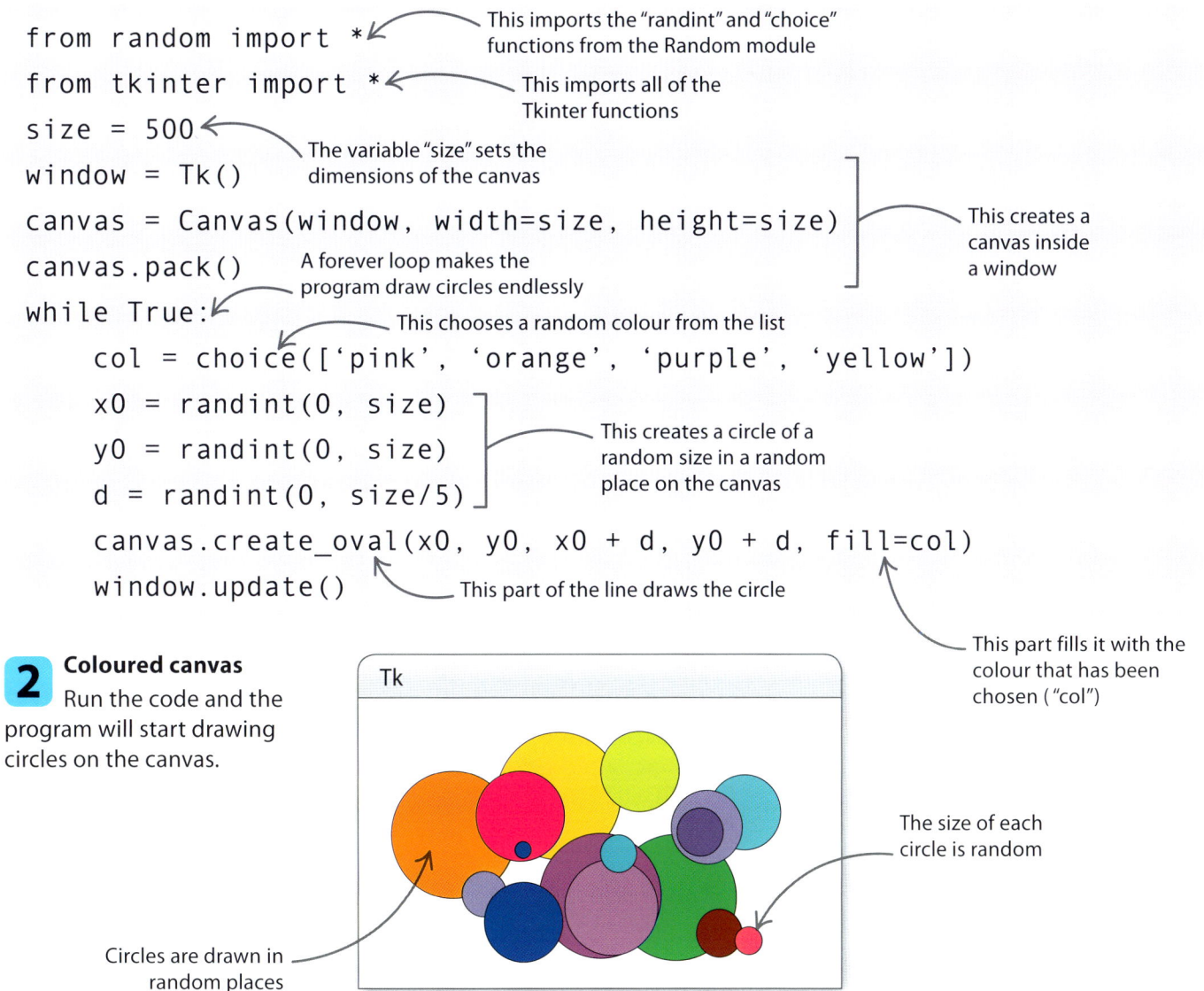

```python
from random import *
from tkinter import *
size = 500
window = Tk()
canvas = Canvas(window, width=size, height=size)
canvas.pack()
while True:
    col = choice(['pink', 'orange', 'purple', 'yellow'])
    x0 = randint(0, size)
    y0 = randint(0, size)
    d = randint(0, size/5)
    canvas.create_oval(x0, y0, x0 + d, y0 + d, fill=col)
    window.update()
```

- `from random import *` — This imports the "randint" and "choice" functions from the Random module
- `from tkinter import *` — This imports all of the Tkinter functions
- The variable "size" sets the dimensions of the canvas
- This creates a canvas inside a window
- A forever loop makes the program draw circles endlessly
- This chooses a random colour from the list
- This creates a circle of a random size in a random place on the canvas
- This part of the line draws the circle
- This part fills it with the colour that has been chosen ("col")

2 Coloured canvas
Run the code and the program will start drawing circles on the canvas.

The size of each circle is random

Circles are drawn in random places

Making shapes

As well as adding windows, buttons, and colours to a graphical user interface (GUI), Tkinter can also be used to draw shapes.

> **SEE ALSO**
>
> Changing **156–157 〉** things
>
> Reacting **158–159 〉** to events

Creating basic shapes

Rectangles and ovals are useful shapes for drawing all sorts of things. Once a canvas has been created, the following functions can be used to draw shapes on it.

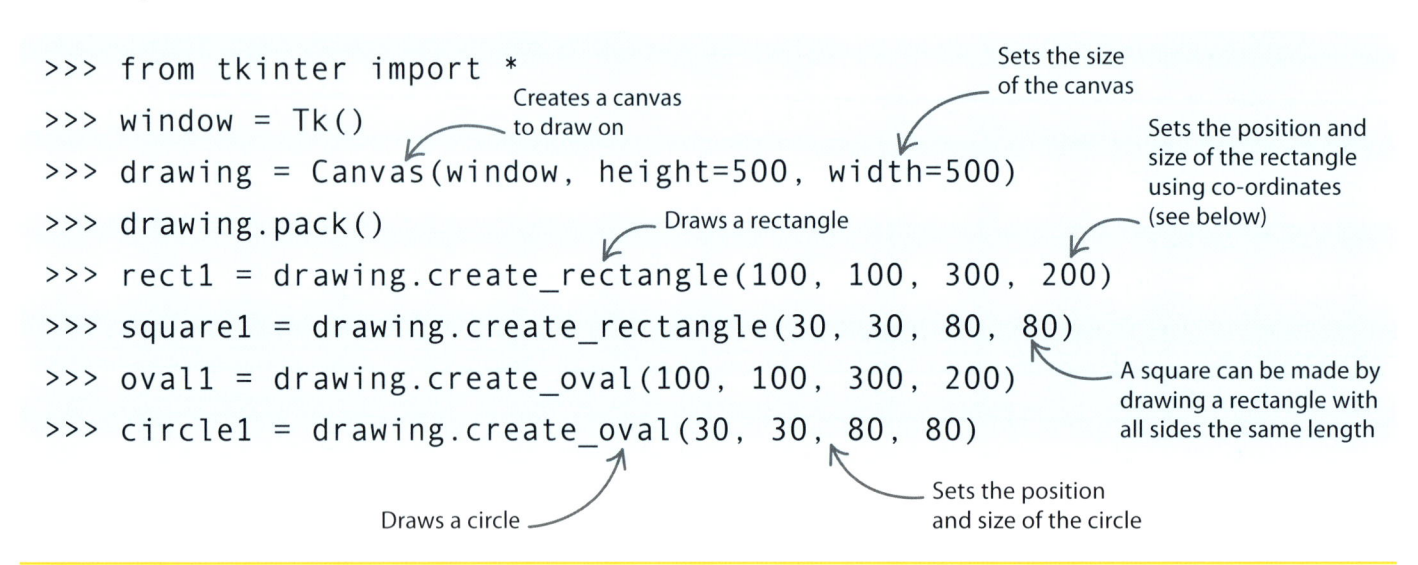

```
>>> from tkinter import *
>>> window = Tk()
>>> drawing = Canvas(window, height=500, width=500)
>>> drawing.pack()
>>> rect1 = drawing.create_rectangle(100, 100, 300, 200)
>>> square1 = drawing.create_rectangle(30, 30, 80, 80)
>>> oval1 = drawing.create_oval(100, 100, 300, 200)
>>> circle1 = drawing.create_oval(30, 30, 80, 80)
```

- Creates a canvas to draw on
- Sets the size of the canvas
- Sets the position and size of the rectangle using co-ordinates (see below)
- Draws a rectangle
- A square can be made by drawing a rectangle with all sides the same length
- Draws a circle
- Sets the position and size of the circle

Drawing with co-ordinates

Co-ordinates are used to tell the computer exactly where to create shapes. The first number ("x") tells the computer how far along the screen to go. The second number ("y") tells the computer how far down to go.

```
>>> drawing.create_rectangle(50, 50, 250, 350)
```

- This is the name of the canvas
- Co-ordinates for the top left of the rectangle
- Co-ordinates for the bottom right of the rectangle

△ **Setting the co-ordinates**
The first two numbers give the co-ordinates for the top-left corner of the rectangle. The second two numbers locate the bottom-right corner.

▽ **Co-ordinates grid**
The top-left corner of the rectangle is at co-ordinates (50, 50). The bottom-right corner is at (250, 350).

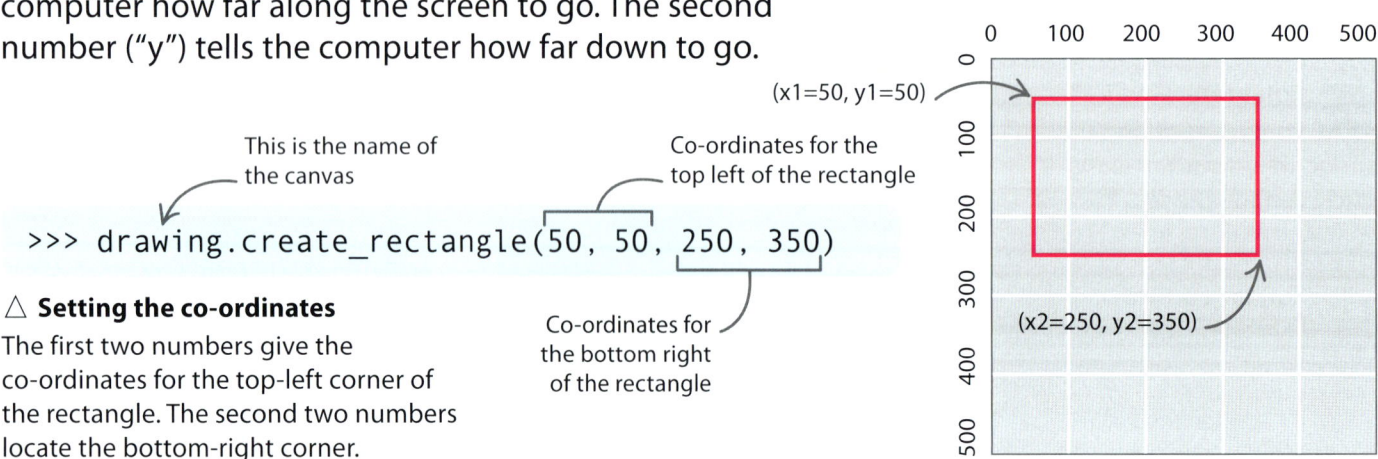

(x1=50, y1=50)
(x2=250, y2=350)

Adding colour to shapes

It's also possible to create coloured shapes. Code can be used to set different colours for the outline and the inside ("fill") of each shape.

Creates a solid blue circle with a red outline

```
>>> drawing.create_oval(30, 30, 80, 80, outline='red', fill='blue')
```

Draw an alien

You can draw almost anything by combining different shapes. Here are some instructions for creating an alien using ovals, lines, and triangles.

1 Create the alien
For each part of the alien, you must define the type of shape, size, position on the canvas, and colour. Each shape has a unique ID number that can be stored in a variable.

```
from tkinter import *
window = Tk()
window.title('Alien')
c = Canvas(window, height=300, width=400)
c.pack()
body = c.create_oval(100, 150, 300, 250, fill='green')
eye = c.create_oval(170, 70, 230, 130, fill='white')
eyeball = c.create_oval(190, 90, 210, 110, fill='black')
mouth = c.create_oval(150, 220, 250, 240, fill='red')
neck = c.create_line(200, 150, 200, 130)
hat = c.create_polygon(180, 75, 220, 75, 200, 20, fill='blue')
```

Sets "Alien" as the title of the window
Creates the canvas
Draws a green oval for the body
Draws a black dot inside the eye
Draws a red oval for the mouth
Draws a blue triangle for the alien's hat

2 Meet the alien
Run the code to draw the alien. It has a green body, a red mouth, and one eye on a stalk. It's also wearing a lovely blue hat.

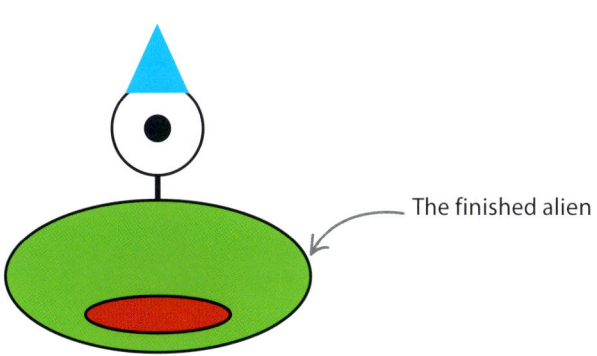

The finished alien

Changing things

Once a graphic has been drawn on the canvas, it doesn't need to stay the same. Code can be used to change the way it looks, or move it around the screen.

SEE ALSO

❮ 154–155 Making shapes

Reacting to events 158–159 ❯

Moving shapes

To make a shape move on the canvas, you need to tell the computer what to move (the name or ID you gave the shape) and where to move it.

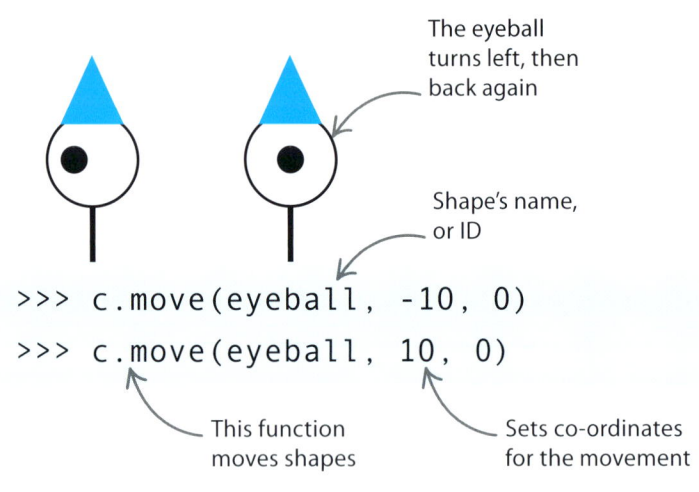

The eyeball turns left, then back again

Shape's name, or ID

```
>>> c.move(eyeball, -10, 0)
>>> c.move(eyeball, 10, 0)
```

This function moves shapes

Sets co-ordinates for the movement

REMEMBER
Meaningful names

It's a good idea to use sensible names to identify the shapes on the canvas. These pages use names like "eyeball" and "mouth" so the code is easy to read and understand.

◁ **Moving eyeballs**
Type this code into the shell window to make the eyeball turn to the left, then turn back again.

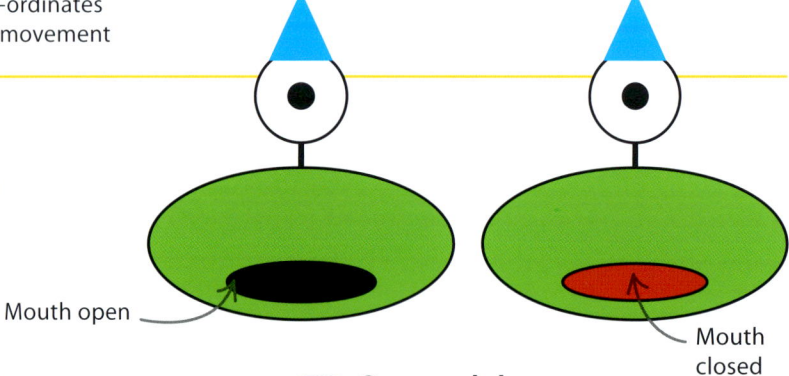

Changing colours

You can make the mouth look as though it is opening and closing by simply changing the colour of the oval.

Mouth open

Mouth closed

1 Write the code
Type this code to create two functions that will make the mouth seem to open and close.

The function "itemconfig()" changes the properties of shapes you've already drawn

The opened mouth will be black

```
def mouth_open():
    c.itemconfig(mouth, fill='black')
def mouth_close():
    c.itemconfig(mouth, fill='red')
```

The shape's ID

The closed mouth will be red

2 Open and close
Type this code into the shell window to make the mouth open and close.

```
>>> mouth_open()
>>> mouth_close()
```

Enter these commands to make the alien open and close its mouth

CHANGING THINGS 157

Hide and show

Shapes can be hidden using the "itemconfig()" function. If you hide the eyeball, and then show it again a moment later, the alien looks as though it is blinking.

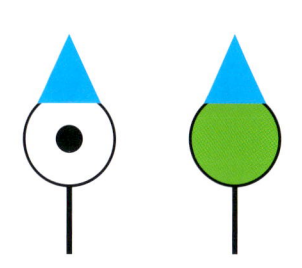

◁ **Blinking alien**
To make the alien blink, you need to hide the pupil and make the white of the eye green.

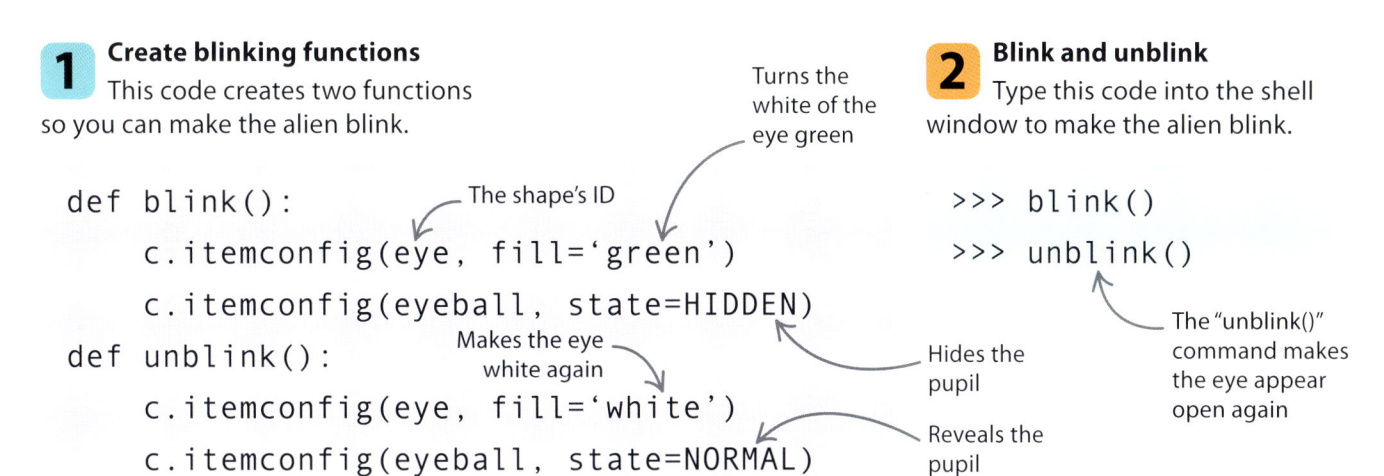

1 Create blinking functions
This code creates two functions so you can make the alien blink.

Turns the white of the eye green

```
def blink():
    c.itemconfig(eye, fill='green')
    c.itemconfig(eyeball, state=HIDDEN)
def unblink():
    c.itemconfig(eye, fill='white')
    c.itemconfig(eyeball, state=NORMAL)
```

The shape's ID

Makes the eye white again

Hides the pupil

Reveals the pupil

2 Blink and unblink
Type this code into the shell window to make the alien blink.

```
>>> blink()
>>> unblink()
```

The "unblink()" command makes the eye appear open again

Saying things

Text can also be displayed on the screen to make the alien talk. You can even make it say different things in response to user commands.

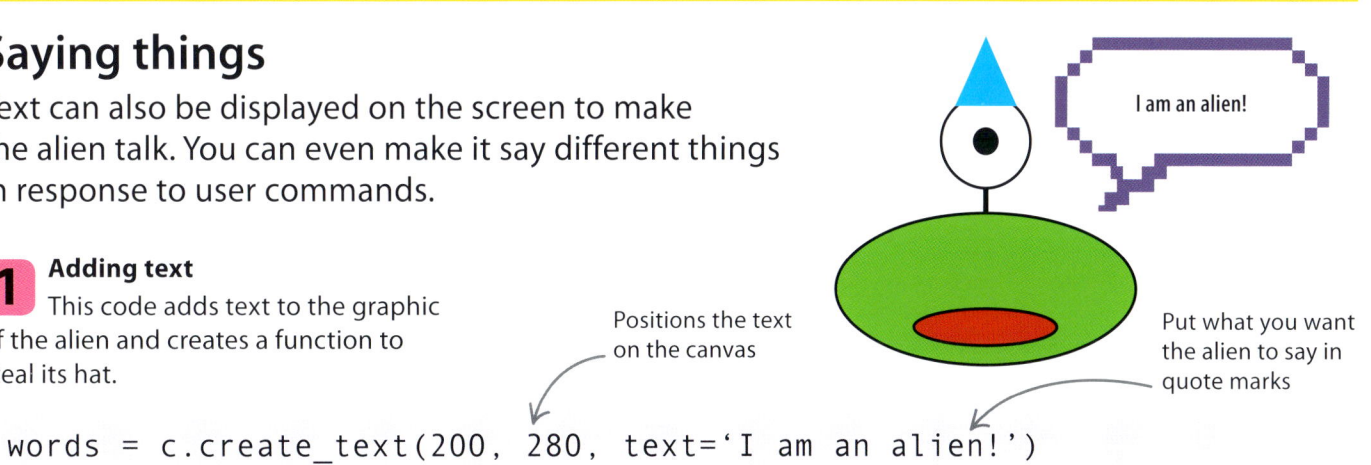

1 Adding text
This code adds text to the graphic of the alien and creates a function to steal its hat.

Positions the text on the canvas

Put what you want the alien to say in quote marks

```
words = c.create_text(200, 280, text='I am an alien!')
def steal_hat():
    c.itemconfig(hat, state=HIDDEN)
    c.itemconfig(words, text='Give my hat back!')
```

This hides the hat

As soon as the hat disappears the alien will ask for it back

A new message appears when the hat disappears

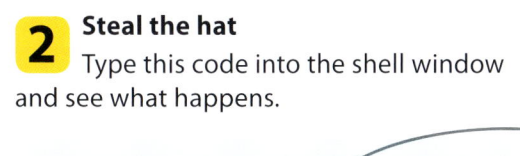

2 Steal the hat
Type this code into the shell window and see what happens.

Type this to steal the hat

```
>>> steal_hat()
```

Reacting to events

Computers receive a signal when a key is pressed or a mouse is moved. This is called an "event". Programs can instruct the computer to respond to any events it detects.

> **SEE ALSO**
>
> ⟨ **154–155** Making shapes
>
> ⟨ **156–157** Changing things

Event names

Lots of different events can be triggered using input devices like a mouse or keyboard. Tkinter has names to describe each of these events.

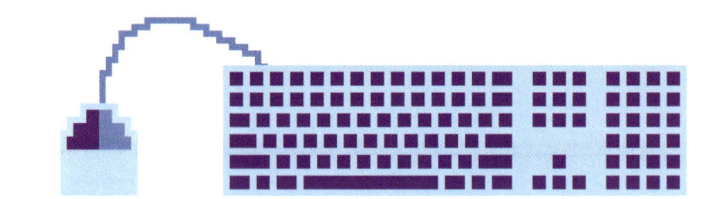

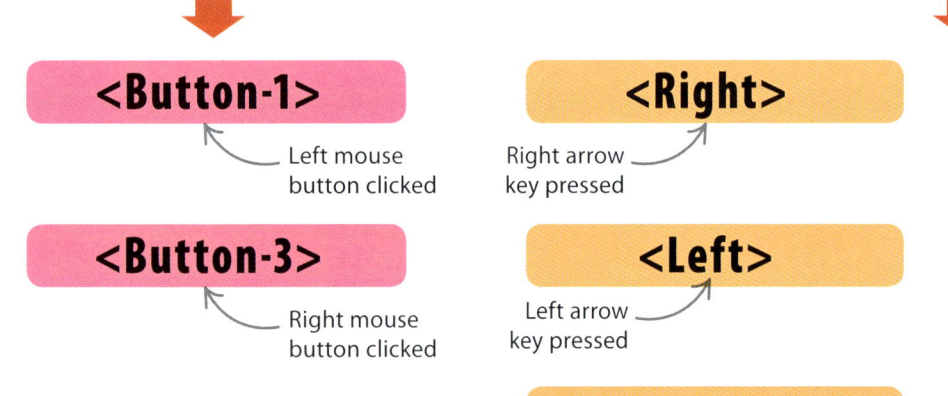

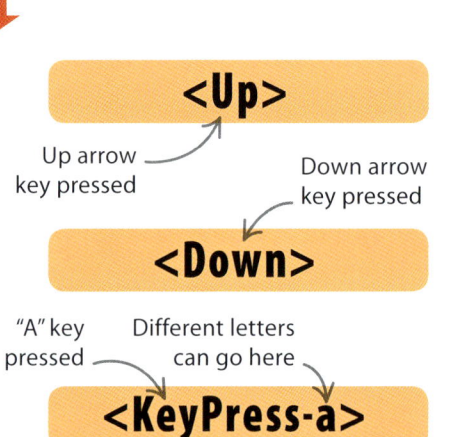

Mouse events

- `<Button-1>` — Left mouse button clicked
- `<Button-3>` — Right mouse button clicked

Keyboard events

- `<Right>` — Right arrow key pressed
- `<Left>` — Left arrow key pressed
- `<space>` — Spacebar pressed
- `<Up>` — Up arrow key pressed
- `<Down>` — Down arrow key pressed
- `<KeyPress-a>` — "A" key pressed / Different letters can go here

Mouse events

To make a program respond to mouse events, simply link (or bind) a function to an event. Here, the function "burp" is created, then bound to the "<Button-1>" event.

```
window.attributes('-topmost', 1)
def burp(event):
    mouth_open()
    c.itemconfig(words, text='Burp!')
c.bind_all('<Button-1>', burp)
```

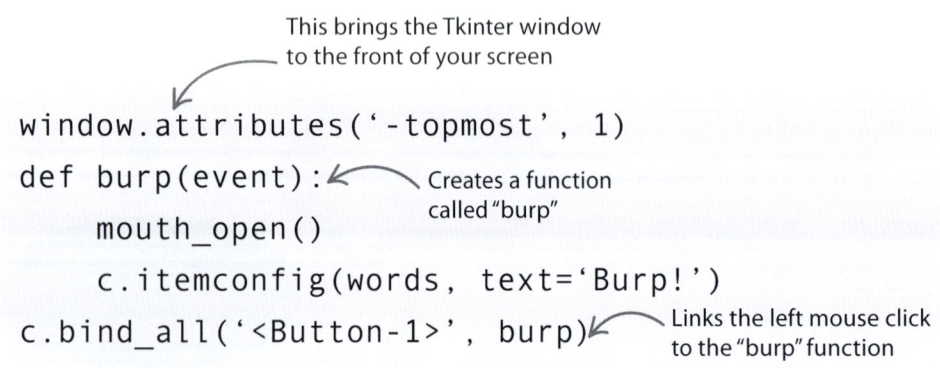

- `window.attributes('-topmost', 1)` — This brings the Tkinter window to the front of your screen
- `def burp(event):` — Creates a function called "burp"
- `c.bind_all('<Button-1>', burp)` — Links the left mouse click to the "burp" function

△ **Burping alien**

Click the left mouse button and the alien lets out a burp. This is because the "burp" function has been used.

Key events

Functions can also be bound to keys on the keyboard in the same way. Type in the code below to make the alien blink when the "A" and "Z" keys are pressed.

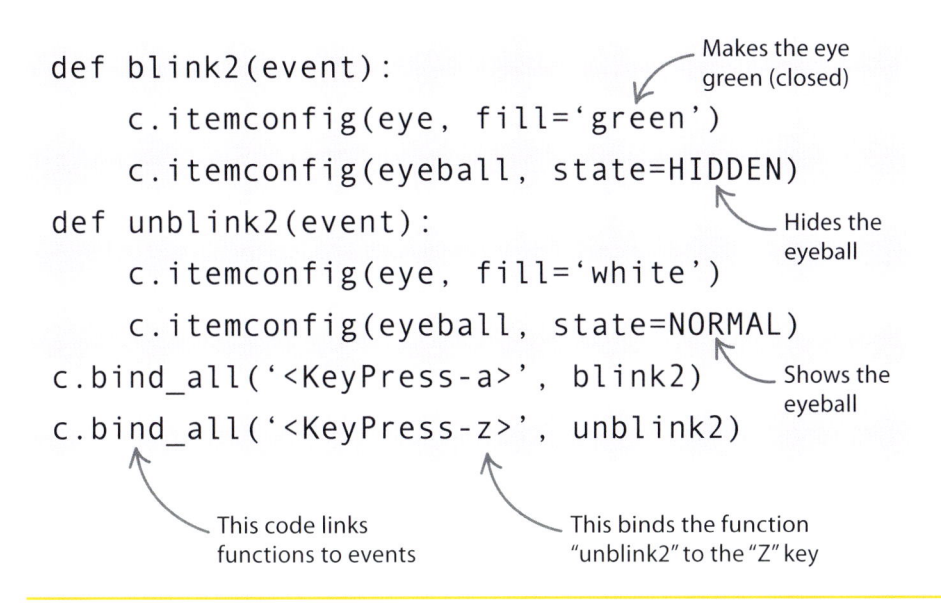

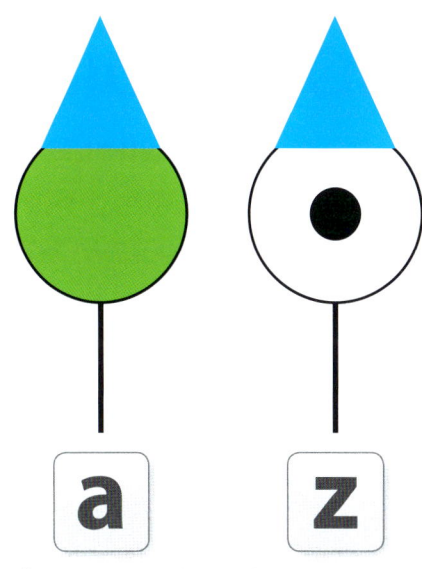

```
def blink2(event):
    c.itemconfig(eye, fill='green')
    c.itemconfig(eyeball, state=HIDDEN)
def unblink2(event):
    c.itemconfig(eye, fill='white')
    c.itemconfig(eyeball, state=NORMAL)
c.bind_all('<KeyPress-a>', blink2)
c.bind_all('<KeyPress-z>', unblink2)
```

- Makes the eye green (closed)
- Hides the eyeball
- Shows the eyeball
- This code links functions to events
- This binds the function "unblink2" to the "Z" key

△ **Make the alien blink**
When this code is run, the "A" key will make the eye close, and the "Z" key will make it open again.

Moving with keys

Key presses can also be used to trigger movement. This code binds the arrow keys to functions that make the alien's eyeball move.

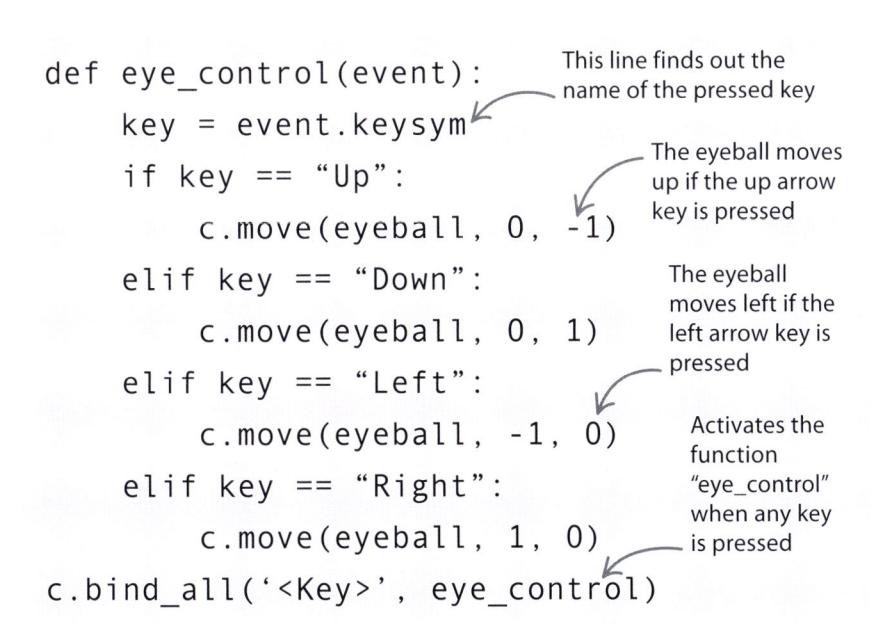

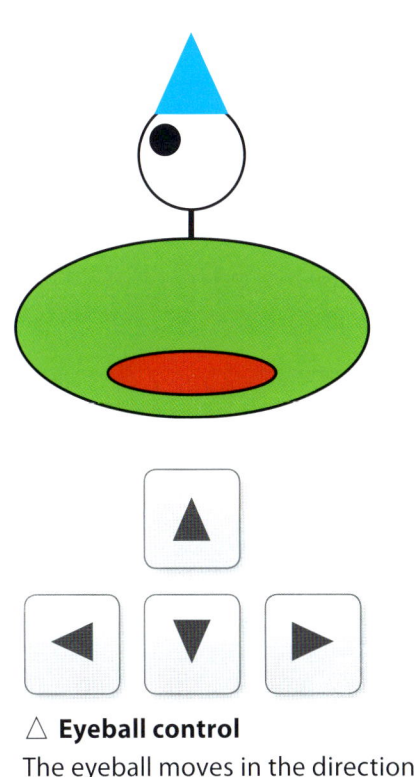

```
def eye_control(event):
    key = event.keysym
    if key == "Up":
        c.move(eyeball, 0, -1)
    elif key == "Down":
        c.move(eyeball, 0, 1)
    elif key == "Left":
        c.move(eyeball, -1, 0)
    elif key == "Right":
        c.move(eyeball, 1, 0)
c.bind_all('<Key>', eye_control)
```

- This line finds out the name of the pressed key
- The eyeball moves up if the up arrow key is pressed
- The eyeball moves left if the left arrow key is pressed
- Activates the function "eye_control" when any key is pressed

△ **Eyeball control**
The eyeball moves in the direction of the pressed arrow key.

PROJECT 7

Bubble blaster

This project uses all the skills taught in this chapter to make a game. It's a big project, so tackle it in stages and remember to save the program regularly. Try to understand how each part fits together before moving on to the next stage. By the end you'll have a game that you can play and share with friends.

> **SEE ALSO**
> ‹ **150–151** Making windows
> ‹ **152–153** Colour and co-ordinates
> ‹ **154–155** Making shapes

Aim of the game

Before writing any code, think about the overall plan for the game and how it should work. Here are the main rules that set out how the game will be played:

- The player controls a submarine
- The arrow keys move the submarine
- Popping bubbles scores points
- A timer is set to 30 seconds at the start
- Scoring 1,000 points earns extra time
- The game ends when the time runs out

BUBBLE BLASTER | **161**

Create the game window and the submarine

Start by setting the scene. Open a new code window in IDLE. Type in the code below to create the window for the game, and the submarine that the player controls.

1 Use the Tkinter library to build the graphical user interface (GUI). This code will create the main window for the game.

```
from tkinter import *          # Imports all of the Tkinter functions
HEIGHT = 500                    # Sets the size
WIDTH = 800                     # of the window
window = Tk()
window.title('Bubble Blaster')  # Give the game a snappy title
c = Canvas(window, width=WIDTH, height=HEIGHT, bg='darkblue')
c.pack()
```

Creates a canvas that can be drawn on

Sets dark blue as the colour of the background (the sea)

2 A simple graphic will represent the submarine in this game. This can be made using some of the drawing functions from Tkinter. Type out this code, then run it.

The submarine will be represented by a triangle inside a circle

Draws a red triangle for the submarine

```
ship_id = c.create_polygon(5, 5, 5, 25, 30, 15, fill='red')
ship_id2 = c.create_oval(0, 0, 30, 30, outline='red')
SHIP_R = 15          # The radius (size) of the submarine
MID_X = WIDTH / 2
MID_Y = HEIGHT / 2
c.move(ship_id, MID_X, MID_Y)
c.move(ship_id2, MID_X, MID_Y)
```

The variables "MID_X" and "MID_Y" give the co-ordinates of the middle of the screen

Draws a red circle outline

Moves both parts of the submarine to the centre of the screen

Don't forget to save your work

BUBBLE BLASTER

Controlling the submarine

The next stage of the program is to write the code that makes the submarine move when the arrow keys are pressed. The code will create a function called an "event handler". The event handler checks which key has been pressed and moves the submarine.

3 ▶ Type this code to create a function called "move_ship". This function will move the submarine in the correct direction when a cursor key is pressed. Try running it to see how it works.

```
SHIP_SPD = 10
def move_ship(event):
    if event.keysym == 'Up':
        c.move(ship_id, 0, -SHIP_SPD)
        c.move(ship_id2, 0, -SHIP_SPD)
    elif event.keysym == 'Down':
        c.move(ship_id, 0, SHIP_SPD)
        c.move(ship_id2, 0, SHIP_SPD)
    elif event.keysym == 'Left':
        c.move(ship_id, -SHIP_SPD, 0)
        c.move(ship_id2, -SHIP_SPD, 0)
    elif event.keysym == 'Right':
        c.move(ship_id, SHIP_SPD, 0)
        c.move(ship_id2, SHIP_SPD, 0)
c.bind_all('<Key>', move_ship)
```

- The sub will move this far when a key is pressed
- Moves the two parts of the sub up when the up arrow key is pressed
- These lines are activated when the down arrow key is pressed, and the sub moves down
- The sub moves left when the left arrow key is pressed
- Moves the sub right when the right arrow key is pressed
- Tells Python to run "move_ship" whenever any key is pressed

Don't forget to save your work

▷ **How it works**
The "move_ship" function moves the sub in different directions. Adding to the sub's x and y co-ordinates moves it right and down, while subtracting from them moves it left and up.

- y co-ordinate gets smaller moving up
- x co-ordinate gets smaller going left
- y co-ordinate gets larger moving down
- x co-ordinate gets larger going right

Get ready for bubbles

Now the submarine can move, start creating the bubbles for the player to pop. Each bubble will be a different size and move at a different speed.

4 ▸ Every bubble needs an ID number (so the program can identify each specific bubble), a size, and a speed.

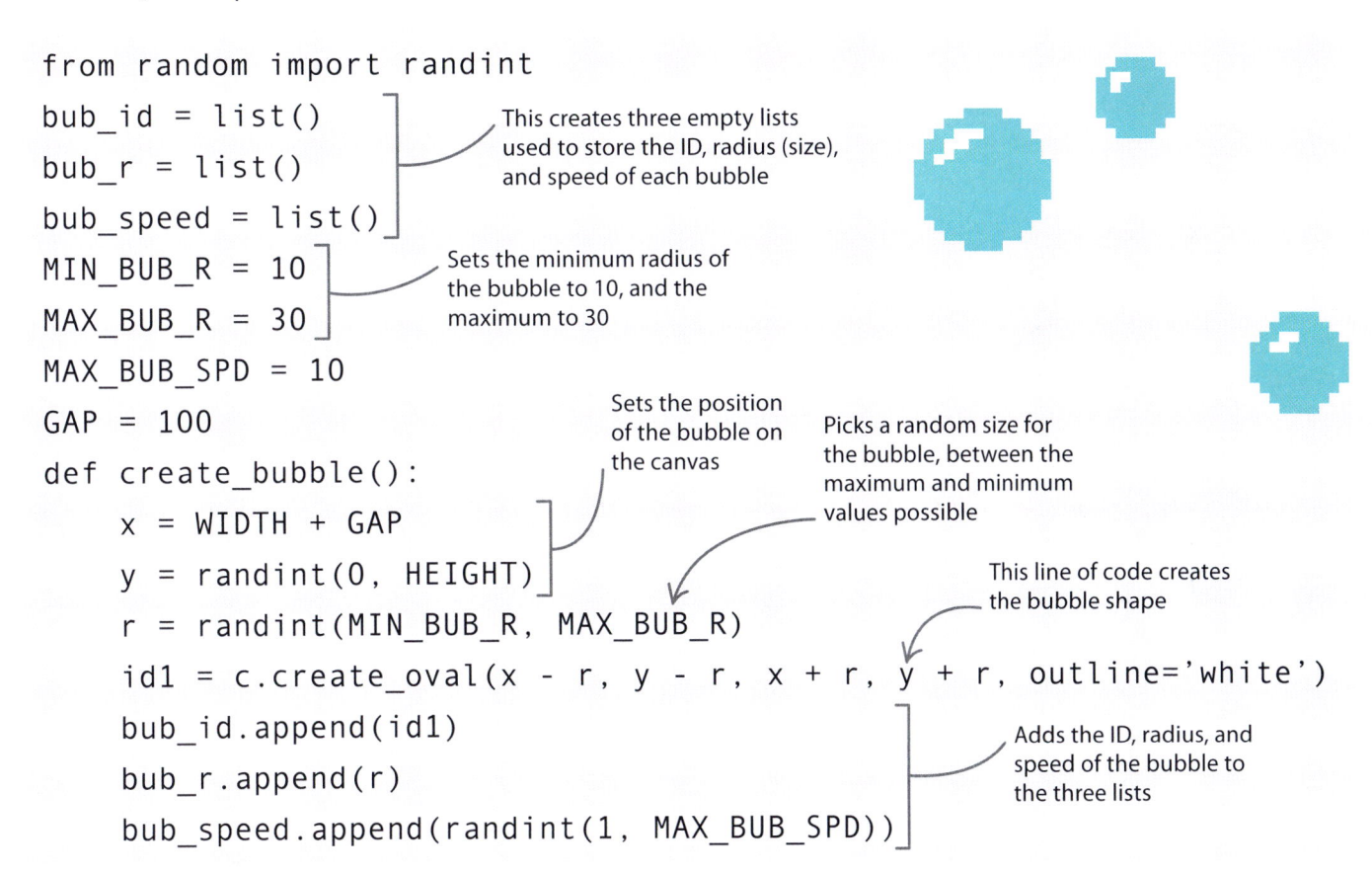

```
from random import randint
bub_id = list()
bub_r = list()
bub_speed = list()
MIN_BUB_R = 10
MAX_BUB_R = 30
MAX_BUB_SPD = 10
GAP = 100
def create_bubble():
    x = WIDTH + GAP
    y = randint(0, HEIGHT)
    r = randint(MIN_BUB_R, MAX_BUB_R)
    id1 = c.create_oval(x - r, y - r, x + r, y + r, outline='white')
    bub_id.append(id1)
    bub_r.append(r)
    bub_speed.append(randint(1, MAX_BUB_SPD))
```

- This creates three empty lists used to store the ID, radius (size), and speed of each bubble
- Sets the minimum radius of the bubble to 10, and the maximum to 30
- Sets the position of the bubble on the canvas
- Picks a random size for the bubble, between the maximum and minimum values possible
- This line of code creates the bubble shape
- Adds the ID, radius, and speed of the bubble to the three lists

EXPERT TIPS
Bubble lists

Three lists are used to store information about each bubble. The lists start off empty, and information about each bubble is then added as you create it. Each list stores a different bit of information.

bub_id: stores the ID number of the bubble so the program can move it later.
bub_r: stores the radius (size) of the bubble.
bub_speed: stores how fast the bubble travels across the screen.

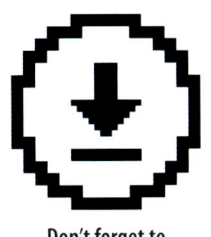

Don't forget to save your work

BUBBLE BLASTER

Make the bubbles move

There are now lists to store the ID, size, and speed of the bubbles, which are randomly generated. The next stage is to write the code that makes the bubbles move across the screen.

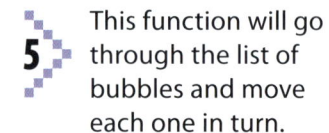

5 This function will go through the list of bubbles and move each one in turn.

```
def move_bubbles():
    for i in range(len(bub_id)):
        c.move(bub_id[i], -bub_speed[i], 0)
```

- Goes through each bubble in the list
- Moves the bubble across the screen according to its speed

6 This will be the main loop for the game. It will be repeated over and over while the game is running. Try running it!

```
from time import sleep, time
BUB_CHANCE = 10
#MAIN GAME LOOP
while True:
    if randint(1, BUB_CHANCE) == 1:
        create_bubble()
    move_bubbles()
    window.update()
    sleep(0.01)
```

- Imports the functions you need from the Time library
- Generates a random number from 1 to 10
- If the random number is 1, the program creates a new bubble (on average 1 in 10 times – so there aren't too many bubbles!)
- Runs the "move_bubbles" function
- Updates the window to redraw bubbles that have moved
- Slows the game down so it's not too fast to play

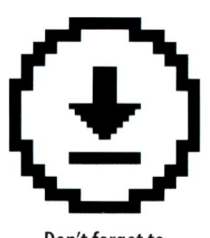

Don't forget to save your work

7 Now you're going to create a useful function to find out where a particular bubble is, based on the ID. This code should be added to the program directly after the code you created in step 5.

```
def get_coords(id_num):
    pos = c.coords(id_num)
    x = (pos[0] + pos[2])/2
    y = (pos[1] + pos[3])/2
    return x, y
```

- Works out the x co-ordinate of the middle of the bubble
- Works out the y co-ordinate of the middle of the bubble

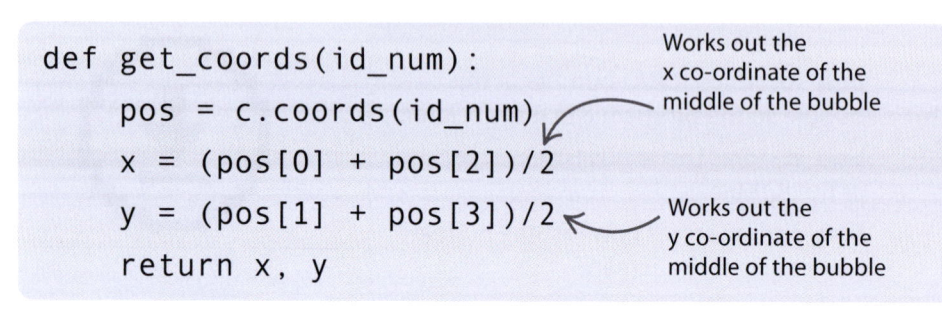

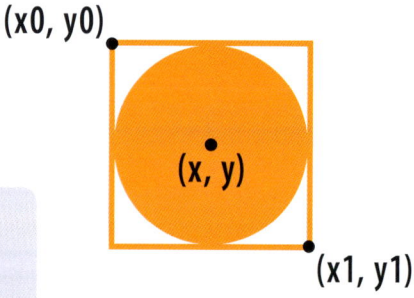

(x0, y0)
(x, y)
(x1, y1)

△ **Locating bubbles**
The function finds the middle of the bubble by taking the point halfway between the corners of the box around it.

How to make bubbles pop

The player will score points when the bubbles are popped, so the program has to make bubbles disappear from the screen. These next functions will allow it to do that.

8. This function will be used to remove a bubble from the game. It does this by deleting it from all the lists, and from the canvas. This code should be added directly after the code you typed out in step 7.

```
def del_bubble(i):
    del bub_r[i]
    del bub_speed[i]
    c.delete(bub_id[i])
    del bub_id[i]
```

This function deletes the bubble with ID "i"

Deletes the bubble from the radius and speed lists

Deletes the bubble from the canvas

Deletes the bubble from the ID list

9. Type this code to create a function that cleans up bubbles that have floated off the screen. This code should go directly after the code from step 8.

```
def clean_up_bubs():
    for i in range(len(bub_id)-1, -1, -1):
        x, y = get_coords(bub_id[i])
        if x < -GAP:
            del_bubble(i)
```

This goes through the bubble list backwards to avoid the "for" loop causing an error when bubbles are deleted

Finds out where the bubble is

If the bubble is off the screen then it is deleted – otherwise it would slow the game down

10. Now update the main game loop (from step 6) to include the helpful functions you have just created. Run it to make sure you haven't included any errors.

```
#MAIN GAME LOOP
while True:
    if randint(1, BUB_CHANCE) == 1:
        create_bubble()
    move_bubbles()
    clean_up_bubs()
    window.update()
    sleep(0.01)
```

Makes a new bubble

Updates the positions of all the bubbles

Removes bubbles that are off the screen

Redraws the window to show the changes

Don't forget to save your work

BUBBLE BLASTER

Working out the distance between points

In this game, and lots of others, it is useful to know the distance between two objects. Here's how to use a well-known mathematical formula to have the computer work it out.

11 ▸ This function calculates the distance between two objects. Add this bit of code directly after the code you wrote in step 9.

- Loads the "sqrt" function from the Math library
- Gets the position of the first object
- Gets the position of the second object
- Gives back the distance between them

```python
from math import sqrt
def distance(id1, id2):
    x1, y1 = get_coords(id1)
    x2, y2 = get_coords(id2)
    return sqrt((x2 - x1)**2 + (y2 - y1)**2)
```

Pop the bubbles

The player scores points by popping bubbles. Big bubbles and fast bubbles are worth more points. The next section of code works out when each bubble is popped by using its radius (the distance from the centre to the edge).

▷ **Collision sensing**
If the distance between the centre of the sub and the centre of a bubble is less than their radiuses added together, they have collided.

12 ▸ When the submarine and a bubble crash into each other, the program needs to pop the bubble and update the score. This bit of code should come directly after the code in step 11.

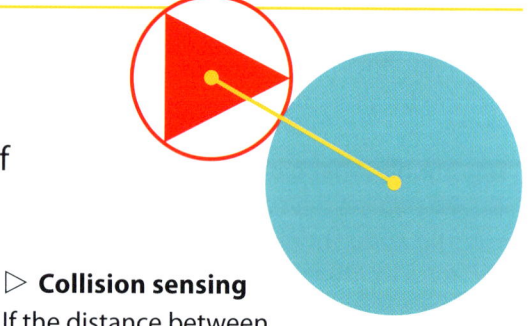

- This variable keeps track of points scored
- This loop goes through the entire list of bubbles (it goes backwards to avoid errors when deleting bubbles)
- Checks for collisions between the sub and any bubbles
- Calculates the number of points this bubble is worth and adds it to "points"
- Deletes the bubble
- Gives back the number of points

```python
def collision():
    points = 0
    for bub in range(len(bub_id)-1, -1, -1):
        if distance(ship_id2, bub_id[bub]) < (SHIP_R + bub_r[bub]):
            points += (bub_r[bub] + bub_speed[bub])
            del_bubble(bub)
    return points
```

13 Now update the main game loop to use the functions you have just created. Remember that the order is important, so make sure you put everything in the right place. Then run the code. Bubbles should burst when they hit the sub. Check the shell window to see the score.

```
score = 0
#MAIN GAME LOOP
while True:
    if randint(1, BUB_CHANCE) == 1:
        create_bubble()
    move_bubbles()
    clean_up_bubs()
    score += collision()
    print(score)
    window.update()
    sleep(0.01)
```

- Sets the score to zero when the game starts
- Creates new bubbles
- Adds the bubble score to the total
- Shows the score in the shell window – it will be displayed properly later
- This pauses the action for a very short time – try removing this and see what happens

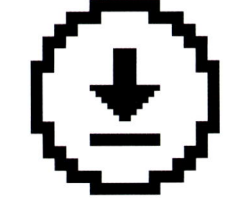

Don't forget to save your work

EXPERT TIPS
Python shortcut

The code "score += collision()" is a shortcut for writing "score = score + collision()". It adds the collision score to the total score, then updates the total score. Code like this is common, so a shortcut is useful. You can also do the same thing using the "–" symbol. For example, "score –= 10" is the same as "score = score – 10".

168 PLAYING WITH PYTHON

BUBBLE BLASTER

Adding a few final touches

The main stages of the game are now working. All that remains is to add the final parts: displaying the player's score, and setting a time limit that counts down until the game ends.

14 Type in this code after the code you entered in step 12. It tells the computer to display the player's score and the time left in the game.

Creates "TIME" and "SCORE" labels to explain to the player what the numbers mean

```
c.create_text(50, 30, text='TIME', fill='white' )
c.create_text(150, 30, text='SCORE', fill='white' )
time_text = c.create_text(50, 50, fill='white' )
score_text = c.create_text(150, 50, fill='white' )
def show_score(score):
    c.itemconfig(score_text, text=str(score))
def show_time(time_left):
    c.itemconfig(time_text, text=str(time_left))
```

Sets the scores and time remaining

Displays the score

Displays the time remaining

15 Next, set up the time limit and the score required to gain bonus time, and calculate the end time of the game. This bit of code should come just before the main game loop.

```
from time import sleep, time
BUB_CHANCE = 10
TIME_LIMIT = 30
BONUS_SCORE = 1000
score = 0
bonus = 0
end = time() + TIME_LIMIT
```

Imports functions from the Time library

Starts the game with a 30-second time limit

Sets when bonus time is given (when a player has scored 1,000 points)

Stores the finish time in a variable called "end"

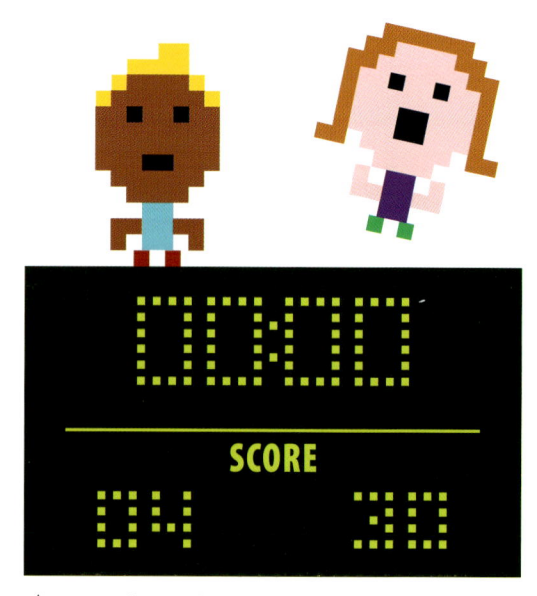

△ **Scoreboard**
Scoreboards are a great visual way to show the player at a glance how well they are doing in a game.

16. Update the main game loop to include the new score and time functions.

```
#MAIN GAME LOOP
while time() < end:
    if randint(1, BUB_CHANCE) == 1:
        create_bubble()
    move_bubbles()
    clean_up_bubs()
    score += collision()
    if (int(score / BONUS_SCORE)) > bonus:
        bonus += 1
        end += TIME_LIMIT
    show_score(score)
    show_time(int(end - time()))
    window.update()
    sleep(0.01)
```

Repeats the main game loop until the game ends

Calculates when to give bonus time

"print(score)" has been replaced by "show_score(score)" so that the score now appears in the game window

Displays the time remaining

Don't forget to save your work

17. Finally, add a "GAME OVER" graphic. This will be shown when the time runs out. Add this to the very bottom of your program.

Puts graphic in the middle of the screen

Sets the font – "Helvetica" is a good font for big letters

```
c.create_text(MID_X, MID_Y, \
    text='GAME OVER', fill='white', font=('Helvetica',30))
c.create_text(MID_X, MID_Y + 30, \
    text='Score: '+ str(score), fill='white')
c.create_text(MID_X, MID_Y + 45, \
    text='Bonus time: '+ str(bonus*TIME_LIMIT), fill='white')
```

Tells you what your score was

Sets the text colour to white

Shows how much bonus time was earned

Don't forget to save your work

BUBBLE BLASTER

Time to play

Well done! You've finished writing Bubble blaster and it's now ready to play. Run the program and try it out. If something isn't working, remember the debugging tips – look back carefully over the code on the previous pages to make sure everything is typed out correctly.

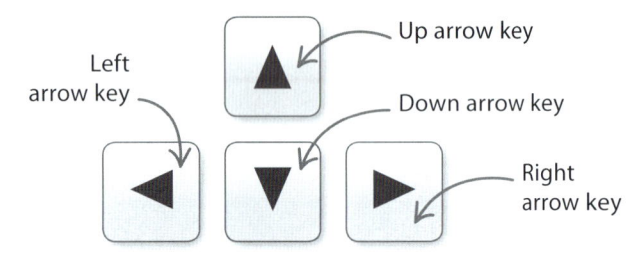

The timer counts down to the end of the game

The player scores points for popping bubbles with the sub

△ **Controls**
The submarine is steered using the arrow keys. The program can be adjusted so it works with other controls.

> **EXPERT TIPS**
> ## Improving your game
>
> All computer games start as a basic idea. They are then played, tested, adjusted, and improved. Think of this as version one of your game. Here are some suggestions of how you could change and improve it with new code:
>
> **Make the game harder** by adjusting the time limit and the score required for bonus time.
>
> **Choose a different colour** for your submarine.
>
> **Create a more detailed** submarine graphic.
>
> **Have a special type of bubble** that increases the speed of the submarine.
>
> **Add a smart bomb** that deletes all of the bubbles when you press the spacebar.
>
> **Build a leaderboard** to keep track of the best scores.

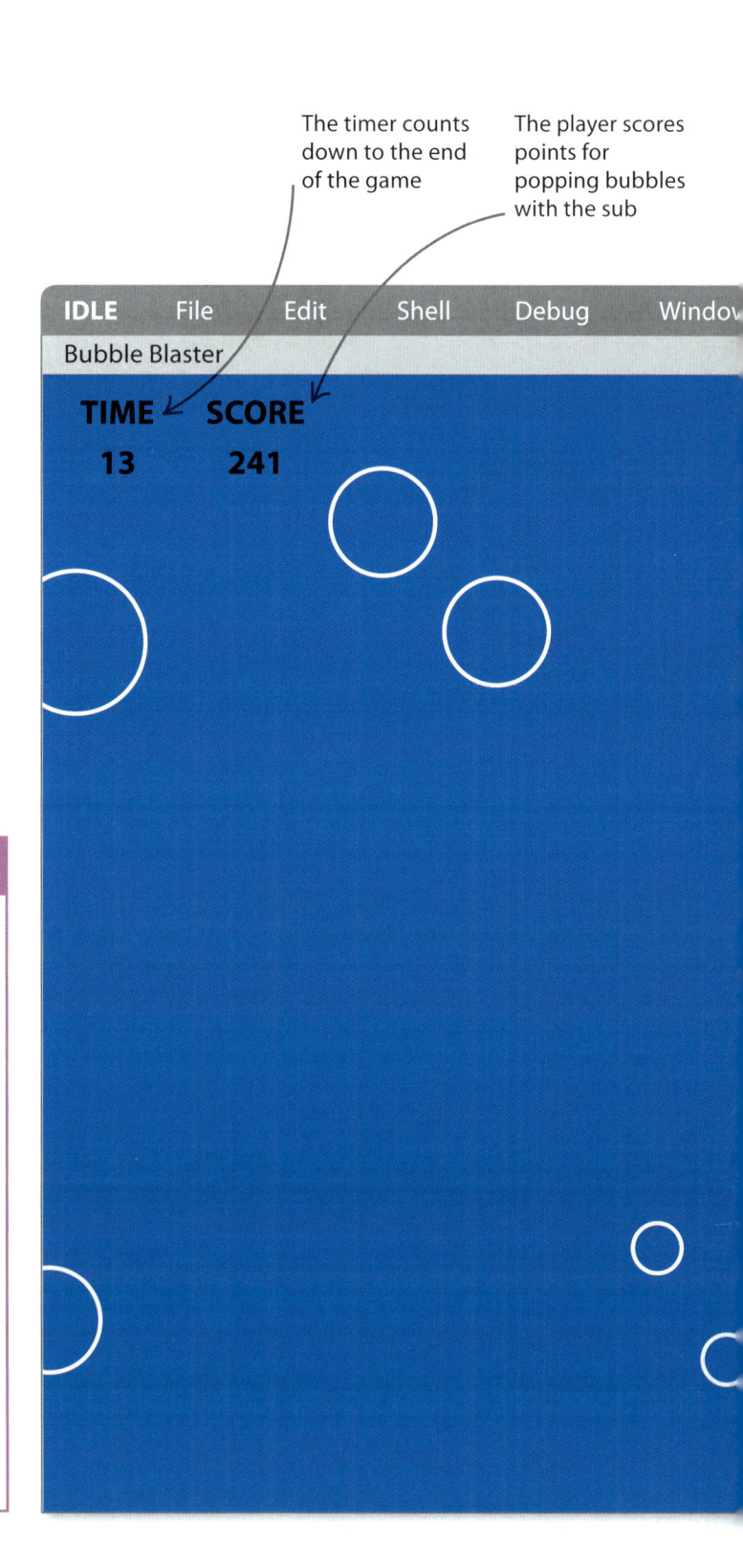

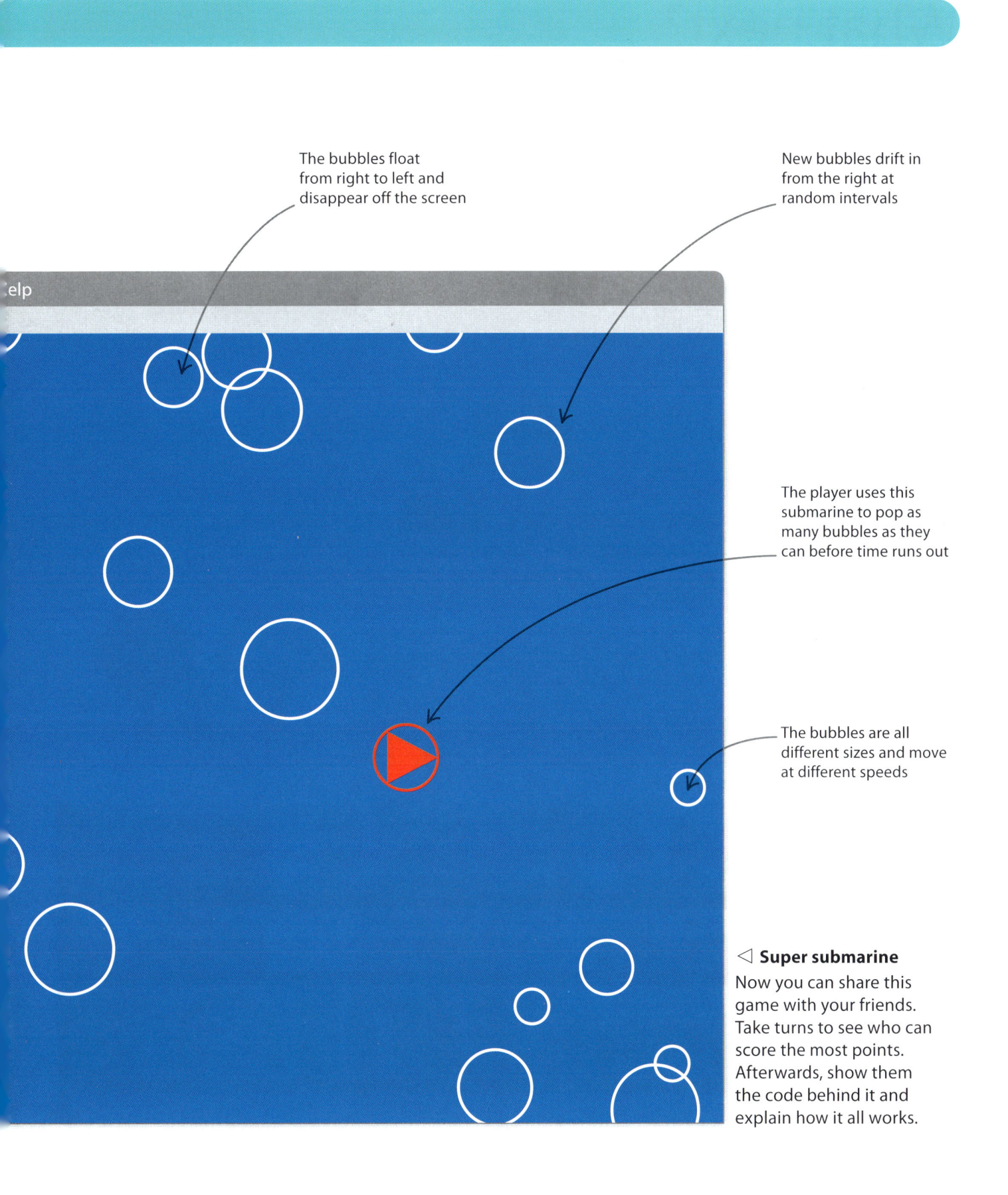

BUBBLE BLASTER 171

The bubbles float from right to left and disappear off the screen

New bubbles drift in from the right at random intervals

The player uses this submarine to pop as many bubbles as they can before time runs out

The bubbles are all different sizes and move at different speeds

◁ **Super submarine**
Now you can share this game with your friends. Take turns to see who can score the most points. Afterwards, show them the code behind it and explain how it all works.

What next?

Now that you've tackled the Python projects in this book, you're on your way to becoming a great programmer. Here are some ideas for what to do next in Python, and how to take your programming skills further.

SEE ALSO

‹ 148–149 Libraries

Experiment

Play around with the code samples in this book. Find new ways to remix them or add new features – and don't be afraid to break them too! This is your chance to experiment with Python. Remember that it is a professional programming language with a lot of power – you can do all sorts of things with it.

Build your own libraries

Programmers love to reuse code and share their work. Create your own library of useful functions and share it. It's a great feeling to see your code being used by another programmer. You might build something as useful as Tkinter or Turtle!

REMEMBER
Read lots of code

Find interesting programs or libraries written by other people and read through the code and their comments. Try to understand how the code works, and why it is built that way. This increases your knowledge of coding practices. You will also learn useful bits of information about libraries that you can use in future programs.

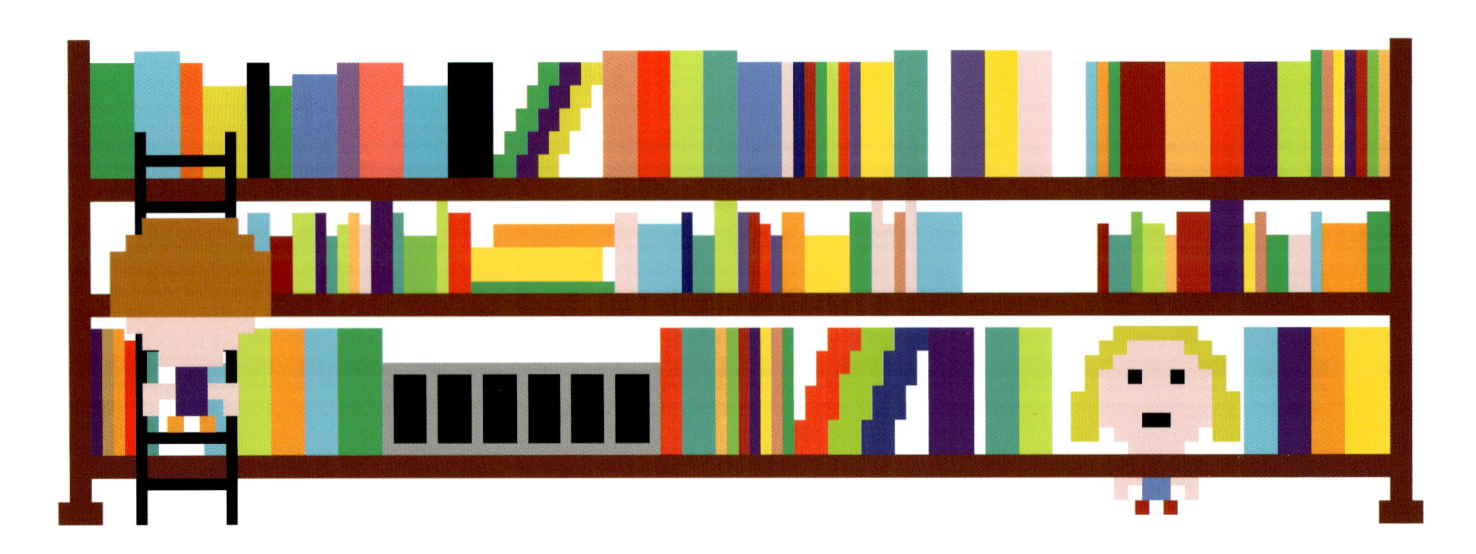

Make games with Python

You could create your own game using Python. The PyGame library, which is available to download from the web, comes with lots of functions and tools that make it easier to build games. Start by making simple games, then progress to more complex ones.

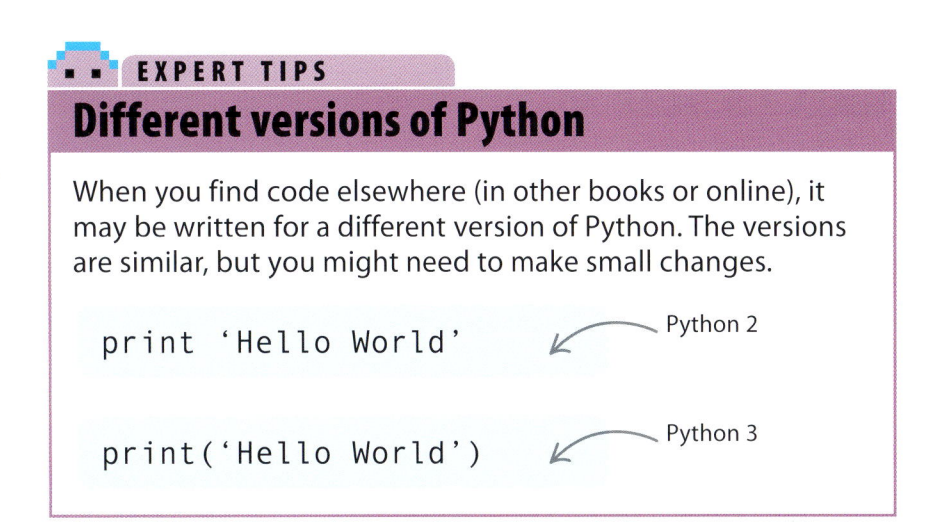

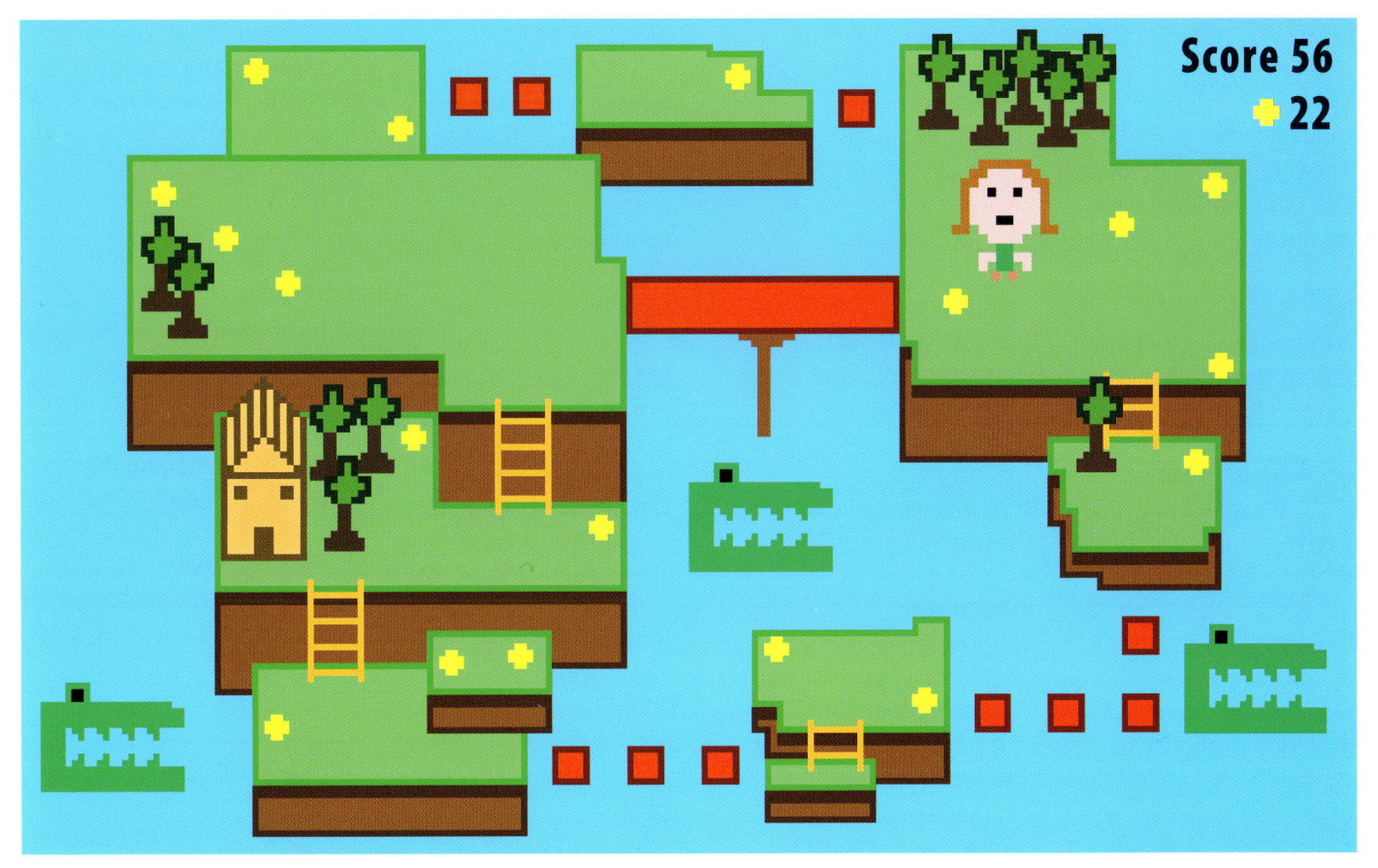

EXPERT TIPS
Different versions of Python

When you find code elsewhere (in other books or online), it may be written for a different version of Python. The versions are similar, but you might need to make small changes.

```
print 'Hello World'
```
← Python 2

```
print('Hello World')
```
← Python 3

Debug your code

Debugging is an important part of programming. Don't just give up if something isn't working. Remember that computers will only do what you tell them, so look through the code and figure out why it's not working. Sometimes looking over it with another programmer helps you to find bugs quicker.

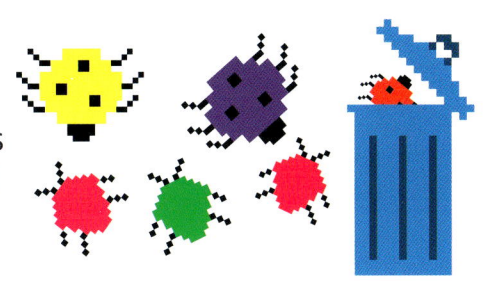

Glossary

algorithm
A set of step-by-step instructions followed when performing a task: for example, by a computer program.

ASCII
"American Standard Code for Information Interchange" – a code used for storing text characters as binary code.

binary code
A way of writing numbers and data that only uses 0s and 1s.

bit
A binary digit – 0 or 1. The smallest unit of digital information.

Boolean expression
A question that has only two possible answers, such as "true" and "false".

branch
A point in a program where two different options are available to choose from.

bug
An error in a program's code that makes it behave in an unexpected way.

byte
A unit of digital information that contains eight bits.

call
To use a function in a program.

compression
A way of making data smaller so that it takes up less storage space.

computer network
A way to link two or more computers together.

container
A part of a program that can be used to store a number of other data items.

data
Information, such as text, symbols, and numerical values.

debug
To look for and correct errors in a program.

debugger
A program that checks other programs for errors in their code.

directory
A place to store files to keep them organized.

encryption
A way of encoding data so that only certain people can read or access it.

event
Something a computer program can react to, such as a key being pressed or the mouse being clicked.

execute
See run.

file
A collection of data stored with a name.

float
A number with a decimal point in it.

function
A piece of code that does part of a larger task.

gate
Used by computers to make decisions. Gates use one or more input signals to produce an output signal, based on a rule. For example, "AND" gates produce a positive output only when both input signals are positive. Other gates include "OR" and "NOT".

GPU
A graphics processing unit (GPU) allows images to be displayed on a computer screen.

graphics
Visual elements on a screen that are not text, such as pictures, icons, and symbols.

GUI
The GUI, or graphical user interface, is the name for the buttons and windows that make up the part of the program you can see and interact with.

hacker
A person who breaks into a computer system. "White hat" hackers work for computer security companies and look for problems in order to fix them. "Black hat" hackers break into computer systems to cause harm or to make profit from them.

hardware
The physical parts of a computer that you can see or touch, such as wires, the keyboard, and the display screen.

hexadecimal
A number system based on 16, where the numbers 10 to 15 are represented by the letters A to F.

index number
A number given to an item in a list. In Python, the index number of the first item will be 0, the second item 1, and so on.

input
Data that is entered into a computer: for example, from a microphone, keyboard, or mouse.

GLOSSARY

integer
Any number that does not contain a decimal point and is not written as a fraction (a whole number).

interface
The means by which the user interacts with software or hardware.

IP address
A series of numbers that makes up a computer's individual address when it is connected to the Internet.

library
A collection of functions that can be reused in other projects.

loop
Part of a program that repeats itself (to prevent the need for the same piece of code to be typed out multiple times).

machine code
The basic language understood by computers. Programming languages must be translated into machine code before the processor can read them.

malware
Software that is designed to harm or disrupt a computer. Malware is short for "malicious software".

memory
A computer chip inside a computer that stores data.

module
A section of code that performs a single part of an overall program.

operator
A symbol that performs a specific function: for example, "+" (addition) or "-" (subtraction).

OS
A computer's operating system (OS) provides the basis for other programs to run, and connects them to hardware.

output
Data that is produced by a computer program and viewed by the user.

port
A series of numbers used by a computer as the "address" for a specific program.

processor
A type of electronic chip inside a computer that runs programs.

program
A set of instructions that a computer follows in order to complete a task.

programming language
A language that is used to give instructions to a computer.

random
A function in a computer program that allows unpredictable outcomes. Useful when creating games.

run
The command to make a program start.

server
A computer that stores files accessible via a network.

single-step
A way of making a computer program run one step at a time, to check that each step is working properly.

socket
The combination of an IP address and a port, which lets programs send data directly to each other over the Internet.

software
The programs that run on a computer and control how it works.

sprite
A movable object.

statement
The smallest complete instruction a programming language can be broken down into.

string
A series of characters. Strings can contain numbers, letters, or symbols, such as a colon.

syntax
The rules that determine how a program must be structured in order for it to work properly.

Trojan
A piece of malware that pretends to be another piece of software to trick the user.

tuple
A list of items separated by commas and surrounded by brackets.

Unicode
A universal code used by computers to represent thousands of symbols and text characters.

variable
A named place where you can store information that can be changed.

virus
A type of malware that works by multiplying itself to spread between computers.

Acknowledgements

DORLING KINDERSLEY would like to thank: Vicky Short, Mandy Earey, Sandra Perry, and Tannishtha Chakraborty for their design assistance; Olivia Stanford for her editorial assistance; Caroline Hunt for proofreading; Helen Peters for the index; and Adam Brackenbury for creative technical support.

DORLING KINDERSLEY INDIA would like to thank: Kanika Mittal for design assistance; Pawan Kumar for pre-production assistance; and Saloni Singh for editorial management of the jackets team.

Scratch is developed by the Lifelong Kindergarten Group at MIT Media Lab. See **http://scratch.mit.edu**

Python is copyright © 2001-2013 Python Software Foundation; All Rights Reserved.